# Hiking
# Illinois

## SECOND EDITION

# Hiking Illinois

## SECOND EDITION

Susan L. Post

Human Kinetics

**Library of Congress Cataloging-in-Publication Data**

Post, Susan L.
  Hiking Illinois / Susan L. Post. -- 2nd ed.
    p. cm.
  ISBN-13: 978-0-7360-7474-2 (soft cover)
  ISBN-10: 0-7360-7474-0 (soft cover)
  1. Hiking--Illinois--Guidebooks. 2. Trails--Illinois--Guidebooks.
  3. Parks--Illinois--Guidebooks. 4. Natural history--Illinois--Guidebooks.
  5. Illinois--Guidebooks. I. Title.
  GV199.42.I3P67 2009
  796.51'09773--dc22

                                                                2008041586

  ISBN-10: 0-7360-7474-0
  ISBN-13: 978-0-7360-7474-2

The Web addresses cited in this text were current as of September 2008, unless otherwise noted.

**Acquisitions Editor:** Justin Klug; **Developmental Editor:** Amanda Eastin-Allen; **Assistant Editor:** Laura Podeschi; **Copyeditor:** Jan Feeney; **Proofreader:** Kathy Bennett; **Permission Manager:** Martha Gullo; **Graphic Designer:** Nancy Rasmus; **Graphic Artist:** Julie L. Denzer; **Cover Designer:** Keith Blomberg; **Photographer (cover and interior):** Michael R. Jeffords; **Photo Production Manager:** Jason Allen; **Art Manager:** Kelly Hendren; **Associate Art Manager:** Alan L. Wilborn; **Illustrator:** Tim Shedelbower; **Printer:** Versa Press

The maps on the following pages were adapted from maps from the Illinois Department of Natural Resources: 4, 8, 12, 20, 24, 32, 36, 40, 50, 78, 83, 87, 95, 99, 103, 110, 118, 125, 140, 158, 169, 173, 180, 186, 190, 200, 210, and 229. Map on page 16 adapted by permission of the Winnebago County Forest Preserve District; map on page 28 adapted by permission of the McHenry County Conservation District; maps on pages 47, 59, 61, 62, and 63 courtesy of Forest Preserve District of DuPage County; map on page 65 adapted by permission of The Morton Arboretum; map on page 69 adapted by permission of the Forest Preserve District of Cook County; map on page 81 adapted by permission of the Nauvoo Tourism Office; map on page 91 adapted by permission of the Peoria Park District; map on page 121 adapted by permission of the Ballard Nature Center; maps on pages 128 and 144 adapted by permission of the Vermilion County Conservation District; map on page 132 adapted by permission of the University of Illinois at Urbana-Champaign; map on page 136 adapted by permission of the Urbana Park District.

Human Kinetics books are available at special discounts for bulk purchase. Special editions or book excerpts can also be created to specification. For details, contact the Special Sales Manager at Human Kinetics.

Printed in the United States of America    10 9 8 7 6 5 4 3 2 1

**Human Kinetics**
Web site: www.HumanKinetics.com

*United States:* Human Kinetics
P.O. Box 5076
Champaign, IL 61825-5076
800-747-4457
e-mail: humank@hkusa.com

*Canada:* Human Kinetics
475 Devonshire Road, Unit 100
Windsor, ON N8Y 2L5
800-465-7301 (in Canada only)
e-mail: info@hkcanada.com

*Europe:* Human Kinetics
107 Bradford Road
Stanningley
Leeds LS28 6AT, United Kingdom
+44 (0) 113 255 5665
e-mail: hk@hkeurope.com

*Australia:* Human Kinetics
57A Price Avenue
Lower Mitcham, South Australia 5062
08 8372 0999

e-mail: info@hkaustralia.com
*New Zealand:* Human Kinetics
Division of Sports Distributors NZ Ltd.
P.O. Box 300 226 Albany
North Shore City
Auckland
0064 9 448 1207
e-mail: info@humankinetics.co.nz

# Acknowledgments

As I hiked and wrote, many people made the job easier. My thanks go to all the staff members and volunteers at nature centers, state parks, and forest preserves for answering innumerable questions and providing maps to their sites. Several members went beyond just answering questions by either hiking with me or providing detailed information: Stacy Iwanicki at Volo Bog State Natural Area, Carol Thompson at Weldon Springs State Park, and Molly Oliver at Cache River State Natural Area.

Jim Waycuilis at Cache River State Natural Area and Liz Jones at Cypress Creek National Wildlife Area went above and beyond mere maps and information. They welcomed me with southern Illinois hospitality. Already one of my favorite areas of the state, southern Illinois is now even more special. Connie Cunningham put me in tune with the wonders of Vermilion County. Jen Mui was a partner for James "Pate" Philip State Park and also field-tested Waterfall Glen. My sisters, Jennifer Douglas and Valerie Post, field-tested the Peoria area hikes and discovered listening points! Bob Reber and Lynn Smith of *Illinois Steward Magazine* helped update areas I had previously visited. Le Ann Benner of the Illinois State Geological Survey always had the right map or geological publication. Carie Nixon helped with all things computer related. My entomological colleagues—Joe Spencer, Kelly Estes, Jennifer Schuster, and Cathy Eastman—were always curious about my progress and willing to listen to my trials along the trail, always with an encouraging word. Patty Dickerson and her son Neil cared for Bolt during my absences; Patty also provided many words of encouragement and helped with last-minute details. The staff of the Illinois Natural History Survey kept asking how the project was going, and those thoughtful queries made my day. And finally, thanks to Bolt (my guinea pig), who always had "wheeks" of encouragement.

To my hiking partners:

My nieces, Samantha and Hannah Post, the next generation of hikers.
Together we scaled a 13,000-foot peak and climbed the highest sand dune.

My husband, Michael. Not only is he my favorite hiking partner and best friend,
but he kept me motivated and headed in the right direction.

# Contents

# How to Use This Book

Hiking is an antidote to the rigors of modern life. It gives the body some much-needed (and enjoyable) exercise, and it gives the mind both rest and stimulation. Hiking even lifts the spirit to reconnect with this earth, which we're a part of but seldom have time to think about. We hope to provide you with an incentive to start or continue hiking for the pleasure and the challenge of it.

The assortment of trails in this book range from short, easy hikes for occasional hikers and families with young children to longer, more rugged ones for experienced trailblazers. None of the trails take more than a day to hike, although some trails may be linked together to create a hike of several days.

The trails are divided into three main areas—North, Central, and South. Within each area, trails are listed from west to east. Divider pages signal the beginning of each new area, and those pages include information on the local topography, major rivers and lakes, flora and fauna, weather, and the best features of the area.

The innovative format of the book makes exploring new parks and trails easy. Information on each park begins with the park's name and a small state map that shows the park's general location. Bulleted highlights point out the park's most interesting features. A description of the park's history and terrain appears next; there you can find directions to the park and the hours of operation, available facilities, permits and rules, and the address and phone number of a contact who can give you more information. After the general information is a list of trails in the park. The length and difficulty of hiking each are stated along with a brief description of its terrain. The difficulty rating, shown by boot icons, ranges from 1 (easiest) to 5 (most difficult). The section titled Other Areas of Interest mentions nearby parks and recreational opportunities and lists phone numbers to call for more information.

After the introduction are descriptions of the best trails in the park along with a trail map. (A few parks have only one hike with just one map that primarily shows the trail.) Each hike begins with information on the length and difficulty of the trail and the estimated time to walk it, plus cautions to help you avoid potential annoyances or problems. The description of the trail provides more than directions; it's a guided tour of what you will see as you hike along. The scenery, wildlife, and history of the trail are all brought to life. Points of interest along the trail are numbered in brackets within the text, and those numbers are shown on the trail map to guide you. The approximate distance from the trailhead to each point of interest is given.

If you want to quickly find a park or trail to explore, use the trail finder on pages ix to xix. It gives essential information about each highlighted trail in the book, including the trail's length, difficulty, special features, and the park's facilities.

We hope this book inspires you to get out and enjoy some outdoor experiences. We've included interesting trails from all parts of the state. Some are unexpected treasures—places you'd never dream exist in the state. Some may be favorites that you've already hiked and recommended to friends. But whether you live in a city or in the country, are away vacationing or are at home, some of these trails will be near you. Find one you like, lace up your hiking boots, and go!

# Trail Finder

| Park | Trails | Miles | Difficulty | Landscape | | | | | | | Page # |
|------|--------|-------|------------|-----------|---|---|---|---|---|---|--------|
| | | | | Hills | Prairie/Grass | Forest | Lake | Wetlands | Overlook | River/Stream | |
| **NORTH** | | | | | | | | | | | |
| 1 **Apple River Canyon State Park** | Primrose and Sunset Trails | 1.5 | 👣👣👣 | ✗ | | ✗ | | | ✗ | ✗ | 5 |
| | Pine Ridge, River View, and Tower Rock Trails | 2.6 | 👣👣👣 | ✗ | | ✗ | | | ✗ | ✗ | 6 |
| 2 **Mississippi Palisades State Park** | Sentinel Trail | 1 | 👣👣👣👣 | ✗ | | ✗ | | | ✗ | ✗ | 9 |
| | High Point Trail | 5 | 👣👣👣👣 | ✗ | | ✗ | | | ✗ | ✗ | 10 |
| 3 **Rock Cut State Park** | Rock Cut State Park–South Trail Sampler | 3.15 | 👣👣👣 | ✗ | | ✗ | | ✗ | | | 13 |
| | Puricrest Trail | 2.1 | 👣 | | ✗ | ✗ | | | | | 14 |
| 4 **Winnebago County Forest Preserves** | Colored Sands | 1.15 | 👣👣 | | ✗ | ✗ | | | ✗ | ✗ | 17 |
| | Sugar River Alder | 3.8 | 👣👣 | | ✗ | ✗ | | | | | 18 |

» continued

 RV camping   tent camping   swimming   canoeing   fishing   boating   picnicking   biking

» continued

| Park | Trails | Miles | Difficulty | Landscape | | | | | | | Page # |
|---|---|---|---|---|---|---|---|---|---|---|---|
| | | | | Hills | Prairie/Grass | Forest | Lake | Wetlands | Overlook | River/Stream | |
| **NORTH** | | | | | | | | | | | |
| 5 **White Pines Forest State Park**  | Red Squirrel and Gray Squirrel Trails | 1.25 | 👣👣 | X | | X | | | X | X | 21 |
| | Sunset Trail | 2.25 | 👣👣 | | | X | | | | | 22 |
| 6 **Lowden-Miller State Forest** | Fire Trail Sampler | 3.25 | 👣👣 | | | X | | | | | 25 |
| 7 **McHenry County Conservation District** | Glacial Park Trail | 2 | 👣👣👣 | X | X | X | | | X | | 29 |
| | Marengo Ridge | 3.6 | 👣👣 | X | X | X | | | X | | 30 |
| 8 **Chain O' Lakes State Park** | Goldfinch and Badger | 3.4 | 👣👣 | | X | X | | | X | X | 33 |
| | Mud Lake | 1.3 | 👣👣 | | | X | X | X | | X | 34 |
| 9 **Volo Bog State Natural Area** | Tamarack Trail | 3.2 | 👣👣 | X | X | X | | X | X | | 37 |
| | Bog Boardwalk Trail | .5 | 👣 | | | | | X | X | | 38 |
| 10 **Moraine Hills State Park** | Blue Trail–Leatherleaf Bog | 3.45 | 👣 | | X | X | X | X | X | | 41 |
| | Fox River Trail | 3.5 | 👣 | | X | X | X | X | X | | 42 |

 RV camping    tent camping    swimming    canoeing    fishing    boating    picnicking    biking

| | Park | Trails | Miles | Difficulty | Hills | Prairie/ Grass | Forest | Lake | Wetlands | Overlook | River/ Stream | Page # |
|---|---|---|---|---|---|---|---|---|---|---|---|---|
| | | | | | | | | | | **Landscape** | | |
| **NORTH** | | | | | | | | | | | | |
| 11 | Bluff Spring Fen | Bluff Spring Trail | 1 | 👣👣 | X | X | | | | | | 45 |
| 12 | James "Pate" Philip State Park   | Bluestem, Blazing Star, and Indigo | 4.25 | 👣👣 | | X | | X | X | | | 48 |
| 13 | Illinois Beach State Park | Dead River Trail | 2.4 | 👣👣 | | X | X | X | X | X | X | 51 |
| | | North Unit Trail | 2.2 | 👣 | | X | X | X | X | | | 52 |
| 14 | Lake County Forest Preserves | Rollins Savanna | 5.75 | 👣 | | X | X | X | X | X | | 55 |
| | | Cuba Marsh Trail | 3.5 | 👣👣 | | X | X | X | X | | | 56 |
| 15 | Waterfall Glen Forest Preserve | Waterfall Glen Trail | 9.65 | 👣👣👣 | | X | X | X | X | | X | 58 |
| 16 | Regional Trail | Blackwell Forest Preserve | 6.65 | 👣 | | X | X | X | X | | X | 62 |
| | | Herrick Lake Forest Preserve | 4.6 | 👣 | | X | X | X | X | | | 63 |
| 17 | Morton Arboretum | Prairie Trail | 1.1 | 👣 | | X | | | | | | 66 |
| | | East Main Trail | 4.5 | 👣 | | X | X | X | | | | 67 |

» continued

 RV camping    tent camping    swimming    canoeing    fishing    boating    picnicking   biking

» continued

| Park | Trails | Miles | Difficulty | Landscape | | | | | | | Page # |
| | | | | Hills | Prairie/ Grass | Forest | Lake | Wetlands | Overlook | River/ Stream | |
|---|---|---|---|---|---|---|---|---|---|---|---|
| **NORTH** | | | | | | | | | | | |
| 18 **Palos and Sag Valley Forest Preserves**  | Black Oak Trail | 2.75 | 👣 | | X | X | X | X | | | 70 |
| 19 **Will County Forest Preserves** | Messenger Woods Nature Preserve | 2 | 👣👣 | | | X | | | | | 73 |
| | Thorn Creek Nature Preserve | 2.5 | 👣 | | | X | | | X | | 74 |
| **CENTRAL** | | | | | | | | | | | |
| 20 **Big River State Forest** | Lincoln Trail | 1.5 | 👣👣 | | X | X | | | | | 79 |
| 21 **Nauvoo** | Historic Nauvoo | 4 | 👣 | | X | | | | X | X | 81 |
| 22 **Siloam Springs State Park** | Red Oak Backpack Trail | 4 | 👣👣👣 | X | X | X | | | X | X | 84 |
| | Hoot Owl Trail | 1.5 | 👣👣👣 | X | | X | | | X | | 85 |
| 23 **Pere Marquette State Park** | Dogwood-Goat Trails | 2 | 👣👣👣 | X | X | X | | | X | | 88 |
| | Fern Hollow Trail | 3 | 👣👣👣 | X | | X | | | | | 89 |

 RV camping    tent camping    swimming   canoeing    fishing   boating    picnicking    biking

| | Park | Trails | Miles | Difficulty | Landscape | | | | | | | Page # |
|---|---|---|---|---|---|---|---|---|---|---|---|---|
| | | | | | Hills | Prairie/Grass | Forest | Lake | Wetlands | Overlook | River/Stream | |
| **CENTRAL** | | | | | | | | | | | | |
| 24 | **Forest Park Nature Preserve**  | Inside Trail (Several Combined) | 1.75 | 🥾🥾🥾🥾 | X | | X | | | X | | 92 |
| | | Outside Trail (Several Combined) | 2.75 | 🥾🥾🥾🥾 | X | X | X | | | X | | 93 |
| 25 | **Sand Ridge State Forest**  | Sand Ridge State Forest Sampler | 3.5 | 🥾🥾 | X | X | X | | | | | 96 |
| | | Henry Allan Gleason Nature Preserve | 1.15 | 🥾🥾 | X | X | | | | X | | 97 |
| 26 | **Starved Rock State Park** | Starved Rock, Sandstone Point, and LaSalle Canyon | 5.5 | 🥾🥾🥾🥾 | X | | X | | | X | X | 100 |
| | | Canyon Sampler– Owl to Illinois | 6.8 | 🥾🥾🥾 | X | | X | | | X | X | 101 |
| 27 | **Matthiessen State Park** | Dells Trail | 3 | 🥾🥾🥾 | X | | X | X | | X | X | 104 |
| 28 | **Where Lincoln Walked** | New Salem | 3.5 | 🥾🥾🥾 | X | | X | | | | X | 107 |
| | | Springfield's Lincoln | 6.5 | 🥾🥾 | | | | | | | | 108 |
| 29 | **Goose Lake Prairie State Natural Area** | Tall Grass Nature Trail | 2.7 | 🥾 | | X | | | X | | | 111 |
| | | Prairie View Trail | 3.3 | 🥾🥾 | X | X | | X | X | X | | 112 |

» continued

 RV camping   tent camping   swimming   canoeing  fishing   boating   picnicking   biking

» continued

| Park | Trails | Miles | Difficulty | Hills | Prairie/Grass | Forest | Lake | Wetlands | Overlook | River/Stream | Page # |
|---|---|---|---|---|---|---|---|---|---|---|---|
| **CENTRAL** | | | | | | | | | | | |
| 30 **Midewin National Tallgrass Prairie**  | Hoff Road Trailhead–East Side Trails | 4.5 | 👞 | | X | | | | | | 115 |
| | Interim West Side Trails–Newton and Henslow | 3 | 👞👞 | | X | | | | | | 116 |
| 31 **Spitler Woods State Natural Area** | Squirrel Creek Trail | 2 | 👞👞 | | | X | | | | X | 119 |
| 32 **Ballard Nature Center** Note: Fishing available for children only. | Wetland and Prairie Trails | 1.75 | 👞 | | X | X | | X | | | 122 |
| | Second Creek Trail | 1.4 | 👞👞 | | X | X | | | | X | 123 |
| 33 **Iroquois County State Wildlife Area** | Hooper Branch Savanna | 2.5 | 👞👞 | | X | X | | X | | | 126 |
| 34 **Forest Glen Preserve** | Willow Creek, Deer Meadow, and Old Barn Trails | 3.75 | 👞👞 | X | X | X | X | X | X | X | 129 |
| | Big Woods Trail | 2.5 | 👞👞👞 | X | | X | | | X | X | 130 |
| 35 **Robert Allerton Park** | North River Trails | 5.25 | 👞👞 | X | | X | | | X | X | 133 |
| | Buck Schroth Nature Trail | 2.1 | 👞👞 | | X | X | | | | X | 134 |

 RV camping    tent camping    swimming    canoeing    fishing    boating    picnicking    biking

| Park | Trails | Miles | Difficulty | Landscape | | | | | | | Page # |
|---|---|---|---|---|---|---|---|---|---|---|---|
| | | | | Hills | Prairie/Grass | Forest | Lake | Wetlands | Overlook | River/Stream | |
| **CENTRAL** | | | | | | | | | | | |
| 36 **Urbana Park District**   | Meadowbrook Park | 2 | 👣 | | X | | | | X | | 137 |
| | Busey Woods and Crystal Lake Park | 3.35 | 👣👣 | | | X | X | | | X | 138 |
| 37 **Fox Ridge State Park** | Riverview Sampler | 1.5 | 👣👣 | X | | X | | | X | X | 141 |
| | Acorn Avenue and Trail of Trees | 2.75 | 👣👣👣 | X | | X | | | X | X | 142 |
| 38 **Kennekuk Cove County Park** | Windfall Prairie and Collins Site | 2.25 | 👣👣 | | X | X | X | | X | X | 145 |
| | Lake Mingo Trail | 7.3 | 👣👣👣 | X | | X | X | X | | | 146 |
| **SOUTH** | | | | | | | | | | | |
| 39 **Fults Hill Prairie** | Fults Hill Prairie Trail | 1.6 | 👣👣👣👣 | X | X | X | | | X | | 150 |
| 40 **Piney Creek Ravine Nature Preserve** | Piney Creek Trail | 2.5 | 👣👣👣 | X | | X | | | X | X | 152 |
| 41 **LaRue-Pine Hills** | Snake Road (Base of the Bluff Road) | 5 | 👣 | | | X | X | X | | | 155 |
| | Inspiration Point Trail | 2 | 👣👣👣 | X | | X | | | X | | 156 |

» continued

 RV camping    tent camping    swimming    canoeing    fishing    boating    picnicking    biking

» *continued*

| Park | | Trails | Miles | Difficulty | Hills | Prairie/Grass | Forest | Lake | Wetlands | Overlook | River/Stream | Page # |
|---|---|---|---|---|---|---|---|---|---|---|---|---|
| | | | | | | | Landscape | | | | | |
| **SOUTH** | | | | | | | | | | | | |
| 42 | **Giant City State Park**  | Giant City Trail | 2.25 | | ✗ | | ✗ | | | ✗ | ✗ | 159 |
| | | Trillium Trail | 1.5 | | ✗ | | ✗ | | | ✗ | ✗ | 160 |
| 43 | **Little Grand Canyon** | Loop Trail | 3.6 | | ✗ | | ✗ | | ✗ | ✗ | ✗ | 163 |
| 44 | **Cedar Lake** | Cove Hollow Trail–Cedar Lake | 6 | | ✗ | | ✗ | ✗ | | | ✗ | 166 |
| | | Little Cedar Lake | 5.75 | | | | ✗ | ✗ | ✗ | | ✗ | 167 |
| 45 | **Trail of Tears State Forest** | Fire Trails 21 to 29 | 4.1 | | ✗ | | ✗ | | | ✗ | | 170 |
| | | Ozark Hills Nature Preserve | 3.5 | | ✗ | | ✗ | | | | | 171 |
| 46 | **Horseshoe Lake Conservation Area** | Horseshoe Lake | 5.75 | | | ✗ | ✗ | ✗ | ✗ | | | 174 |

 RV camping   tent camping   swimming   canoeing   fishing   boating   picnicking   biking

| Park | Trails | Miles | Difficulty | Landscape | | | | | | | Page # |
|---|---|---|---|---|---|---|---|---|---|---|---|
| | | | | Hills | Prairie/ Grass | Forest | Lake | Wetlands | Overlook | River/ Stream | |
| **SOUTH** | | | | | | | | | | | |
| 47 **Crab Orchard National Wildlife Refuge**  | Panther Den Wilderness | 2.6 | | ✗ | | ✗ | | | | ✗ | 177 |
| | Rocky Bluff Trail–Devil's Kitchen Lake | 2 | | ✗ | | ✗ | | | ✗ | ✗ | 178 |
| 48 **Ferne Clyffe State Park** | Hawk's Cave, Blackjack Oak, and Waterfall Trails | 3 | | ✗ | | ✗ | | | ✗ | ✗ | 181 |
| | Round Bluff Nature Preserve Trail | 1 | | ✗ | | ✗ | | | | | 182 |
| | Big Buck Creek Trail | 3.8 | | ✗ | | ✗ | | | | ✗ | 183 |
| | Borks Waterfall Trail | 1.25 | | ✗ | | ✗ | | | | ✗ | 184 |
| 49 **Tunnel Hill State Trail** | Tunnel Hill | 5.2 | | | | ✗ | | | ✗ | | 187 |
| | Barkhausen Wetlands Center | 5.6 | | | ✗ | ✗ | | ✗ | | ✗ | 188 |
| 50 **Cache River State Natural Area** | Heron Pond Trail | 2.5 | | | | ✗ | | ✗ | | ✗ | 191 |
| | Tupelo Trail | 2.5 | | | | ✗ | | ✗ | | | 192 |
| | Little Black Slough and Wildcat Bluff Trails | 6.4 | | ✗ | | ✗ | | ✗ | | ✗ | 193 |
| | Lower Cache Access | 3.2 | | | | ✗ | | ✗ | ✗ | ✗ | 194 |

» continued

 RV camping    tent camping    swimming    canoeing    fishing    boating    picnicking   biking

*» continued*

| Park | Trails | Miles | Difficulty | Hills | Prairie/Grass | Forest | Lake | Wetlands | Overlook | River/Stream | Page # |
|---|---|---|---|---|---|---|---|---|---|---|---|
| **SOUTH** | | | | | | | | | | | |
| 51 **Cypress Creek National Wildlife Refuge** | Limekiln Slough | 2.4 | 🥾 | | | X | | X | | X | 197 |
| | Hickory Bottoms | 2.45 | 🥾 | | | X | | X | | X | 198 |
| 52 **Mermet Lake Conservation Area** | Mermet Lake Trail | 5 | 🥾 | | | | X | X | | | 201 |
| 53 **Max Creek** | Max Creek | 4.25 | 🥾🥾🥾 | X | | X | | | | X | 204 |
| 54 **Bell Smith Springs Recreation Area** | Mill Branch Trail | 2 | 🥾🥾 | X | | X | | | X | X | 207 |
| | Sentry Bluff Trail | 3.5 | 🥾🥾🥾 | X | | X | | | X | X | 208 |
| 55 **Dixon Springs State Park** | Pine Tree, Oak Tree, and Bluff Trails | 2.3 | 🥾🥾 | | | X | | | | X | 211 |
| | Ghost Dance Canyon | 1 | 🥾🥾🥾 | | | | | | | | 212 |
| 56 **Stone Face Recreation Area** | Stone Face | 1.6 | 🥾🥾🥾 | X | | X | | | X | | 215 |

 RV camping   tent camping   swimming   canoeing   fishing   boating   picnicking   biking

| | Park | Trails | Miles | Difficulty | Hills | Prairie/ Grass | Forest | Lake | Wetlands | Overlook | River/ Stream | Page # |
|---|---|---|---|---|---|---|---|---|---|---|---|---|
| **SOUTH** | | | | | | | | | | | | |
| 57 | Garden of the Gods Recreation Area | Observation Trail | .25-.6 | 👣 | | | | | | X | | 218 |
| | | Wilderness Trail | 2.25 | 👣 | X | | X | | | X | X | 219 |
| 58 | Rim Rocks/Pounds Hollow Recreation Complex | Rim Rock National Trail | 2.25 | 👣 | X | | X | | | X | X | 222 |
| | | Beaver Trail | 3.9 | 👣 | X | | X | X | X | | X | 223 |
| 59 | War Bluff Valley Audubon Sanctuary | North Pond | 2.25 | 👣 | | X | X | | X | | X | 226 |
| | | Deer and Cedar Ponds | 2 | 👣 | | X | X | | X | | X | 227 |
| 60 | Beall Woods State Park | Schneck and Sweet Gum Trails | 2.2 | 👣 | | | X | | | | X | 230 |
| | | White Oak Trail | 4.3 | 👣 | X | | X | | | X | X | 231 |

 RV camping    tent camping    swimming    canoeing    fishing    boating    picnicking    biking

# Illinois

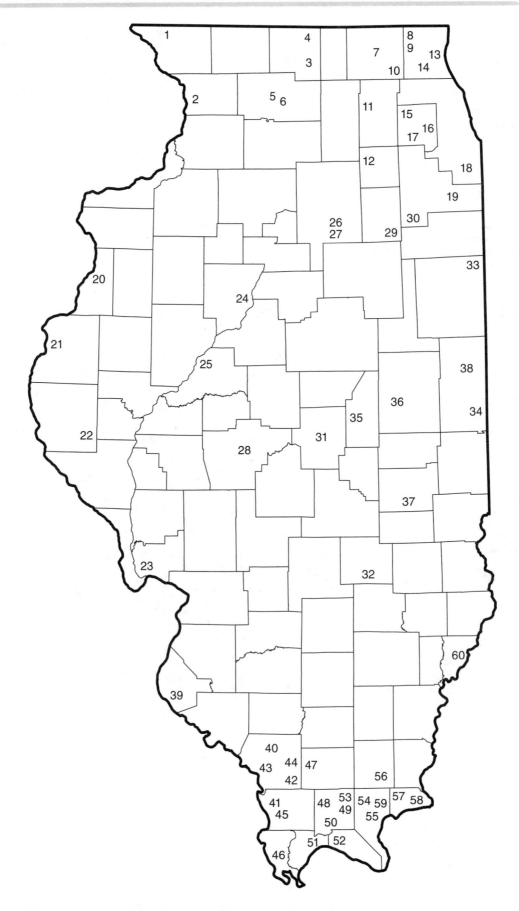

# North

Northern Illinois is defined as the area south of the Wisconsin border and north of an imaginary line (from Indiana to the Mississippi River) that follows the east-to-west portion of the Illinois River Valley.

## Topography

A drive from east to west across northern Illinois leads from a region that saw glaciers 6,000 to 10,000 years ago to the rugged northwestern corner of the state that never saw the bottom of a glacier. In the northeast (the most recently glaciated area), glacial landforms are common, and moraines (long ridges of glacial debris) and kames (conical mounds of glacial debris) make for a rolling, hilly terrain. Kettle holes and other depressions scooped out by the glaciers create a montage of complex wetlands. Near Lake Michigan, the lake-bed deposits of old glacial Lake Chicago (much bigger than the current Lake Michigan) and old shoreline ridges contribute to a unique landscape of sandy beaches, low dunes, and moist swales.

The Rock River dominates the north-central part of Illinois. Gravel hill prairies once extended along the eroded bluffs; outcrops of St. Peter sandstone are common in the lower reaches of the valley, and the overall topography is rolling. At one time, the Rock River Valley between Beloit and Dixon was designated the "Hudson of the West" because of its many limestone bluffs and rugged sandstone outcrops.

Extreme northwestern Illinois escaped glaciation, and consequently the region is called the Driftless Area (drift is glacial debris). The Driftless Area has one of the most maturely developed land surfaces in the state and is characterized by rugged terrain, including loess-capped bluffs (loess is windblown sediment) and high, rocky palisades. The highest point in the state, Charles Mound (1,235 feet above sea level), occurs here.

## Major Rivers and Lakes

Lake Michigan borders the state on the northeast and the Mississippi River forms the entire western boundary of Illinois. The northeast area is home to numerous glacial lakes. These formed when chunks of ice broke off from the glaciers, became buried, and eventually melted or when a depression was created between two moraines. The Des Plaines River lies west of Lake Michigan; its upper reaches, at least during high water, provided early French explorers the beginning stretch of an easy and continuous canoe route from the Great Lakes to the Mississippi. Today, most of the Des Plaines watershed is the Greater Chicago metropolitan region.

The Illinois River extends diagonally across the state and drains 45 percent of Illinois. Other major rivers found here are the Fox, the third-largest tributary of the Illinois; the Rock, which drains part of southern Wisconsin and most of northwestern Illinois; and the Apple, whose two forks unite at Apple River Canyon State Park, forming high cliffs with a unique flora.

## Common Plant Life

Three broad types of forests occur in the north: upland, with bur and white oak that were referred to in early writings as oak openings; mesic (moist) upland, dominated by sugar maple and basswood; and floodplain, found along major watercourses, containing silver maple, green ash, and cottonwood. The more unusual tree species found in northern

Illinois are tamaracks (growing in bogs), the state's only stand of native white pines, and white birch (native to the Driftless Area).

Wildflowers to look for in these forests are expanses of white trillium, trout lily, jack-in-the-pulpit, wild geranium, false Solomon's seal, and many other favorite spring ephemerals. The Driftless Area has plants that found a refuge from the glaciers: jeweled shooting star, bird's-eye primrose, and Canada violet.

The prairies found here can be spectacular and include wet-to-mesic tallgrass prairies, dry gravel hill prairies, and sand prairies. Common wet or mesic prairie plants are big bluestem, compass plant, prairie dock, shooting star, blazing star, and the rare prairie white-fringed orchid. One-third of the country's population of this plant grows here. Dry gravel hill prairies contain plants more common to the northwest—pasque flower, prairie smoke, bird's-foot violet, and expanses of purple coneflower. Sand prairie species include coreopsis, puccoon, and gentians (both fringed and bottle).

Wetlands make up a significant portion of the landforms in the northeast. Besides the familiar cattail marsh, you will encounter bogs, forested and grassy fens, and seeps. Look for pitcher plants, sundew, grass pink and rose pogonia orchids, leatherleaf, marsh marigold, and skunk cabbage.

# Common Birds and Mammals

In wetland habitats, seek out red-winged blackbirds, great blue herons, great white egrets, little green herons, Canada geese, wood ducks, kingfishers, common yellowthroats, yellow warblers, and swallows. A few of the rarer species that call this area home are yellow-headed blackbirds, black-crowned night herons, sandhill cranes, and black terns. Open grasslands provide habitat for bobolinks, American goldfinches, dickcissels, eastern meadowlarks, and various hawks.

Mammals found throughout the north include white-tailed deer, cottontails, chipmunks, gray squirrels, woodchucks, and muskrats. Red-eared slider, snapping, and softshell turtles may be seen basking on logs in most wetlands. In addition, frogs are universal inhabitants of these wet places.

# Climate

As you might expect, this area of Illinois is the last to warm up each spring. The mean average temperature is 23 degrees F for January and 74 degrees F for July. Cooler temperatures are found along Lake Michigan in the summer and warmer temperatures occur during winter. Rainfall averages 33.5 inches, per year. The mean average snowfall is 27 to 33 inches, and this area has 20 to 35 days a year with 3 or more inches of snow on the ground. A final note: The Driftless Area has the coldest and driest climate in the state.

# Best Natural Features

- Sandy habitats along Lake Michigan
- Illinois' only open-water bog
- Extensive wetlands
- Outcrops of St. Peter sandstone
- Glacial features—kames, moraines, kettle holes, and glacial boulders
- Palisades along the Mississippi River
- Expanses of wildflowers, both rare and common
- Small jewels of original prairie landscape

- Climb dolomite cliffs carved not by glaciers but by the Apple River.
- Bring a plant identification guide to help you identify over 60 species of trees and 600 species of plants found in this small park.
- Discover glacial relicts—plants surviving at the southernmost tip of their range.
- Enjoy the picturesque Apple River and its surrounding canyon.
- Find Pepoon's primrose cliffs.

## Area Information

In 1823 a geologist from Pennsylvania, W.H. Keating, traveled through this area and observed that the huge granite boulders characteristic of much of the glaciated Midwest were missing. He found ravines and valleys crisscrossing the land in every direction and a landscape dominated by slopes. Few lakes and ponds were present. From this evidence he deduced that Jo Daviess County and part of Carroll County had escaped the glaciers of the Pleistocene epoch. The area, literally an island in a sea of ice, became known as the Driftless Area (drift is glacial debris).

Although the glaciers missed this area, their meltwaters blocked the southeast outlet of Apple River, causing it to cut a new channel. As the river cut through the masses of limestone, dolomite, and shale to form its new channel, it also formed the rugged and picturesque canyon. This iceless region provided a haven that allowed certain plants and animals to survive the glacial periods. Dozens of species managed to survive the Pleistocene in the Driftless Area as their neighbors were driven to extinction. Both paper birch and bird's-eye primrose are examples of these relict species.

The river changes course at about the center of the park. The small town of Millville, so named because it contained two sawmills, took advantage of the river's power here. By 1838, Millville had a population of 330 and a post office, and the stagecoach went through town. Millville had begun to rival Chicago, which had a population of only 550. Unfortunately, the railroad later bypassed the town, and in 1892 a flood drove the people away forever.

**Directions:** Apple River Canyon State Park is only 3 miles from the Wisconsin border. From Route 78 take East Canyon Road west into the park.

**Hours Open:** The site is open year-round, except on Christmas Day.

**Facilities:** The park has camping (no electrical hookups), fishing, a concession stand, and picnic facilities.

**Permits and Rules:** Pets must be kept leashed at all times. Do not pick or remove any wildflowers.

**For Further Information:** Apple River Canyon State Park, 8763 E. Canyon Road, Apple River, IL 61001; 815-745-3302.

## Other Areas of Interest

Eighty-five percent of Galena is a National Register Historic District, encompassing Main Street and adjacent residential streets. Here you will find numerous examples of 19th-century architecture. Galena was home to Ulysses S. Grant, and his home is a state historic site open for tours. For more information, call 800-747-9377.

Located near the town of Lena in Stephenson County, **Le-Aqua-Na State Park** offers modern campsites, boating, fishing, swimming, and a small restaurant. Le-Aqua-Na has 7 miles of hiking trails, and the 13-mile Stephenson-Black Hawk Trail passes through the park. In spring, the marsh area of the park hosts nesting geese and a large expanse of marsh marigold. For information about the park, call 815-369-4282; for information about the trail, call 835-369-5351.

The **Jane Addams Recreation Trail** is a 12.85-mile trail in northwest Illinois that begins in Freeport and ends at the Wisconsin state line. This hiking and bicycle trail features a crushed limestone path that travels past wetlands, oak woods, prairies, exposed-rock embankments, small towns, and farms. For more information, go to www.janeaddamstrail.com or call 800-369-2955.

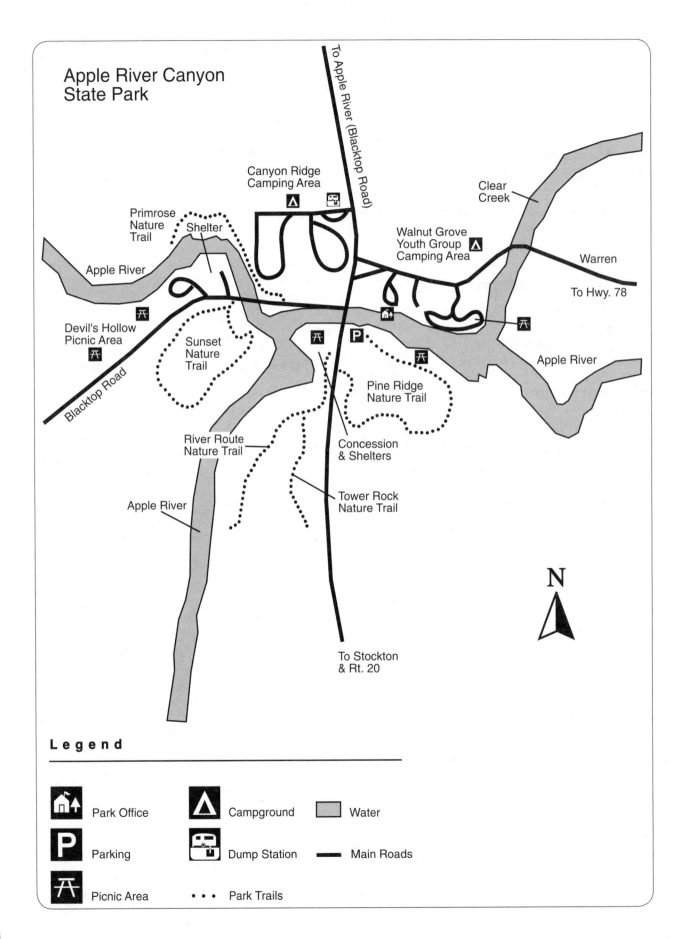

Apple River Canyon
State Park

To Apple River (Blacktop Road)

Canyon Ridge
Camping Area

Clear
Creek

Primrose
Nature
Trail

Shelter

Walnut Grove
Youth Group
Camping Area

Warren

Apple River

To Hwy. 78

Devil's Hollow
Picnic Area

Sunset
Nature
Trail

Apple River

Pine Ridge
Nature Trail

Blacktop Road

River Route
Nature Trail

Concession
& Shelters

Apple River

Tower Rock
Nature Trail

N

To Stockton
& Rt. 20

**Legend**

Park Office

Campground

Water

Parking

Dump Station

Main Roads

Picnic Area

• • •  Park Trails

# Primrose and Sunset Trails

 **Distance Round-Trip:** 1.5 miles
**Estimated Hiking Time:** 1 hour

*While heading down to see the primrose cliffs, I was scared out of my wits by a wild turkey exploding into the air in front of me on the trail. I don't know who was more frightened, but we both quickly headed in opposite directions!*

**Caution:** The trail can be very muddy. Logs and roots pose tripping hazards, and a stream crossing has no bridge.

**Trail Directions:** Begin at the Primrose Trail board and immediately climb steps [1]. During the upward trek, check out the spring wildflowers on the bluff. At the top, go left and pass a grove of pines on your right and the campground. Lots of shooting star occurs along this trail through the pines. If the shooting star is blooming, take time to smell it; it has an odor similar to grape juice. The campground is out of sight at .2 mi. and the trail passes an observation deck for Apple River on your left [2]. Almost the entire river basin lies in the Driftless Area, but the river cut a new channel and created the canyon when glacial meltwaters blocked its outlet.

At the overlook, watch swallows swooping for insects; they are very helpful in keeping mosquitoes and biting flies at bay. From the overlook, the trail curves right past a prairie restoration. The trail crosses a bridge at .3 mi. and then heads back uphill [3]. You are hiking through an oak-maple woods. In spring look for hepatica, wild geranium, and wild ginger in this area. Within a few yards you reach another bridge crossing. When the formal trail ends at .4 mi. you will enter a grassy area [4]. Go left, skirting the bluff and a profusion of wildflowers each spring. Cross a small creek and skirt the bluff on the far side.

These bluffs are unglaciated dolomite; where pockets of soil form, plants have been able to gain a foothold. Look for columbine, ferns, and bird's-eye primrose in the crevices. In 1909, Herman Pepoon, a botanist, described bird's-eye primrose as "tinting the bare rock a lavender purple with the multitudes of its blossoms." Bird's-eye primrose, a northern relict of cooler times, blooms in late April. Walk along these bluffs to discover these unique plants [5], but be careful not to topple into the river.

Discovery over, retrace your steps across the creek back to where the formal trail ended [4]. Before heading up, look for full-cheeked chipmunks scurrying under large, moss-covered boulders. On the bluff look for Solomon's seal, jack-in-the-pulpit, and prairie trillium. Retrace your steps back to the trail board [1]

(1.0 mi.). From here go right, walking along the edge of the park road. Cross the bridge, taking time to enjoy the canyon from this angle; on your left is the trail board for Sunset Trail [6] (1.1 mi.).

Climb upward; after a few steps, the trail goes left and up again. In the spring, it is lined with wild ginger, wood anemone, nodding trillium, and twinleaf. The latter was the favorite flower of Thomas Jefferson, and its Latin name reflects this—*Jeffersonia diphylla*. The trail follows a narrow ridge that overlooks the river and the park. At 1.2 mi. [7] the low, sprawling evergreen on either side is Canada yew, a plant that occurs only in northern North America.

You have been hiking in mixed hardwoods with an unusual composition of northern pin oak and chinquapin oak and black maple. At 1.3 mi. you will come to a bench where the trail heads downward [8]. As you hike downward, look for spotted coral-root orchid. You have completed the loop and the path soon ends at the trail board [6] (1.5 mi.). Recross the road and retrace your steps to the parking area.

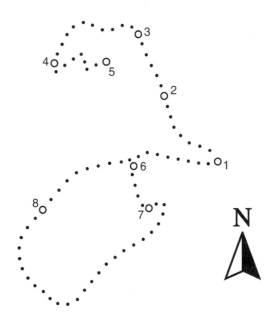

1. Start
2. Overlook
3. Bridge
4. Grassy area
5. Primrose
6. Sunset Trail
7. Canada yew
8. Downhill slope

# Pine Ridge, River View, and Tower Rock Trails

**Distance Round-Trip:**
2.6 miles
**Estimated Hiking Time:**
1.3 hours

*Although the trail may be rated difficult, the climb up the dolomite bluff has plenty of benches for resting, nice views, carpets of native pine needles, and a scenic walk along the Apple River.*

**Caution:** The trail can be very muddy and the rocks very slippery.

**Trail Directions:** Begin at the Pine Ridge Trail board and head upward [1]. In spring, note a thick stand of white trout lilies on both sides of the trail. Once you reach the top, you will find a bench. The trail curves to the left and soon comes to a T; follow the trail sign and veer left. At .10 mi. observe a stand of native white pine on the right [2] as the trail heads through an aspen and pine forest. You will soon go right through a pine and maple forest and head up. The trail is lined with prickly ash, the food for the giant swallowtail butterfly. The caterpillar resembles an oversize bird dropping!

A bench appears at .25 mi. [3] and the trail curves left; you are hiking on a carpet of pine needles. Along this piece of the trail, note the difference in the pines—pine plantations, where the trees are of uniform age and planted in rows, and native pines mixed with other tree species. The latter pines are of mixed age and randomly scattered about. The trail heads downhill at .45 mi. [4]. Soon after you hike under the arching branches of an elm, the trail will T; go left, head downward, cross a bridge and the park road, and pick up the River Route/Tower Rock Trail on the opposite side [5] (.55 mi.) and head upward.

During spring, the moss-covered rocks by the trail's entrance are covered with Dutchman's breeches. Head upward through a maple woods with an occasional white pine. You will come to a T at .65 mi. [6]; go right on the River Rock Trail. At the next intersection, near a wooden observation deck, go left on a narrow,

mountain goat–like trail. (Before going left, take a spur to the observation deck to look at and listen to the Apple River far below.)

As you descend, Apple River will be on your right at the 1 mi. point [7]. Just before reaching the river, look on either side of the trail for *Equisetum*, commonly known as horsetails. They are also called scouring rushes (because their stems contain abrasive silica) or puzzle plants (because they can be pulled apart and reassembled at their gray bands). Once the river has been reached, a faint trail skirts the water. Look for sneezeweed among the stinging nettle; across the river beautiful bluffs appear.

Trail and river have come together at 1.2 mi. and, unfortunately, the river wins and the trail disappears [8]. Retrace your steps back to [7] and head up the narrow goat path you just descended. At 1.25 mi. you are back to the observation deck [9]; go right on Tower Trail. Continue past a bench. You are hiking on a ridge through a mixed woods; another bench appears between two oaks at 1.5 mi. A bridge crossing [10] is at 1.55 mi.; off the bridge, curve to the left. As you hike along this winding path, you will be able to note the difference between disturbed and undisturbed woods.

You will cross two more bridges [11] at 1.65 mi. as you wind up and down. During late summer see if you can find puffballs, appearing like magic globes to soon decay in the forest. At the trail intersection [12] (1.7 mi.) go left; soon you will head down to the right on rocky steps, where you encounter Tower Rock [13]. From the top of the rock you have a panoramic view of the park. Use caution when you come down from the rock because it is slick and steep!

Once rested, retrace your steps back up the hill and back to the bench before [9]; go right (2.35 mi.) and head downhill; cross the road and head back to the parking area where you began.

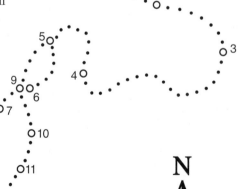

1. Start
2. Native white pines
3. Bench, curve left
4. Downhill slope
5. River Route/Tower Rock Trail
6. Right turn
7. Descend to river
8. End of trail
9. Observation deck
10. Bridge
11. Bridges
12. Intersection, left turn
13. Tower Rock

- View unique rock features eroded from the dolomite, with names like Indian Head, the Sentinel, and Twin Sisters.
- Climb the bluffs to enjoy a great view of the Upper Mississippi River Valley and its flood-plain.
- Bring your binoculars and field guide to observe and identify some of the park's 150 bird species.
- Savor an artist's palette of color—in the spring a profusion of wildflowers lines the trails, and in fall burnished leaves cloak the bluffs.

## Area Information

Mississippi Palisades State Park, near Savanna, is in the southern part of the geologic region known as the Driftless Area, a section untouched by glaciers during all the Ice Ages. With bitterly cold winters, the park is also slow to warm in the spring, allowing for late viewing of spring wildflower assemblages.

The unglaciated topography of the park contains steep limestone bluffs and rock palisades that overlook the Mississippi River. The bluffs are cut by wooded ravines. The name *palisades* was given to the steep bluffs because of their resemblance to similar geological formations along the Hudson River.

Contained within the park is Sentinel Nature Preserve, dedicated as the 200th preserve in the state. This preserve is named for a geological feature called the Sentinel, a freestanding dolomite column rising nearly 200 feet above the talus (rock) slopes. In addition to its geological features, the preserve contains expanses of wildflowers. Extensive stands of Virginia bluebell, great white trillium, and bellwort grow on the north-facing slopes and in ravines. Large concentrations of jeweled shooting star line the bluff tops and southern exposures. They clothe the rocky slopes in a blanket of pink, visible from the highway below.

Whether a hillside of amethyst-colored shooting stars; expanses of trilliums in deep, lush valleys; wild turkeys at dusk; or 400-million-year-old rock palisades, a unique mix of wonders awaits the visitor to Mississippi Palisades State Park.

**Directions:** Mississippi Palisades State Park is located north of Savanna on Illinois Route 84.

**Hours Open:** The site is open year-round except on Christmas Day and New Year's Day.

**Facilities:** A campground with showers (showers in operation from May through October). Boating, fishing, picnicking, and rock climbing are also featured.

**Permits and Rules:** The Sentinel Trail lies within a dedicated Illinois Nature Preserve. No pets are allowed on the trail. On all other trails pets must be leashed. Rock climbers should check in with the site superintendent. All trails are foot travel only.

**For Further Information:** Mississippi Palisades State Park, 16327A Rt. 84, Savanna, IL 61074; 815-273-2731.

## Park Trails

**North Trail System** (, 5.9 miles). The system includes these trails: Rocktop, Goldenrod, Aspen, Bittersweet, Deer, and High Point. The trails' accesses are near the campground. Goldenrod offers pieces of prairie; otherwise the trails are mainly forested.

**South Trail System** (, 3.3 miles). The South trails are Sunset, Sentinel, Indian Head, Prairie View, and Pine. Several of these trails traverse along the bluff edges; use extreme caution. Sunset offers grand vistas, Pine should be hiked in the spring so you can enjoy the diverse wildflowers, and Indian Head features a view of an eroded bluff in the shape of its namesake.

## Other Areas of Interest

**The Upper Mississippi River National Wildlife and Fish Refuge** extends more than 260 miles from Wabasha, Minnesota, to Rock Island, Illinois. Its many ramps offer boating and canoeing opportunities, and the hunting of ducks and geese is allowed during season. It is a great area for wildlife watching, boasting 306 bird species and 51 species of mammals. Wintering bald eagles can number in the hundreds. For more information, call 815-273-2732.

**Lost Mound,** located in northwestern Carroll County, is an area in transition. This area was originally the Savanna Army Depot that began military operations in 1918 as an artillery firing range and later was a testing and munitions storage area. In 2000, the area was closed and divided among several groups. The Fish and Wildlife Service, along with the Illinois Department of Natural Resources, have over 10,000 acres. Here you can find floodplain forests, backwater lakes, a shoreline that contains the tallest natural dune system on the Mississippi River in Illinois, and the largest upland sand prairie in the region. The area is home to nesting bald eagles, regal fritillary butterflies, and grasshopper sparrows. For more information, call 815-273-3184.

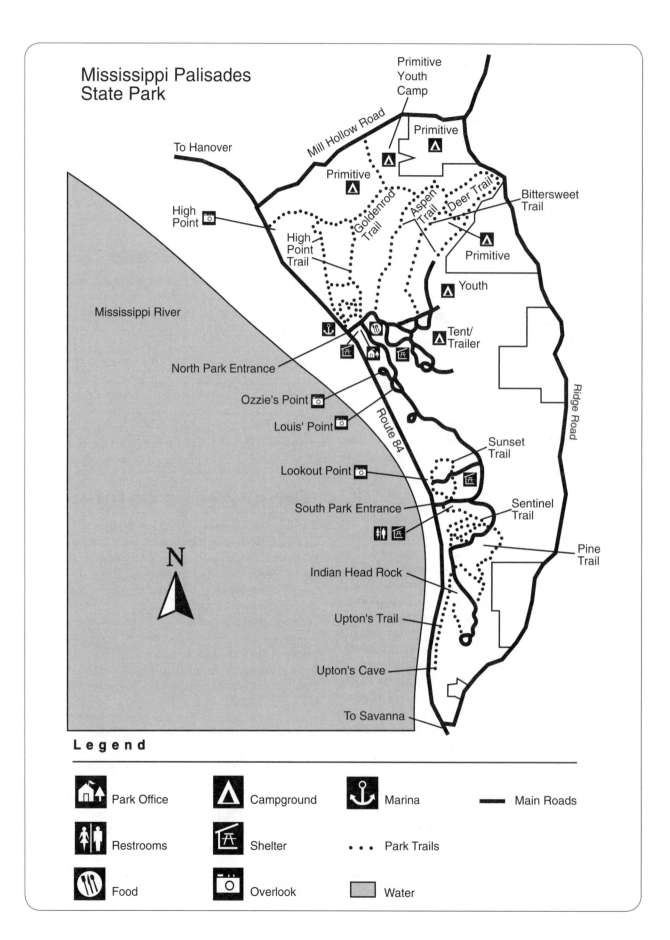

# Mississippi Palisades State Park

To Hanover

Mill Hollow Road

Primitive Youth Camp

Primitive

Primitive

High Point

High Point Trail

Goldenrod Trail

Aspen Trail

Deer Trail

Bittersweet Trail

Primitive

Youth

Mississippi River

Tent/Trailer

North Park Entrance

Ozzie's Point

Louis' Point

Route 84

Sunset Trail

Lookout Point

Sentinel Trail

South Park Entrance

Pine Trail

Ridge Road

Indian Head Rock

Upton's Trail

Upton's Cave

To Savanna

**N**

## Legend

| | | | |
|---|---|---|---|
| Park Office | Campground | Marina | —— Main Roads |
| Restrooms | Shelter | ··· Park Trails | |
| Food | Overlook | Water | |

# Sentinel Trail

 **Distance Round-Trip:** 1 mile
**Estimated Hiking Time:** 1 hour
(or a lifetime, if you like flowers!)

*Celebrate May Day by hiking the Sentinel Trail and its profusion of wildflowers. Peak bloom is usually around this flower-appreciating holiday.*

**Caution:** The trail climbs over rocks and steps that can be very slippery with moss and mud. Tree roots are prominent in the trail, especially near bluff edges. Portions of the trail are also very steep and narrow.

**Trail Directions:** Begin at the Sentinel Trail board and immediately cross the arched stone bridge [1]. Go left off the bridge and enter an Illinois Nature Preserve—one of the state's finest. Although not marked, the trail is a narrow, well-trodden path. If you are hiking from April to May, within a few steps you should have encountered a fantastic array of wildflowers [2]; 10 to 15 species are blooming simultaneously.

Identifying and enjoying the wildflowers should keep you occupied while you gradually climb. At .05 mi. steps lead upward and the trail forks; go right [3]. On your right are two large moss-covered chunks of sandstone. Continue to climb along a narrow ledge. Look on your left for a bluff covered with wildflowers in spring and draped with ferns in summer. On the right will be an overview of the carpet of wildflowers you just walked through.

At .1 mi. [4] go up steps and note the cavelike structure on your left. Skirt a huge boulder, and climb more steps. If visiting in early May, look to the left: Jeweled shooting stars usually carpet the hillside a bright pink. At one time it was classified as a threatened and endangered (T&E) species in Illinois. The state's botanist used binoculars to search likely habitats from roads and was able to locate several new populations of this plant, which turn inaccessible hillsides pink each spring. His search led to removing the jeweled shooting star from the state's T&E list.

Before the overlook of the Mississippi River you will encounter several humanmade spur trails on both the left and right. Please stay on the main path! Go right [5] to the overlook (.2 mi.). Here's a bird's-eye view of the Mississippi River. In the summer the river's lotus beds are quite spectacular from here. From the overlook retrace your steps to [5] and walk along the ridgetop through a mixed woods on either side. The woods along this section were white oak

at one time, but moister species are becoming more common now.

At .4 mi. there will be a bench and a trail intersection; go left [6]. You are hiking once again on a narrow ridge with a bluff on your left and a ravine on your right. This area resembles the old-growth forests of the Pacific Northwest. The hillside is clothed with ferns (many of them lady ferns), and fallen logs are covered with thick green moss. While passing the rock outcrops, look for doll's eye (very colorful berries in the fall) and wild columbine.

A series of slick steps are encountered that lead down, and soon (.6 mi.) you are back at the first intersection [3]. You have completed the loop, so continue downward, retracing your steps through the wildflower-strewn valley (in the spring). Before the bridge (.7 mi.), angle left [7] for a side trail to view the Sentinel. During the summer the bluff on the left will have great blue lobelia and yellow touch-me-not. On your right will be a maintance building.

At .75 mi. go left at the trail board, just before the road. In the spring look here for Canada violet, an uncommon boreal species. The trail curves around the bluff and ends at the Sentinel, a freestanding dolomite column rising nearly 200 feet above the talus (rock) slopes. Admire the column, look for Canada violet in sping, and watch and listen to the climbers before retracing your steps back to the bridge and the parking area.

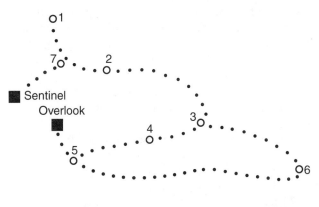

1. Start
2. Flower display
3. Right turn
4. Cavelike structure
5. Right turn to overlook
6. Left turn
7. Angle left to Sentinel

# High Point Trail

**Distance Round-Trip:** 5 miles
**Estimated Hiking Time:** 2 hours

*This trail is for the birds—from the bird's-eye view of the Upper Mississippi River National Wildlife Refuge to the robins darting back and forth and from side to side along the trail. Other notable bird encounters during my hike included a turkey vulture, spooked from the hollows that took off to begin its daily ride on the thermals, and a close encounter with a pair of fuzzy, but naive, great horned owlets.*

**Caution:** The trail is very steep and can be slick, especially after a heavy rain.

**Trail Directions:** Park at the Great River Road sign and begin hiking at the High Point Trail board, climbing on a one-lane gravel road [1]. You will soon go through a gate; the trail on the left leads to Rocky Point, but continue on the original path. Note the white birch and wolf tree (a large oak with outspread branches) on the left. The trail begins to head upward at .2 mi. [2]. Look for loess (windblown silt) and notice its uniform texture and how it is free from rocks. If you touch it, you will find that although it holds together, it is crumbly—good for digging and nest building. Just ask the local swallows!

A bench is on your left at .35 mi. and the gravel and asphalt trail has become a grassy path (and level) [3]. Within a few yards you will encounter Rock Top Trail on your left; continue to the right, noting the shrubby vegetation on either side of the trail. During spring for the next .25 mi. you will encounter large clumps of bellwort, likely one of the best stands in the state. The yellow-petaled flowers that hang down reminded early naturalists of a bell; *wort* means plant. At .80 mi. Goldenrod Trail comes in on the right [4]; continue straight on High Point.

A trail intersection is at 1.05 mi.; go right [5]. As you hike to the overlook the trail begins to narrow. Along this stretch, look for big-tooth aspen intermingling with oaks. The sheltered overlook occurs at 1.5 mi. [6]. Take time to scan the backwaters of the Upper Mississippi River Wildlife Refuge. From the shelter retrace your steps back to [5] and then go right.

A major intersection appears at 2.1 mi. [7]. Go right for .25 mi. to the overlook at a dead end. You will hike on rolling terrain until the trail comes to a wide area with a danger sign—steep cliff ahead [8] (2.3 mi.). From the overlook you may explore (look for jeweled shooting star), but use caution because this part of the trail is very steep and slick. Through the fence of cedars, look at the marsh across the way and listen to the geese. Explore a little and then retrace your steps back to the intersection [7].

Back at [7] (2.6 mi.), take the first right downhill. You will be walking through a valley, dwarfed by the large bluffs on either side. Rock outcrops and more shooting stars appear on the right. A maidenhair fern-covered slope is on the left. The trail forks at 3.05 mi. [9]; go left and up. On the right note a fence, a shed, and the road. You will pass a house at 3.2 mi. [10]; go left. By 3.25 mi. you are away from development and hiking through wooded bluffs on either side again.

Look to your right at 3.3 mi. to see a nice valley [11]. The bluffs are lush with ferns, and farther down the trail on the left is a sandstone outcrop with a patch of walking fern. At 3.65 mi. the grassy path curves left and goes up [12], and in .1 mi. you are back at [7]. Go right and uphill. Mile 3.85 brings you back to [5] and the main trail; go right. As you retrace your steps, look for stands of white birch appearing like ghosts in the forest. At 4.5 mi. you are back to where Rock Top Trail comes in; continue on High Point and back to the trail board.

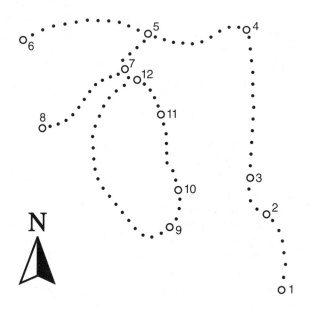

1. Start
2. Loess
3. Bench
4. Trail intersection
5. Right turn
6. Sheltered overlook
7. Trail intersection
8. Overlook
9. Left turn
10. House
11. Valley
12. Curve left

# 3. Rock Cut State Park

- Get away from it all within the confines of the second-largest city in Illinois.

- Hike through a kaleidoscope of spring warblers.

- Bring your plant and bird field guides for prairie and woodland flora and spring warblers.

- View aspens colored for autumn in Illinois.

## Area Information

The city of Rockford is located in a region of rolling topography drained by the Rock River. If you were to look at the soil of the area, you would find not the deep, fine-particle soils of areas to the east and south, but glacial till and outwash—a mixture of sand, gravel, and dolomite with only a thin layer of soil on top.

Rocks, whether the tiny particles that make up the area's soils or larger examples found along the Rock River, played a part in the development of the area. Rockford is where wagons once forded the Rock River—hence its name. Rock Cut State Park, which opened in 1962, is the site of the old Kenosha-Rockford Rail Line. Most of the railroad bed is now under the waters of Pierce Lake. The name of the park can be traced to the days of rock-quarrying operations near the site. In 1859, engineers blasted through solid rock to provide a suitable roadbed for the Kenosha-Rockford Railroad. The procedure was referred to as the cut through the rock.

A visit to the park wouldn't be complete without a glimpse of Lone Rock, a great rock standing high and isolated in the grove. Legend has it that in the 19th century Native Americans inhabited the area. A young warrior wooed and won the daughter of the Potawatomi chief. The young couple's happiness was interrupted with a summons to the warpath. When the warriors returned, the young warrior was not among them. The Potawatomi maiden was devastated, and one night when the camp was asleep, she wandered to the base of the rock and climbed to the top; while singing her song, she hurled herself over the edge. The tribe told of how, if one ventures near the rock at night, the maiden might be seen flitting about in the moonlight.

**Directions:** Rock Cut State Park is located 7 miles northeast of Rockford and is accessible from Illinois Route 173.

**Hours Open:** The site is open year-round, except on Christmas Day and New Year's Day.

**Facilities:** The park offers camping that includes electricity and showers, fishing, boating, swimming, picnicking, a concession stand, and two fishing piers accessible to the disabled. During the winter only electricity and pit toilets are available. Winter brings cross-country skiing, ice fishing, ice skating, and snowmobiling.

**Permits and Rules:** Rock Cut State Park does not allow alcoholic beverages in the park from March 1 through May 31. Do not pick any of the flowers, and keep your pets leashed at all times. From November 30 to March 31 the trails are closed to bicycles.

**For Further Information:** Rock Cut State Park, 7318 Harlem Road, Loves Park, IL 61111; 815-885-3311.

## Park Trails

**Pierce Lake Trail** (🥾, 4.25 miles). Circumnavigate the shoreline of Pierce Lake at Rock Cut State Park on this loop trail. You will hike not only by the water's edge but through wooded areas as well.

## Other Areas of Interest

Located southwest of Rock Cut State Park, **Harlem Hills Nature Preserve** is the only gravel-terrace prairie that has not succumbed to the city of Rockford, and it is the largest and finest remaining example in Illinois. Enjoy a profusion of wildflowers, from pasque flowers in the spring and pale purple coneflower in the summer to blazing star at summer's end. Although there are no formal trails, several short footpaths allow exploration of this unique area. For more information, call 815-732-6185.

Located only 30 minutes from Rockford, **Long Prairie Trail** begins north of Illinois Route 173. The 14.2-mile linear asphalt trail, marked every half mile, highlights natural history features and points to where interesting human events occurred. For a trail map and more information, call 815-547-7935.

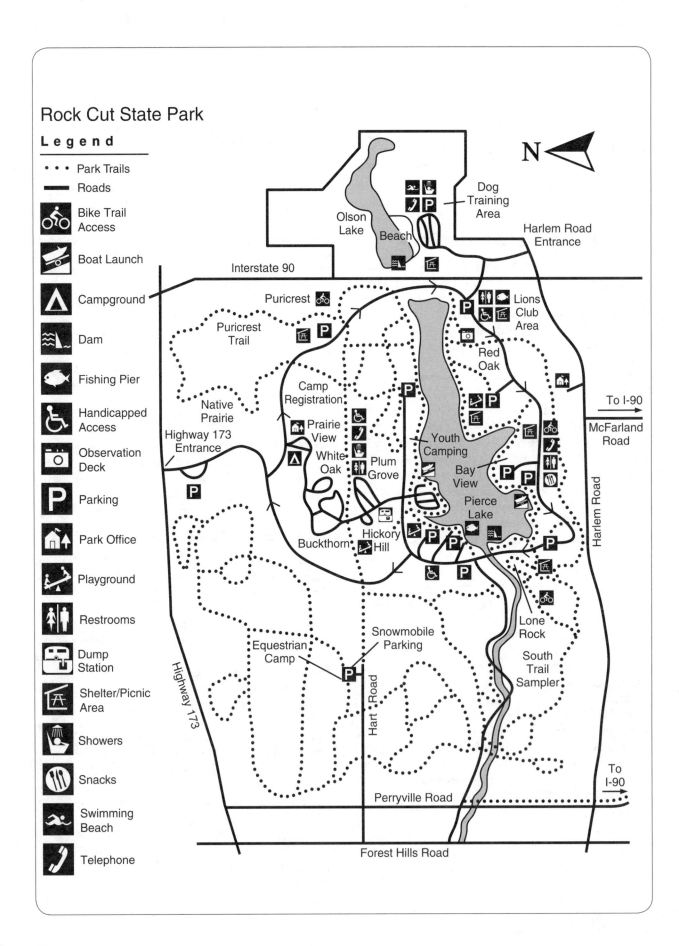

# Rock Cut State Park

### Legend

- • • Park Trails
- —— Roads
- Bike Trail Access
- Boat Launch
- Campground
- Dam
- Fishing Pier
- Handicapped Access
- Observation Deck
- Parking
- Park Office
- Playground
- Restrooms
- Dump Station
- Shelter/Picnic Area
- Showers
- Snacks
- Swimming Beach
- Telephone

Olson Lake

Beach

Dog Training Area

Harlem Road Entrance

Interstate 90

Puricrest

Puricrest Trail

Native Prairie

Highway 173 Entrance

Camp Registration

Prairie View

White Oak

Plum Grove

Buckthorn

Hickory Hill

Lions Club Area

Red Oak

Youth Camping

Bay View

Pierce Lake

To I-90

McFarland Road

Lone Rock

South Trail Sampler

Harlem Road

Equestrian Camp

Snowmobile Parking

Hart Road

Highway 173

Perryville Road

Forest Hills Road

To I-90

N

# Rock Cut State Park—
# South Trail Sampler

 **Distance Round-Trip:** 3.15 miles
**Estimated Hiking Time:** 1.5 hours

*As I entered the park, I had to slow for a dozen wild turkeys crossing the parkway. At the trailhead, I had yet another turkey encounter. Thirty were feeding on hickory nutmeats, their wattles glowing translucent orange in the early morning light—a true Kodak moment and one of several I had on the trails at Rock Cut State Park.*

**Caution:** Roots and rocks have eroded from the trail. Remember that some parts of the trail are shared with bicyclists; be cautious.

**Trail Directions:** Park at West Lake Picnic Area and begin at the trail board [1]. The trail is marked with red, and within less than .05 mi. you will come to a wooden platform with a staircase—Lone Rock [2]. Head down the stairs, looking at both the rock and the pond on the right; cross a bridge and head up the stairs. Go right off the stairs.

You will go left and left [3] again, all within .1 mi. as you hike through an oak, hickory, black walnut, and basswood forest. An intersection is at .3 mi.; go right [4]. The trail is marked in blue and is now shared with bicyclists. Look for the Vs of turkey scratchings as you hike this section. Be on the lookout for rocks and roots (and, in the fall, black walnuts) in this undulating trail that has more tire marks than shoeprints.

A trail junction appears at 1 mi. [5]; continue left and cross the road to enter the forest on the opposite side. The trail has become narrow and is rated difficult for cyclists. This part of the trail has some obstacles for cyclists; hikers are able to step up and over them. A trail intersection will be encountered soon; go right (straight) and then right again and cross a creek. You will come out into a hilly clearing; go right across the stream.

Along this section of the trail, find periodical offshoots and spurs; stay on the main, well-traveled trail. Unfortunately, along this section you can hear I-90 in the distance. As you enter the pines go right and downhill [6]. The trail comes to a T at 2.1 mi.; go right [7], passing a natural area on your left. At 2.25 mi. go left back into the woods; you have returned to [5]. Retrace your steps, but once at [4] (2.9 mi.) go straight (to the right) on the blue trail.

You will come out into a parking and picnic area [8]; bear left and you will soon pick up the trail on the left and head back into the woods. At 3.15 mi. you are back to the trail board where you started. If it is dusk, take a short spur back to Lone Rock to see if you can hear or see the Indian maiden's spirit.

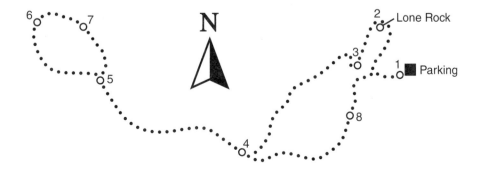

1. Start
2. Lone Rock
3. Left turn, left turn
4. Right turn
5. Junction, left turn
6. Pines
7. Trail Ts, right turn
8. Parking/picnic area

North

## Puricrest Trail

  **Distance Round-Trip:** 2.1 miles
**Estimated Hiking Time:** 1 hour

*If you can't make it out west to see the aspen's fall color show, don't despair; this trail and its groves offer plenty of aspen-viewing opportunities.*

**Caution:** You will be sharing the trail with bicyclists and horses.

**Trail Directions:** Park at the Puricrest picnic area parking lot and begin the trail at the trail board [1]. The trail begins as a wide, grassy path through a second-growth mixed woods. An intersection is at .15 mi.; go left [2]. The trail is now marked with blue and yellow. You will soon cross the road, where the trail is a straight path with a grassy "old field" on the right and cedars on the left.

The trail Ts at .3 mi.; go right [3] through a grassy area with goldenrod in the summer and fall. Look for goldfinches in this section. Also look for poison ivy as it climbs the adjacent trees. In the fall this plant is quite stunning; its leaves mimic the colors of the sugar maples and its fruiting berries are white.

The first of a series of quaking aspen groves appears at .55 mi. [4]. You will pass a grove of river birch on the right at .7 mi. [5]. A horse trail (marked with yellow) intersects the trail; continue straight (to the left) [6] on the trail marked with blue and yellow. You will cross the road at 1.1 mi. [7]; on the other side you have entered an even-aged stand of silver maples. The silver maples soon give way to a mixed woods, which includes tulip trees, a more southern species.

You will pass a large river birch with scaly, flaky bark at 1.5 mi., and then the trail passes a grove of even-aged alders. Wild parsnip lines the path here. Although the plant is phototoxic, swallowtail butterflies do not have a problem with it. Look for black swallowtails and giant swallowtails in this area.

At 1.8 mi. the trail Ys; go right [8] and continue on the multipurpose trail (blue and yellow markers). A grove of hickory trees soon appears. Hickories have compound leaves with toothed leaflets. The wood of hickories is strong and tough but decays on contact with moisture. The nuts are a favorite food of squirrels and turkeys. The trail Ys again at 2 mi.; go left [9], and you are now retracing your steps back into the woods (the trail is marked only with blue). Retrace your steps back to the parking area and the trail board.

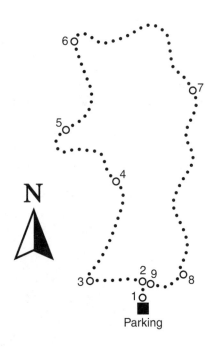

1. Start
2. Left turn
3. Right turn
4. Aspen groves
5. River birch
6. Go straight (left)
7. Road crossing
8. Right turn
9. Left turn

- Visit one of the largest small-bird banding operations in the country.
- Discover Colored Sands.
- Straddle the Illinois and Wisconsin border.
- Hike through extensive sand prairies and sand savannas.

## Area Information

Original land surveys show that Winnebago County was 30 percent forest and 70 percent prairie. Forests grew along the rivers—the Rock, Sugar, and Pecatonica—where the prairie fires were kept at bay. Settlers timbered the forests and converted the prairies to pastures for dairy farming. The Winnebago County Forest Preserve District was formed in 1922 by citizens who wanted to preserve some of the county's flora, fauna, and scenic beauty for future generations.

Two preserves along the Sugar River—**Colored Sands** and **Sugar River Alder**—are perhaps some of the area's best, yet when the county bought them in the 1930s they were considered derelict land. Both of these preserves are on an inland sand deposit that covers a band 12 miles long and 4 miles wide, bordered by the Rock River to the east and the Sugar River to the west. The sand was deposited by wind after the last glaciation and formed dunes and ridges along the Sugar River. The dunes and ridges were eventually stabilized by forest and prairie vegetation. At Colored Sands, one of the larger dunes (40 feet tall) is part of an Illinois Nature Preserve.

Colored Sands is the local name for St. Peter sandstone. While the sandstone lies invisible beneath most of Illinois, it is exposed in the upland areas of northern Winnebago County. The stone contains naturally occurring iron oxides that turn red when exposed to weather and darken the stone, forming colors. Settlers mined the eroded, tinted sand from these outcrops to make colorful jar decorations for their homes.

Within Colored Sands is Sand Bluff Bird Observatory, one of the largest small-bird banding operations in the country that is open to the public. The observatory is a research facility operated by volunteers. The birds are caught in mist nets that, together, stretch for almost a mile through Colored Sands prairies and woods. Captured birds are returned to the observatory to be banded and released. Banding helps biologists learn about bird migration patterns. Through this station's hard work, the Sugar River Corridor is documented as a vital migration route for more than 150 species.

**Directions:** **Colored Sands** is located in northern Winnebago County. From Rockford, take Meridian Road south to Shirland Road. Turn left on Shirland Road, turn right on Boswell Road, turn left on Yale Bridge Road, turn right on Hauley Road, and finally turn left on Haas Road. Proceed 1 mile to the entrance. **Sugar River Alder** is north of Colored Sands, and you pass this preserve before entering Colored Sands.

**Hours Open:** The sites are open year-round. Sand Bluff Bird Observatory is open Saturdays 8:00 a.m. to 4:00 p.m. and Sundays 8:00 a.m. to 10:00 a.m. March through May and September through November.

**Facilities:** Restrooms, drinking water, and picnic tables are found at both sites. Colored Sands also has a canoe launch.

**Permits and Rules:** Keep your pets leashed at all times. Access to the mist nets at Sand Bluff Bird Observatory is only with a certified staff member.

**For Further Information:** Winnebago County Forest Preserve District, 5500 Northrock Drive, Rockford, IL 61103; 815-877-6100 or www.wcfpd.org. Sand Bluff Bird Observatory: c/o Mike Eichman, P.O. Box 2, Seward, IL 61077; 815-964-2378.

## Other Areas of Interest

Located south of Colored Sands is **Sugar River Forest Preserve**. This 530-acre tract contains a campground with a shower area, picnic areas, a playground, and an equestrian area. Several hiking trails, totaling 6 miles, explore woodlands, sand prairie, and the river. Call 815-877-6100 for more information.

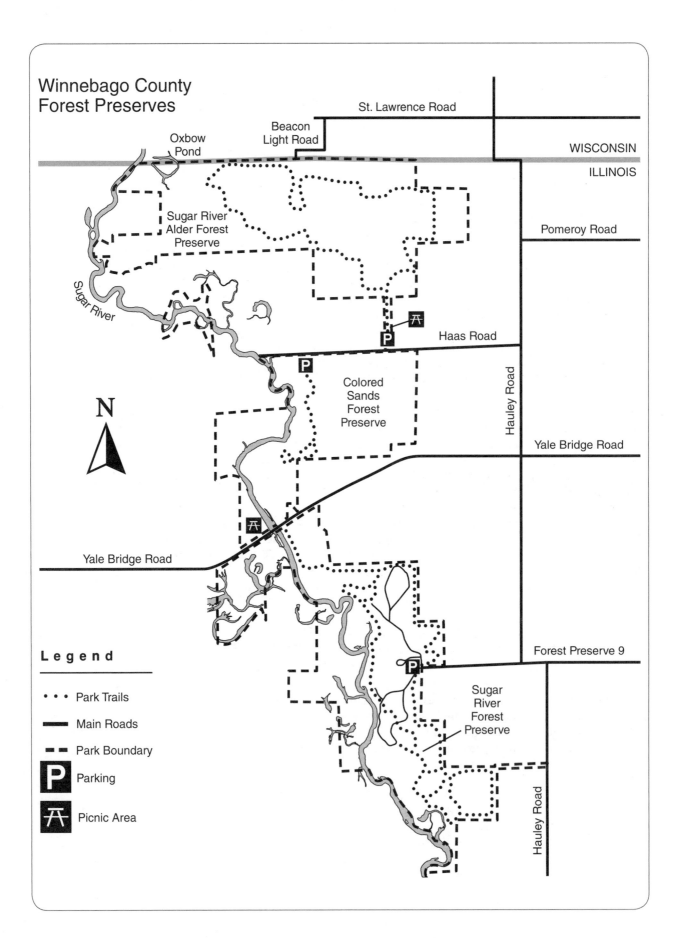

# Winnebago County Forest Preserves

St. Lawrence Road

Beacon Light Road

Oxbow Pond

WISCONSIN

ILLINOIS

Pomeroy Road

Sugar River Alder Forest Preserve

Sugar River

N

Haas Road

Hauley Road

P

P

Colored Sands Forest Preserve

Yale Bridge Road

Yale Bridge Road

Forest Preserve 9

P

Sugar River Forest Preserve

Hauley Road

**L e g e n d**

• • • Park Trails

—— Main Roads

- - - Park Boundary

**P** Parking

🛆 Picnic Area

# Colored Sands

 **Distance Round-Trip:** 1.15 miles
**Estimated Hiking Time:** .9 hour

*This trail gave me the blues. It was a blue-sky Indian summer day; clusters of little bluestem dominated the prairie; a shiny, blue-green blister beetle crawled across my path; and the bird banders caught an eastern bluebird while I was there.*

**Caution:** Do not enter the Sugar River overlook area.

**Trail Directions:** Begin the trail at the trail board **[1]** across from the bird-banding building. If the banders are present while you are hiking, be sure to take advantage of their presence—they are a wealth of information. The trail is a sandy path through the prairie. You can see the banders' mist nets off to the left. Stay on the wide main trail.

At .1 mi. you will see a sign on the right indicating a nature preserve **[2]**. This area was dedicated as a nature preserve in 1976 because of its natural features of eroding bluffs, sand savanna, dolomite prairie, and sand prairie. Within a tenth of a mile a trail comes in from the left; ignore it. Instead, enjoy the aspen grove and note the octagonal building on the left, a hawk-banding station.

The trail Ys at .35 mi.; go right **[3]**. On your right will be the nature preserve; prairie is on your left. The trail leads you through a sand savanna. Notice how many of the small oak trees are sprouting from their fire-scarred bases. These are called grubs. Along this section, don't forget to look down at the trail for evidence of wild turkeys—oval depressions where they dust-bathe and V-shaped scratchings where they have been searching for food.

Half a mile brings you to the overlook of the Sugar River **[4]**. You are standing on top of a large sand dune that was deposited during the last glaciation. The Sugar River is a stream of fast, clear water that, for the most part, runs over a bed of rock and sand. Stretches of this river have been designated as a biologically significant stream in Illinois. The Native Americans called the stream "sweet water." While at the overlook, don't forget to look for outcrops of sandstone—the colored sands that gave the area its name.

After the overlook, continue on the trail. At .55 mi., go right **[5]**. At .6 mi. you emerge from the savanna; go right **[6]** again, and at the trailboard go straight (ignoring the sign). At .75 mi. you are back at **[3]** and have completed the loop. Retrace your steps back to the parking area, and if the banders are present, see what they may have captured.

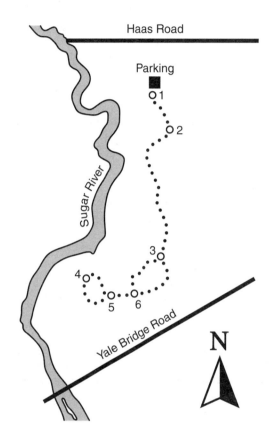

1. Start
2. Nature preserve sign
3. Right turn
4. Sugar River overlook
5. Right turn
6. Right turn

North

# Sugar River Alder

  **Distance Round Trip:** 3.8 miles
**Estimated Hiking Time:** 2 hours

*Like the applause at the finish line of a big race, greeting me at trail's end were two dozen cedar waxwings cavorting in a leafless tree and giving their high-pitched calls.*

**Caution:** Watch your step on the trail; tree roots have eroded from the soil of the path and can catch an unsuspecting toe. You will share this trail with bicyclists.

**Trail Directions:** You could hike from Colored Sands to Sugar River Alder using the 2-mile connecting path between the two preserves. But begin your hike of Sugar River Alder at the preserve's trail board [1]. At certain intersections there will be maps marked with a "you are here" arrow.

You first hike through huge patches of brown-eyed Susans, Indian grass, and big bluestem on a connector trail through an oak-hickory forest. An intersection is at .2 mi.; go right [2]. Watch where you step; hordes of grasshoppers will launch into the air in front of you. Although most people think the bison ate the most grass on the prairie, it was really the grasshoppers! The trail Ts at .55 mi.; go right [3] through a field of little bluestem. The roots of little bluestem are 3 to 4 feet deep, enabling it to withstand periods of drought.

The trail will curve right through a woods that was logged at one time. Periodically, you will see a large oak amidst the saplings. The trail emerges from the woods at 1.1 mi. into a thick stand of Indian grass [4] and little bluestem. The trail then goes straight into an area dominated by pines. At 1.35 mi. the trail Ts; go right [5], and on either side will be a recovering prairie. Soon you are hiking through an allée of oaks. At the intersection at 1.5 mi. [6], go left (right leads to a privy and a pump). Within .1 mi. the trail will Y at a grove of oaks; go right (a sign for a nature preserve will be on your left). This nature preserve is an extension of the one at Colored Sands.

The trail Ts again at 1.9 mi.; go right [7] and note a sand prairie restoration on the left. On your right are oaks with some large ash trees. On the other side of the tree line is Wisconsin! The trail will soon go through the woods and curve left, somewhat following the creek on the right. A Y junction appears at 2.4 mi. [8]; go left. Glance through the trees for a view of a dolomite prairie. The trail Ts again at 2.7 mi.; go right [9] through an oak-pine woods that eventually becomes a pine plantation.

The trail comes to a crossroad at 3 mi. [10]; go right. Look for large oaks along this segment. You will soon come out into a restoration area. The trail curves left at 3.4 mi., and by 3.5 mi. you have completed the loop and are back at [2]. Retrace your steps to the parking area.

1. Start
2. Right turn
3. Right turn, little bluestem
4. Indian grass
5. Right turn
6. Intersection
7. Right turn, Wisconsin
8. Left turn
9. Right turn
10. Crossroad, right turn

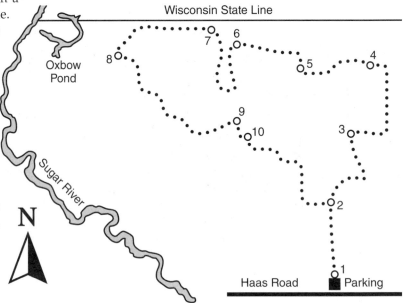

- Hike through woods that support white pines—not the uniform plantations found in much of Illinois, but massive examples that occur naturally on the site (the southernmost natural population of white pines in the United States).
- Travel through straight-trunked trees that form a distant canopy high overhead.
- Admire waves of wild ginger that create green carpets, even in fall.
- Ford Pine Creek without leaving your car.
- Look for unusual forms of fungus attached to decaying trees and logs.

## Area Information

Although noted for its human history as the southern boundary of the old Chicago-Iowa Trail, the natural history of White Pines Forest State Park is what takes precedence. Nowhere else in Illinois can one experience such a mixed hardwood-conifer forest. None of these trees grew in the open because each white oak and white pine is straight trunked and very tall, specimens that obviously grew amidst other trees. Originally containing over 700 acres along Pine Creek when first encountered by European settlers, the park today supports nearly 400 acres of trees and open lands.

As early as 1903, Ogle County residents were petitioning their politicians to save this southernmost and last Illinois remnant of white pines. Although they initially failed, in 1927 Congress finally appropriated funds to purchase and preserve the area. Any season is a good time to visit the pines, but spring and winter are particularly beautiful—spring for its displays of wildflowers, and winter for the soft, silky blanket of snow that creates a stark contrast with the dark green needles of the pines and accentuates the fact that this forest is indeed a unique place in Illinois.

**Directions:** White Pines Forest State Park is located east of Polo and 8 miles west of Oregon on Pines Road.

**Hours Open:** Open year-round.

**Facilities:** Picnicking, camping, cross-country skiing, and restrooms are included. Its 1930s Civilian Conservation Corp (CCC)–constructed lodge (with cabins), the White Pines Inn, houses a gift shop and restaurant. For lodge reservations, call 815-946-3817.

**Permits and Rules:** Pets must be leashed at all times. Wading in Pine Creek is prohibited.

**For Further Information:** White Pines Forest State Park, 6712 West Pines Road, Mt. Morris, IL 61504, 815-946-3717.

## Park Trails

**Razor Back Trail** (🥾, .75 mile). This linear trail allows you to discover Pine Creek and view the surrounding limestone bluffs. Look for tadpoles, ducks, and geese.

**Sleepy Hollow Trail** (🥾🥾, 1.2 miles). You will cross Pine Creek three times as you wind your way through the park, viewing the pines and the vine-covered limestone bluffs.

## Other Areas of Interest

**Nachusa Grassland,** an Illinois Nature Conservancy preserve south of Oregon on the east side of the Rock River (along Lowden Road), is a 1,200-acre natural area that features a mosaic of forest and prairie. Listed as a major work in progress, the site is undergoing extensive restoration activities. For more information, go to www.nature.org or call 815-456-2340.

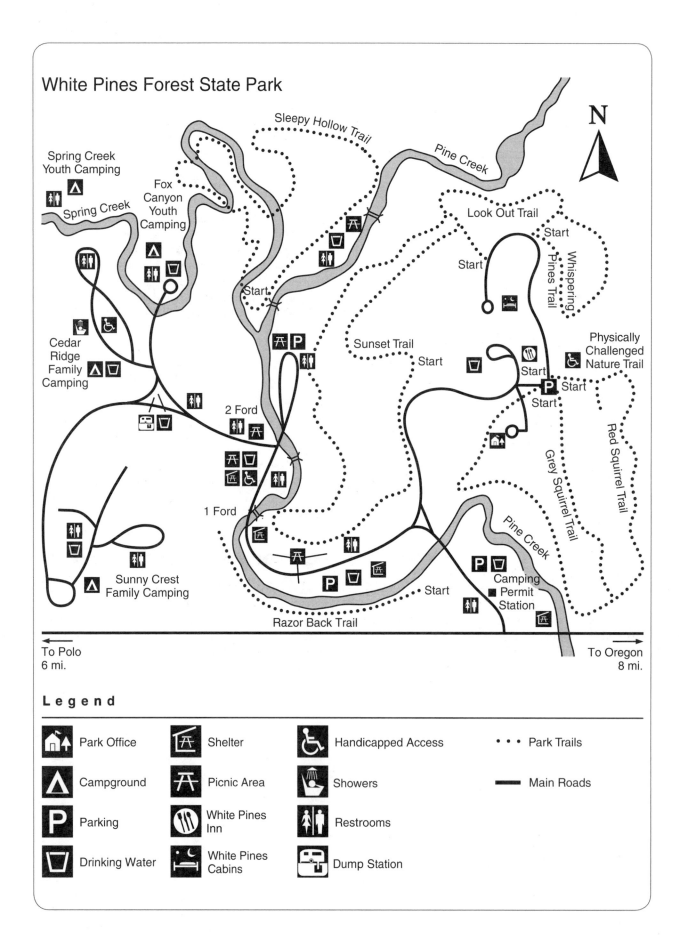

# White Pines Forest State Park

Sleepy Hollow Trail

Spring Creek Youth Camping

Fox Canyon Youth Camping

Spring Creek

Pine Creek

Look Out Trail

Start

Whispering Pines Trail

Start

Start

Cedar Ridge Family Camping

Sunset Trail

Start

Physically Challenged Nature Trail

2 Ford

Start

Start

P Start

1 Ford

Grey Squirrel Trail

Red Squirrel Trail

Sunny Crest Family Camping

Pine Creek

Start

Camping Permit Station

Razor Back Trail

To Polo
6 mi.

To Oregon
8 mi.

## Legend

| | | | | | | |
|---|---|---|---|---|---|---|
| 🏠 | Park Office | 🏕 | Shelter | ♿ | Handicapped Access | ••• Park Trails |
| ⛺ | Campground | 🏕 | Picnic Area | 🚿 | Showers | — Main Roads |
| P | Parking | 🍴 | White Pines Inn | 🚻 | Restrooms | |
| 🥤 | Drinking Water | 🌙 | White Pines Cabins | 🚐 | Dump Station | |

North    20

# Red Squirrel and Gray Squirrel Trails

 **Distance Round-Trip:** 1.25 miles
**Estimated Hiking Time:** 1 hour

*The virgin white pine forests of the eastern United States were so vast that pioneers boasted a squirrel could travel its lifetime (7 to 10 years) without ever setting a paw on the ground. This small remnant provided me with historical insight as I gazed upward and watched gray squirrels scramble from lofty branch to lofty branch.*

**Caution:** Many large trees have been toppled in recent years, and portions of the trail might be littered with their branches. This is deer tick country, so take precautions (light clothes, socks over pant legs, and tick repellent).

**Trail Directions:** Park in the lot between the park headquarters and the lodge. The trailhead for Red Squirrel Trail is on the northeast corner and will be designated with brown posts with a blue top. Enter the trail and soon turn right. Note a CCC-constructed stone well house on the right [1]. Signs designating a nature preserve will be along the trail on the left. This area will look like a typical Illinois forest, at least until you look up! The canopy is made up of large oaks and white pines—the latter not planted but native to the site. These trees are forest grown. The clues are their long, straight trunks and fan-shaped canopies that reach far overhead. The forest around you is a curious mixture of several species of hardwoods and large pines. It may look like Illinois, but it smells like the north woods!

At .15 mi. go right and take the stairs up [2]. There are several downed trees in this segment, so look for fungus attached to the logs. An intersection appears at .25 mi.; go right onto Gray Squirrel [3]. You are now following brown posts with green tops. The large, green, heart-shaped leaves that carpet areas of the understory (plants growing under the canopy) are wild ginger. During the spring a maroon flower is hidden beneath their leaves. This plant was used as a substitute for tropical ginger by pioneers.

Another intersection appears within a tenth of a mile; go left down a gnarled root path. At .5 mi. you will come into the parking lot [4]. Cross the lot, walk the park road to the right side of the maintance building, and go into the woods. There will be a trail marker (brown with a green cap) within a few steps. Go down

the steps and cross a bridge. A CCC-constructed kiln is on the left [5] (.55 mi.).

For an interesting side spur, take the trail at .65 mi. down to the tree identification area [6]; over 30 species of trees are identified. Retrace your steps back to the trail, where you are following the ridgeline overlooking Pine Creek. An observation platform [7] is found at .7 mi. on the right; go down the steps to view Pine Creek and look for great blue herons. Retrace your steps back up and continue past a CCC-constructed bench. The trail leads along a ridge between two creeks; look for waves of wild ginger and spring wildflowers.

Go down and up a set of steps, coming up between two large white pines competing with a large oak [8]. You are hiking under arching branches. Come to an intersection [3] at 1.1 mi.; go left, retracing your steps. The trail soon ends at the Gray Squirrel sign where you parked.

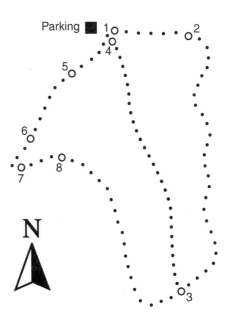

1. Start
2. Right turn, stairs
3. Right turn onto Gray Squirrel Trail
4. Parking lot
5. Kiln
6. Spur to tree identification area
7. Observation platform
8. Two large white pines

# Sunset Trail

   **Distance Round-Trip:** 2.25 miles
**Estimated Hiking Time:** 1.4 hours

*This forest of tall trees is the closest to California that Illinois has; the trees just aren't as tall or as large.*

**Caution:** Many large trees have been toppled in recent years, and portions of the trail might be littered with their branches. Don't get tripped up by a root in the trail. This is deer tick country, so take precautions (light clothes, socks over pant legs, and tick repellent).

**Trail Directions:** After passing the second ford, park and begin the trail at the large sycamore [1]. A trail connector is adjacent to a rock outcrop. Go left up a narrow set of stairs. You are hiking this trail backward, and it is marked with posts with white caps. The trail wanders through large cedars with even larger white pines as you hike on a ridge above Pine Creek. Several access trails come in from the left; ignore these and stay on the well-worn dirt path.

At the trail intersection at .2 mi, continue left [2] on Lookout Trail, which is marked with red. You are hiking through mixed hardwoods; look for early spring wildflowers—hepatica and anemone. Look to your left at .4 mi. to view an old railroad bridge [3]. As you hike along this section, gazing at the pines, notice the difference in the pine bark. Young white pines have smooth, green bark, but as the tree ages the bark turns brown to black and becomes fissured and rectangular. Notice whether there are many young pines to take the place of these giants.

Another trail intersection appears at .55 mi.; go left [4] on Whispering Pines Trail, marked with yellow. The pines seem even taller along this stretch of the trail. You will come to a crossroads at .75 mi.; go right [5]. The trail is lined with several species of ferns, and if you look closely at the trunks of the trees, you might catch a glimpse of a white-breasted nuthatch. This tiny white and blue-black bird moves up and down tree trunks, gleaning insects and giving a high, beeping call.

At the intersection at .9 mi. [6], go right. The trail will intersect the road at 1.05

mi.; cross the park road and go back into the woods. You will come to [4] again at 1.1 mi.; go left, retracing your steps on Lookout Trail and admiring the railroad bridge once more.

A pair of intersections [7] appears at 1.5 mi.; at the first one, go left away from the creek. Within a few steps the second one will appear; go right on this one. Immediately on your left is a large white pine. Trees over 100 feet tall will be common along this section. Look for doll's eye, a member of the buttercup family that grows to about 2 feet tall. Its fruits are white clusters of berries that have a dark purple spot at one end and look like eyes.

Stay right as several access trails come in from the left. At 1.6 mi. go left [8] even though you see a trail marker (post with a white cap) straight ahead. (Remember, we are doing the trail backward.) You are now hiking on grassy steps; a split oak will be on your left. Take another left within a tenth of a mile; this will lead to the trail board [9]. Walk along the grassy area between the woods and the road. This section is periodically marked with white posts. The trail heads right, into the woods, prior to the park road heading downhill.

This segment of the trail is now dominated by lofty white oaks; note the scaly bark. At 2 mi. the trail Ts [10]; go right at the large pine and you are hiking on the ridge above Pine Creek again. Stairs appear at 2.2 mi.; these are the same ones you used to ascend to the trail. Go down, back to the large sycamore and your vehicle.

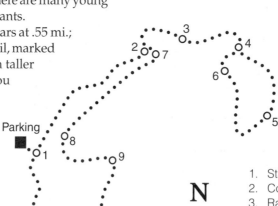

1. Start
2. Continue left on Lookout Trail
3. Railroad bridge
4. Left turn onto Whispering Pines
5. Right turn
6. Right turn
7. Pair of intersections
8. Left turn
9. Trail board
10. Trail Ts, right turn

- Bring your binoculars; 20 species of warblers breed at Lowden-Miller State Forest.
- Follow the numbers as you string fire trails together.
- Learn about the timber industry as you hike.
- Savor the piney smell of the north woods.

## Area Information

Lowden-Miller State Forest, located along the eastern shoreline of the Rock River, originally belonged to Frank Lowden, governor of Illinois from 1917 to 1921. He named the area "Sinnissippi"—a Native American word for rocky water, referring to the Rock River. On sandy hillsides unsuitable for conventional farming, Lowden began planting white pines, a native species suited to the sandy soil. Encouraged by these results, he expanded his plantings and began to augment the natural oak-hickory forest with pines as well. Lowden's effort was one of the first large-scale reforestations of the state.

In 1992 and '93 Lowden's grandsons sold most of the forest land to the State of Illinois to create the 2,200-acre Lowden-Miller State Forest, named after their parents and grandparents. The forest is a mosaic of even-aged stands of trees and provides a unique habitat for birds.

During 1995, the Illinois Natural History Survey conducted a breeding-bird census of the area. Scientists found 100 bird species either breeding or defending territories. These breeding-bird species were a mix of northern and southern species found nowhere else in Illinois. Of these, 20 species were warblers (the much larger Shawnee National Forest has 19 breeding warbler species) and included the state's first nest of the black-throated green warbler, a breeder of northeastern coniferous forests. On October 6, 2004, Lowden-Miller State Forest was designated an important bird area of Illinois.

**Directions:** Lowden-Miller State Forest is found along the eastern shoreline of the Rock River. From Oregon, take Illinois Route 64 east, across the Rock River. At the stoplights of Route 64 and Daysville Road, turn south onto Daysville Road, go 2 miles, and turn right on Lowden Road. Go 1 mile and turn right on Nashua Road and proceed to the forest.

**Hours Open:** This site is open year-round. The hiking trails are closed during firearm hunting season.

**Facilities:** Lowden-Miller State Forest offers parking and hunting.

**Permits and Rules:** Pets must be leashed at all times.

**For Further Information:** Castle Rock State Park, 1365 W. Castle Road, Oregon, IL 61061; 815-732-7329.

## Park Trails

**Lowden-Miller State Forest** has 22 miles of trails available for hiking and cross-country skiing.

## Other Areas of Interest

**Nachusa Grassland,** a Nature Conservancy preserve south of Oregon on the east side of the Rock River (along Lowden Road), is a 1,200-acre natural area that features a mosaic of forest and prairie. Listed as a major work in progress, the site is undergoing extensive restoration activities. For more information, go to www.nature.org or call 815-456-2340.

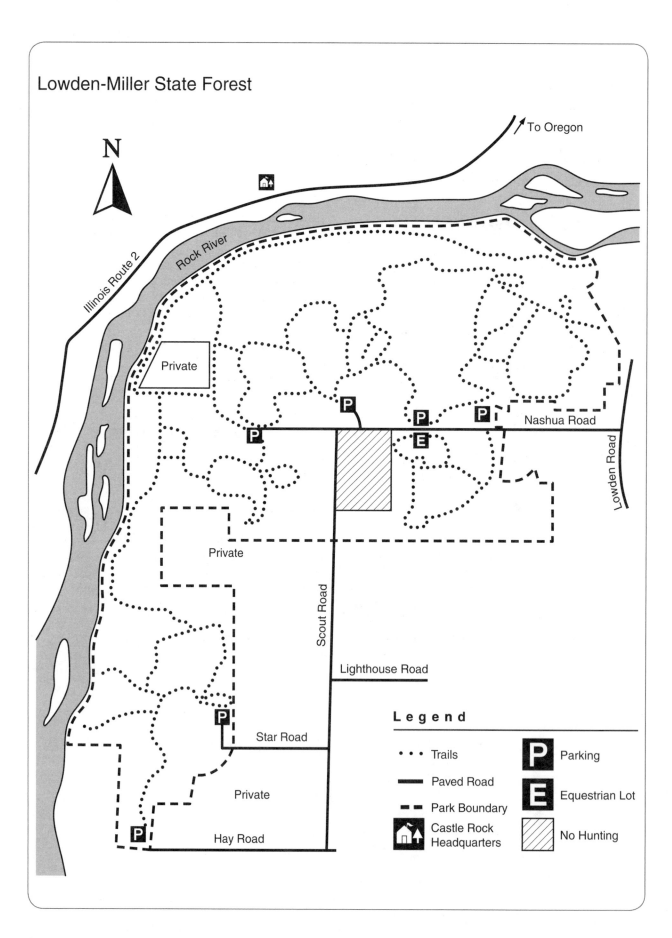

Lowden-Miller State Forest

N

To Oregon

Illinois Route 2

Rock River

Private

P

P

P

P

E

Nashua Road

Lowden Road

Private

Scout Road

Lighthouse Road

P

Star Road

Private

P

Hay Road

**Legend**

- • • Trails
- —— Paved Road
- – – Park Boundary
- 🏠 Castle Rock Headquarters

P Parking

E Equestrian Lot

▨ No Hunting

# Fire Trail Sampler

 **Distance Round-Trip:** 3.25 miles
**Estimated Hiking Time:** 1.5 hours

*The numbers 22, 24, 19, 33, 13, and 9 sound like a winning combination for the state lottery. Actually, it's a winning spring and summer bird hike.*

**Caution:** This is deer tick country, so take precautions (light clothes, socks over pant legs, and tick repellent).

**Trail Directions:** Park in lot 3 and begin the hike at the blue gate; take the grassy path of trail 22 **[1]**. Even-age stands of hardwoods are on either side of the trail. At some of the intersections you will find a forest map with the numbered trails. Within a tenth of a mile come to two trail intersections. At the first one go right and the second one go left **[2]**. The path has now become sand and you begin to pass planted pines.

At .35 mi. is another intersection; go right on trail 24 **[3]**. The trail now passes an older white oak forest with fan-shaped canopies and an understory of tick trefoil. The tall trees will fade in and out along the trail, replaced by pines or a recovering forest. At .85 mi. the trail Vs; go left on trail 20 **[4]**. Another intersection is at .9 mi.; go left on trail 19 **[5]**. This trail will T at 1.15 mi.; go right **[6]** through the tall pines on trail 32.

Trail 32 gives way to trail 33 at 1.5 mi. **[7]**, and you are hiking on a ridge with a view of the Rock River on your left in the distance. Trails 32 and 33 are used by horses, so watch where you step. At 1.7 mi. you will pass another trail on your left; ignore it and within a few steps come to another intersection. Go right on trail 9 **[8]**, a horseless trail. A pond will appear on the right.

At 2 mi. you have merged into an open area; go right **[9]**. You are now on the loggers trail (trails 10 and 11). The trail will now be dotted with periodic posters explaining terms and facts about the timber industry. An example of a question is *What is a board foot?* Along this section you are still hiking through oaks, but there are also quite a few maple trees. Since these forests stopped periodically burning, maples, a species not tolerant of fires, have been able to gain a foothold and outcompete the fire-tolerant oaks. Who knows—one day Illinois may become as famous as New England for sugar maple fall colors.

The trail Ts at 2.4 mi.; go right and uphill, where you will eventually come out into parking area 2 **[10]**. Walk across the parking area and take trail 15 on the opposite side. At the intersection, go left, hiking through woods dominated by hickory trees, and you will come out into parking lot 3.

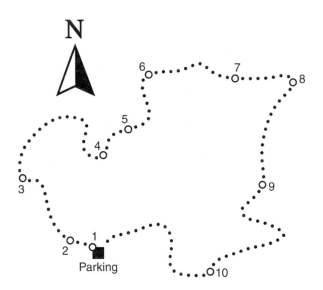

1. Start
2. Right turn, left turn
3. Right turn on #24
4. Left turn on #20
5. Left turn on #19
6. Right turn through pines on #32
7. #32 becomes #33
8. Right turn on #9
9. Loggers Trail
10. Parking area #2

# 7. McHenry County Conservation District

- Discover kames, kettle holes, erratics, and a glacial end moraine in parks where glacial history comes alive.

- Climb a 100-foot camelback kame to enjoy a bird's-eye view.

- Bring your binoculars to watch the aerial acrobatics of swallows, the day-to-day drama in the lives of red-winged blackbirds, and the creek-patrolling behavior of kingfishers.

- Experience the parklike setting of savannas, one of the rarest plant communities in the state.

## Area Information

The Pleistocene glaciers and their meltwaters forever changed the Illinois landscape. Nearly 90 percent of the state was once covered by one or more sheets of glacial ice. When the last of the glaciers began to melt from Illinois, about 14,000 years ago, the country that emerged looked far different from preglacial lands. The glaciers had scraped and smeared the landforms they overrode (much the same way a person kneads dough). The moving ice carried colossal amounts of rock and earth, and when the ice melted, it dumped whatever it was carrying in place. Perhaps the best place to encounter Ice Age Illinois is McHenry County. R. Wiggers, a geologist, wrote, "The landscape of McHenry County rises and rolls and falls away with the grandness of an ocean worked with deep swells." Two of the best areas to experience the glacial geology are the county's conservation district parks—Glacial Park and Marengo Ridge.

In **Glacial Park** look for outwash deposits (a mixture of sand, stone, and gravel) in which the glacier created distinctive landforms called kames. Kames are circular mounds of outwash that resulted when holes in the glacial ice were filled with debris from the streams that flowed along the surface of the glacier—imagine the debris-laden water from a waterfall. Today, kames have great value and go by another name: sand and gravel pits. Kettle holes were formed when large pieces of ice became detached from the glacier and were buried by outwash. When the blocks of ice melted, the outwash fell downward, creating craters and pockmarks. Leatherleaf bog and kettle

hole marsh are examples of kettle holes. Although you weren't present during the glacial event, the reminders of this great ice form an ancient and interesting part of Illinois history.

**Marengo Ridge,** which runs north and south through western McHenry County, is a massive moraine that extends southward from the Wisconsin border for almost 40 miles. Whenever the advance of the glacial ice was balanced by melting, the leading edge of the ice remained in one place. As the ice melted, thick piles of fine rock dust mixed with coarser silt, sand, gravel, and rock were left, forming moraines. Marengo Ridge is one of these moraines; it is 3 miles wide and 200 feet thick, and it rises 930 feet above the surrounding landscape. It is the state's oldest moraine—geologists estimate its age at 24,000 years.

**Directions: Glacial Park** is located in northeastern Illinois in McHenry County. From the town of Richmond, go south on Route 31 until you reach Harts Road and a sign for the park. Follow Harts Road to the Wiedrich Barn Education Center. **Marengo Ridge** is located in southwest McHenry County. From the town of Marengo, head north on County Road 23. At about 1.5 miles, look for an entrance sign to the park, turn right, and continue until you see a sign for the conservation area.

**Hours Open:** Both sites are open year-round from sunrise to sunset.

**Facilities:** Glacial Park has Wiedrich Barn Education Center, seasonal displays, and interpreters who conduct walks through the area. The park has several restrooms. Picnic facilities with fire grates are located at the visitor parking lot. Canoeing and bank fishing are allowed on Nippersink Creek; cross-country skiing and snowmobiling are allowed when there is enough snow. Glacial Park Field Research Station is open 9:00 a.m. to 4:00 p.m. on weekdays and 9:00 a.m. to 5:00 p.m. on weekends. Marengo Ridge offers camping (some sites have electricity), picnic shelters, fishing, cross-country skiing, restrooms, and drinking water.

**Permits and Rules:** Part of the trail at Glacial Park is in a dedicated Illinois Nature Preserve. Because of its status, no pets are allowed on the trail. Campsites at Marengo Ridge must be reserved. At both sites bicycles are allowed only on the roadways, parking areas, and designated bicycle trails (not the hiking trails).

**For Further Information:** McHenry County Conservation District, Brookdale Administrative Office, 18410 US Highway 14, Woodstock, IL 60098; 815-338-6223 or www.MCCDistrict.org.

## Park Trails

**The Prairie Trail** (, 26 miles). This is a linear trail that is open to hikers and equestrians in the spring and summer and snowmobilers in winter. The trail is on an old railroad bed that was once a Chicago and Northwestern rail line. Along its length you will find patches of prairie and nice views of the Fox River Valley. The path begins at the McHenry County line south of Algonquin and ends at the Illinois–Wisconsin border. For more information, call 815-338-6223.

## Other Areas of Interest

**Trail of History** is a living history event where interpreters from across the county portray life as it was from 1670 to 1850 in the former Northwest Territory. This yearly event is held during October weekends at Glacial Park Conservation Area. There is an admission charge. For more information, call 815-338-6223.

Located near the small town of Coral, **Coral Woods Conservation Area** is one of the largest remaining wooded areas in McHenry Country, a 297-acre maple forest that is a blaze of color in the fall and carpeted with wildflowers in the spring. The area offers three hiking trails totaling 2.8 miles, picnicking with a shelter, restrooms, and water. For more information, call 815-338-6223.

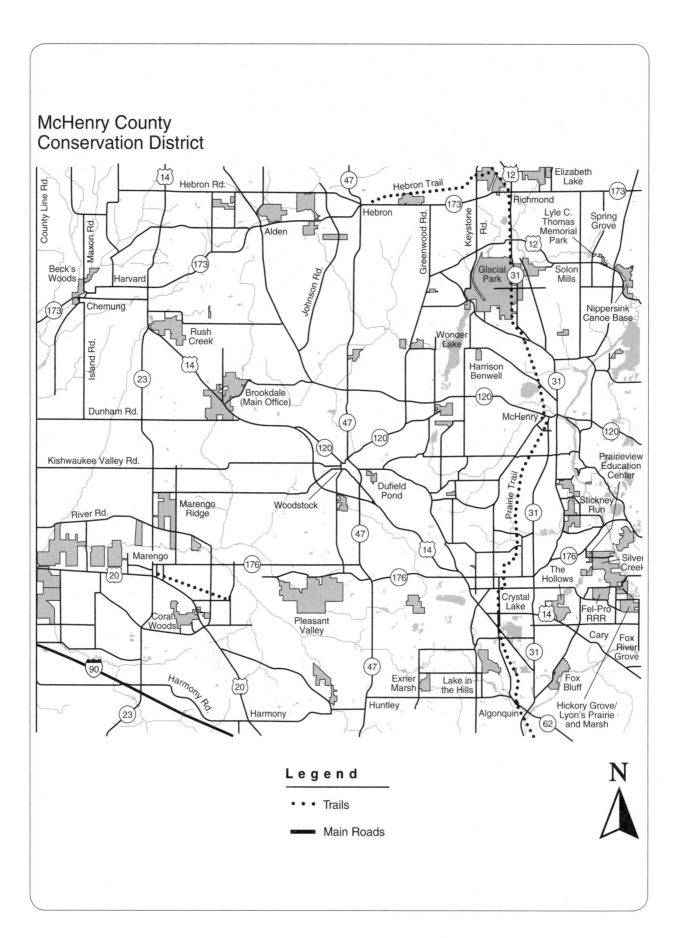

# McHenry County
# Conservation District

**Legend**

•••  Trails

▬▬  Main Roads

N

# Glacial Park Trail

 **Distance Round-Trip:** 2 miles
**Estimated Hiking Time:** 1 hour

*While the kame is in the distance, the hike is a one-booter. When I hiked over it, however, it quickly acquired two more boots. Kames are far easier to admire than to climb.*

**Caution:** Stay on the boardwalk at the bog. The ground is very unstable, and a heavy body is likely to sink!

**Trail Directions:** Park at the main parking lot (not at the barn) and begin at the trail board [**1**]; go right (north) and cross the road. Continue past the trail for the observation deck. The trail skirts the edge of a marsh, which was formed by the slow fill-in of an old kettle hole.

As you hike, look to your left for a series of kames that are topped with bur oaks. Your opportunity to climb a kame will soon come. At .25 mi. come to a trail crossroad [**2**]; go straight across to discover a bog. Use the boardwalk to look for sphagnum moss and the dominant plant of this bog, leatherleaf, a plant that keeps its leaves year-round. Occasional stems of poison sumac emerge from the leatherleaf.

The boardwalk ends at .35 mi. [**3**]; go right and walk through a savanna, a plant community characterized by large, open-grown oaks with an understory of woodland and prairie plants. A few yards bring you back to point [**2**]; continue straight. The trail Ts at .45 mi.; go right [**4**] on Coyote Loop Trail. You are hiking through a bur oak savanna. Look on the ground on either side and note the glacial debris (rocks and gravel). These rocks were hauled in not by trucks but by glaciers.

The trail curves to the right around the bog, and at .6 mi. it comes to a T [**5**]. Go right at a large bur oak. The trail will take you by another savanna. While you will see several examples of this community here, it is a very rare plant community within the state. Savannas, with their parklike settings, were a favorite area for pioneers to settle. Without fire to maintain them, woody plants such as sugar maple and buckthorn soon grow up and turn savannas into closed forests.

At the southwest corner of the savanna are two trails; take the narrow trail and begin the trek up the kame [**6**] (.75 mi.). Local people call these 100-foot mounds camelback kames. Over 10,000 years ago the edge of the glacier rested here. During the summers, meltwaters carried sand and gravel over the edge, resulting in these unique landforms. At the top, enjoy a vulture's-eye view of the surrounding savanna and valley of Nippersink Creek.

At the end of the kame (.9 mi.) go right and then left [**7**]. As you hike along this stretch, look for kames on both sides and don't forget to admire the huge bur oak on the left at 1 mi. [**8**]. Take the side spur to the left to the Thomas family cemetery, and then retrace your steps back to the main trail. From the bur oak you begin to hike through an oak-hickory savanna. In the spring the ground is covered with mayapple. Note that only plants with a pair of leaves bear a flower. The trail goes upward to an overlook and a bench [**9**] (1.3 mi.).

From here you can see the broad valley shaped by the ancient Fox River. The savanna is left behind and at 1.5 mi. the trail comes to a T; go right [**10**], hiking up a moraine. At the top experience a great view of the area. The trail Ts at 1.65 mi.; go left [**11**] and, within a few steps at the V, go right. The trail skirts Kettle Hole Marsh and parallels the park road. Take advantage of the marsh observation deck at 1.9 mi. [**12**] to look for mallards, red-winged blackbirds, tree swallows, and at least half a dozen species of dragonflies. Off the observation deck, go right and back on the main trail within a few steps. Go left here, recrossing the road and heading back to the parking area.

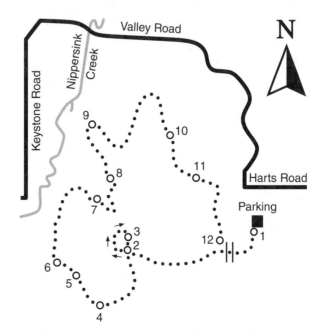

1. Start
2. Trail to bog
3. Right turn
4. Coyote Loop Trail
5. Right turn
6. Kame
7. Winding trail
8. Bur oak
9. Overlook
10. Right turn, moraine
11. Left turn, right turn
12. Observation deck

North

# Marengo Ridge

**Distance Round-Trip:** 3.6 miles
**Estimated Hiking Time:** 2 hours

*This trail has everything—a great view from the top of the ridge, the squeaks and squeals of chipmunks, prairie, woodlands, and a few glacial erratics thrown in for good measure.*

**Caution:** Watch for rocks and roots in the trail. The trail will also cross the park road, so use caution.

**Trail Directions:** Park at Shelter 2 and begin the hike at the shelter, taking advantage of the top-of-the-world view [1]. The trail begins as a mown path through a prairie restoration. The trail enters a white oak grove at .2 mi. [2], a remnant of a savanna that at one time was pastured. As the trail winds through the trees, look and listen for woodpeckers and chipmunks. Once the trail leaves the grove, you are hiking through a field dotted with milkweeds.

At .6 mi. you will cross a small bridge [3]. Here you are hiking through prairie grasses—Indian, big and little bluestem, side oats grama, and Canada wild rye. In the fall this area is russet with the drying grasses. Take advantage of the bench at .75 mi. [4]; the view gives you an appreciation of the glacial heritage. An intersection comes up at .9 mi.; continue straight [5]. Within a few steps you will cross the road and enter a mixed woods of pine and walnut.

The trail Ts at 1 mi.; go right [6] through a mix of conifers. Emerson Kunde, who owned the land in the 1950s, planted these trees. He claimed, "The soil was so hard you could hardly put a pickaxe into it." Thus, he planted evergreens, believing only they could survive. You are now hiking on a piece of the interpretive trail with periodic signage.

Within .1 mi. encounter several intersections (this area is near the campground). At the first one go right [7], and within a few steps, at yet another intersection, continue straight ahead. At 1.2 mi. continue straight [8] through a narrow allée of pine trees. Within a few yards, ignore a trail to the right (it leads to the campground).

An intersection with a bench appears at 1.4 mi.; go right [9] and you are soon hiking through a pine plantation, obviously a reforestation area. Those medium-sized boulders you see along the trail were not put there by the park staff, but are glacial erratics. These boulders (made of rock normally not found in Illinois) were picked up by glaciers as they moved southward, only to be left stranded when the ice finally melted.

From the pines you will emerge into a prairie restoration on your right with a woods on your left (1.6 mi.). Soon the trail takes you back into the woods near a sign for the Nature Trail [10]. The path has now become very narrow. You are hiking through an oak woods with an understory of honeysuckle, poison ivy, and wildflowers—bloodroot, wild geranium, and jack-in-the-pulpit. Glacial boulders are scattered about. An intersection will appear in a few yards; go right, staying on the narrow trail.

At 1.9 mi. you will cross a bridge [11] and the trail will follow the curve of the stream for a short period before turning away. You will cross two more bridges before coming to another intersection at 2.4 mi.; go straight, retracing your steps back to [9] where the path has widened. At the intersection at 2.75 mi., go right [12]. You will encounter a sign about glacial erratics as the trail leads you through a less disturbed oak forest; note the more open understory.

The trail forks at 3.1 mi.; go right [13] as you continue to hike through an oak woods with a high, open canopy and a prickly ash understory. The trail comes out at Shelter 1 and a parking area (3.4 mi.) [14]. Pick up the asphalt path near the restrooms, cross the park road, and enter the prairie on the opposite side. At the fork, go right and soon you are back at Shelter 2.

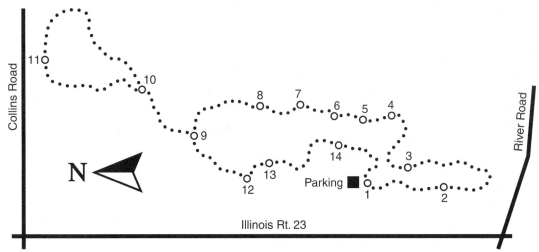

1. Start
2. Savanna
3. Footbridge
4. Bench with view
5. Go straight
6. Right turn
7. Right turn
8. Go straight, pine trees
9. Bench, right turn
10. Nature Trail
11. Bridge
12. Right turn
13. Trail forks, right turn
14. Shelter 1

- Visit the largest concentration of natural lakes in Illinois.
- Hike through a tunnel of oaks that arch over the trail.
- Listen for the rattle of the sandhill crane, the squeaks of chipmunks and goldfinches, and the ever-present wind rustling the prairie grasses.
- Discover remnants of the famous lotus beds.
- Look for Mud Lake.

## Area Information

Chain O' Lakes State Park, just south of the Wisconsin border, is called the finest water playground in northeastern Illinois. The park borders three natural lakes—Grass, Marie, and Nippersink. The Fox River flows through the park from north to south and connects seven other lakes, giving a combined surface area of over 6,000 acres.

There is more to this park than water recreation. Chain O' Lakes State Park has oak woodlands on a gravel moraine, wet prairies, and wetlands. The area's lakes are the result of scrapes and gouges by glaciers over 12,000 years ago. The lakes have no defined edges, and most of them have boggy or peaty bottoms. Associated with these lakes are various wetland habitats—fens (a type of wet meadow fed by alkaline water) and marshes, with their associated plants, especially American lotus.

The lotus became a botanical landmark for the Chain O' Lakes. The large lotus beds, "a floating forest of saffron flowers," were such an attraction that the railroad and steamboats ran tours of the area and local businesses sold postcards and lotus perfume. By 1873 the Wisconsin Central Railroad guidebook described the sight in poetic terms as a "dreaminess that makes the soul forget the woes of the earth." Promoters alleged that "China, Egypt, and Chain O' Lakes were the only places on earth that offered this spectacle." Remnants of the great lotus beds still exist, and they, along with the park's other natural features, still offer a dreaminess that can be experienced on its trails.

**Directions:** Chain O' Lakes State Park is located near the Illinois–Wisconsin border in northeast Illinois. From Illinois Route 173 take Wilmot Road 1.7 miles to the park entrance.

**Hours Open:** The park is open every day except Christmas. Summer hours (April 1 to October 31) are 6:00 a.m. to 9:00 p.m. Winter hours are 8:00 a.m. until sunset. The park is closed to all activities except hunting from the beginning of November through mid-December.

**Facilities:** Camping (300 sites), cabin rental, fishing, boating, boat rental, picnicking, bicycling, horseback riding, cross-country skiing, and hunting (deer, turkey, waterfowl, and pheasant) are all included.

**Permits and Rules:** In winter hikers are requested to stay off the cross-country ski trails and to walk to the side of the groomed ski trails. Pets must be leashed. Bicyclists must yield to pedestrians, stay on the surfaced trails, and ride slowly. Swimming or wading is not allowed.

**Further information:** Chain O' Lakes State Park, 8916 Wilmot Road, Spring Grove, IL 60081; 847-587-5512.

# Chain O' Lakes State Park

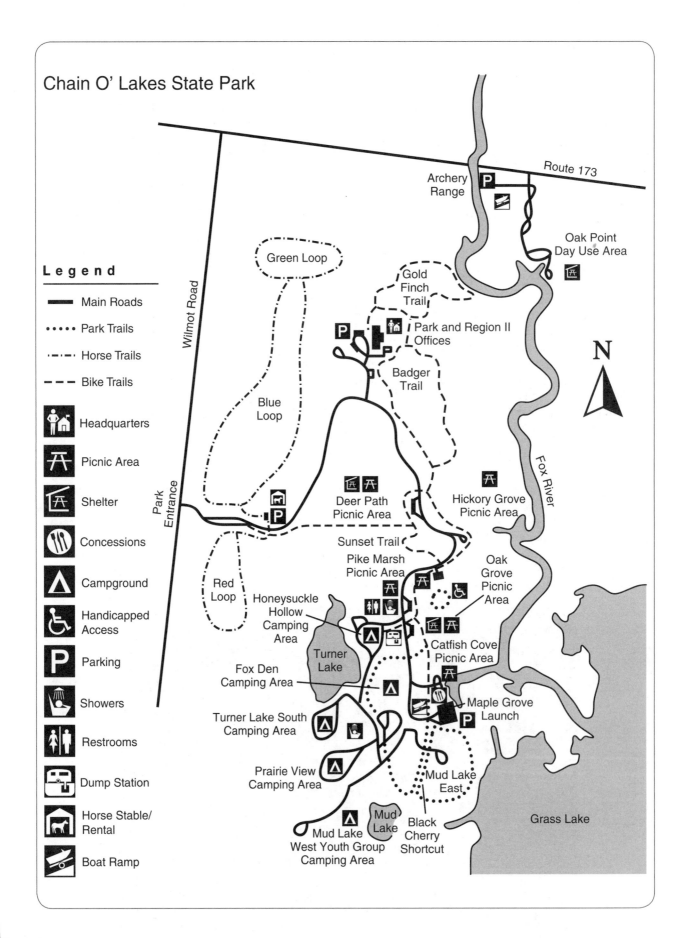

**Legend**

| | |
|---|---|
| —— | Main Roads |
| •••• | Park Trails |
| -·-·- | Horse Trails |
| - - - | Bike Trails |

Headquarters

Picnic Area

Shelter

Concessions

Campground

Handicapped Access

Parking

Showers

Restrooms

Dump Station

Horse Stable/Rental

Boat Ramp

Route 173

Archery Range

Oak Point Day Use Area

Green Loop

Gold Finch Trail

Park and Region II Offices

Badger Trail

Wilmot Road

Blue Loop

Park Entrance

Deer Path Picnic Area

Hickory Grove Picnic Area

Fox River

N

Sunset Trail

Pike Marsh Picnic Area

Oak Grove Picnic Area

Red Loop

Honeysuckle Hollow Camping Area

Fox Den Camping Area

Turner Lake

Catfish Cove Picnic Area

Turner Lake South Camping Area

Maple Grove Launch

Prairie View Camping Area

Mud Lake East

Mud Lake West Youth Group Camping Area

Mud Lake

Black Cherry Shortcut

Grass Lake

# Goldfinch and Badger

  **Distance Round-Trip:** 3.4 miles
**Estimated Hiking Time:** 1.3 hours

*It was a blue-sky fall day and I kept looking up to marvel at the oaks. As I stared up, I saw two turkey vultures, a broad-winged and Cooper's hawk, and a northern harrier, all within 5 minutes. Farther along I listened and then watched a deer rip cattails out of the marsh and eat them. Other than the wildlife, we had the trails to ourselves.*

**Caution:** You will be sharing the trail with bicyclists, joggers, and dog walkers.

**Trail Directions:** Park at the office parking lot and begin the trail at the flagpole [1]; go left away from the office on the paved path. At .1 mi. the trail Ts; go left [2] on a limestone path that is marked with yellow squares and mileage points. (The mileage points do not correspond to the mileage points in this book.)

Large oaks with a questionable understory are on your left; prairie is on the right. Both the prairie and the oaks wax and wane throughout the hike. An old gravel mine is on your left at .6 mi. [3]. The gravel is a remnant of the glaciers; as they moved they carried enormous amounts of rock, gravel, and sand. When the ice melted it dumped what it had carried. The area on the right is an old lakebed with a wet spot in the middle. The cottonwoods are an indicator of wet soil. While hiking this section, look ahead to the tunnel of oaks arching over the trail.

At .8 mi. the Fox River comes into view by a giant bur oak [4]. As you approach the river, look over your shoulder to view a remnant of the once-great lotus beds. On your right are wetlands and on the opposite, undeveloped side of the river is perhaps what this side once looked like. Spend a few minutes at the river, looking for waterfowl, large wading birds, and other wildlife. The trail curves away from the river and the habitat alternates between wet prairie, ponds, and sloughs.

The trail goes through pines [5] at 1.4 mi. and within a tenth of a mile a pine plantation is on the left. The trail intersects with the Badger Trail at 1.6 mi.; go left [6] at the stop sign. This segment of the trail will be marked with white squares. Prairie will line both sides of the path.

The trail enters an oak-hickory savanna (widespread oaks with prairie vegetation) at 2.1 mi. [7]. Listen for goldfinches and chipmunks and watch bluebirds as they fly back and forth over the trail.

A T intersection appears at 2.5 mi.; go right [8], noting the many-branched hackberry on your right as well as a wild grape arbor. At 2.7 mi. you will cross an old park road [9]; continue on the limestone path, noticing the big bluestem–covered hummock on the right. Farther along, compare the flat-topped bur oak to the three white oak trees; notice their different structures. An overlook is on the right [10] (3.1 mi.), providing bird's-eye views of the river and landscape. The groves of oaks with deer feeding in the distance make for a very pastoral scene.

Pines appear again at 3.2 mi. [11]; go left, retracing your steps back to [6] and the Goldfinch Trail. Go left at the stop sign, retracing your steps back to [2]. From here you retrace your steps back to the flagpole where you began.

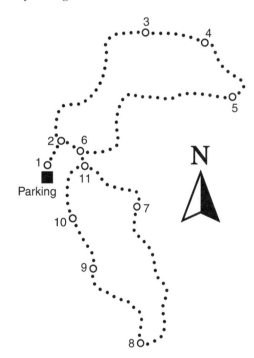

1.  Start
2.  Trail Ts, left turn
3.  Gravel mine
4.  Fox River
5.  Pines
6.  Left turn, stop sign (Badger Trail)
7.  Savanna
8.  Right turn
9.  Park road crossing
10. Overlook
11. Left turn

North

# Mud Lake

**Distance Round-Trip:** 1.3 miles
**Estimated Hiking Time:** .85 hour

*On a trail called Mud Lake, be thankful you are hiking on the upland, viewing it from above.*

**Caution:** The trail is a dirt path. Roots and rocks can trip you.

**Trail Directions:** Park in the boat launch parking lot and begin hiking on the park road [1]. At the stop sign go left, still hiking on the park road. Cross the road and go into the woods at the first left. The trail is a mown dirt path, and the first section passes through the back of Mud Lake East campground. There are several side trails leading to camping areas, but the main trail is fairly easy to follow. Buckthorn, an introduced shrubby plant from Eurasia, lines the trail.

At .2 mi. come to a trail intersection; go left [2]. An opening [3] appears at .35 mi. and through it you can see Grass Lake and a wetland leading to the Fox River. Even in fall there are still remnant lotus blooms here. At one time Grass Lake had over 700 acres of blooming lotus, but flooding and harvesting of the seedpods for decoration decimated the population. The lotus beds are starting to come back, lending a serene elegance to the lake's backwaters.

Another trail intersection appears at .4 mi. [4]; stay left as you hike through an oak-hickory woods with the occasional large oak specimen. Don't forget to look down on the trail for evidence of wild turkeys. Acorns are a favorite food and the trail provides some perfect areas for scratching and dust baths, evidenced by the oval depressions and occasional feathers in the trail. Several openings in the woods have allowed prairie plants to gain a foothold. Horsetail milkweed with its whorled leaves, white flowers, and upward-pointing pods is especially common.

You are hiking on a ridge with oaks and patches of mayapple. From this vantage point you can see and hear the action on the Fox River, a river popular with boaters. The trail descends at .7 mi. [5]; look for gnarled cottonwoods. As the trail curves right, Mud Lake and its surrounding wetlands can be seen in the distance. An opening on the left provides a view of the lake, now overgrown with cattails. Don't be surprised if you see a northern leopard frog jumping across the path. These medium-sized green frogs have dark spots and are strong jumpers. Just try to catch one!

The buckthorn soon returns, with the occasional hickory and large cottonwoods. An intersection for the Black Cherry Shortcut appears at 1 mi.; go right [6]. Notice the giant bur oak on the left. Another intersection is within a tenth of a mile; continue straight. You will cross the road by the campground at 1.2 mi. and come to a trail intersection where you will go left, completing the loop [7]. Hike back on the park road, taking a right to the parking area, and soon you should be back at your vehicle.

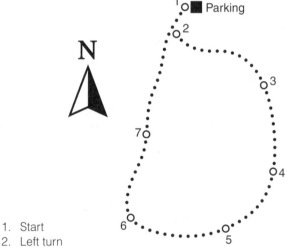

1. Start
2. Left turn
3. Grass Lake
4. Left turn
5. Trail descends
6. Black Cherry Shortcut, right turn
7. Left turn, completed loop

North

- Venture forth in an area where heavy bodies are likely to sink (if you stumble off the boardwalk)!

- Visit a habitat more commonly associated with the northeastern states and Canada.

- Look for orchids, ferns, tamaracks, sphagnum moss, and carnivorous plants along the trail.

- Explore a cattail-filled moat and encounter not alligators but dragonflies, frogs, and muskrats.

- Climb an observation tower for a bird's-eye view of the bog.

- Traverse from the edge to the eye of a bog.

## Area Information

Volo Bog was formed during the Wisconsin glaciation, about 15,000 years ago. Large blocks of ice broke away from the main mass of the glacier and were pushed into the ground with great force. As the ice melted, it left depressions called kettle holes. Volo Bog consists of two kettle holes left after the glacier receded. The kettle holes slowly filled in with partially decomposed plant material called peat. All that remains of the kettle hole is the open-water area of the bog, called the eye. Volo Bog is the only bog in the state with such an eye.

With all the water around, it's hard to believe that plants experience the bog as a dry habitat, but most have trouble getting water and essential nutrients into their roots because of the high acidity level. Yet Volo Bog is lush with ferns, orchids, winterberry holly, tamaracks, and poison sumac. All of these plants have developed unique ways of extracting nutrients from the bog: Some are simply able to tolerate the acidic waters, some have developed leathery leaves that slow water loss and are not shed each winter, and a few have specialized soil fungi that help them absorb nutrients.

At one time the eye of Volo Bog was 50 feet deep; today it contains 10 feet of water and 40 feet of muck, marl, and peat. Although the eye is slowly disappearing, it is alive with activity. Kingfishers survey the edges, pollywogs appear to pave the peaty bottom, dragonflies canvass the open water for mates and food, and many frogs (camouflaged from the kingfishers) enjoy the sunshine. An eight-year-old child, being coaxed to leave the boardwalk by parents, perhaps best summed up Volo Bog: "Dad, there's no better place than this!"

**Directions:** Volo Bog is located 4 miles east of McHenry. From the intersection of US 12/IL 59 and IL 120 in the town of Volo, go north on US 12/IL 59 to Brandenburg Road; turn and go west (left) 1.3 miles to the entrance on the left.

**Hours Open:** The trails, picnic area, and parking open at 8:00 a.m. daily. Closing time varies with the season. The visitor center is open from 9:00 a.m. to 3:00 p.m. Wednesday through Sunday.

**Facilities:** A visitor center houses exhibits, a classroom, a natural history reference library, restrooms, and a book and gift shop. Picnic facilities and a bird-watcher's blind are included on the site.

**Permits and Rules:** Pay attention to all park signage; it is for your protection. Do not pick or collect any natural object. No pets are allowed into the bog. Pets must be leashed in the picnic area. Camping and fishing are not permitted. Please stay on the trails.

**For Further Information:** Volo Bog State Natural Area, 28478 W. Brandenburg Road, Ingleside, IL 60041; 815-344-1294.

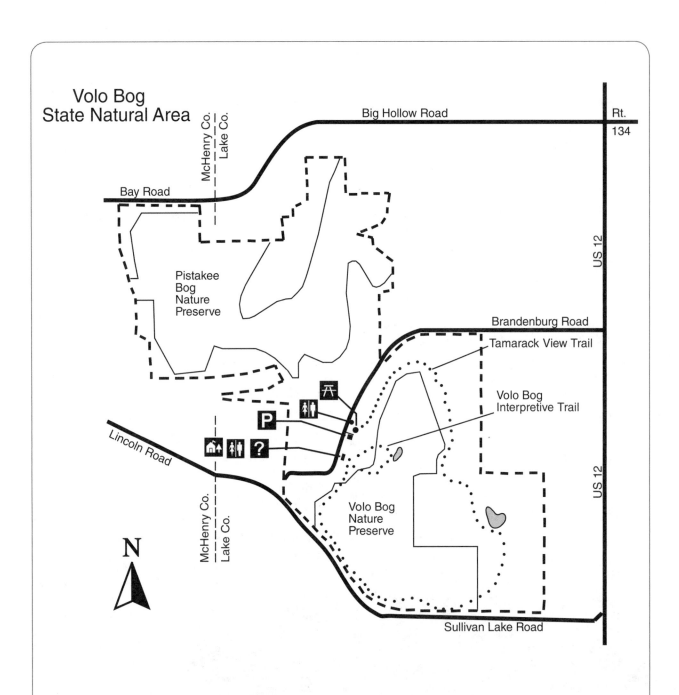

# Volo Bog State Natural Area

Big Hollow Road

Rt. 134

McHenry Co.
Lake Co.

Bay Road

US 12

Pistakee
Bog
Nature
Preserve

Brandenburg Road

Tamarack View Trail

Volo Bog
Interpretive Trail

Lincoln Road

McHenry Co.
Lake Co.

Volo Bog
Nature
Preserve

US 12

N

Sullivan Lake Road

## Legend

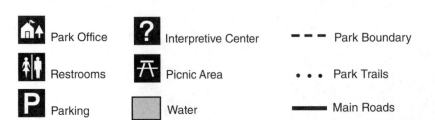

|  |  |  |
|---|---|---|
| Park Office | Interpretive Center | - - - Park Boundary |
| Restrooms | Picnic Area | • • • Park Trails |
| Parking | Water | Main Roads |

# Tamarack Trail

 **Distance Round-Trip:** 3.2 miles
**Estimated Hiking Time:** 1.3 hours

*This trail gives an introduction into how the bog was formed, especially if hiked during an extremely cold day. You feel as if you are part of the Ice Age, waiting for the glaciers to recede.*

**Caution:** Stay on the trail, especially the boardwalks, because some areas can be extremely wet and muddy with unstable soil. Poison sumac may overlap the trail. Learn what it looks like and avoid it.

**Trail Directions:** Begin the trail at the visitor center. At the bottom of the hill, note a sign for Tamarack View Trail; go right to begin hiking the hummocks (small hills) **[1]** on a mown path. Trail distance is marked every half mile (my mileage and theirs did not correspond). A kettle hole is on your left and an upland oak-hickory forest is on your right. Within a tenth of a mile you will hike close to the road and houses, but the trail soon ventures back into an oak-hickory forest.

In the distance view the hummocky topography associated with glacial terrain. When you think of bogs, oak trees usually don't come to mind, but along this trail note the many splendid examples (mostly bur oaks). During the winter and spring, while the trees are leafless, each example looks like a gnarled root system turned upside down.

At .45 mi. you will climb a small hummock and go left **[2]**, staying on the gravel path. The dense trees provide just glimpses of the marsh. You will come to a boardwalk at .65 mi. **[3]** that crosses a marsh. Cattails line both sides. Around the base of the cattails a "false bottom" often develops—silt floating on the water with buoyant plant fragments gives the area a solid appearance. Stay on the boardwalk—even though the marsh may look solid, it isn't and will result in wet, muddy feet. As you cross the area in the fall, look for the violet blooms of bottle gentian.

Off the short boardwalk, keep to the left as several maintenance paths come in. A hummock on your right, formed by the melting glacier, is now covered with prairie grasses and obscures all vestiges of civilization for a few minutes. At 1.1 mi. **[4]** the flat area on your left is an old lake bed; on your right are glacial potholes—shallow depressions gouged by the glaciers that soon filled with water. At the top of the rise on the right are two large bur oaks; on the left is nothing but big bluestem (the state grass).

A side trail to the observation platform appears at 1.25 mi; go left for this bird's-eye view **[5]**. The bog and marsh are on the right and prairie grasses are on the left. You are looking at the back of the bog. Climb the stairs for a view of how big the kettle hole once

was and note the different zones of the bog (tamarack, shrub, and cattail zones). Down from the tower, retrace your steps back to **[5]** (1.9 mi.).

At the 1.5 mi. marker **[6]** go through the small grove dominated by bur oaks. Take time to look on the ground for their leaves. Bur oaks have the largest leaves of any of the oak trees—6 to 12 inches long and 3 to 6 inches wide. A trail marker indicates to go left, and hummocks and open areas are again on either side.

The trail curves to the left **[7]** at 2.3 mi. through an oak woods with a buckthorn understory. Once through the woods, stay to the left. Take a side spur at 2.55 mi. to an observation blind on the left **[8]**. Pause to look for waterfowl or perhaps to see a kingfisher. Retrace your steps back to the trail and go left. You will soon come to a bench; pause and see what is going on in the area. The path forks from the bench; you may take either path because they both end up at the same point.

At 2.75 go left **[9]**, but not before examining the two types of arrowhead in the open-water marsh and then heading up through an oak-hickory woods. You will pass a trail off to your right; continue straight and through the grove. You will come out at the picnic area near the parking area within a few steps.

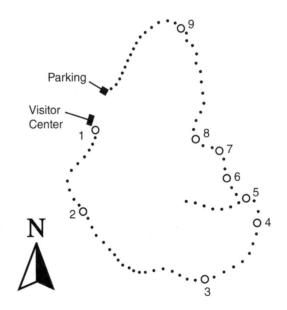

1. Start
2. Left turn
3. Boardwalk
4. Old lake bed
5. Spur to platform
6. Bur oak
7. Curve left
8. Blind
9. Left turn

# Bog Boardwalk Trail

 **Distance Round-Trip:** .5 mile
 **Estimated Hiking Time:** .5 hour

*A visit to Volo Bog used to require a good bit of courage and tall boots. Today, all you need is a trail map and enough balance to negotiate a floating wooden boardwalk to explore the mysterious interior of a bog.*

**Caution:** Stay on the boardwalk! The ground, although it may look solid, is not, and you could find yourself encased in layers of mud and muck. Learn what poison sumac looks like and do not touch it!

**Trail Directions:** Because of the trail's short length, mileage distances will not be given here.

Begin the hike at the visitor center [1]. The barn you have just left is the original barn of the George Sayer farm. Volo Bog, or Sayer Bog as it was originally called because it adjoined the Sayer farm, was the first piece of property acquired by the newly formed Illinois Nature Conservancy in 1958. Downhill from the center is the entrance to the boardwalk [2] and your path for the hike. Be thankful that a boardwalk exists; in earlier times visitors jumped from hummock to hummock, causing the trees growing on the floating mat of vegetation to swing like pendulums. You are hiking on the fifth layer of boardwalk (the rest have sunk into the bog!).

The first area you encounter is the cattail marsh moat that surrounds the bog [3]. The cattail was a veritable supermarket for Native Americans. Every part was edible or used in some other way.

You soon enter the shrub zone, marked by winterberry holly [4]. In late summer this area is spectacular with the bright red berries of holly intermingling with the final yellow-orange flowers of tickseed sunflower. Here you will also encounter six species of ferns—crested, spinulose, cinnamon, marsh, royal, and sensitive. The latter's name comes from the fact that it is sensitive to cold and always succumbs to the first frost.

While walking through the shrub zone, begin to look on your left for tamaracks. Tamaracks grow on spongy hummocks and are usually short and scrubby, and their roots grow sideways instead of straight down. The dead trees that you see off to the left are the result of wet years [5]; they drowned.

From here to the eye of the bog, look for some of the more colorful and unusual plants of the bog [6]. Blooming during June are the maroon blossoms of marsh cinquefoil and the light pink of the rose pogonia orchid. In July, look for the bright pink upside-down flower of the grass pink orchid, a plant that is fleeting and rare. Also look for pitcher plants. Please enjoy them from afar. At one time they were much more

numerous, but illegal collecting has taken its toll on the pitcher plant population. If your visit is during summer, look for the plant's unusual flowers that resemble apples on a stick.

You will soon reach the eye of the bog [7]. Volo Bog is the only bog in Illinois that has an area of open water—the eye. This small, circular expanse is all that is left of the original 50-acre lake. The lake has slowly filled in with peat and within a century or two the eye will eventually fill in and disappear, a natural process in the life of a bog. From the floating platform, look for pollywogs, kingfishers, dragonflies, large frogs, and waterliles. The eye is ringed with sphagnum moss, and the plants you observe are all growing on a floating mat of sphagnum. The sphagnum grows from the top, dying away below, and can hold 18 times its weight in water.

As you come off the platform, look to your right [8] for leatherleaf. This plant never loses its leaves, although during the winter they turn brown. Once spring arrives, the leaves turn green again but soon fall off as new ones emerge. This process helps the plant conserve nutrients.

From here [9] continue on the boardwalk, looking for ferns, bright orange mushrooms, and, if you are quiet, maybe a glimpse of the bog's resident animals—muskrat, mink, or turtle. You now cross the marsh moat and the boardwalk ends [10]. The trail heads uphill and to the left. A right turn will take you to a picnic area. On the way back to the visitor center you will pass a small pond on the right and go through a prairie restoration area. Whether you are a pollywog, a dragonfly, a carnivorous plant, or, more likely, just someone who appreciates unusual areas, could there be a better place than this?

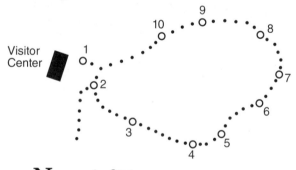

1. Start
2. Boardwalk entrance
3. Marsh moat
4. Shrub zone
5. Dead tamaracks
6. Bog plants
7. Eye of bog
8. Leatherleaf
9. Bog observation
10. Boardwalk ends

- Bring your binoculars to scan Black Tern Marsh from the observation deck. Who knows—you might see the rare yellow-headed blackbird or black tern.

- Listen for the rattle of sandhill cranes and watch them strut like giant chickens in the tall reeds.

- On a sunny day look for hundreds of basking turtles.

- Discover glacial artifacts—marshes, a bog, a fen, a glacial lake, kames, and moraines.

## Area Information

The legacy of the Pleistocene glaciers left northeastern Illinois with a mosaic of many wetland habitats—bogs, fens, marshes, and glacial lakes. Moraine Hills State Park is an excellent place to view many of these because half the park's acreage is made up of wetlands and lakes.

Lake Defiance, near the center of the park, was formed when a large piece of ice broke away from the glacier and was pushed into the ground with great force. As the ice melted, it left a depression, called a kettle hole. The hole soon filled with water because it was below the water table. The shore of the lake is unstable because of an accumulation of peat, and the lake itself is fed by the park's wetlands. Leatherleaf Bog was also formed from a kettle hole, but unlike Lake Defiance, the bog is poorly drained and has no inlet or outlet. The hole gradually filled with ever-thickening layers of peat to form the unstable, acidic mat that you see today.

Another area formed from a shallow kettle hole is Pike Marsh. But unlike a bog, it receives groundwater. The gravel bedrock near Pike Marsh is high in minerals. Thus, surrounding the marsh is a fen, a wetland community that resembles a bog but whose water is alkaline (instead of acidic) from a high mineral content. Its peat is formed from decaying grasses and sedges, not sphagnum moss.

In addition to the watery glacial evidence, note the occasional boulders, kames, and moraines. A kame is a circular mound of gravel and sand deposited when holes in the glacier filled with debris. Moraines formed when the glaciers retreated and left mounds of stones, boulders, and other debris. These appear as slight ridges and hills in the park. With a variety of plant communities and interesting glacial terrain, Moraine Hills State Park is a great site for a leisurely hike and provides the opportunity for excellent wildlife viewing.

**Directions:** Moraine Hills State Park is located in the northeast corner of Illinois, 3 miles south of McHenry. From Route 176, go north on River Road approximately 2 miles. The park entrance is off River Road.

**Hours Open:** The site is open year-round from 6:00 a.m. to 9:00 p.m. except on Christmas Day and New Year's Day.

**Facilities:** Fishing is allowed at both Lake Defiance and in the Fox River, and you can rent a boat (see the concession area). Picnicking is a favorite pastime and some of the day-use areas have playground equipment. Other features include concessions and an interpretive center.

**Permits and Rules:** Boat trailers are not allowed in the park. Private watercrafts are not allowed on Lake Defiance. At Lake Defiance you may fish only from one of the lake's three piers. Pets must be leashed.

**For Further Information:** Moraine Hills State Park, 1510 S. River Road, McHenry, IL 60051; 815-385-1624.

## Park Trails

**Lake Defiance** (👣👣, 3.7 miles). On a circuit of Lake Defiance you will encounter several marshes, wooded moraines, and the park's day-use areas.

**Lake Defiance Interpretive Trail** (👣, .5 mile). Use the guide available from the park office to aid you in the discovery of plant succession, plant communities, and wetlands. The trail also has an observation blind.

**Pike Marsh Interpretive Trail** (👣👣, .6 mile). A boardwalk allows you to discover a marsh, fen, and upland forest communities. Look for marsh marigold in the spring and an abundance of cattails during all seasons.

## Other Areas of Interest

From Algonquin at the junction of Route 31 and Route 62 (Huntley-Algonquin Road), go west on Route 62 for 1 mile to Pyott Road. Turn north on Pyott for 1.5 miles to the entrance of Barbara Key Park. A trailhead in the park provides access to **Lake-in-the-Hills Fen Nature Preserve**. Here you can continue your discovery of wetland communities and find a calcareous floating mat, graminoid (grassy) fen, low-shrub fen, calcareous seep, and several prairies. For more information, contact the McHenry County Conservation District at 815-338-6223.

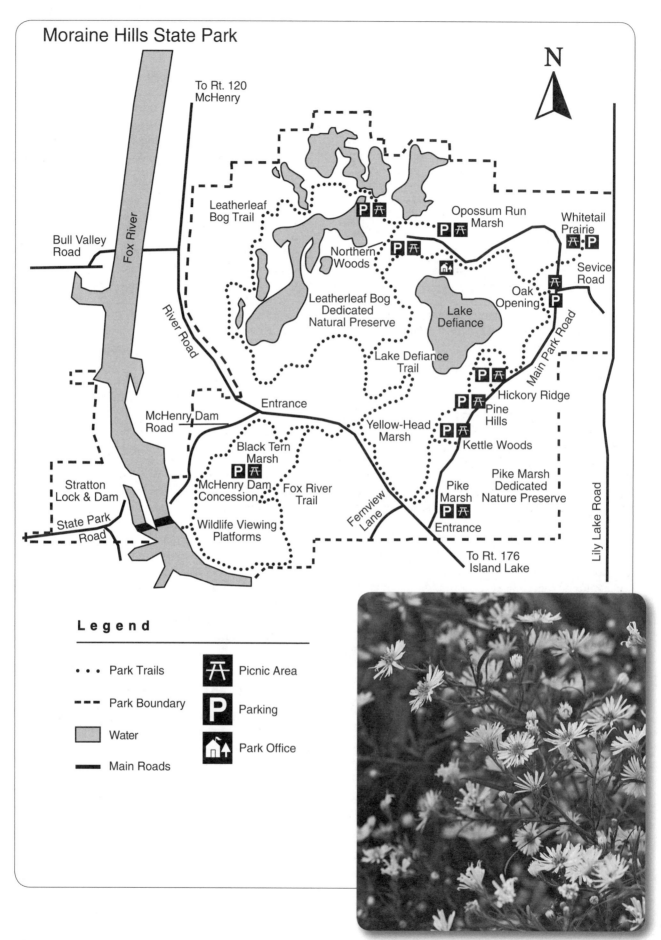

# Moraine Hills State Park

N

To Rt. 120 McHenry

Bull Valley Road

Fox River

River Road

Leatherleaf Bog Trail

Northern Woods

Opossum Run Marsh

Whitetail Prairie

Sevice Road

Leatherleaf Bog Dedicated Natural Preserve

Oak Opening

Lake Defiance

Lake Defiance Trail

Main Park Road

Entrance

McHenry Dam Road

Yellow-Head Marsh

Hickory Ridge

Pine Hills

Kettle Woods

Black Tern Marsh

McHenry Dam Concession

Fox River Trail

Stratton Lock & Dam

State Park Road

Wildlife Viewing Platforms

Fernview Lane

Pike Marsh

Pike Marsh Dedicated Nature Preserve

Lily Lake Road

Entrance

To Rt. 176 Island Lake

## Legend

•••  Park Trails

- - -  Park Boundary

▨  Water

▬  Main Roads

🛉  Picnic Area

P  Parking

⌂  Park Office

## Blue Trail–Leatherleaf Bog

 **Distance Round-Trip:** 3.45 miles
 **Estimated Hiking Time:** 1.5 hours

*The trail is a symphony of sound: cricketing frogs, honking geese, skreeing red-winged blackbirds, chattering and chiding chipmunks, and rattling sandhill cranes.*

**Caution:** This is a multiuse trail, so the path will be shared by bicyclists and dog walkers.

**Trail Directions:** Park at the Northern Woods picnic area, where a short access path will take you to the beginning of the trail and mile markers [1]. The trail is marked every .25 mi. with blue squares and immediately passes through an oak-hickory woods. By .2 mi. [2] you come down a hill to a cattail marsh on both sides. Look for turtles basking in the sun. Not only are they increasing their body temperature, but they're also exposing their shells to air to reduce algal growth.

The trail soon curves away from the water and the large oaks disappear to be replaced by a shrubby old field. At .55 mi. cattail marshes [3] again appear on both sides.

From the marsh you will enter an oak savanna. Don't be alarmed if you see burning in this section. The understory of savannas is burned quite frequently, getting rid of fire-intolerant species and allowing the oaks to grow unimpeded. From the savanna you will hike through a shrubby woods on your left and a grassy field with bluebird houses. Bluebirds are making a comeback, thanks in part to the widespread use of these houses. Bluebirds are cavity nesters, building their nests near open fields in rotted trees or fence posts. When farm fencerows began disappearing, so did the bluebirds.

At 1 mi. [4] note an open-water marsh on your left. Scan the area for turtles (both snapping and red-eared sliders) and for herons (great blue and green) as they fish. The trail soon curves to the right. At 1.5 mi. look to the left for Leatherleaf Bog [5], an area surrounded by marsh.

Watch sandhill cranes come in for a landing with the grace and precision of an experienced parachutist, and try to identify any warblers flitting around the edge. The plant in the middle of the bog is leatherleaf—an evergreen shrub. During the spring the plant produces white flowers that dangle from the branches like little bells. At 2 mi. [6] look for two large oak trees on your right—one is a bur and the other a white. Also on the right is a vast, grassy, prairielike area.

At 2.15 mi. look at the woods on the left for large, open-grown oaks [7]. A drainage channel appears on the left at 2.35 mi. and also a trail junction [8]. The blue and red trails intersect at this point; go left, still following the blue. The trail soon heads over moraines—small hills on both the right and the left [9] (2.6 mi.). On the moraines you will find an oak-hickory woods carpeted in the spring with mayapple and toothwort.

At 2.75 mi. the trail skirts the ill-defined edge of Lake Defiance [10]. At 2.8 mi. take the boardwalk on your right [11] for a .25 mi. side spur that wanders through the lake. Use the observation platforms to look for water lilies, frogs, and turtles. Retrace your steps back to [11]. Did you notice, unlike manmade lakes, glacial lakes have no edges? Another trail junction appears at 3.15 mi. [12]; go left and skirt the Northern Woods picnic area. Soon you will return to where you started and to your vehicle.

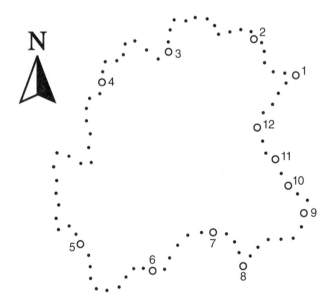

1.  Start
2.  Cattail marsh
3.  Cattail marshes
4.  Open-water marsh
5.  Leatherleaf Bog
6.  Two oaks
7.  Large oaks
8.  Trail junction
9.  Moraines
10. Lake Defiance
11. Side spur to explore Lake Defiance
12. Left turn

# Fox River Trail

**Distance Round-Trip:** 3.5 miles
**Estimated Hiking Time:** 2 hours

*This trail brings you up close and personal with large, fat bullfrogs camouflaged by green duckweed; proud geese with new goslings; chipmunks scurrying across the trail; and tall, stately great white egrets.*

**Caution:** This is a multiuse trail, and the path will also be shared with bicyclists and dog walkers.

**Trail Directions:** Park at the Pike Marsh parking area and cross the road. Begin the trail at the gate [1]. As you begin to hike, notice the line of large bur oaks on the right. The trail comes to a T at .15 mi.; go left [2]. A marsh will be on your right and the highway on your left. Look for green herons at the edge of the marsh. Open water appears at .3 mi. [3]. During the spring, watch as goose parents show off their new goslings to those still sitting on nests. Scan the duckweed for large bullfrogs trying to hide from herons.

The trail now heads up and away from open water. At .5 mi. you'll come to a trail junction; take the second left (trail junction C) [4]. The trail goes through an underpass and comes out on a grassy area. Another trail junction appears at .7 mi. [5]. Go right to McHenry Dam. This segment of the trail is marked with yellow squares and distances. The trail continues through rolling grasslands, and at .85 mi. you pass a grove of bur oak trees on a moraine to the right [6].

Look for a very tall plant along this segment of the trail. It is cow parsnip, a member of the parsley family. The plant may be anywhere from 4 to 9 feet tall and have very large leaves with a cluster of white flowers on the top. An open-water marsh has come into view at 1.25 mi. [7]. This marsh is part of the Moraine Hills Enhancement Project for the perpetuation of North American waterfowl. From the trail you can see lots of turtles basking, geese, and perhaps even a mute swan.

At 1.4 mi. take advantage of the observation platform on your left [8] to look for muskrats, wood ducks, coots, yellow-headed blackbirds, and black terns. Rejoin the trail, from which the Fox River is now visible at 1.5 mi. [9]; it skirts the river for some time. Gone is the quiet, peaceful hike around the marsh, replaced by blaring boat radios as they zip up and down the river. At 1.7 mi. find a series of open-water marshes on the left [10]. Look for gatherings of turtles and a kingfisher. At 1.85 mi. the trail curves left, leaving the Fox River behind, but not the small slough.

A levee appears on the left with a Do Not Walk On sign; please obey [11] (1.9 mi.). At 2 mi. the trail curves left [12], with a copse of cottonwoods on the left and a marsh on the right. At 2.25 mi. come to a trail intersection; go left to a viewing platform and a wildlife area [13]. (The viewing platform is on the left, down a few steps.) From this vantage point look to the right to locate any sandhill cranes that may be present. They are tall, gray birds with a patch of red on the crown. Or seek out great white egrets, white birds almost as tall as the cranes. Go back up the steps and to the left. At 2.5 mi. you will come to another trail intersection; again go left and come down off a moraine into a cottonwood copse [14].

You are back to [5] at 2.75 mi.; go right and begin to retrace your steps. At 3 mi. you are at [4]; take the second right (not River Road Trail), ignoring the wrong-way signs (for bicyclists and cross-country skiers). As you pass the open water, don't forget to look for any new activity. At 3.35 mi. you will return to the Pike Marsh junction [2]; go right and soon you are back to the trailhead, hopefully with some new bird sightings to add to your Illinois life list.

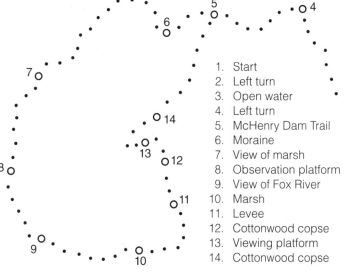

1. Start
2. Left turn
3. Open water
4. Left turn
5. McHenry Dam Trail
6. Moraine
7. View of marsh
8. Observation platform
9. View of Fox River
10. Marsh
11. Levee
12. Cottonwood copse
13. Viewing platform
14. Cottonwood copse

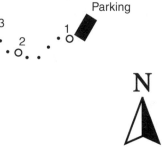

Parking

N

# 11. Bluff Spring Fen

- Explore a fen with its marl flats and spring run.

- Climb a kame.

- Bring your field guides; for a small site this area is teaming with wildflowers, butterflies, and birds.

- On a cool, misty morning, the glaciers seem not far away, at least in your mind.

## Area Information

Bluff Spring Fen is a small treasure. It may be only 100 acres in size, yet it supports over 450 plant species (white lady's slipper, prairie smoke, and skunk cabbage) and 56 butterfly species (Baltimore checkerspot and mulberry skipper). At least 30 bird species nest on-site (including the red-headed woodpecker and yellow-breasted chat). The attraction here is a selection of the rarest habitats found in the state—bur oak savanna, black soil prairie, marsh, sedge meadow, dry gravel prairie, and fen—all within a few short steps of each other. The fen, however, may be the area's jewel in the crown.

Fens are a type of wet meadow fed by alkaline water (basic), usually from a spring or seep. At Bluff Spring Fen you can see the spring runs (small channels of flowing water) that feed the fen. Fens occur on organic soils and can be shrubby, grassy, or even forested. Fen vegetation forms a unique community of calcium-loving plants such as Kalm's lobelia, fringed gentian, turtlehead, and grass-of-Parnassus. All these special species are found here, and more besides. In addition to the spring run, a marl flat has developed, which is a stagnant, level, highly alkaline wetland fed by groundwater laden with dissolved limestone. The greatest threat to fens is a change in the groundwater. Any alteration, whether by pollution or changes in the water level, will drastically affect the habitat.

Appearances aren't always as they seem: Before a land survey revealed the unique features of this area, it was a favored place for fly ash dumping, off-road vehicle traveling, and gravel quarrying. Restoration began in 1979, and in 1987 the site was dedicated as a nature preserve. The hard work of volunteers is paying off. Bluff Spring Fen is a site to visit often during a season. From skunk cabbage poking through the snows in early March to the final, faded bloom of fringed gentians in late October, the area is always full of botanical surprises.

**Directions:** Take US 20 to the southeast side of Elgin. At the stoplight intersection of US 20 and Bluff City Boulevard (also known as Shales Parkway), turn south. Follow Bluff City Boulevard as it bends to the east. Go 1 mile to the main entrance of Bluff City Cemetery. Turn left and follow the signs through the cemetery (Central Avenue) to a small parking area at the entrance to the fen on the cemetery's southern edge.

**Hours Open:** The site is open-year round. The gates to the cemetery close at 7:30 p.m. April through October and 4:00 p.m. November through March.

**Facilities:** None, except for a parking area.

**Permits and Rules:** This is an Illinois Nature Preserve, and no pets are allowed. No collecting of plants or animals. No bicycles.

**For Further Information:** The Nature Conservancy, 8 South Michigan Avenue, Suite 900, Chicago, IL 60603; 312-580-2100 or Friends of the Bluff Spring Fen at 847-464-4426.

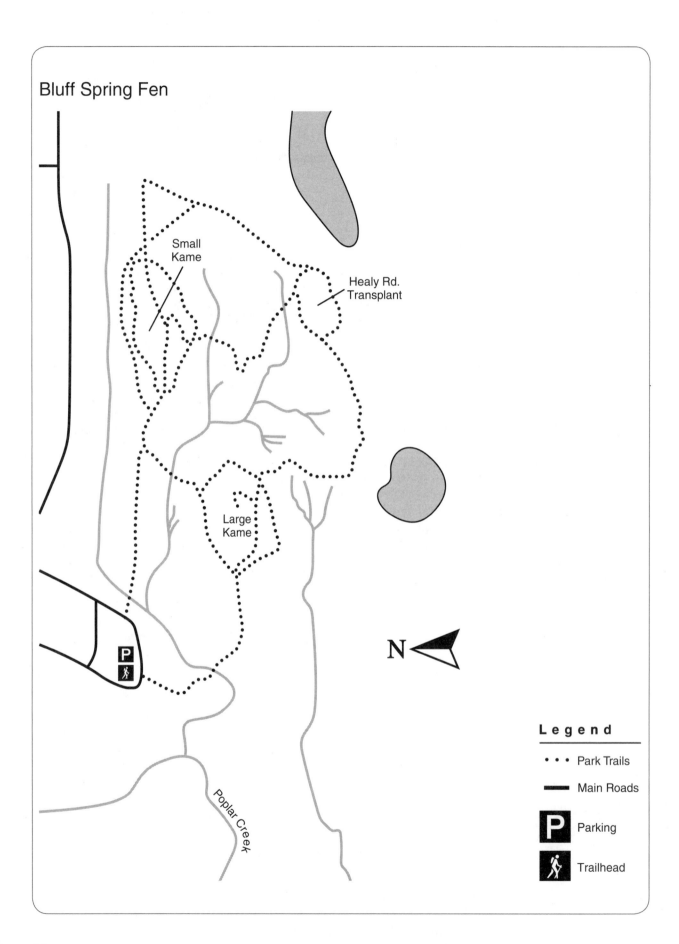

Bluff Spring Fen

Small
Kame

Healy Rd.
Transplant

Large
Kame

N

Poplar Creek

**Legend**

• • • Park Trails

━━ Main Roads

P Parking

Trailhead

# Bluff Spring Trail

   **Distance Round-Trip:** 1 mile
**Estimated Hiking Time:** 1 hour

*Fall is a perfect time to explore the fen; monarch butterflies cluster on Joe-pye weed blooms, white ladies' tresses orchids bloom along the spring runs, giant robber flies with orange-red eyes sally forth seeking prey, a large walking stick may hitch a ride on your backpack, and violet-blue-fringed gentians add a bit of the fall sky to the marl flats.*

**Caution:** Stay on the path because this is a delicate area and too many trails may upset the delicate hydrology.

**Trail Directions:** Because the trail is very short, mileage distances will not be given here. But this is a place to take your time to discover and listen. Begin the trail at the gate with the trail box. The path is narrow and could be wet. You will cross a bridge over a small stream. Take a few minutes to see if you can spot any mottled skullpin in the stream. These bottom-feeding fish are a sign of a high-quality stream. Along this wet area look for skunk cabbage; its maroon spathe can poke through the ground in late February.

The trail heads through an oak grove; look for shooting star, bloodroot, and wild geranium during the spring. By late fall the vegetation along this section can be 4 feet tall. The path will go between two giant bur oaks, and within a few steps the faint trail will go left. If you pass through the grove of oaks, you have missed the trail.

Soon you are walking under the limbs of an arching bur oak and will cross a stream with the aid of stepping-stones. Look for the glint of marsh marigold, with its heart-shaped leaves, in early spring and fringed gentian and ladies' tresses orchid in the fall. From the stream you will hike up the first of a series of small kames. Note the lovely savanna on your left. Kames are gravel hills that were formed by the glaciers, literally where a stream formed a waterfall on the glacier and dumped its load of sediment in a neat, conical pile. Each spring look for prairie smoke, a wildflower associated with the short-grass prairies of the west. By late spring, prairie smoke's wispy seed heads give it the common name of old man's whiskers. At the top you gain an overview of the preserve and are able to see the marl flat and the spring run in the center of the preserve.

Winding your way down the kame brings you to the marl flats. Here the vegetation is similar to the runoff channels at Yellowstone's geyser basins, and like Yellowstone's fringed gentians, they are the dominant fall bloomer here. The trail will V; go left on the gravel path to explore a second marl flat. You will then come to a bridge at the bottom of a kame; cross the bridge and go left. Within a few steps another fork will appear; go right, circling the kame. As you circle around, note the gravelly, glacial outwash, the parent material of kames.

Away from the kame, the trail goes through an area where cottonwood seedlings dominate. You will soon join a gravel path; go right, and a shrubby area will be on your left. By fall the trail is very faint and the grasses and shrubs are closing in. Go left and then right, through two small oaks and prairie grasses. After about 20 steps go right again as soon as you become engulfed in tall prairie grasses.

From the grasses, climb up a kame with oaks; go left. Take a side spur to an overlook, climbing to the top of the kame. Here you are almost at the tops of the oaks; the climb is worth the the effort because it provides another overview of this unique area. Retrace your steps back down, go right, and continue to encircle the kame. Soon you are back to the large oaks where you began. Retrace your steps through the marsh and cross the bridge, heading back to the parking area.

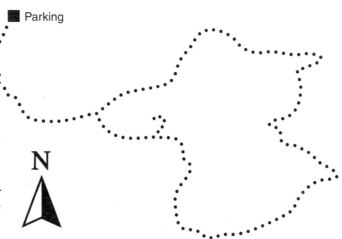

# 12. James "Pate" Philip State Park

- Hike a trail where the frogs are always just one hop ahead.
- View an occupied osprey nest.
- Spot dragonflies, butterflies, and birds on this family-friendly trail.
- Imagine mastodons on the path ahead of you.
- Learn about the prairie ecosystem that once made up 60 percent of Illinois.

## Area Information

James "Pate" Philip State Park, named after the DuPage County congressman who was president of the state senate and an avid outdoorsman, was originally called Tri-County State Park. The park encompasses over 500 acres in DuPage, Kane, and Cook counties and was established as corridor and greenway connections for all three counties.

The park's mission is to celebrate Illinois' natural history. At one time this area was wet prairie—a mix of grasses and forbs and home to numerous insects and bison. While diligent restoration will bring back the grasses, flowers, and insects, the only bison you will see is in the visitor center—a brass bison sculpture is on view with information on its role in the prairie. The visitor center also explains how the prairie ecosystem was formed, maintained, and ultimately destroyed.

James "Pate" Philip State Park is a place to visit frequently to catch the changing seasons on the prairie and to see what organisms are out and about during every season.

**Directions:** James "Pate" Philip State Park is located on Stearns Road in Bartlett, Illinois. From Illinois 59, take Stearns Road to the park.

**Hours Open:** The site is open daily from one hour after sunrise to one hour after sunset. The visitor center is open from 9:00 a.m. to 4:00 p.m. Monday through Friday and 9:00 a.m. to 1:00 p.m. on Saturday. It is also closed during major holidays.

**Facilities:** Visitor center, restrooms, water, and a reservable picnic shelter are available. The trails are suitable for wheelchairs and strollers.

**Permits and Rules:** Dogs must be leashed.

**For Further Information:** James "Pate" Philip State Park, 2050 W. Stearns Road, Bartlett, IL 60103; 847-608-3100.

## Other Areas of Interest

Located directly south of James "Pate" Philip State Park is DuPage County's largest forest preserve, **Pratt's Wayne Woods.** The preserve's 3,400 acres, combined with those from the state park, form a continuous 4,000-acre stretch of savannas, marshes, meadows, and wetlands. There are more than 12 miles of trails for hiking, horseback riding, and bicycling. A piece of the Illinois Prairie Path also runs through the preserve. This preserve offers a model-airplane field and an off-leash dog area. For more information, call 630-933-7248.

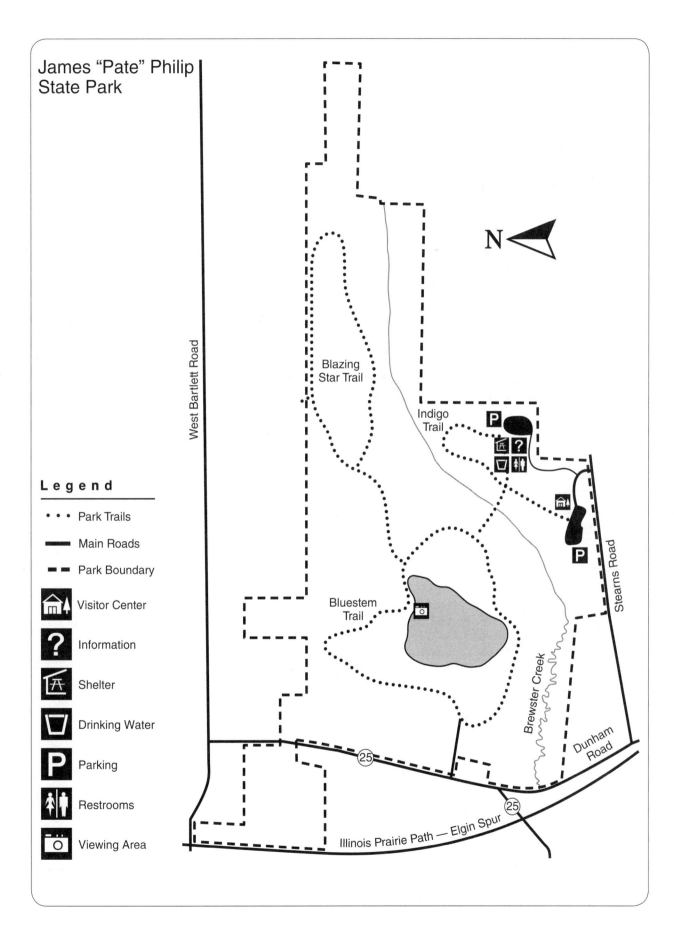

James "Pate" Philip
State Park

N

West Bartlett Road

Blazing
Star Trail

Indigo
Trail

**Legend**

• • • Park Trails

—— Main Roads

– – Park Boundary

Visitor Center

? Information

Shelter

Drinking Water

P Parking

Restrooms

Viewing Area

Bluestem
Trail

P

P

Stearns Road

Brewster Creek

Dunham Road

25

25

Illinois Prairie Path — Elgin Spur

# Bluestem, Blazing Star, and Indigo

 **Distance Round-Trip:** 4.25 miles
**Estimated Hiking Time:** 1.5 hour

*I never know what I might see on this trail of surprises. It could be a rabbit warming itself along the trail margins, northern leopard frogs one hop ahead of me, or a baby snapping turtle crossing on its too-small legs.*

**Caution:** This trail is frequently used by dog walkers and bicyclists. Low spots occur with the possibility of wet feet.

**Trail Directions:** Begin the hike at the large boulder in front of the visitor center [1]. Immediately go left, hiking past a prairie garden with native plants and glacial boulders. At the intersection go right and then left on the all-purpose path. Periodically, informational signs will appear about the ecology of the area; take advantage of these to enhance your knowledge about the area.

At the intersection at .15 mi. go left [2]; soon you will cross the bridge over Brewster Creek. Look at the water for muskrats, duckweed-covered bullfrogs, and patrolling dragonflies. You are hiking through a prairie restoration, and by late summer the plants are tall enough to give the feeling of hiking in the wild. Another intersection is at .25 mi; go left [3], looking in the wet areas for great egrets and common moorhens.

The path is littered with the calling cards of those who traveled before you—tracks and scat. Several species of frogs will hop in front of you—look for northern leopard frogs, chorus frogs, green frogs, and American toads. In the late summer the trail is ablaze with the gold of false sunflowers.

At .8 mi. go right at the intersection [4]. Along this section you can find plants in the genus *Silphium*—prairie dock, compass plant, and cup plant. Take a few minutes to feel how coarse the leaves are. As the trail curves right, check out the ball diamond and the lights surrounding the water tower. An osprey has built a nest there [5] (1.2 mi.). Osprey build large stick nests and will use the same nest year after year. There are only four known nesting sites for osprey in Illinois.

At 1.4 mi. continue straight, and within a tenth of a mile you will come to an intersection; go left on Blazing Star [6] (1.5 mi.). As you pass open water on both sides, look for frogs. Continue straight [7] (1.8 mi.) at the next intersection; you will be heading toward the subdivision. For the next half mile the trail will encircle the subdivision. At 2.4 mi. the trail curves away from it [8]. At 3 mi. you are at another intersection [6]; go left, retracing your steps back to the bridge. Recross the bridge and at 3.6 mi. go left on the Indigo Trail [9].

An area with open water appears at 3.75 mi. [10]. Look at the row of dead trees for a heron rookery (area of several nests) and in the water for ducks and egrets. At 3.9 mi. willows appear in the distance [11]. In 2005 a contractor uncovered a mastodon molar in this area. High school students have been excavating here for two weeks every summer. The picnic area soon appears on the left; stay right on the path.

A small wetland [12] appears at 4.1 mi. and then an intersection; go left, retracing your steps back to the visitor center and the boulder.

1. Start
2. Left turn
3. Left turn
4. Right turn
5. Osprey nest
6. Left turn
7. Continue straight
8. Curve away from subdivision
9. Left turn
10. Open water
11. Mastodon site
12. Wetland

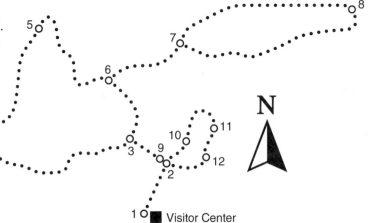

# 13. Illinois Beach State Park

- Build a sandcastle and kick off your hiking boots as you walk along the lakeshore, dipping your toes in the cold water of Lake Michigan.
- Look in the open spaces to find wildflower treats that are ever changing with the seasons. The park has nearly 700 species of plants.
- Pick up a smooth, rounded rock or two along the shore to use as heavy hands.
- Study dunesland succession as you proceed from the sandy beach to a black oak savanna.
- Bring your binoculars to look for birds in the 16 plant communities and to observe avian activity along Lake Michigan.

## Area Information

Dubbed the dunesland, Illinois Beach State Park is a remnant of the sand and beach terrain that once lined the state's Lake Michigan shore. The geology, climate, and location account for the diversity of life present here. The dunesland is home to nearly 700 species of plants that grow on the park's beaches and in its sand dunes, marshes, chalky swales (low area between two dunes), sand prairies, and oak savannas (widely spaced oaks with prairie vegetation underneath).

Here the southwestern prickly pear cactus mingles with the bearberry and tough, creeping juniper of the far north; southeastern blazing stars coexist with northern fringed gentians. You can see northern orchids, wood lilies, Indian paintbrushes, lupines, and the occasional carnivorous sundew. Because of this area's unique plant diversity, in 1964 it became the state's first nature preserve.

Although the dunes pale in comparison to those found along the Indiana shoreline where wind and wave action deposit massive quantities of sand, they are noteworthy because each sand ridge and low, wet swale that parallels the lake represents an old lakeshore—relics from glacial times.

A walk from Lake Michigan back to the parking lot will chronicle how plants have colonized the dunes. Begin by noting the sand-binding grasses along the beach's edge and progress to dune-binding shrubs such as the creeping and upright junipers. Once these plants have stabilized the dunes (a process that takes several hundred years) and contributed humus to the sand, other species appear and continue to enrich the coarse sand. The final stage is an oak savanna, a unique and beautiful landscape.

**Directions:** The South Unit of Illinois Beach State Park is located on the shore of Lake Michigan, a few miles south of the Illinois–Wisconsin border. From Zion, take Sheridan Road south about 1 mile to Wadsworth Road; go east to the park. From the South Unit turn right (north) on Sheridan Road, follow it to 17th Street, and turn right into the main entrance for the North Unit.

**Hours Open:** The site is open daily from sunrise to 8:00 p.m. from Memorial Day to Labor Day and from sunrise to sunset from Labor Day to Memorial Day.

**Facilities:** A nature center, found in the nature preserve (South Unit), is usually open during weekends. A campground is present with 40 sites available by reservation. Showers, a camp store, boating, jetskiing, fishing, swimming, beachcombing, picnic areas with shelters, a playground, and a lodge with a conference center are some of the amenities.

**Permits and Rules:** No pets are allowed on the beach, and they must be leashed in all other areas of the park. No skiing or bicycling is allowed on the trails that go through the nature preserve.

**For Further Information:** Illinois Beach State Park, Lake Front, Zion, IL 60099; 847-662-4811.

## Park Trails

**Bicycle Trail** ( , 10 miles). This asphalt trail (South Unit) connects various amenities in the park and provides a nice overview of the area.

**Power Line Trail** ( , 3.3 miles). From the trailhead near Sand Pond in the North Unit, this trail offers savannas and beach ridges (most of it is on an old asphalt road).

**Marsh Trail** ( , 6.7 miles). This trail, also found in the North Unit, is a continuation of the Power Line Trail. You will skirt the day-use portion of the park and discover a marsh.

## Other Areas of Interest

Located in northwestern Lake County near Wadsworth, **Van Patten Woods Forest Preserve** offers fishing and boating on Sterling Lake, picnicking with shelters among the oak forests, youth group camping, and a boat, bicycle, and fishing equipment rental store. The preserve offers several trails. Two loops go around Sterling Lake, 3 miles of loop trails are found in the eastern half, and a 9-mile section of the Des Plaines River Trail crosses the area (see below). For more information, call 847-367-6640.

The **Des Plaines River Trail (Northern Section),** a multiuse gravel trail, parallels the Des Plaines River through Lake County and can be accessed on Russell Road, east of Route 41. It can also be accessed at each of the forest preserves it traverses. At present, the northern section is 9 miles long and goes through Van Patten Woods, Wadsworth Savanna Forest Preserve, and the Wetlands Demonstration Project.

North

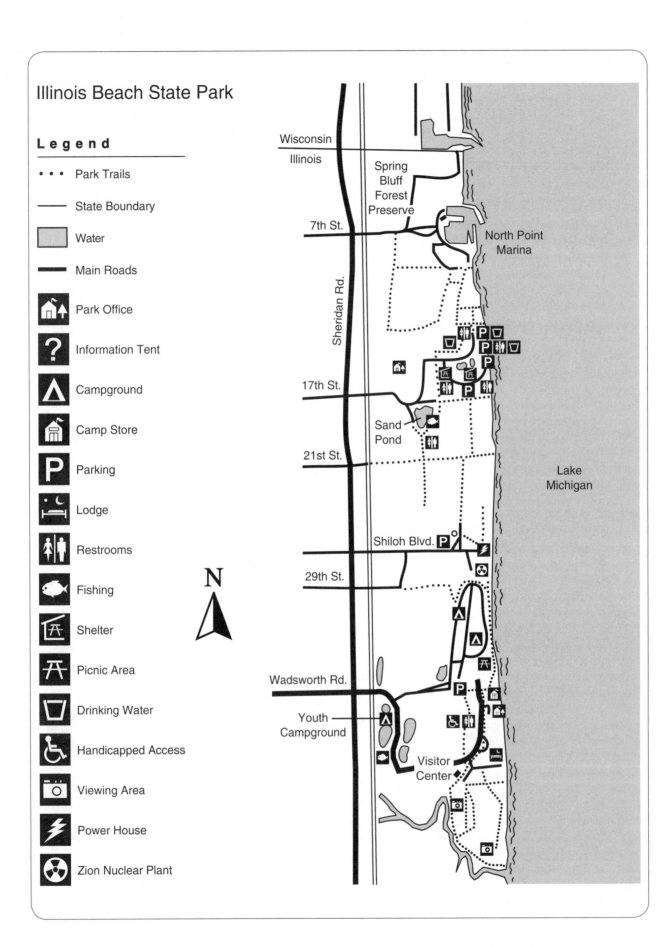

# Illinois Beach State Park

## Legend

**• • •** Park Trails

⎯⎯⎯ State Boundary

▢ Water

▬▬▬ Main Roads

Park Office

Information Tent

Campground

Camp Store

P Parking

Lodge

Restrooms

Fishing

Shelter

Picnic Area

Drinking Water

Handicapped Access

Viewing Area

Power House

Zion Nuclear Plant

Wisconsin
Illinois

Spring
Bluff
Forest
Preserve

7th St.

North Point
Marina

Sheridan Rd.

17th St.

Sand
Pond

21st St.

Lake
Michigan

Shiloh Blvd.

29th St.

N

Wadsworth Rd.

Youth
Campground

Visitor
Center

# Dead River Trail

   **Distance Round-Trip:** 2.4 miles
**Estimated Hiking Time:** 1.5 hours

*No matter what the season, the Dead River Trail is alive with color. In spring orange and yellow Indian paintbrush mix with red-violet phlox. Summer brings orange wood lilies and the upside-down blooms of hot pink orchids. In the fall, hidden among the yellows of goldenrods and red-browns of dying leaves, find the deep blue of fringed gentians.*

**Caution:** Do not try to cross the mouth of the Dead River because there can be a dangerous undertow. When there has been a smelt kill, the beach will smell like an abandoned fish market. Mosquitoes can also be more than a nuisance here.

**Trail Directions:** Begin at a trail map sign on the southwest corner of the parking area for the nature preserve [1]. Within the first few steps you realize this is a very different place. The trail is made of wood chips, and all around are low dunes dominated by black oaks. At .25 mi. take advantage of an overlook of the Dead River [2].

Try to avoid the poison ivy along both sides of the trail. Even though in the fall it turns all shades of yellow, red, and orange and is quite pretty, it has lost none of its noxious properties. As you walk along this section, listen for the squeaks of chipmunks and notice the variety of wildflowers. Always the same colors occur—pink, purple, blue, yellow, and orange. Only the species change with the seasons. On your left and low to the ground, note wild lily of the valley. At .6 mi. the trail crosses a swale [3]; this treeless area is sometimes wet.

Stay on the main trail, even though you will see plenty of unofficial side spurs. Go left at .75 mi. [4], leaving the river and the mosquitoes; within a few steps go right. You are now following the Dune Trail. As you head to the lakeshore, you are walking through a black oak savanna. A bench is provided at .9 mi. [5].

This trail intersects another at 1 mi. [6]; continue straight, leaving the gravel path for a sandy path lined with sand-binding creeping junipers, the beach, and soon Lake Michigan. At the lake [7] (1.15 mi.) go right to discover whether the mouth of the Dead River is open or closed. The Dead River seems a short river when its mouth is open to Lake Michigan, but a long pond when its mouth is closed by a ridge of sand (deposited by a north-to-south lake current). While walking to the mouth of Dead River, explore the flotsam and jetsam of the rock-strewn lakeshore. At 1.25 mi. you will reach the mouth of the Dead River

[8]. Turn around and retrace your steps to the Dune Trail.

Notice how the grasses make perfect arcs in the sand. These grasses are the first stage in dune stabilization; they are resistant to water loss and their roots hold firm against the wind. At 1.45 mi. you are at [6] again; go right and continue to follow the Dune Trail. While walking along these stabilized dunes, look for ground cherry, prickly pear cactus, and small, pale yellow clumps of an odd-looking Indian paintbrush. The plant, commonly called downy yellow painted cup, is an endangered species in Illinois; this is the eastern limit of its range.

The large indentions in the sand at 1.6 mi. are called blowouts, formed by wind erosion in areas where the vegetation has been destroyed [9]. With nothing to hold the sand in place, the wind carries it from the exposed area, forming a hole.

At 1.95 mi. [10] you will pass a cement foundation, one of the few remnants of the old town of Beach. On your right will be a sand pond ringed with *Equisetum* (horsetails or scouring rush). Look for mallards along the edge, so still that you'll swear they are decoys.

The trail now curves left, away from the lakeshore, and heads back through a savanna. Stay on the main gravel path. At 2.25 mi. come to a trail junction [11]; go left, coming upon a bridge over a large pond. Take time to look through the tangle of rushes to see what might be lurking there.

The final bridge crossing at 2.3 mi. is over a wet swale [12]. From the bridge, follow the wood-chip path back to the parking area.

1.  Start
2.  Overlook
3.  Swale
4.  Left turn
5.  Bench
6.  Trail junction
7.  Lakeshore
8.  Mouth of Dead River
9.  Blowouts
10.  Foundation
11.  Trail junction
12.  Swale

## North Unit Trail

 **Distance Round-Trip:** 2.2 miles
**Estimated Hiking Time:** 1.1 hours

*Hiking through the fog and mist transports me back 6,000 years. It wipes out any ills, and the landscape appears as it was not long after the glaciers left. Sand prairie species grow next to northern bog species. If not for the old road bed and nearby subdivision, I wouldn't know what epoch I was in.*

**Caution:** During wet periods there can be standing water on sections of the trail. Just take off your shoes—it's worth the wade.

**Trail Directions:** From the South Unit turn right (north) on Sheridan Road, follow it to 17th Street, and turn right into the main entrance of the North Unit. Begin the trail at the south parking area at the yellow hashed lines [1]. On your left will be Sand Pond; on your right are cottonwoods and oaks. As you hike through a small cottonwood grove, check the shape of the leaves. They are triangular, and when crushed, they give off a sweet fragrance. The cottonwood will be the dominant tree on this hike.

Once through the grove, go right at a large cottonwood [2] (.1 mi.). A marsh is on your right, and through the willow on your left is a wet sand prairie restoration with lots of horsetails. Watch for bright green northern leopard frogs along this section. (I saw 10 within 10 minutes.) An enclosed cattail marsh will soon come into view on the right. At .4 mi. go left at the trail intersection [3] and hike on the road of an abandoned housing development. It makes a great path! You skirt a preserve on the left; on the right, groves of quaking aspen alternate with a marsh.

Ignore the trail to the right at .6 mi. [4]. The area here begins to look like the South Unit black oaks mixing with prairie vegetation—a savanna. Already you can feel the effects of the nearby lake, and fog is a common occurrence. Hiking in the fog gives the feel of the ancient north woods. You are totally alone, and given a little imagination, at any moment a mastodon may materialize from the fog.

At .75 mi. note a trail to the left [5], but continue straight to the beach. On your left is a swale, composed of mucky, sandy soils dominated by rushes and sedges. The soil is alkaline, so the plants found are much like those in a fen or marsh. The trail dead-ends at Lake Michigan [6] (.8 mi.). Walk along the beach looking for that perfect rock, observing the gulls and an occasional cormorant, and try to find signs of beach succession. Retrace your steps from the lake back to point [5].

Go right at [5] (.95 mi.). On the right you will have an excellent view of the old beach ridges. When the glacial ice was melting 8,000 to 12,000 years ago, Lake Michigan was part of a much larger Lake Chicago. As the glacier receded farther and farther north, the water level in the lake fell in stages. Each level lasted for several hundred years and formed characteristic beach ridges—the ridges observed in both units of the park.

On the left are evenly spaced trees and a lush green understory dotted with multihued wildflowers. A well-planned and maintained park comes to mind, instead of a natural area that was narrowly saved from being cut up for housing lots. During late spring look for shooting stars and puccoons in the savanna on your left. At 1.25 come to an intersection, but continue on the main trail.

The path comes to a T at 1.45 mi. [7]. Go left, skirting a Federal Aviation Administration air traffic control facility. After this modern-day interruption, look to your left at the swales. At 1.7 mi. [8] go left; Sand Pond will come into view on your right. Look in the willows around Sand Pond for yellow warblers. The trail leads back to where you began the loop [2] (2.1 mi.), and soon you are back at the parking area.

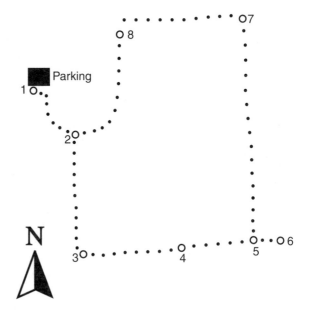

1. Start
2. Right turn
3. Left turn
4. Side trail (don't follow)
5. Side trail (don't follow)
6. Lake Michigan
7. Left turn
8. Left turn

North

- Sight a black-crowned night heron or a yellow-headed blackbird, both endangered species in Illinois.
- Watch for an aerial dogfight as a smaller blackbird wards off a crow.
- Hike under the limbs of grand oaks.
- Work on your bird calls as you pass through a variety of habitats along the trail.

## Area Information

From its name you might associate Lake County only with things wet, yet here you can find a rich, unusual mosaic of habitats—lake, marsh, savanna, woods, and prairie. Lake County is home to more endangered species than any other county in Illinois, and many of these are found in its 26,000 acres of preserves.

**Rollins Savanna** is one of Lake County's largest preserves at over 1,200 acres. Here are scattered groves of majestic oaks and wide-open prairie. Rollins's transformation from farm to forest preserve has been a relatively short one. Work began in 1996 when the area was nothing but a fallow farm without much bird life. Thirteen miles of drain tiles were disabled and 200,000 native wetland plants and 2,000 native trees and shrubs have been planted, as well as several hundred acres of prairie restored. The hard work has provided a wonderful habitat for birds, and some of the state's least common species may be found here—least bittern, bobolinks, Henslow's and grasshopper sparrows, and short-eared owls. In 2004, Rollins Savanna was named an important bird area by the National Audubon Society.

The story of **Cuba Marsh** is much like that of Rollins Savanna. When the settlers first came here, they plowed, logged, and drained the land as best they could. By the 1950s and '60s, though, most of the farmers here had sold their land to developers. Local residents, however, wanted Cuba Marsh preserved as open space and helped the Lake County Forest Preserve District obtain it. These local residents, called the Citizens for Conservation, have helped not only with land acquisition but also with tree planting and general care of the land. The drainage tiles are gone, thousands of trees have been planted, and the regenerative powers of fire have been returned. This is a preserve in the making, so visit it often to see changes as the trees grow, the prairie returns, and the once-lush wetland habitat is restored. More and more wildlife, and humans, will likely find this a metropolitan oasis in years to come.

**Directions: Rollins Savanna** is located in central Lake County near Grayslake. The main entrance is located on Washington Street at Atkinson Road, just west of Route 45 and east of Route 83. **Cuba Marsh Forest Preserve** is in southwestern Lake County, between Barrington and Lake Zurich, west of Route 12. The entrance is on the south side of Cuba Road, just west of Ela Road.

**Hours Open:** The sites are open daily year-round from 6:30 a.m. to sunset.

**Facilities:** Restrooms and drinking water are available at both sites. In addition, Rollins Savanna has a native seed nursery and Cuba Marsh has picnic tables. If there is adequate snow, cross-country skiing is allowed at both sites.

**Permits and Rules:** Leash and pick up after all pets. Park only in designated areas. Hunting, collecting, firearms, and off-road vehicles are prohibited. Horses, fires, and camping are not allowed.

**For Further Information:** Lake County Forest Preserves, 2000 N. Milwaukee Avenue, Libertyville, IL 60048; 847-367-6640 or www.LCFPD.org.

## Other Areas of Interest

One of the best examples of an old-growth sugar maple forest in northeastern Illinois is found at **Ryerson Conservation Area,** near Deerfield. During the spring, wildflowers and migrating warblers make the 6.5 miles of trails a treasure trove of discovery. Here you can also find a "green" welcome center, library, lecture and meeting rooms, natural history exhibits, and a working farm. Pets are not allowed. For more information, call 847-968-3321.

Located near Wauconda, **Lakewood** is the county's largest forest preserve. Here you can find picnic shelters, fishing, playing fields, and winter sports fun. The preserve also has Lake County Museum, which traces the county's history and includes a locally discovered mastodon bone. The area has 9 miles of hiking trails, including a 6.5-mile horse and hiking trail, a .75-mile fitness trail, and a 3-mile cross-country ski trail. For more information, call 847-367-6640.

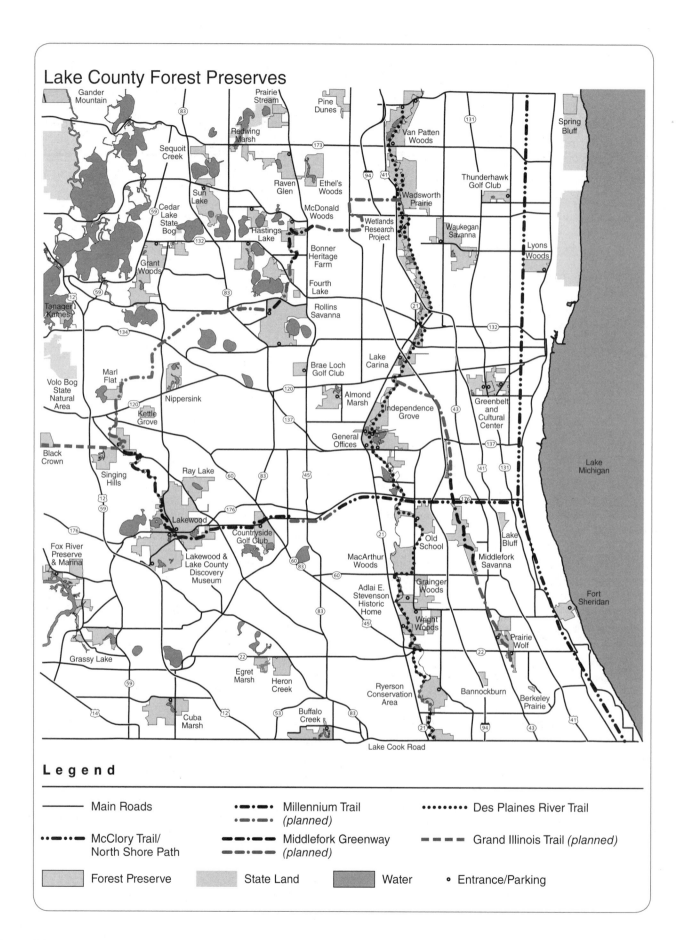

# Lake County Forest Preserves

Gander Mountain

Prairie Stream

Pine Dunes

Spring Bluff

Redwing Marsh

Sequoit Creek

Raven Glen

Ethel's Woods

Van Patten Woods

Thunderhawk Golf Club

Sun Lake

McDonald Woods

Wadsworth Prairie

Waukegan Savanna

Cedar Lake State Bog

Wetlands Research Project

Hastings Lake

Bonner Heritage Farm

Lyons Woods

Grant Woods

Fourth Lake

Tanager Kames

Rollins Savanna

Volo Bog State Natural Area

Marl Flat

Brae Loch Golf Club

Lake Carina

Greenbelt and Cultural Center

Nippersink

Almond Marsh

Independence Grove

Kettle Grove

General Offices

Black Crown

Singing Hills

Ray Lake

Lakewood

Lake Michigan

Fox River Preserve & Marina

Lakewood & Lake County Discovery Museum

Countryside Golf Club

MacArthur Woods

Old School

Middlefork Savanna

Lake Bluff

Adlai E. Stevenson Historic Home

Grainger Woods

Wright Woods

Prairie Wolf

Fort Sheridan

Grassy Lake

Egret Marsh

Heron Creek

Ryerson Conservation Area

Bannockburn

Berkeley Prairie

Cuba Marsh

Buffalo Creek

Lake Cook Road

## Legend

— Main Roads

–•–•–•– Millennium Trail
–•–•–• *(planned)*

•••••••• Des Plaines River Trail

•–•–•– McClory Trail/ North Shore Path

––•–– Middlefork Greenway
–•–•– *(planned)*

– – – Grand Illinois Trail *(planned)*

▨ Forest Preserve    ▨ State Land    ▨ Water    ∘ Entrance/Parking

# Rollins Savanna

 **Distance Round-Trip:** 5.75 miles
**Estimated Hiking Time:** 2 hours

*As I hiked, I heard a sora rail, watched and listened to a pair of sandhill cranes as they landed, and walked under the limbs of grand oaks. It was a good day, but like that cherry on top of a sundae, a sharp-shinned hawk chased a goldfinch right in front of me as I was finishing my hike. Wow! A perfect finishing touch.*

**Caution:** You will be sharing the trail with bicyclists, joggers, and dog walkers.

**Trail Directions:** Park at the main entrance and begin the trail at the flagpole [1] and go right, hiking on a wide gravel path. The preserve is a restoration in progress, and you will want to hike it often to observe its changes. The trail will be littered with coyote scat, and in the summer and fall butterflies will be imbibing nutrients from this rich source of nitrogen. Benches are provided periodically.

As you hike, you will encounter several potholes that are ringed with cattails, and in spring they will be alive with birds. At 1.1 mi. go right [2] on a loop trail. Don't forget to admire the line of oaks on the left. The trail will soon cross a bridge over Mill Creek; continue on the gravel path. The tall, torchlike plant along the trail is woolly mullen, a non-native plant related to snapdragons that arrived with early settlers. Those settlers used the plant to cure several aliments, and the large, soft leaves were used for baby diapers.

At 1.5 mi. come to an intersection; go right [3]. A large grove of cottonwoods will soon appear on the right as well. A pond appears at 1.8 mi. [4]; look for waterfowl and listen for soras. In the summer the pond will be ringed with bright yellow bidens (a sunflower) whose seeds are a favorite of waterfowl. At the intersection at 2.75 mi. go right [5], retracing your steps back to [2]. Go right again and continue on the main trail.

Along this segment of the trail you are hiking through the remnants of a classic savanna (large open-grown oaks with an understory of prairie vegetation). Marvel at the gnarled oaks with their open canopies and furrowed bark. You will hike up a short rise and leave the savanna behind, and at 3.5 mi. a large wetland complex comes into view [6]. An observation deck will give a closer view of some of the waterfowl.

An intersection for a second parking area and a bench appears at 3.75 mi.; stay to the left [7] and on the main trail. The wetland complex is still visible on the left, and as you circle it, gain various vantage points for any waterfowl action. Another intersection appears at 4.1 mi.; continue left [8]. Look for northern

harriers gliding over the grass in fall and grasshopper and Henslow's sparrows here in the summer.

At 5 mi. go right on the Discovery Trail [9]. The trail traverses over boardwalks with closer views of some of the wetlands and their residents. Look for waterfowl, herons, egrets, and dragonflies along this cattail jungle. An intersection at 5.45 mi. brings you back to the main trail; go right [10], and all too soon you are back at the flagpole. With so much activity at this preserve, you will want to hike this trail often.

1. Start
2. Loop trail
3. Right turn
4. Pond
5. Right turn
6. Wetlands
7. Stay left
8. Stay left
9. Discovery Trail
10. Right turn

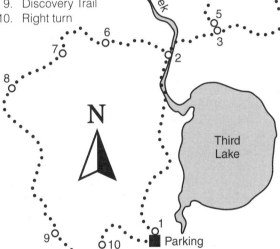

# Cuba Marsh Trail

   **Distance Round-Trip:** 3.5 miles
**Estimated Hiking Time:** 1.3 hours

*Before I even set foot on the trail, a red-winged blackbird greeted me from the trail board, a pair of mallards had taken over a large puddle by the parking area, and a kestrel hovered over its kill. With this at the trail's entrance, who knew what surprises lay ahead?*

**Caution:** This is a multiuse trail, so keep alert for bicyclists.

**Trail Directions:** Begin your hike at the trail board [1]. This is a hike for wetlands, and even though the lakes are no longer in clear view, the trail provides an excellent window for viewing the day-to-day happenings of an Illinois wetland ecosystem. The marsh will come into view at .1 mi., where a bench is provided for your enjoyment [2]. At .2 mi. the trail forks; go right [3], and soon you are skirting a bur oak savanna on your right.

The trail bears right at .4 mi. [4]. At .55 mi. the trail forms a Y in front of a row of white pines; go right [5], through the grove of oaks. In the spring look for trout lily and waterleaf under the oaks, but be sure to also look up and admire the crowns of these wide-spreading trees. At .7 mi. is another Y; go left [6]. Watch for black (melanic) gray squirrels crossing the path ahead of you.

For the next .1 mi. you will pass two marshes on your right. Look for the familiar red-winged blackbirds defending their territories from atop any convenient cattail. At 1 mi. a bench overlooks the lake on top of a short incline [7]. Look for herons, egrets, ducks, swallows, and even hummingbirds as they go about their daily routines.

The trail will pass through a wetland corridor not far from the bench. Keep your binoculars ready for a glimpse of a black-crowned night heron. At 1.45 mi. the trail goes through a grove of larger trees—maple and walnut—and bluebirds and goldfinches may be found in the adjacent grassy meadows. Watch where you step on the trail because small brown snakes, which look like twigs, like to bask along here. The trail comes out at Ela Road at 1.7 mi. [8].

It's time to retrace your steps and complete several of the loops. Along the way, look for any wildlife you might have missed, especially woodchucks among the grassy openings between trees. Before the arrival of Europeans, woodchucks were not especially numerous, but as settlers cleared away the dense forests to make way for croplands, they created acres of very good woodchuck habitat. If you look up, you might discover herons, egrets, or cormorants silently flying

overhead, or you might witness a noisy mobbing encounter between a small hawk and a blue jay. Also notice the native prairie plants attempting to reclaim the old fields.

At 2.35 mi. you are back at the lake and the bench [7]. Turn right at 2.5 mi. [9], soon coming to a shrubby area that goldfinches appear to favor. At 2.7 mi. the trail comes to a Y; go right [10]. The trail comes to another Y at 2.85 mi.; go right again [11], checking the marshy area for wood ducks and yellow warblers. You come to the last Y at 3.05 mi.; go right again [12], where you will soon encounter the same familiar bench [2]. Scan the wetland with your binoculars one last time before heading back to the parking area.

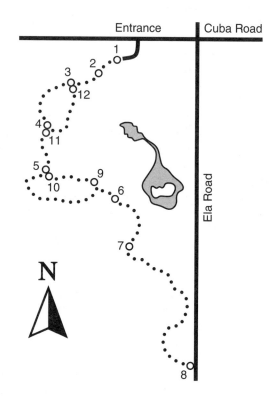

1. Start
2. Bench
3. Right turn
4. Veer right
5. Y in trail, go right
6. Y in trail, go left
7. Bench
8. Turnaround point
9. Right turn
10. Y in trail, go right
11. Y in trail, go right
12. Y in trail, go right

- Visit a waterfall, brought to you from the hands of the Civilian Conservation Corps (CCC).

- Hike where every big tree is a wolf tree.

- Pause at the ponds and look for herons, egrets, turtles, waterfowl, and other water-loving creatures.

- Bring your plant field guide—75 percent of DuPage County's plant species are found here.

## Area Information

In 1834, when Harriet Martineau traveled in this area on her way from Chicago to Joliet, what impressed her most were the groupings of trees. "The grass was wilder, the occasional footpath not so trim, and the single trees less majestic; but no park ever displayed anything equal to the grouping of the trees within the windings of the blue, brimming River Aux Plaines [Des Plaines]." As you hike, look for Harriet's groupings, unusually large oaks with outspread branches.

The forest preserve is part of a 20-mile-long valley that is enclosed by dolomite bluffs. As glacial Lake Chicago drained through the area, it eroded through the glacial deposits to bedrock and carved bluffs 50 feet in height, deposited low gravel ridges, and left an extremely shallow soil containing elements from the dolomite bedrock. At one time three quarries were actively mined in the area, taking advantage of the Lemont limestone. The Chicago Water Tower is constructed from limestone from one of these quarries.

In addition, a small area of the park was once used as a nursery by Lincoln Park; a lot of its topsoil was used for creating Lincoln Park along the Chicago lakeshore. The pine plantations were planted as a buffer by Argonne Lab. The word *Waterfall* in the name of the area is not in honor of the CCC-constructed waterfall, but after Seymour "Bud" Waterfall, an early president of the District's Board of Commissioners.

**Directions:** Take the Argonne National Laboratory/Cass Avenue exit (273A) off I-55 and head south on Cass Avenue. Drive .2 mile and turn right (west) on Northgate Road. Follow the signs to Waterfall Glen trailhead parking area.

**Hours Open:** The site is open year-round from one hour after sunrise to one hour after sunset.

**Facilities:** At the trailhead you will find horse-trailer parking, water, and toilets. You are welcome to picnic, but there are no tables. Fishing, orienteering, and use of the model airplane field are other activities that may be conducted at the preserve.

**Permits and Rules:** Alcohol, collecting, and hunting are prohibited. Pets are welcome; however, they must be leashed. Please use the trash receptacles.

**For Further Information:** Forest Preserve District of DuPage County, P.O. Box 5000, Wheaton, IL 60189; 630-933-7200 or www.dupageforest.com.

# Waterfall Glen Trail

 **Distance Round-Trip:** 9.65 miles
**Estimated Hiking Time:** 3.75 hours

*Hike through history—the ancient oaks, pines planted by the Argonne Lab when it first opened, remnants of an old nursery from the 1920s, a CCC waterfall, and pieces of prairie.*

**Caution:** This is a multiuse trail; be alert for bicyclists. There are several road crossings, and the trail can be very muddy or flooded. Occasional side trails (dirt paths) branch off from the main trail and do not show up on the park maps. You are welcome to take these, but be sure to have a topographic map and a compass.

**Trail Directions:** Begin at the information board and head west into the woods [1]. A trail immediately comes in from the left; ignore this. Stay on the easy-to-follow main path, which will be an 8-foot-wide crushed-rock path. There are trail markers at each intersection. The first of several pine plantations occurs at .45 mi. At 1.1 mi., as you head up a small incline, look into the woods [2]. On your right are large, evenly spaced oaks with widespread canopies. This was a savanna, but without fire, the understory has grown up.

At 1.4 mi. cross an old road and head into a spruce-pine mixed woods [3]. Cross West Gate Road [4] at 1.85 mi., noting a fenced area and a checkpoint on your left. Angle right, parallel to the road. By 2.25 mi. you will leave the road and go left into the woods [5]. At 2.65 mi. come to a pond on your left [6], ringed with cottonwoods and inhabited by mallards. Within .2 mi. you will pass another pond, less idyllic than the previous example. At 3.1 mi. ignore the Waterfall Glen Trail to the right and stay on the main path [7].

The trail next enters an open, grassy area. At 4 mi. turn left at the information kiosk [8] and head into Poverty Prairie, an 80-acre short-grass prairie with poverty oat grass, pussytoes, and whorled milkweed. Beyond the prairie in the distance is Poverty Savanna.

At 4.3 mi. [9] the prairie gives way to a pine plantation. At 4.55 mi. [10] the trail comes to a T; first go right for a scenic view of the Des Plaines River, and then follow the main trail left. On your right note a trail board. Five miles is marked by huge bur oaks on your right and left. Look on your left at 5.2 mi. for old cement foundations of Lincoln Park Nursery (LPN). At 5.25 mi. the trail comes out at the power station; turn left [11]. You will now come to two trails on your right; take the first one. (Note a trail map here.)

At 5.8 mi. you will cross picturesque Sawmill Creek on an iron bridge [12]. The trail will head uphill, and once you've reached the top, the main trail will eventually turn right and head into the woods.

The trail forms a Y at 6.4 mi. and the information board [13]; go left and then angle farther left, going down stone steps to a manmade waterfall. Look around, explore, and find names written in the cement by the waterfall's creators. Retrace your steps and soon you are back on the gravel path heading northeast. At the crossroads at 6.75 mi. go straight (through the pines). They soon grade into a mixed woods [14]. You will come to a parking area and restrooms at 6.8 mi.; go left [15] as the trail crosses a road on the right side of a small house.

Cross Bluff Road at 7 mi. [16]. At 7.70 mi. the trail forks; go left [17], ignoring the power line right of way. You will begin to pass a series of ponds at 8 mi. [18]. At 8.35 mi. you will come to a large wet area [19]. Take time to look for sunning sliders, a double-crested cormorant drying its wings, fishing herons, and many swallows combing the air for insects. Cross the road at 8.4 mi. [20].

The last mile of the hike is through a mixed oak woods. At 8.9 mi. come to the first of two more road crossings [21]. Cross 91st Street, an extremely busy road; use caution (9.3 mi.). At 9.45 mi. cross Northgate Road [22] and head into the woods where the trail will T; go right and you are back at the trailhead.

# Waterfall Glen Forest Preserve

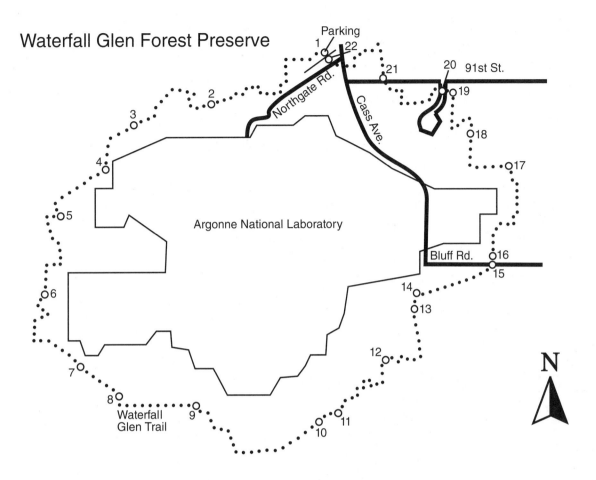

1. Start
2. Oaks/savanna
3. Old road
4. West Gate Road
5. Woods
6. Pond
7. Ignore Waterfall Glen spur
8. Left turn
9. End of prairie
10. Trail Ts
11. Left turn
12. Sawmill Creek crossing
13. Y to waterfall
14. Mixed woods
15. Left turn
16. Bluff Road
17. Fork in trail
18. Ponds
19. Large wet area
20. Park road
21. 91st Street
22. Northgate Road

- Enjoy pleasant hikes through grasslands, woods, and wetlands.
- Watch bobolinks, one of the state's declining songbird species, as they court mates and defend their territories.
- Catch glimpses of how the area looked in the past—hike past large, open-grown oaks concealed in thickets of vegetation.
- Imagine a mammoth as you circle a lake where the remains of one were found.
- Discover the spittlebug.

## Area Information

DuPage County was the second county in the state to establish an open-space district in 1915 with the goal of preserving continuous bands of open lands along major waterways. These provide natural floodwater storage, wildlife habitat, and recreational opportunities.

The Regional Trail is a 7.5-mile linear, multiuse limestone path that connects three of the county's 60 preserves—Blackwell, Herrick Lake, and Danada.

**Blackwell Preserve** used to be the site of a gravel quarry, but with hard work and careful restoration, the area's marshes have been reclaimed. Mt. Hoy (Blackwell), created as a winter sports hill, is a prime area for hawk sightings.

**Herrick Lake** was one of the early parcels purchased by the district. A natural pond, Herrick Lake has had little disturbance and is home to 19 mammal and 108 bird species, including Illinois' endangered black-crowned night heron.

**Danada Preserve** was once a private estate whose owners' main interest was thoroughbred racehorses. This preserve now houses the Danada Equestrian Center.

**Directions:** To reach **Blackwell Preserve** from Interstate 88 (southwest of Wheaton), go north on Illinois 59 for 1.2 miles to Butterfield Road (Illinois 56). Turn right (east), and in 1.5 miles the entrance for the preserve will be on the left. The parking area and trail information are off to the right. To reach **Herrick Lake,** take Butterfield Road and turn south onto Herrick Road. The south picnic and parking area is the second left off Herrick Road. To reach **Danada** from Butterfield Road, exit south onto Naperville Road and continue for .6 mile to the entrance.

**Hours Open:** The sites are open year-round from one hour after sunrise to one hour after sunset.

**Facilities: Blackwell** has horseback riding, boating, boat rental, fishing, picnicking, camping, showers, a dog training field, and snow tubing during the winter.

**Herrick Lake** has horseback riding, picnicking, fishing, and boat rental. This preserve is one of the most accessible for visitors with special needs.

**Danada** has an equestrian center, which provides educational and recreational equestrian experience, hay rides and sleigh rides, fishing, and the Danada House, which is available for functions.

**Permits and Rules:** Collecting and hunting are prohibited in the forest preserves. Pets are welcome, but they must be leashed at all times. Dispose of litter properly. Stay in single file on busy days, stay on the right if you are moving slowly, be careful when approaching horses, and if you are on a bicycle, footpaths and single tracks are off limits.

**For Further Information:** Forest Preserve District of DuPage County, P.O. Box 5000, Wheaton, IL 60189; 630-933-7200 or www.dupageforest.com.

## Park Trails

**Egret Trail (Blackwell)** (🐾, .9 mile). North of Silver Lake, this trail offers the chance to see waterfowl and the occasional muskrat. It is located near the family camping area.

**Lake Trail (Herrick)** (🐾, 1 mile). Encircle Herrick Lake along its shore for some pleasant views of the lake, geese with their goslings, and several large oak trees.

**Regional Trail (Danada)** (🐾, 1.9 miles). This linear path goes through the preserve, passing grasslands, restored woodlands, and the equestrian center.

**Parson's Grove Nature Trail (Danada)** (🐾, .9 mile). This double-loop trail winds through an open savanna. Enjoy the large bur oaks and the spring wildflowers.

## Other Areas of Interest

Although the **Fermi National Accelerator Laboratory** is a workplace for hundreds of physicists, the grounds are home to a 975-acre tallgrass prairie restoration, 250 species of birds, and the Chicago area's only herd of bison. Take time to visit Wilson Hall not only to learn about the lab, but also to see Native American artifacts on the grounds. Fermi has a 3.6-mile bike path and two prairie trails—.5 mile and 1.2 miles. For more information, call 630-840-3351.

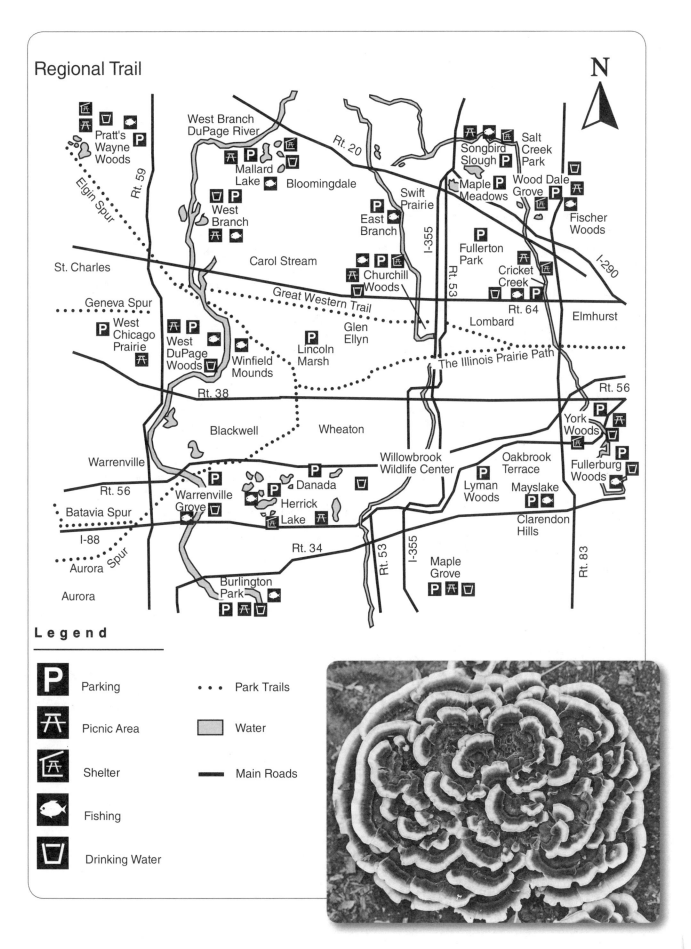

# Regional Trail

N

West Branch
DuPage River

Rt. 20

Pratt's
Wayne
Woods

P

Rt. 59

Elgin Spur

Songbird
Slough

Salt
Creek
Park

P

Wood Dale
Grove

P

Fischer
Woods

Mallard
Lake

P

Bloomingdale

Maple
Meadows

West
Branch

P

Carol Stream

Swift
Prairie

East
Branch

P

I-355

Fullerton
Park

P

Cricket
Creek

I-290

St. Charles

Great Western Trail

Churchill
Woods

P

Rt. 53

Rt. 64

Lombard

Elmhurst

Geneva Spur

West
Chicago
Prairie

P

West
DuPage
Woods

P

Winfield
Mounds

Lincoln
Marsh

P

Glen
Ellyn

The Illinois Prairie Path

Rt. 38

Rt. 56

Blackwell

Wheaton

York
Woods

P

Warrenville

Rt. 56

Batavia Spur

Warrenville
Grove

P

Danada

P

Herrick
Lake

Willowbrook
Wildlife Center

Oakbrook
Terrace

Lyman
Woods

P

Mayslake

P

Fullerburg
Woods

P

Clarendon
Hills

Rt. 83

I-88

Aurora Spur

Aurora

Rt. 34

Rt. 53

I-355

Maple
Grove

P

Burlington
Park

P

## Legend

P — Parking

• • • — Park Trails

— Picnic Area

— Water

— Shelter

— Main Roads

— Fishing

— Drinking Water

# Blackwell Forest Preserve

 **Distance Round-Trip:** 6.65 miles
**Estimated Hiking Time:** 2.1 hours

*I kept seeing little brown sticks on the Regional Trail. A closer look revealed not sticks but small, brown, pencil-sized snakes—Dekay's snakes—catching some rays on an Indian summer afternoon.*

**Caution:** This is a multiuse trail that is shared by hikers, cyclists, horses, dog walkers, and the local cross-country teams; keep alert and watch where you step. You will cross the road twice; remember to look both ways.

**Trail Directions:** Park by the information board near the forest preserve entrance. The trail begins across the road at the McKee Marsh sign and proceeds on a crushed-rock path [1]. Mount Hoy and a pond appear on your right. Ignore the path that comes in from the left; it leads to the highway. You will be walking through an open, grassy area with scattered trees and shrubs. A few large cottonwoods appear here and there, and you will pass through a grove of white pines (planted). At .6 mi. the trail goes through a wooded area [2]; a small ravine is off to your left, and the trail curves left.

Springbrook Creek is on your left at .7 mi. with several spurs leading to a closer look [3]. Oaks now dominate the trail at .75 mi. [4], forming a stately avenue. The understory is carpeted with false Solomon's seal. Remember to stay on the gravel path.

You will cross an iron span bridge at 1.1 mi. [5], just after the oaks have given way to cottonwoods. From the bridge you hike through a grassy, open area where every available small tree is usually occupied by a male red-winged blackbird. Watch barn swallows swoop for insects, and listen for the call of the meadowlark and pheasant. The grass gives way to a black locust thicket at 1.5 mi. [6]. Look for large elm trees among the black locust.

At 1.7 mi. [7] the trail crosses Mack Road. Once you're across, cattails appear immediately on the left and soon line the trail. An intersection appears at 2 mi.; go left [8] and soon go right on a spur that offers an overlook of the marsh. Retrace your steps back to the trail, and at 2.25 mi. on the right is a grassy path to a large granite boulder [9] with a plaque indicating the Robert and Ada McKee Wildlife Marsh (Robert was the first superintendent of DuPage County).

As you walk along this section of the trail [10] (2.4 mi.) in the spring or early summer, you might think you are following a lot of expectorating hikers. Not so; these masses of "spit" are really spittlebug nymphs getting rid of liquid waste.

Another trail enters from the left at 2.5 mi.; stay right on the main path. At 2.6 mi. the trail enters an old savanna [11]. Note how widely spaced the trees are and their open crowns. A savanna is usually dominated by oaks, and the understory vegetation is composed of a blend of prairie and forest species.

Take time to marvel at these giant oaks and their outreaching limbs. After you exit the savanna, stay on the gravel path. Three miles brings a side spur [12]; go right to the overlook and imagine what this site looked like to a woolly mammoth. This was the spot where the Blackwell Mammoth, the oldest known mammoth found in the entire Great Lakes region, was found. Retrace your steps back to the trail.

Catbird Trail comes in from the left and joins the trail at 3.3 mi. The trail forks at 3.5 mi.; go to the right (straight) [13]. You are now hiking on Bobolink Trail. On either side is grassland, so look for bobolinks. Smaller than red-winged blackbirds, the bobolink male is black with a yellow nape and white on the rump and shoulders.

At 3.75 mi. the trail winds through a wooded area [14]; climb up a short hill and reenter the grassland. From here you have a distant view of the marsh and should see great blue herons and great white egrets flying in and out of the marsh. Along this section the marsh's open area is hard to see because of all the cattails. At 4.6 mi. you have returned to [8]; go left and retrace your steps. Recross Mack Road [7] and the iron bridge [5]. Eventually you will be back at the parking area. Did you note any living brown "sticks" on the path while you hiked?

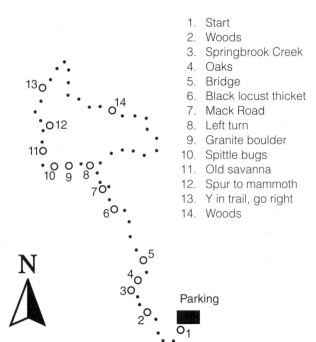

1. Start
2. Woods
3. Springbrook Creek
4. Oaks
5. Bridge
6. Black locust thicket
7. Mack Road
8. Left turn
9. Granite boulder
10. Spittle bugs
11. Old savanna
12. Spur to mammoth
13. Y in trail, go right
14. Woods

# Herrick Lake Forest Preserve

 **Distance Round-Trip**: 4.6 miles
**Estimated Hiking Time**: 1.75 hours

*Although the trail was labeled Green Heron, I didn't see one, maybe because it was through a grassland! Yet this area was alive with the familiar call of meadowlarks from small shrubs, a flash of orange and the song of a Baltimore oriole, goldfinches racing across the trail, and the black-and-white wings of myriads of bobolinks.*

**Caution:** This is a multiuse trail that is shared by hikers, cyclists, horses, and dog walkers. Keep alert and watch where you step.

**Trail Directions:** Enter the preserve off Herrick Road and park at the south picnic area. Begin the trail at the information board and go right [1]. Trail boards will appear at the intersections. Within a few steps another trail intersects; continue on the wide path. At .1 mi. go right [2]. Although the trail is lined with small oak and hickory trees, look beyond these for larger examples. You'll soon leave the oaks behind, replaced with cottonwoods, maples, and elms.

The .5 mi. mark finds you in an open woods with tall oaks and maples [3]. The understory is Virginia creeper and false Solomon's seal. At .6 mi. the trail enters an open, grassy area; proceed to a trail intersection at .7 mi. [4]. Go right and enter the Green Heron Trail. Look on either side during late summer and fall for elliptical swellings on the stems of goldenrods. These swellings are caused by flies and called galls. During the early fall this landscape, with its subtle gold, yellow, brown, and purple, looks like a worn Persian carpet.

In this grassy area, with the trail stretching out before you, the plant diversity is low but the bird diversity certainly isn't! Listen for distinctive calls and spot the flash of wings; locate them with binoculars, identify them with your field guide, and add them to your bird life list. Seek out meadowlarks, bobolinks, goldfinches, savanna sparrows, and the common yellowthroat. As you near the trees, look for deer. At the 1.75 mi. intersection, go left [5] and head through the woods. Look for cottonwood, basswood, and large oak trees with outreaching limbs.

Herrick Marsh appears on the left at 2 mi. [6] with a bench. You can use the bench to rest and scan the water for great blue herons, camouflaged against the dead trees in the pond. Continue on the trail as it wanders through a grove of walnuts and then into a mixed woods. At 2.7 mi. come to a trail crossroads; go left and you are back on the Regional Trail [7]. You will pass the Hesterman Drain Project on the left; go through a grassy area and reenter the woods.

You will enter a mixed woods at 3 mi.; look for large oaks in thickets of honeysuckle and chipmunks as they scurry across the path. From the woods you will emerge into another grassland. At the trail crossroad [8] (3.4 mi.), go to the right to hike on Meadowlark Trail. In mid-September parts of the trail are ablaze with the gold of goldenrod. Entering the woods again; you can marvel at the tall, straight oak trees that grade into a disturbed area of young trees and saplings.

At 3.75 mi., barely visible through the vegetation on the right, is a golf course and a reforestation area. A small creek lined with cottonwoods appears on your left at 4.25 mi. [9]. At this point, and until you are back at the parking area, several unofficial paths will intersect the trail, all leading to the lake. Stay on the main trail. At 4.4 mi. [10] the trail forms a Y; go left—the lake will be on your right. In the late spring, scan this area for geese and their goslings. A final trail crossroad is encountered at 4.45 mi. [11]; go straight to the south picnic parking area where the trail ends.

1. Start
2. Right turn
3. Open woods
4. Green Heron Trail
5. Left turn
6. Bench and pond
7. Left turn
8. Meadowlark Trail
9. Creek
10. Y in trail
11. Trail junction

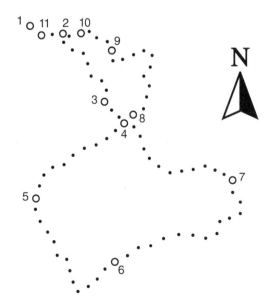

- Bring your tree, vine, and shrub identification guides to help separate the forest into trees and other things.

- Discover a landscape that at one time covered 60 percent of Illinois—the prairie.

- Learn about woody plants from other regions of the world by walking the Geographic Trail.

- Enjoy spectacular spring wildflowers in May and equally notable fall foliage in October.

## Area Information

Morton Arboretum was built on the estate of Joy Morton, founder of the Morton Salt Company. In addition to the home, the family grounds consisted of land used for agricultural crops and grazing, although some undisturbed woodland did exist. The transformation of the estate began in December 1922. It is appropriate that Joy developed the arboretum on the grounds; his father was the originator of Arbor Day, and the family's motto was "Plant trees."

Joy referred to the arboretum as a ginkgo, meaning it was one of a kind, unrelated to any other institution, just as a ginkgo tree is unique and unrelated to any other plant. In this 1,700-acre living outdoor museum you can see more than 4,000 types of plants from around the world. Not only is it a museum, but also a trial garden for woody plants that can survive the ever-changing continental climate of the Midwest. The plants in the collection—grouped by botanical characteristics, landscape use, or geographic origin—may be seen by car, along 11 miles of one-way roads, or by various walking and hiking trails.

**Directions:** The arboretum is located just north of Lisle at the intersection of Illinois Route 53 and Illinois Route 88 (the East-West Tollway). Enter it via Route 53.

**Hours Open:** The grounds are open year-round 7:00 a.m. to 7:00 p.m. (or sunset, whichever is earlier). The visitor center and Ginkgo Café are open 8:00 a.m. to 6:00 p.m. (March to October) and 8:00 a.m. to 5:00 p.m. (November to February).

**Facilities:** Visitor center, restaurant, coffee shop, plant clinic, library, education center, auditorium, restrooms, picnic area, and an open-air tram are included. Restrooms are also located here, and a small picnic area is available. A fee is charged for parking and admission.

**Permits and Rules:** Park in designated areas only. The speed limit on one-way roads is 20 miles per hour. No bicycles, snowmobiles, or horses are allowed. No pets are allowed, not even in cars. No sports, games, fishing, kite flying, or swimming. Most important, *no climbing trees* and *no collecting of specimens*.

**For Further Information:** Morton Arboretum, 4100 Route 53, Lisle, IL 60532; 630-968-0074 or www.mortonarb.org.

## Park Trails

**West Side Main Trail** (🥾, 1.75 miles). This wood-chip trail links the Thornhill Education Center with the Prairie Visitor Station and Lake Marmo.

**Joy Path** (🥾, .3 mile). Park in lot 21 and wander this linear trail through woodlands and large-specimen trees to connect with the Godshalk Meadow.

**Thornhill Trail** (🥾, .6 mile). Park in lot 20 or 21 and take this wood-chip path from the education center past Sunfish Pond and to Joy Path. Along the way you will pass several plant collections and mature trees.

**Meadow Lake Trail** (🥾, .6 mile). Park in lot 1 and take this scenic paved path around Meadow Lake.

**Heritage Trail** (🥾, 1.3 miles). Park in lot 13 at the Big Rock Visitor Station and take this wood-chip path through an oak woods to a glacial erratic (a granite rock left at the site by the last glacier).

**Woodland Trail** (🥾, .6 mile). Park in lot 13 at the Big Rock Visitor Station and discover woods of sugar maple and oak that has spectacular fall colors.

## Other Areas of Interest

Located on the east side of Highland Avenue at 33rd Street in Downers Grove, **Lyman Woods Forest Preserve** offers short hiking trails through prairie, oak forest, meadow, and marsh. Spring wildflowers are plentiful, and a trail guide will help you with their identification. For more information, call 630-933-7200 or 630-963-1304 (Downers Grove Park District).

Located between the communities of Hinsdale and Oak Brook, **Fullersburg Woods Forest Preserve** offers hiking, biking, an environmental education center, and the state's only operating waterwheel grist mill. A 2.5-mile multiuse trail traverses Salt Creek and the mill and climbs a bluff overlooking the creek. Also, a .10-mile Wildflower Trail and a 1.3-mile Interpretive Trail run along Salt Creek and its environs. For more information, call 630-850-8110.

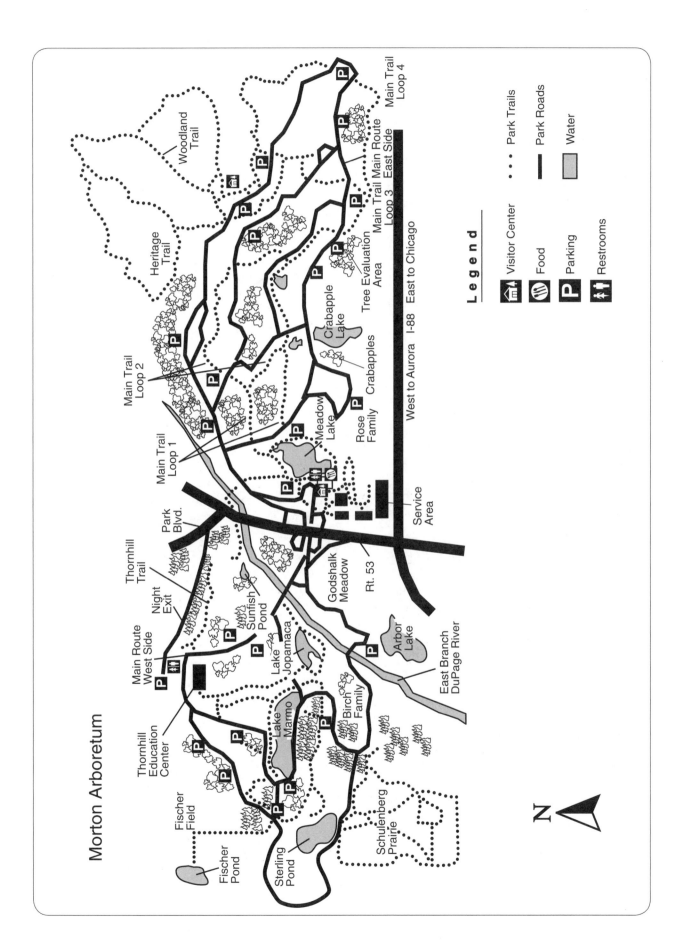

# Morton Arboretum

Fischer Field

Fischer Pond

Thornhill Education Center

Thornhill Trail

Night Exit

Main Route West Side

Sunfish Pond

Lake Jopamaca

Lake Marmo

Birch Family

Sterling Pond

Schulenberg Prairie

East Branch DuPage River

Arbor Lake

Godshalk Meadow

Rt. 53

Service Area

Park Blvd.

Main Trail Loop 1

Main Trail Loop 2

Meadow Lake

Rose Family Crabapples

Crabapple Lake

Tree Evaluation Area

Heritage Trail

Woodland Trail

Main Trail Loop 4

Main Trail Main Route Loop 3    East Side

West to Aurora    I-88    East to Chicago

## Legend

Visitor Center

Food

Parking

Restrooms

· · · Park Trails

—— Park Roads

▨ Water

N

# Prairie Trail

 **Distance Round-Trip:** 1.1 miles
**Estimated Hiking Time:** .75 hour

*From the savanna I emerged onto the prairie. The words of Ellen Bigelow, an early settler of Illinois, came to mind: "Nothing can equal the surpassing beauty of the rounded swells and the sunny hollows. The brilliant green of grass, the numberless varieties and splendid hues of multitudes of flowers, I gazed in admiration too strong for words."*

**Caution:** While on the Prairie Trail, be sure to walk single file and clockwise. Do not damage or pick plants. Stay on the path.

**Trail Directions:** This trail is on the west side of the arboretum; park in lot 25 and begin the trail at the Prairie Visitor Center [1]. Take the path to the farthest left, which begins as a gravel path. Although this trail is short, it is an excellent introduction to a landscape that covered 60 percent of Illinois. Take time to study the grasses, read the signage, touch and feel the textures, and learn about the prairie. At .1 mi. you will cross a bridge; the trail will then intersect with two trails on the right. Stay on the main path [2].

At .2 mi. is another intersection; continue straight on the Prairie Trail [3], which is surrounded by milkweed, asters, and Indian grass. In the fall look for pale gentian; its flowers are cream colored with a closed, elliptical shape. The bumblebee is one of the few insects strong enough to open these bottle-shaped flowers and achieve pollination.

The trail enters a savanna (an oak woodlands with prairie plants growing underneath them) at .3 mi. [4]. In the fall look for a mix of goldenrods, sunflowers, and asters. You emerge (much like Ellen Bigelow) from the savanna and turn right into the prairie at .4 mi. [5], and then immediately bear left. The trail is now concrete blocks with informational signage about the plants. Immediately find a great diversity of vegetation; while 80 percent of the prairie was grass, 80 percent of the species was forbs.

If you happen to visit in late summer, the trail will be overgrown and it will be hard to see around you. You may have the experience of seeing nothing but grass and sky. Look for compass plant (large dissected leaves) and prairie dock (large, spade-shaped leaves); these plants usually grow near each other. Explore the various textures of these leaves. Feel their coarseness. Pioneers used compass plant leaves for directions; the plant leaves orient themselves along a north-south axis so that their huge flat surfaces can rotate to follow the rays of the rising and setting sun.

At the large oak in the middle of the path, the trail curves right [6] (.55 mi.). Patches of cordgrass are on either side of the trail. The edges of cordgrass are extremely sharp, leading to the common name of ripgut. Your introduction to the prairie is complete at .7 mi., and you have also completed the loop trail [7]. Take the middle path and go left and then take another left, retracing your steps back to the Prairie Visitor Center.

While walking the Prairie Trail, you encountered not only many new plants but also a myriad of insects. In fact, as you walked along, you likely stepped on the most numerous and important herbivore (plant eater) on the prairie. No, not the bison, but the lowly grasshopper!

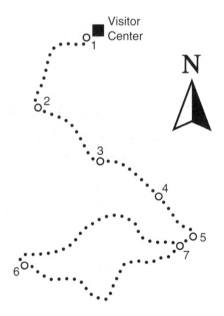

1. Start
2. Bridge, stay on main path
3. Continue straight
4. Savanna
5. Right turn, prairie
6. Oak
7. Completed loop

# East Main Trail

 **Distance Round-Trip:** 4.5 miles
**Estimated Hiking Time:** 1.1 hours

*Who needs a tree identification guide? Most of these large (and small) guys were already identified for me!*

**Caution:** Beware of neck strain as you look up to see some of the large trees. The path will cross the park road; be sure to look both ways.

**Trail Directions:** Begin at the large acorn on the east side of the visitor center. The trail begins as an asphalt path with Meadow Lake on your left [1]. As you walk around the lake, notice the prairie plantings surrounding it. At .2 mi. go right [2] and cross the road. The trail is now a wood-chip path, and you are hiking on East Side Main Trail Loop 1. At major intersections there will be trail maps. Once you leave the area of the lake, you are able to find solitude.

Go left at the intersection at .3 mi. [3]. Many of the trees in this section are labeled, so take advantage of this to improve your tree identification skills. The Geographic Trail comes in at .4 mi.; ignore it and continue on the main trail. Soon you are walking through an oak savanna (widespread oak trees with an understory of prairie plants). Watch for gray and fox squirrels and chipmunks—they scurry across the path ahead of you.

Continue straight [4] at the intersection at .7 mi., walking under the branches of an Ohio buckeye. You will cross the park road in a half mile and head to the other side, where you will encounter a grove of big-tooth aspen. As you walk through this mixed-hardwood forest in the spring, look for your favorite spring wildflowers. At 1.4 mi. the trail Ys; continue to the left [5]. You are now hiking on East Side Main Trail Loop 3. Within a few steps you will cross the road and several side trails will come in. Stay on the main trail and hike through a beech-maple woods.

At 1.7 mi. you will first cross a gravel path, then cross asphalt, and finally cross the parking area,

ending at Big Rock Visitor Center [6]. Take time to read the signage here and explore the short trails. At the kiosk [7] go right, continuing on East Main Trail, skirting the parking area, and reentering the woods on the right side. You will cross a bridge and enter an oak-maple woods. Notice the glacial boulders and the lofty trees.

At 1.8 mi. come to another intersection; keep straight [8] because you are now hiking on East Side Main Trail Loop 4. The trail crosses the road at 2.1 mi. with a stream on your right. Cross a bridge at 2.2 mi. [9], and within .1 mi. you will cross the road; stay on the main trail as you enter the East Woods restoration. Notice a large ash on your right (it has alligator-like bark). During the summer and fall this area has an understory of white snakeroot. White snakeroot was responsible for "milk sickness"—when cows eat the plant they secrete a poison into their milk. Abraham Lincoln's mother died from milk sickness in 1818.

Several trails intersect at 2.9 mi. [10]; go straight and then bear left on the wood-chip path. Notice the large bur oak on your right. You are now back on East Side Main Trail Loop 3 and are hiking through the oak collection, passing under the branches of a large white oak. Leaving the oak collection, another intersection appears; continue straight on East Side Main Trail Loop 2.

A marsh appears at 3.3 mi. [11]. This marsh was formed by a glacial pothole; a chunk broke off the glacier, melted, and filled with water. Cross the marsh using the bridge and continue on the trail. You will cross the road at 3.6 mi. [12], and within a few steps the trail will Y; go left through lofty oaks, staying on East Side Main Trail. The trail Ys again at 3.75 mi.; go left [13] through the Midwest collection of magnolias. The trail passes through a grove of pines at 3.9 mi. [14] and Vs; stay right and hike through a grove of tall oaks and then a grove of hickory trees. You are back at [2] (4.2 mi.); retrace your steps to the visitor center and the large acorn, passing by a dolomite prairie and rejoining the masses visiting the garden.

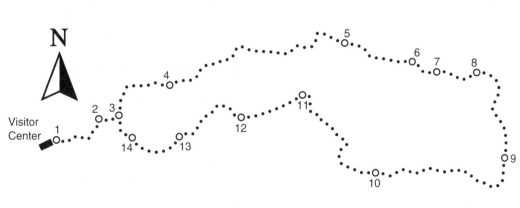

1. Start
2. Right turn
3. Left turn
4. Continue straight
5. Trail Ys, go left
6. Big Rock Visitor Center
7. Kiosk, right turn
8. Continue straight
9. Bridge
10. Major trail intersection
11. Marsh
12. Road crossing
13. Left turn
14. Pines

# 18. Palos and Sag Valley Forest Preserves

- Discover the largest and most diverse holding in the Forest Preserve District of Cook County, containing everything from nature preserves to a nuclear Stonehenge.

- Bring a bird identification guide to help you identify the many waterfowl and shorebirds that congregate on and around the sloughs during spring and fall.

- Enjoy the many wildflowers, from the early-blooming skunk cabbage found in Black Partridge Woods to the final goldenrods in the prairie restoration at Little Red Schoolhouse.

- Don't forget your compass! The preserve has many trails, both official and unofficial, and it is very easy to become confused and lost.

## Area Information

The Palos and Sag Valley Forest Preserves is the largest and most diverse natural area in any North American urban setting. Here you can find woods, thickets, meadows, sloughs, marshes, and small twisting streams. The Palos Hills are moraines, accumulations of earth and stones carried and deposited by the last glacier. The many sloughs found here also resulted from the last glacier. When the glacier receded, it left behind large chunks of ice; as the ice melted, it created depressions in the land.

Four of the state's oldest nature preserves are located here. Black Partridge Woods is an area of river bluffs, ravines, and spring-fed streams and is the first place in the Chicago region where wildflowers bloom each spring. Cap Sauers Holdings, the best-defined glacial ridge *(esker)* in the state, is the most undeveloped tract of native landscape in Cook County. A climb to the top of the esker yields a spectacular overlook of the preserve. Cranberry Slough supports a population of wild cranberries and is the only quaking bog in Cook County. The final preserve in the area is Pawpaw Woods, a bluff and floodplain forest that is the northernmost limit for pawpaws in Illinois.

Despite the peaceful nature of the preserves, a not-so-peaceful enterprise was at one time located here: the original Argonne Lab, where the first atomic bomb was developed. Deep in the woods you might stumble on a radioactive burial site. It is marked by six corner markers and a large granite stone—a Stonehenge from the atomic age.

**Directions:** The Little Red Schoolhouse (where the hike begins) is north of the Cal–Sag Channel in Willow Springs. From the Willow Springs Road intersection with Archer Avenue, take Willow Springs south of 95th Street. Here Willow Springs Road becomes 104th Avenue; proceed south, and the entrance to Little Red Schoolhouse is on the west side.

**Hours Open:** The forest preserves are open sunrise to sunset 365 days a year. The Little Red Schoolhouse is open from 8:00 a.m. to 5:00 p.m. (summer hours) and 8:00 a.m. to 4:00 p.m. (winter hours). It is closed on Fridays and Thanksgiving Day, Christmas Day, and New Year's Day.

**Facilities:** Little Red Schoolhouse Nature Center has a variety of live mammals, reptiles, and amphibians that are native to the area. Picnickers will find tables, water, reservable shelters, and open places to play. Fishing is allowed on many of the lakes and sloughs. Swallow Cliff has a winter sports center that supports six toboggan slides, including the longest and highest in the Chicago region. Horseback riding is also available here.

**Permits and Rules:** Ride and walk on the right side of the trail. Give warning before passing other trail users. All pets must be leashed. Ground fires are not permitted. Do not pick the flowers.

**For Further Information:** Forest Preserve District of Cook County, 536 North Harlem Avenue, River Forest, IL 60305; 800-870-3666 or www.fpdcc.com. For information about Little Red Schoolhouse, call 708-839-6897.

## Park Trails

**Swallow Cliff Woods** (🐾🐾🐾, 7 miles). This is a gravel multipurpose trail where you will climb small hills, cross streams, and discover large sycamores and ironwood trees.

**Maple Lake Trail** (🐾🐾, 12 miles). Discover some of the preserve's many sloughs and resident waterfowl as you hike through woods and meadows on this multipurpose path. Little Red Schoolhouse, as well as the old site of Argonne Laboratory, can be accessed from this trail.

## Other Areas of Interest

Contact the Forest Preserve Headquarters for maps of all nine forest preserve regions (800-870-3666). Here are many woods, sloughs, and meadows to explore on miles of trails. Just be sure you have a reliable compass before you set out exploring. Some of the trails are not marked well, and unauthorized bicycle trails create a confusing maze.

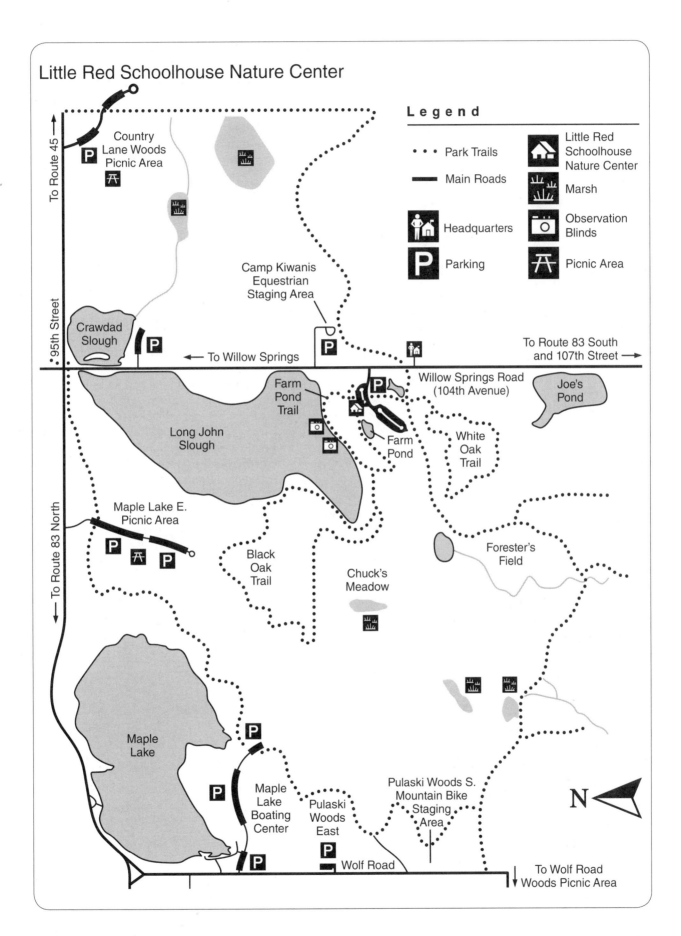

# Little Red Schoolhouse Nature Center

**Legend**

· · · Park Trails

—— Main Roads

Headquarters

Parking

Little Red Schoolhouse Nature Center

Marsh

Observation Blinds

Picnic Area

To Route 45

Country Lane Woods Picnic Area

95th Street

Crawdad Slough

Camp Kiwanis Equestrian Staging Area

To Willow Springs

To Route 83 South and 107th Street

Willow Springs Road (104th Avenue)

Joe's Pond

Farm Pond Trail

Long John Slough

Farm Pond

White Oak Trail

To Route 83 North

Maple Lake E. Picnic Area

Black Oak Trail

Chuck's Meadow

Forester's Field

Maple Lake

Maple Lake Boating Center

Pulaski Woods East

Pulaski Woods S. Mountain Bike Staging Area

Wolf Road

To Wolf Road Woods Picnic Area

N

# Black Oak Trail

🐾 **Distance Round-Trip:** 2.75 miles
🐾 **Estimated Hiking Time:** 1 hour

*What an excellent trail for introducing young children to hiking and nature! Colorful songbirds—Baltimore orioles, rose-breasted grosbeaks, and cardinals sang from the oaks; chipmunks scampered across the path ahead of me; and dragonflies danced over my head.*

**Caution:** The trail can be very muddy. Remember that the gate to the trail is locked each evening. If you are still on the trail after closing time, you might get locked in the preserve.

**Trail Directions:** Begin the trail behind the Little Red Schoolhouse Nature Center [1]. The trail is a wide path with informational signage throughout. At .05 mi. you reach Long John Slough.

At .25 mi. the trail forks; go right and through a gate at .3 mi. that is locked each night [2]. From here you will have open woods on the left and the slough on your right. The trail forks again at .35 mi.; again, go right [3]. By .5 mi. the slough is fairly close to the trail. Look for frogs along the edge and turtles basking on the logs. The shrub that surrounds Long John Slough is button-bush. By summer, the plant has cream-colored flowers that resemble pins stuck in a round pincush-ion. The seeds produced by the flower are a vital winter food source for musk-rats and mallard ducks, both of which are common residents of the slough.

At .7 mi. the trail curves to the left and heads up, leaving the water behind [4]. In the spring look in the woods for mayapple, toothwort, green dragons, and jack-in-the-pulpit. At 1.1 mi., look to your right for a very small ravine—the result of rainwater carving into the rock [5].

Pause at the pond on your left and look for aquatic insects—dragonflies, water striders, and damselflies. You will cross a bridge and soon pass another pond, this time on the right. Ignore the trails coming in from the right and stay on the wide path. The straight path you have been hiking on is old 99th Street. At 1.5 mi. you are back to point [3]; go right and out the gate. Soon you are back at [2]; go right and follow the sign to Farm Pond. On your right is a prairie restoration, so take your time and slowly walk by to see how many different insects you can observe. Illinois has an estimated 17,000 species of insects!

Farm Pond comes into view at 1.6 mi. [6]. This pond was created in 1921 and then enlarged by the forest preserve. Look for basking red-eared sliders, bullfrogs, and water striders that skate on top of the water. At 1.7 mi. the trail Ts; go right [7], angling across the parking lot to the entrance of White Oak Trail.

Immediately you should notice a large white oak on your right. While this section of the trail is not main-tained as well as the last, you have more of a sense of wilderness. This 1-mile trail may be hiked either clock-wise or counterclockwise and passes through a white oak–dominated forest. Metallic green tiger beetles will keep one step ahead of you, and chipmunks will scamper and squeak at your intrusion. Look for black oaks among the white oaks; black oaks have pointed lobed leaves, while white oaks have rounded lobed leaves. Once you have completed your trip, cross the parking lot back to Little Red Schoolhouse.

1. Start
2. Gate
3. Right turn
4. Leave Long John Slough
5. Ravine
6. Farm Pond
7. Right turn, White Oak Trail

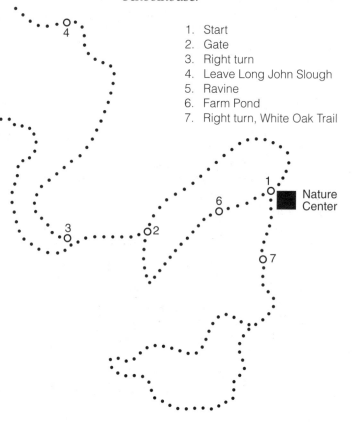

N

North

- Revel in an abundance of spring wildflowers, especially great white trilliums and Virginia bluebells.

- Hike where silence is broken only by the snort of a deer and the chattering of chipmunks.

- Discover a woods that is very similar to what the original land surveyors saw in 1834.

- Enjoy the fall colors of a sugar maple woods.

## Area Information

Will County Forest Preserve District was "born" in 1927 when the citizens approved a referendum establishing the organization as an independent taxing agency. At that time Will County was undeveloped and agriculture was prevalent. Messenger Woods was the first property the county acquired, paying $125 per acre for 142 acres. Today, the district owns and manages over 15,000 acres.

**Messenger Woods Nature Preserve,** the oldest forest preserve, is one of the few remaining forests in northeastern Illinois that has not been altered by grazing, cutting, or development. It is an old prairie grove forest of oaks, basswood, and elm that, during the summer, is like walking through a canopy of green stained glass with huge dark columns for support. This preserve is known throughout the region for its spring wildflowers, especially its Virginia bluebells. It is said that there are more here than at any other location in Will County.

**Thorn Creek Nature Preserve** is a 1,000-acre oak-hickory forest dominated by 150-year-old white and red oak trees. A forestry expert found that the trees in Thorn Creek were of two ages. The oldest trees in the woods took root between 1830 and 1850, during a period when the land was being cleared for farming. Most farmers kept small woodlots for game, forage, and wood. They selectively logged, opening gaps in the forest's canopy and exposing the forest floor to light that fed the seedlings. The second age

group took root in the 1920s, when most of the local farmers had gone out of business or shifted to row-crop agriculture. The woodlots were purchased and gathered into larger parcels that again were unlogged and ungrazed. Conditions were once again favorable for trees. Between 1850 and 1920, grazing in most of the woods was intense and most trees were not able to reproduce.

**Directions: Messenger Woods** is located on Bruce Road, north of Route 6 (Southwest Highway) and east of Cedar Road in rural Lockport. **Thorn Creek** is located on the east side of Monee Road, just north of Stuenkel Road in Park Forest.

**Hours Open:** The sites are open year-round from 8:00 a.m. to 8:00 p.m. April through October and 8:00 a.m. to 5:00 p.m. November through March. The nature center at Thorn Creek is open from noon to 4:00 p.m. Thursday through Sunday.

**Facilities:** Both sites offer restrooms and drinking water. Messenger Woods has picnic areas and allows tent camping and cross-country skiing. Thorn Creek has a nature center.

**Permits and Rules:** Dogs are not allowed on the trails. No picking, trampling, or disturbing plants or animals.

**For Further Information:** Sugar Creek Administration Center, 17540 W. Laraway Road, Joliet, IL 60433; 815-727-8700 or www.fpdwc.org

## Other Areas of Interest

Each fall Will County Forest Preserve District sponsors **Woods Walk,** a challenge to walk in a variety of the forest preserves and earn a commemorative medal. To participate, you must pick up a booklet and a packet of maps, hike 7 of the 10 selected trails between September 1 and November 30, record your hikes in the booklet, and turn the booklet in to receive your medal. It's a great way to discover the Will County trails. For more information call 815-727-8700.

# Will County Forest Preserves

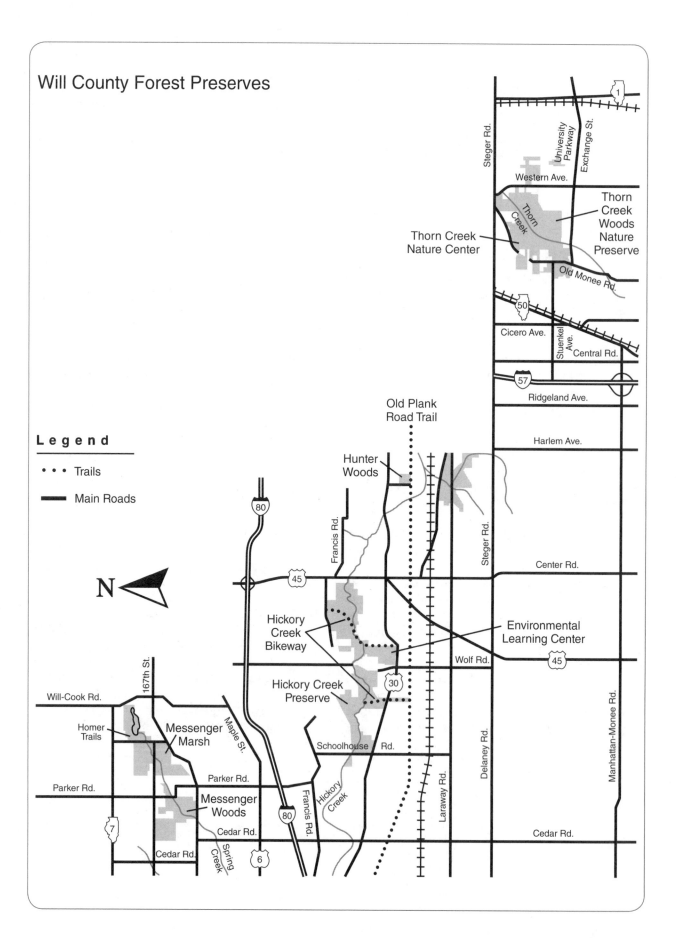

**Legend**

• • • Trails

▬▬ Main Roads

N

# Messenger Woods Nature Preserve

 **Distance Round-Trip:** 2 miles
**Estimated Hiking Time:** 1 hour

*By early summer the profusion of wildflowers has melted away, leaving behind bare brown stems and seed pods. But here at Messenger Woods it's not just about wildflowers—Dreamsicle-colored slugs creep across the trail, 12-spot dragonflies dance and dart above your head, and brilliant blue indigo buntings sing from dead snags.*

**Caution:** Watch for roots and ruts in the trail. Remember that by late May the spring wildflowers are a distant memory.

**Trail Directions:** Begin at the information board for the trail **[1]** and look immediately to your left at a huge white oak. Continue straight on a wide mown path. Within a few steps you will come to a junction **[2]** (.05 mi.); go left, cross a bridge over Spring Creek, and at the Y go to the right. This is a short loop through one of the finest displays of spring wildflowers in the area. While looking at the flowers, don't let the roots trip you up. At .25 mi. you will encounter several large oak trees on your right **[3]**. Here there are also several offshoot trails; stay on the main path.

Notice the large trees and their open understory. This section of the woods has not been grazed, at least not by cattle. One of the problems the preserve is having is with deer; spring wildflowers, especially trilliums, are a favorite food of white-tailed deer. At .6 mi. you have finished the loop **[4]**; go right and retrace your steps back to **[2]**, where you will go left.

As you enter this woods, do you notice a difference? This section was disturbed at one time and the trees are second growth; the understory is not spring wildflowers, but gooseberry and multiflora rose. The trail is a muddy dirt path. Stay on the main path, ignoring the various side spurs. At .7 mi. find a large basswood on the right **[5]** and further along the trail a large chestnut oak. At .85 mi. come to a grassy opening on the left **[6]**; from here you will enter a dark woods that is not so disturbed.

Within a few steps the woods understory has disappeared and all you see are large trees. It is almost parklike. Don't forget to look down at the trail in this area. The bright green spots are tiger beetles, a fierce insect predator; the light orange glints are slugs that litter the trail after a rain. When dry weather comes, slugs will bury themselves in the soil and secrete a mucousy cocoon around themselves. During this time their body processes slow to an almost death-like state. Once there is enough rain to dissolve the mucous and soak into their bodies, the slugs become active again.

At 1.1 mi. you will cross a footbridge **[7]** and soon cross the park road at 1.25 mi. **[8]**. As you hike through the woods on the opposite side, don't be tripped up by the mole tunnels streaming across the trail. Look for huge patches of wild geranium and the glistening green bodies of black-wing damselflies.

At 1.45 mi. continue straight **[9]**; do not go right, because this trail leads to the Oak Knoll Shelter. You are hiking through a floodplain woods, dominated by ash and cottonwoods. By 1.6 mi. you are again hiking in an upland forest **[10]** dominated by large white oaks and straight maples. The trail comes out near the parking area where you have one last view of the huge oak at the beginning.

1. Start
2. Junction
3. Oaks
4. Finished loop
5. Basswood
6. Grassy opening
7. Footbridge
8. Park road crossing
9. Continue straight
10. Upland forest

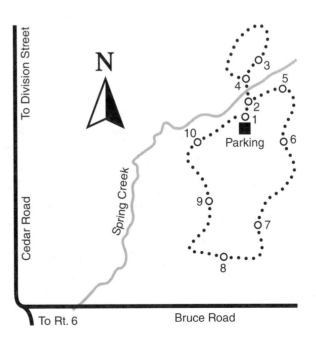

# Thorn Creek Nature Preserve

 **Distance Round-Trip:** 2.5 miles
 **Estimated Hiking Time:** 1.5 hours

*I encountered an entomological treasure while hiking this trail—Megarhyssa lunator—a large wasp with an incredibly long ovipositor (4 inches). I watched as the female probed a tree for a wood-boring larva in which to lay her eggs; she inserted her coiled ovipositor, pumped in an egg, and then proceeded to pull it out and clean it. The much smaller male just buzzed around her.*

**Caution:** Watch your step on the trail; tree roots have eroded from the soil of the path and can catch an unsuspecting toe. Also, watch where you step on the boardwalk: Several places are in need of repair.

**Trail Directions:** Begin the trail behind the nature center [1] at a kiosk. Within a few steps you will come to an intersection; go right and you are hiking through a successional woods. At .2 mi. the trail forks; go right [2] and cross Thorn Creek. After crossing a small footbridge, you will enter an open understory, upland woods. Look for sugar maple, elm, ash, and large oak trees. These oaks are some that began growing in the 1850s.

At .4 mi. go left [3], hiking on a ridge with a small ravine on the left. The large trees will soon disappear to be replaced by a pine plantation. These will soon give way to an oak-hickory woods and then pines again. At the trail intersection at .7 mi., continue straight through the pines to Owl Lake [4]. A pond will appear on the right with blue flag iris and a touch of the south—a bald cypress. You will cross a bridge at .9 mi. [5] and enter a mixed woods of large hickories and oaks.

Owl Lake Loop begins at 1.15 mi. [6]; go right around the lake. The lake is barely visible from the trail. Take one of the side spurs to investigate—look for bullfrogs, cattails, dragonflies, and the elusive sora rail. (It was calling, but it never made an appearance.) After your investigation, continue circling this small lake until you come back to [6], where you entered the loop. Now retrace your steps back to [4], and at the intersection go right on the boardwalk.

You are now on a wooden boardwalk [7] that leads though a maple, oak, and hickory woods. Listen for the snorts of deer and watch the antics of chipmunks as they squeak and scurry under the boardwalk. The trail angles right at 2.15 mi. [8]. At 2.25 you will cross Thorn Creek [9]. As you cross, look for black-wing damselflies; they are usually an indicator of fairly clear water. Within a few steps you will come to an intersection; go right [10] and you are again hiking through a successional woods. The trail will then T; go right, and all too soon your discovery of Thorn Creek Woods has ended.

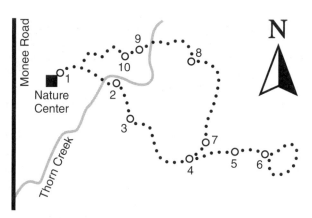

1. Start
2. Right turn
3. Left turn, ravine
4. Intersection, continue straight to Owl Lake
5. Bridge
6. Owl Lake Loop
7. Boardwalk
8. Angle right
9. Thorn Creek crossing
10. Right turn

# Central

Central Illinois is defined as the area south of an imaginary line (from Indiana to the Mississippi River) that follows the east-to-west portion of the Illinois River Valley and north of Interstate 70.

## Topography

The central portion of Illinois is dominated by a vast, flat, or gently rolling plain—a product of recent glaciers. This was the Grand Prairie. Here you have towns with names like Flatville and Broadlands. In this area of the state, towns were named after prairie groves (islands of trees amidst the prairie): Groveland, Table Grove, Forest City, and Middle Grove. Yet the whole area is not flat, as most outsiders believe; west of the Illinois River the terrain is older and becomes rolling with many ravines.

Illinois' east-central border, along the Vermilion River, has a fairly rugged landscape. The western border, along the Mississippi River, has a narrow, imposing band of river bluffs and limestone cliffs. In Calhoun and parts of Pike and Adams counties, the topography is rugged because (like the Driftless Area in the north) it escaped the crunching, leveling effects of the glaciers.

The soils are a unique feature of central Illinois. Most are composed of windblown sediment called loess. In some areas, near road cuts or where erosion has exposed the loess, you can see and feel this most unique material. Sand deposits along the Kankakee and the Illinois rivers are a result of the meltwaters of the last glacier. The water cascaded down old river channels, carrying loads of sand and gravel; when it reached and passed a narrow spot in the river, the water slowed and dumped its load of sand. Other sandy deposits occur in old, glacial lakebeds.

## Major Rivers and Lakes

The Mississippi River borders the central area of Illinois on the west, and the Vermilion and Embarras are among the rivers in the east. The Middle Fork of the Vermilion is the state's only federally designated wild and scenic river.

The major river in the center of the state and the largest tributary of the Mississippi River above the mouth of the Missouri is the Illinois River. It was the most frequently traveled interior waterway by early explorers, traders, and settlers. Thomas Jefferson portrayed the Illinois River in 1787 as "a fine river, clear, gentle, and without rapids." Settlements along its banks are among the oldest in the state.

The Kankakee, Mackinaw, Spoon, and Sangamon rivers are all tributaries of the Illinois. Clinton Lake, an impoundment (reservoir), is part of the Sangamon River drainage. The other major river in this area is the Kaskaskia, which flows into the Mississippi. Two of the state's largest impoundments, Lake Carlyle and Lake Shelbyville, are found in this drainage.

## Common Plant Life

In the early 1800s Henry Blevins described the prairie as "an ocean of flowers of every possible hue, glittering and blazing in the sunlight." Although grasses such as big and little bluestem, Indian grass, and switch grass form 90 percent of prairie vegetation, the wildflowers provide a welcome relief to the infinite shades of green. More than 200 species of plants can be found on Illinois prairies. A gradual procession of blooms begins in spring with diminutive violets and blue-eyed grass; the yellows and pinks of late summer and fall come from sunflowers, such as prairie dock and compass plant, and the familiar blazing stars.

Two unique types of prairies occur here: hill and sand. Hill prairies occur on the windswept bluffs above the major rivers and their tributaries. Look for little bluestem, side oats gramma, obedient plant, purple prairie clover, and ladies' tresses (orchids). Sand prairies occur on the sand deposits of the Illinois River. Growing here to bind the sand are prickly pear cactus, cleft phlox, puccoon, butterfly weed, and blackjack oak.

Savannas are prairie-forest associations that are not quite woods and not quite prairies but have the best of both—an understory (plants growing under the tree canopy) of prairie grasses and forbs along with scattered trees, usually oaks. The oaks, which resist fire, are usually huge and have outstretched branches, an indication that they grew with no competition from surrounding trees. Biologists call these wolf trees. Look for prairie plants such as shooting star, lupine, rattlesnake master, and little bluestem in the understory.

Like islands in an ocean of prairie grasses, prairie groves usually occurred along watercourses, protected from the sweeping prairie fires. These woods are usually oak, hickory, or maple and in the spring have a wonderful display of blooming wildflowers—Virginia bluebell, trillium, trout lily, spring beauty, phlox, and blue-eyed Mary. By summer, the wildflowers have been replaced with stinging nettle. Floodplain-forest species include silver maple, cottonwood, and sycamore. Masses of jewelweed, with spring-loaded seeds, bloom in the summer.

Along the Vermilion River are two unique plant communities—beech-maple forests growing in ravines (complete with tulip trees) and seeps. The first is a forest associated with the northeastern United States. Seep springs, in turn, are wet areas that support skunk cabbage, marsh marigold, and bog twayblade orchid, plants that here are at the southern limit of their range.

# Common Birds and Mammals

Grassland birds to look for are horned lark, dickcissel, meadow lark, pheasant, quail, and American kestrel. Bald eagles roost during the winter along the Mississippi and Illinois rivers. Hummingbirds are abundant in floodplain sites that have jewelweed. In wet areas and along watercourses, great blue herons and wood ducks are commonly seen. The area along the Illinois River is also a temporary home to not only thousands of waterfowl during spring and fall migrations but also white pelicans. Waterfowl species to look for are canvasbacks, mallards, shovelers, scaup, coots, green-winged teals, and Canada geese.

Mammals found here include the ever-present white-tailed deer, cottontail, raccoon, gray squirrel, coyote, beaver, woodchuck, 13-lined ground squirrel, and muskrat. Look for myriads of insects in the prairies and grasslands—monarch butterflies, grasshoppers, katydids, bees, and colorful beetles.

## Climate

The average temperature in January is 27 degrees F; in July, it's 77 degrees F. Rainfall averages 36 inches annually; the highest totals occur in June (4.3 inches). The average snowfall is 17 to 25 inches annually; 10 to 15 days a year have 3 or more inches of snow on the ground. Central Illinois experiences the highest of the highs and the lowest of the lows temperature-wise and is in the middle of the tornado belt.

## Best Features

- Prairie pieces
- Spectacular spring wildflowers
- Loess bluffs
- Outcrops of St. Peter sandstone
- Canyons and dells
- Middle Fork of the Vermilion River
- Illinois' version of deserts

# 20. Big River State Forest

- Discover a forest growing on glacially deposited sand.
- Travel the same route Captain Abraham Lincoln did as he led his men to the Black Hawk War.
- Look for six-lined race-runners, wild turkeys, brown tiger beetles, prickly pear cactus, and Patterson's bindweed.
- View one of only two remaining fire towers in Illinois.

## Area Information

Big River State Forest (3,000 acres) is located on one of the major sand deposits of Illinois. With the Mississippi River as its western border, and at one time sand prairie as its eastern border, this forest occurred as a narrow belt along the river and inland near the bluff line. Because of the sandy growing conditions, the forest was made up of short, scrubby, and mostly black and blackjack oaks.

The state first acquired 200 acres in 1925 and by 1928 had established the Milroy Plantation. The plantation demonstrated timber stand conversion. Through the removal of the scrub hardwood, salvaging of the salable material for pulpwood, controlling of the hardwood reproduction, and planting of rapidly growing white and red pines, the ancestral forest was drastically altered. The Milroy Plantation is one of the oldest plantations in the state and now has mature pines over 50 feet high.

Botanically, it is the sand prairie that is most interesting. While the typical display consists of puccoon, coneflower, and prairie clover, two state-endangered plants are found here—large flowered beardstongue and Patterson's bindweed. The latter was first discovered and described from a sandy prairie on August 11, 1873. This prairie would later become part of Big River State Forest. Harry Norton Patterson, a printer and a botanist from Oquawka, was the collector. Patterson's bindweed belongs to the morning glory family. It has a stout root and wiry stems that spread over the sand. Its leaves are narrow, reducing the plant's exposure to the sun. During the summer the plant produces white flowers.

Several trails wind their way through Big River State Forest, and 60 miles of firebreaks also traverse the forest, an invitation for further exploration.

**Directions:** Big River State Forest is located in northern Henderson County. Go just east of Oquawka on Illinois Route 164 and turn north on the Oquawka-Keithsburg blacktop. Go north about 9 miles. The forest office is located on the right.

**Hours Open:** The site is open year-round.

**Facilities:** Big River State Forest includes camping (water is shut off in winter months), fishing, picnic shelters, a playground, hunting, cross-country skiing, boating, equestrian campsites, and trails.

**Permits and Rules:** Equestrians must stay on designated trails and pets must be kept on leashes at all times.

**For Further Information:** Big River State Forest, R.R. 1, Box 118, Keithsburg, IL 61442; 309-374-2496.

## Park Trails

**Big Pines Hiking Trail** ( , 1.4 miles). The trail winds through red and white pine plantations that were planted in 1927.

**Auto Trails.** Big River State Forest has three auto trails: Windmill Road Scenic Auto Trail (2 miles), Raspberry Road Scenic Auto Trail (2 miles), and Wildlife Road Scenic Drive (4.9 miles). Obtain a map at the forest office.

## Other Areas of Interest

With easy access to the backwaters of the Mississippi River, **Delabar State Park,** located 1.5 miles north of Oquawka, offers fishing, boating, camping, and picnicking. Two trails of under 2 miles are located here. For more information, call 309-374-2496.

A small **monument to Norma Jean,** the circus elephant, is located in Oquawka. On July 17, 1972, Norma Jean was chained to a tree when lightning struck the tree, killing the elephant. She is buried where she went down.

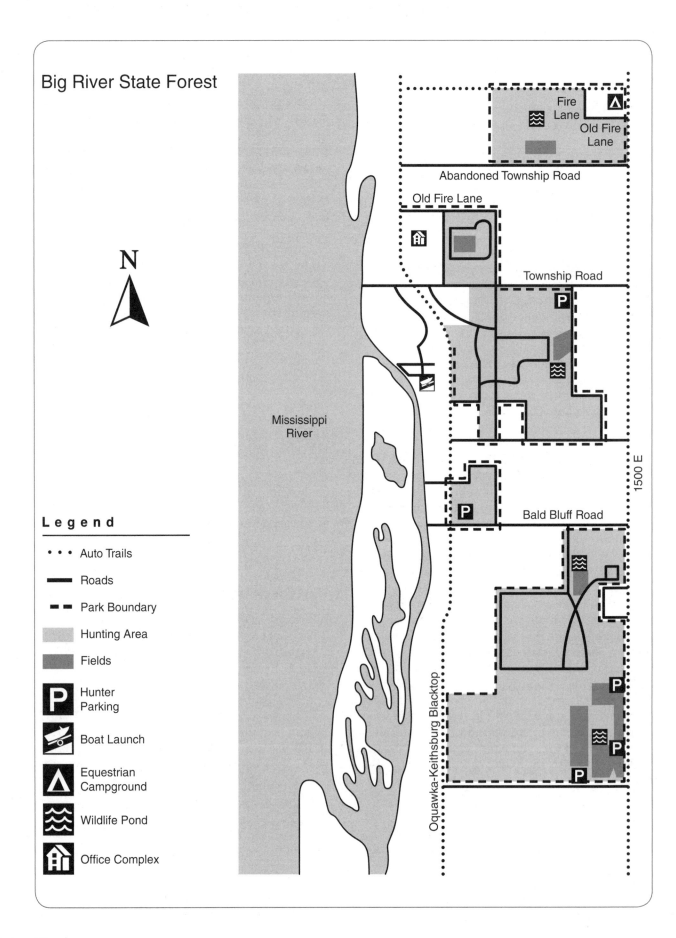

**Big River State Forest**

N

Mississippi
River

Abandoned Township Road

Fire
Lane

Old Fire
Lane

Old Fire Lane

Township Road

1500 E

Bald Bluff Road

Oquawka-Keithsburg Blacktop

**Legend**

• • • Auto Trails

— Roads

- - - Park Boundary

Hunting Area

Fields

**P** Hunter Parking

Boat Launch

△ Equestrian Campground

Wildlife Pond

Office Complex

# Lincoln Trail

 **Distance Round-Trip:** 1.5 miles
**Estimated Hiking Time:** 1 hour

*The trail probably doesn't look much different than when Capt. A. Lincoln marched through with his troops; I wonder if the turkey scratchings, puffballs, and acorns distracted his men.*

**Caution:** Sand gnats can be a nuisance in summer.

**Trail Directions:** The trail is located off Bald Bluff Road (2650 N). Bear right with the Auto Tour sign; drive through a scrub oak forest. A natural area's boundary sign will be on the left as you drive this one-lane gravel and grass road. Park at the large grassy pull-off.

Begin the trail at the trail board and go through the gate [1]. The trail is a grass and sand path lined with blackjack, black, and white oak trees. Take a few minutes to study these trees. Blackjack oak is usually found on sites with dry, sandy, or clay soils. The bark is very dark or black; the leaves are broadly triangular with three lobes (they resemble ducks' feet); and the acorns are often faintly striped with caps of reddish-brown scales. White oak has seven to nine deep lobes on the leaves, and the acorns have knobby caps. Black oak has five to seven bristle-tipped lobes on the leaves, and the acorn caps have scales that form a slight fringe at the cup margin.

Along this section of the trail, also look for the six-lined race runner, rough blazing star, and prickly pear cactus. At .15 mi. you will go down an old sand dune [2]. The trail crosses a forest road at .3 mi.; go through the gate and resume the trail on the opposite side [3].

The forest composition has changed, and you are now hiking through an oak-hickory forest with much taller trees. The trail is still sand. Don't forget to look down; this is a popular area with turkeys for foraging (look for the V-shaped scratch marks). Note their dust baths (oval depressions in the sand). Also on the sandy trail are earth stars, which are gray-brown, star-shaped fungi. If it is dry, the ray-shaped arms fold around the center puffball to protect it from the elements and predators; but when it rains the rays absorb water and unfold, exposing the puffball and allowing the spores to disperse.

The trail curves to the left at .8 mi. [4], and pines have now joined the mix of trees. Brown tiger beetles and grasshoppers keep one step ahead of you. Milkweeds line the trail as it ascends a small sand dune [5] (1.1 mi.); look for monarch caterpillars, milkweed bugs, and milkweed beetles. The trail continues to wind through the forest.

The trail heads through the forest and crosses the road again at 1.4 mi. [6], which brings you to the parking area. Before returning to your car, take the first trail to the right and go through the gate to a small pioneer cemetery. The trail goes uphill and within a few steps comes to the cemetery. The headstones are from the 1800s. Retrace your steps back to the parking area.

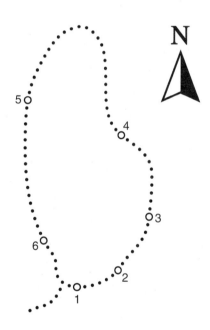

1. Start
2. Descend sand dune
3. Road crossing
4. Curve left
5. Ascend sand dune
6. Road crossing

# 21. Nauvoo

- Celebrate a monument to the traditional stages and roles in a woman's life.
- Hike among the rubble—the sun, moon, and stars—of a failed utopian society.
- Visit a city that was once the largest in the state.
- Learn about the day-to-day lives of early Mormons.
- Look for white pelicans on Mississippi River Islands.

## Area Information

Nauvoo, located on a rise above a horseshoe bend in the Mississippi River, was the religious, governmental, and cultural center of the Church of Jesus Christ of Latter-day Saints (Mormons) from 1839 to 1846. Joseph Smith, its prophet-leader, first described the area as "literally a wilderness. The land was mostly covered with trees and bushes and much of it so wet . . . that it was impossible for teams [of horses] to get through." But he also saw the value of the area as a trading port. Initially, the site was named Commerce, but once the Mormons purchased it, they changed its name to Nauvoo, meaning "beautiful place or pleasant land." It would be the religion's third attempt to build "God's City" on the frontier.

Construction of the temple began during 1841; it was to "rise out of the bluffs as a beacon to all of God's People in their last days of life on earth." The temple took five years to complete, was the tallest structure in Illinois, and was declared an architectural wonder. Yet not everyone who viewed it was impressed. Josiah Quincy, son of the president of Harvard, viewed the area in 1844.

"Perhaps it would of [sic] required a genius to have designed anything worthy of that noble site. The city of Nauvoo, with its wide streets, sloping gracefully to the farms enclosed on the prairie seemed a better temple to Him who prospers the work of industrious hands than the grotesque structure on the hill, with its queer carvings of moons and suns."

By 1844, the town's population had reached 12,000 and Nauvoo was the largest city in the state. Yet all was not well, because neighbors resented the community's religion and prosperity. Tension between the Mormons and their neighbors broke loose when Joseph Smith and his brother were murdered in the Carthage Jail in 1844. By September of 1846 most of the Mormons had left, looking for yet another site on which to build "God's City."

**Directions:** Nauvoo is located near the banks of the Mississippi River along Route 96. The Latter-day Saints Visitors Center is at the north end of the restored village.

**Hours Open:** The site is open year-round. The visitor center hours are Monday through Saturday 9:00 a.m. to 9:00 p.m. and Sunday 10:30 a.m. to 6:00 p.m. (May to August), and Monday through Saturday 9:00 a.m. to 5:00 p.m. and Sunday 12:30 to 5:00 p.m. (September to April).

**Facilities:** The visitor center contains artifacts, an audiovisual presentation, and a scale model of the 1846 city. It also has restrooms, water, and maps.

**Permits and Rules:** Some of the homes are privately owned and cannot be toured. Please respect the owners' privacy.

**For Further Information:** Historic Nauvoo Visitors Center, P.O. Box 215, Nauvoo, IL 62354; 888-453-6434 or www.historicnauvoo.net.

## Park Trails

**1844 Martyrdom Trail: Nauvoo to Carthage** (, 23 miles). The trail begins at the Latter-day Saints Visitors Center and follows the route that Joseph Smith and his brother took to the Carthage Jail. Before hiking, you must register two weeks in advance. For more information, contact Martyrdom Trail Committee, P.O. Box 223, Nauvoo, IL 62354; 217-453-6543.

## Other Areas of Interest

Three years after the Mormons' exodus, another utopian community, the Icarians, attempted to settle at Nauvoo. Although their communal lifestyle proved to be unworkable, they had a lasting effect on the community. They introduced grape growing and wine making to the area. The first vineyard planted at Nauvoo exists in **Nauvoo State Park.** You can also tour the museum, fish, boat, picnic, and camp. A 1.5-mile trail winds around the lake and the wooded areas. For more information, call 217-453-2512.

# Historic Nauvoo

**Distance Round-Trip:** 4 miles

**Estimated Hiking Time:** 2 hours (with a few house tours)

*"Half encircled by a bend of the river, a beautiful city lay glittering in the fresh morning sun; its bright new dwellings, set in cool green gardens, ranging up around a stately dome-shaped hill, which was crowned by a noble marble edifice."*

Colonel Thomas Kane, Fall 1846

**Caution:** There are no sidewalks for part of the trail, so walk along the side of the road.

**Trail Directions:** Park at the Latter-day Saints Visitors Center. Begin the hike in the garden at the Emma and Joseph Smith Statue [1]. At *Fulfillment* go left and begin hiking on Young Street. Cross Partridge and Wells streets before going right on Bluff Street [2] (.4 mi.). Go across the street to the reconstructed temple [3].

After touring the temple site, exit from the south and go right on Mulholland Street [4]. Cross Wells Street and head downhill. At .75, go left on Partridge Street [5]. On your right is the Nauvoo Groves cottonwoods; this is a site where many speeches were given. Cross White and Hotchkiss streets, and at 1.1 mi. view the Heber C. Kimball Home on the left [6].

Continue walking down Partridge. At 1.15 mi. go right on Kimball [7], passing one of the seven brickyards that were in operation during the town's heyday. Go left at the Lucy Mack Smith Home. On your left at 1.3 mi. is the Joseph Coolidge Home. From the Coolidge Home, go right onto Parley [8], and at 1.4 mi., go left onto Main [9]. On your left is the Mansion House.

Cross Water Street; Nauvoo House is on your left as the street dead-ends into the Mississippi River [10] (1.6 mi.). Climb up on the bluff and look around, then proceed north on the other side of the circle. Go up the steps in front of the Smith Family Homestead. At Water Street go left, and as you turn the corner, note the Nauvoo Survey Stone at your feet.

At 1.7 mi., go left into the Smith Family Cemetery [11], following the brick path. Retrace your steps back to Water Street and continue on past the Red Brick Store and the Aaron Johnson Home. On your left is the Mississippi River. At 2.35 mi. Water Street curves to the right, leaving the river behind, and soon deadends into Parley Street.

On your right at this junction is the Monument to Exodus [12]. Continue north on Parley, which was the street used for the exodus—this section is called the Trail of Hope. The Seventies Hall is on your left at 2.55 mi. [13].

Adjacent to the Seventies Hall is the Webb Blacksmith. Cross Granger Street, and at 2.75 mi. go left on Main [14]. For the next .3 mi. you will walk through what was once the business district of the settlement.

The Cultural and Masonic Hall is the last building before the sidewalk gives way on Main Street. Continue past the hall, walking along the side of the street [15] (3.1 mi.). The sidewalk ends at the Hosea Stout property (3.3 mi.). Soon you will pass the visitor center. At 3.6 mi. go left on Broadway and then right at the fenced-in area [16]. Take the ramp for a view of one of the four quarries used for limestone for the original temple. From here, retrace your steps; on Hubbard take a left. You are now back at the visitor center, ending your hike at one of the original temple sunstones.

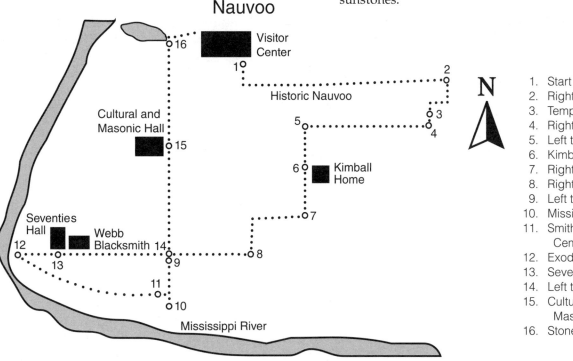

## Nauvoo

Visitor Center

Historic Nauvoo

Cultural and Masonic Hall

Kimball Home

Seventies Hall

Webb Blacksmith

Mississippi River

N

1. Start
2. Right turn
3. Temple site
4. Right turn
5. Left turn
6. Kimball Home
7. Right turn
8. Right turn
9. Left turn
10. Mississippi River
11. Smith Family Cemetery
12. Exodus site
13. Seventies Hall
14. Left turn
15. Cultural and Masonic Hall
16. Stone quarry

# 22. Siloam Springs State Park

- Hike to the deafening din of spring peepers (frogs).
- Enjoy idyllic ravines with fern-covered hillsides and rushing streams.
- Pass by an oak opening.
- Although the curative springs are gone, a hike on one of the park's trails might just cure whatever ails you.

## Area Information

Siloam Springs State Park, an area of rolling hills, prairies, and forests, is one of the larger parks in the state. It was named by Reverend Reuben McCoy, a minister from the neighboring town of Clayton, for the Pool of Siloam, where the miracle of the blind man occurred. The reverend saw a similarity to the healing efficacy of these Illinois waters.

The springs that issued from the ravine slopes had a high mineral content and were believed to be the cure-all for cancer, kidney problems, and drunkenness, among other things. A little community grew up around the springs, and the Siloam Forest Hotel resort (built in 1884) offered a bathhouse, swimming, and a pool to make the waters readily available to the public.

The village suffered when the railroad and medical science passed it by. The springs became contaminated and were sealed off. The present picnic area is where the small village once stood, and all that remains of the park's past are two stone foundations—one of which can be viewed on the Red Oak Trail.

**Directions:** Siloam Springs is 25 miles east of Quincy and north of where Adams, Brown, and Pike counties intersect. From Route 104, go north on 2873 E to the park entrance on the east side.

**Hours Open:** The site is open year-round except on Christmas Day and New Year's Day.

**Facilities:** A concession stand offers boat and canoe rentals. A campground has showers and electricity, a picnic area with shelters and grills, horse trails and equestrian camping, fishing, boating, and hunting.

**Permits and Rules:** Pets must be leashed at all times.

**For Further Information:** Siloam Springs State Park, 938 E. 3003rd Lane, Clayton, IL 62324; 217-894-6205.

## Park Trails

**Crab Apple Trail** (👣👣, .6 mile). This is a linear trail that follows McKee Creek and heads north toward the lake. Rock outcrops along the creek and a pleasant meandering stream are highlights.

**Prairie Bluff Trail** (👣👣, 1.2 miles). This trail can be accessed from Crab Apple Trail. The trail crosses McKee Creek, goes up a hill (with a great view at the top), and continues toward the lake's earthen dam.

## Other Areas of Interest

Located west of Macomb, **Argyle Lake State Park** encompasses part of an old stagecoach route between Galena and Beardstown. Within the park is Argyle Hollow Barrens Nature Preserve. Barrens are characterized by gnarled, stunted open-grown trees and an understory of prairie plants. A short trail leads to the barrens. A 5-mile trail circles the lake within the state park. For more information, call 309-776-3422.

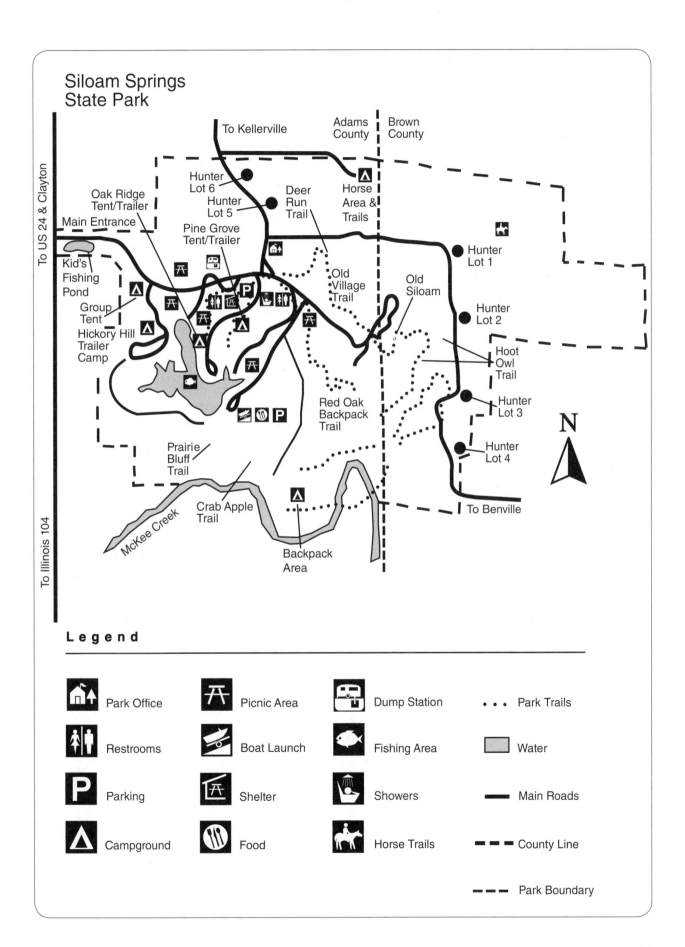

# Siloam Springs State Park

To Kellerville

Adams County | Brown County

To US 24 & Clayton

Oak Ridge Tent/Trailer

Main Entrance

Hunter Lot 6

Hunter Lot 5

Deer Run Trail

Horse Area & Trails

Pine Grove Tent/Trailer

Kid's Fishing Pond

Group Tent

Hickory Hill Trailer Camp

Old Village Trail

Old Siloam

Hunter Lot 1

Hunter Lot 2

Hoot Owl Trail

Hunter Lot 3

Red Oak Backpack Trail

Hunter Lot 4

N

To Illinois 104

Prairie Bluff Trail

Crab Apple Trail

McKee Creek

Backpack Area

To Benville

## Legend

| | | | | | |
|---|---|---|---|---|---|
| Park Office | | Picnic Area | | Dump Station | | · · · Park Trails |
| Restrooms | | Boat Launch | | Fishing Area | | Water |
| Parking | | Shelter | | Showers | | — Main Roads |
| Campground | | Food | | Horse Trails | | - - - County Line |
| | | | | | | - - - Park Boundary |

# Red Oak Backpack Trail

 **Distance Round-Trip:** 4 miles
**Estimated Hiking Time:** 2 hours

*Hike this trail only in dry weather! I hiked it in wet weather and encountered raging streams (impassable), mudslides, and a maze of bewildering, water-filled false trails.*

**Caution:** The trail can be very muddy and slick when wet, and some stream crossings might be difficult in wet weather. There are many roots in the trail, especially going downhill; be careful. This is tick country, so make sure you wear repellent.

**Trail Directions:** Follow the park road to the easternmost picnic area. Park on the grass at the side of the road or in one of the picnic areas and begin at the trail board near the beginning of the park's loop road. The trail ascends on an old roadbed through fern-lined bluffs [1]. The trail is periodically marked with four-by-four poles. By .2 mi. the ascent is over and you are hiking on top of a ridge through a mixed woods with a nice spring understory (especially anemone) [2]. The trail soon passes through an early successional woods with lots of dogwood, elderberry, and sumac.

At .6 mi. go to the right [3] and pass an old mining pit with water in it on the left. Soon the path goes downhill and skirts a park road. The road disappears by .75 mi. and pines line the trail. Look for bracken fern at 1.1 mi. [4]. This fern continues to produce new, wavy, dark-green leaves all season, and usually indicates poor, barren soils.

From 1.65 to 1.75 mi. on the south-facing slope, the trail goes through a unique area in Illinois—an oak opening [5]. Oak openings are an intermediate between prairie and woodlands. They are usually grassy and free of brush with trees growing widely spaced out or in clumps. Look closely at the ground in early spring for bicolored bird's-foot violet. As the trail begins to head down, leaving the oak opening, buckeyes appear as an upper-understory shrub. This is a fairly steep descent, so use caution. (While keeping your mind on the trail, during May look for phlox and columbine.)

After the descent you'll see that the woods gives way to a shrubby, grassy area, which in turn gives way to a floodplain woods. At 2 mi. cross the creek [6]. When the water is low, this presents no problem. If you happen to hike during or after a heavy rainfall, you might have to retrace your steps and find a suitable log on which to cross. The trail now heads up and out of the floodplain. Did you notice the buttercups near the stream? Their generic name *(Ranunculus)* means "little frog," the plants so named because of their affinity for moist areas.

Another creek crossing occurs at 2.15 mi., and to the right are the remains of Old Stone House [7], which are worth a look. The trail soon heads upward at 2.25 mi., and you are walking through autumn olive (a weedy introduced tree) and the state grass, big bluestem. At 2.5 mi. the trail passes a pine plantation on the left and a backpacking campsite (with privy toilets) [8].

The trail intersects with a forest road at 2.6 mi. [9]; go right. You'll wander between pines on the left and autumn olive and prairie grasses on the right. In spring, look down and discover pussytoes. The flower head resembles an off-white kitten's paw. Notice that no other plants grow near the pussytoes. These flowers put out a growth inhibitor to ensure that each of them has enough nutrients and water. The trail curves left at 2.75 mi.

At 3 mi. [10] the trail heads to the right and a forest road emerges and joins the trail. At 3.1 mi. go right, and at 3.35 mi. the trail heads right again and down [11] through a mixed woods. Wind your way downhill with help from steps placed near the end of the descent. Once down, you are on level ground in a floodplain woods; go left before you get to the creek. You are now walking along a narrow path with the creek on the right. Cross the creek several times until the final crossing at 3.7 mi. Look to your right at the shale outcrop [12] and on the left at a sandstone outcrop. The trail comes out on a circular gravel path; follow the gravel path back to where you parked.

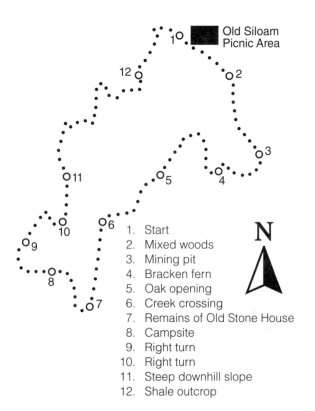

1. Start
2. Mixed woods
3. Mining pit
4. Bracken fern
5. Oak opening
6. Creek crossing
7. Remains of Old Stone House
8. Campsite
9. Right turn
10. Right turn
11. Steep downhill slope
12. Shale outcrop

# Hoot Owl Trail

 **Distance Round-Trip:** 1.5 miles
**Estimated Hiking Time:** .75 hour

*This is a quiet trail where you can hear the bounding of deer through the woods, the drop of acorns, the call of blue jays, and the distant hoot of a barred owl.*

**Caution:** The trail can be very muddy, and roots are in the path. This is tick country, so make sure you wear repellent. During the fall you might get plunked by an acorn or two.

**Trail Directions:** Begin at the farthest trail board near the end of the park loop road, and immediately start an ascent [1]. At one time the trail was marked, but no longer, although you might come across a stray marker or two. This section of the trail is braced with railroad ties. As you head up, look at the large red and white oaks on either side. During spring, the trail will be lined with mayapples, rattlesnake ferns, and anemones. Some parts of the hillside are covered with Christmas fern. The understory shrub is sassafras with its mitten-shaped leaves. This is the food plant of the spicebush swallowtail, which you should see flitting about the trail. Examine the leaves for the larvae of this butterfly, which resemble bird droppings when young and a rough green snake when larger (fourth

to fifth instar). Take advantage of the small overlooks to peer into the ravine below and to catch a glimpse of the trail's namesake.

At .15 mi. [2] the trail has leveled off and you are hiking on top of a ridge with a great view to the left. In spring, when trees just begin to leaf out, this ravine is absolutely beautiful. On your right, look into the woods for large-canopied oak trees, better known as wolf trees. A bench is provided at .3 mi., and soon after the ravine on the left disappears, only to be replaced by an equally impressive ravine on the right. A pine plantation is on the left and the trail skirts a park road at .5 mi. [3]. The trail curves to the right at .65 mi., and you again see the road [4]. By .75 mi. you are finally away from the road and into a woods dominated by oak and elm saplings. Pines will again appear and soon more saplings. If you look closely, however, you can find several large, old oak trees.

At 1.05 mi. you are again on a ridge with a ravine forest on either side [5]. Continue to look down into the beautiful ravines as you hike on this dry, narrow ridge [6]. Keep an eye out for violet wood sorrel. At 1.35 mi. a sign appears warning of an erosion area and to keep out; go left and descend the hill [7]. By 1.45 the trail is back on level ground near two privies. Go right, back to where you parked at the farthest trailhead.

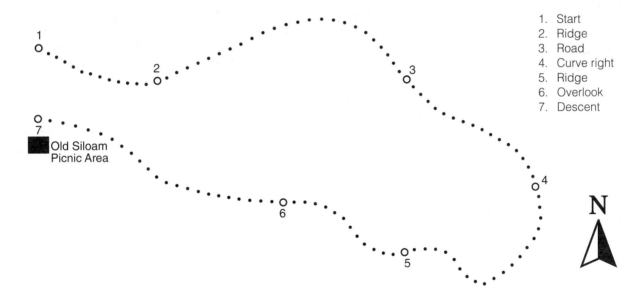

1. Start
2. Ridge
3. Road
4. Curve right
5. Ridge
6. Overlook
7. Descent

Old Siloam Picnic Area

N

# 23. Pere Marquette State Park

- Brush up on your botany as you look for ferns, green dragons, and doll's eyes.
- See spectacular views of the Illinois and Mississippi rivers.
- Experience the highest highs and the lowest lows, all within a few feet.
- Discover loess.

## Area Information

Pere Marquette State Park lies at the confluence of the Mississippi and Illinois rivers, just southwest of the glacial boundary in western Illinois. One of the state's largest parks, consisting of 8,000 acres, it includes limestone and loess bluffs, second-growth timber, and hill prairies.

The park was originally named Piasa Bluff State Park to commemorate the two drawings of the Piasa Bird discovered near the park. The name was later changed to Pere Marquette, in honor of Father Jacques Marquette, a French missionary who in 1673 was among the first group of Europeans to reach the confluence of the Mississippi and Illinois rivers. Father Marquette noted that these bluffs' height and length inspired awe.

One of the extraordinary features of the park is loess (rhymes with bus), deposits of windblown silt. As the glaciers advanced, they acted like giant grist mills, grinding and pulverizing much of the rock and earth into very fine, dust-sized particles. Forests along major river valleys trapped this windblown dust and the material accumulated to form high bluffs. One of the characteristics of loess is its tendency to stand in vertical walls that don't erode. This has resulted in two of the park's higher peaks—McAdams Peak and Lovers Leap.

**Directions:** The park is 5 miles west of Grafton on Illinois Route 100 and approximately 25 miles northwest of Alton.

**Hours Open:** The site is open year-round.

**Facilities:** The lodge and conference center includes a restaurant, gift shop, indoor pool, guest rooms, tennis courts, and a 700-ton fireplace. For information, call 618-786-2331. The park has a visitor center, camping (with rent-a-camp facilities), horseback riding, boating, fishing, picnicking, and hunting.

**Permits and Rules:** Pets must be leashed at all times.

**For Further Information:** Pere Marquette State Park, Route 100, P.O. Box 158, Grafton, IL 62037. The phone number at the visitor center is 618-786-3323.

## Park Trails

Ten interconnected trails traverse the park, each with its own unique blaze. The blazes are kept painted and intersections are marked. A park trail map is keyed to these blazes.

**Ravine Trail** (👣👣👣, .5 mile one way). The trail heads south, using more than 60 stone steps, and follows a narrow ravine.

**Hickory Trail** (👣👣👣, .5 mile one way). This trail heads east from McAdams Peak to Twin Shelters. It links with the park road.

**Hickory North Trail** (👣👣👣, 1 mile). The trail connects with Hickory Trail and Hickory South. Hikers will wind over hills and down valleys.

**Hickory South Trail** (👣👣👣, 1.25 miles). This trail connects with the Fern Hollow Trail and Hickory North Trail. It also provides access to Twin Shelters Overlook and the lodge.

**Rattlesnake Trail** (👣👣👣, .25 mile). This trail skirts rocky bluffs and outcrops; although named for this unpopular reptile, the chances of sighting a rattlesnake are practically nil. Rattlesnake Trail connects with Fern Hollow Trail and the park road.

## Other Areas of Interest

**Sam Vadalabene Trail** is a paved, 21.5-mile rail trail that follows the Great River Road from Alton to Pere Marquette State Park. Hikers are also welcome to use the trail, which includes interesting points along the way (especially the small town of Elsah, listed in the National Register of Historic Places). For more information, call 217-782-3715 or visit www.greatriverroad.com.

From December 1 to March 1, watch for wintering **bald eagles** in this area: downriver from Alton at the mouth of the Missouri River, up the Mississippi to Winfield Lock and Dam, and up the Illinois River to Pere Marquette State Park. On a cold day, dozens of wintering bald eagles can be seen. For eagle-watching information, go to www.greatriverroad.com/Eagles.

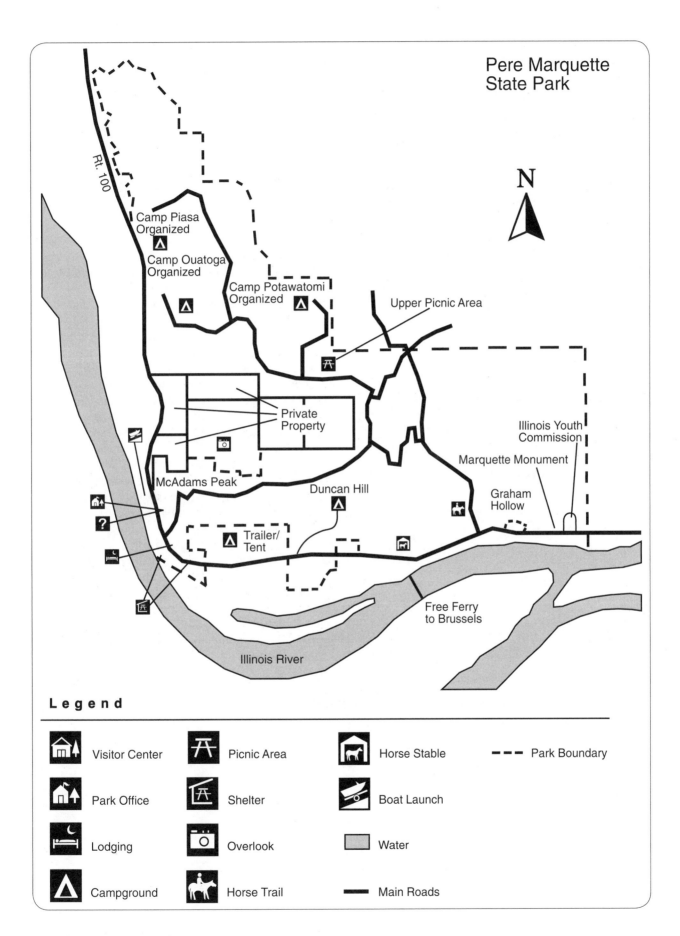

# Pere Marquette State Park

N

Rt. 100

Camp Piasa
Organized

Camp Ouatoga
Organized

Camp Potawatomi
Organized

Upper Picnic Area

Private
Property

Illinois Youth
Commission

Marquette Monument

McAdams Peak

Duncan Hill

Graham
Hollow

Trailer/
Tent

Free Ferry
to Brussels

Illinois River

## Legend

| | | | | | | |
|---|---|---|---|---|---|---|
| 🏠 | Visitor Center | ⛩ | Picnic Area | 🐎 | Horse Stable | - - - Park Boundary |
| 🏠 | Park Office | ⛩ | Shelter | | Boat Launch | |
| 🛏 | Lodging | 📷 | Overlook | | Water | |
| ⛺ | Campground | 🐎 | Horse Trail | | Main Roads | |

## Dogwood-Goat Trails

 **Distance Round-Trip:** 2 miles
**Estimated Hiking Time:** 1 hour

*Walk in feet-deep layers of loess while looking across the valley at an area that never experienced a glacier.*

**Caution:** Roots, limbs, and rocks are scattered about the trail. Try not to trip.

**Trail Directions:** Begin the trail at the trail board north of the visitor center and follow the blue triangles painted on trees (blazes) [1]. The trail, supplied with reinforced steps, immediately ascends. Before .1 mi., come to a trail intersection; continue straight ahead. On your left are great views of the neighboring fish and wildlife area as you pass through a maple-basswood forest growing on rolling ravines.

Take advantage of the Mississippi River Overlook at .2 mi. [2]. At .3 mi. [3] the trail intersects with the Ridge Trail; go left, still following the blue blazes. Within .05 mi. come to another trail intersection, but continue straight ahead, following the sign to McAdams Peak [4]. At .4 mi. [5] you will encounter a large oak tree; take a side spur to your left and view a small prairie opening called a hill prairie. In the spring look for clumps of puccoon—these orange-yellow flowers are related to the Virginia bluebell. Continue on the spur and soon rejoin the trail.

1. Start
2. Mississippi River Overlook
3. Left turn
4. Go straight
5. Hill prairie side spur
6. Trail intersection
7. McAdams Peak Overlook
8. Left turn
9. Left turn
10. Overlook
11. Half-rock arch
12. Trail skirts highway

At .5 mi. [6] several trails intersect; go left, up stairs to McAdams Peak Overlook, only a few feet from the intersection [7]. McAdams Peak is 372 feet above the Illinois River and is named for the McAdams family. William, the father, removed 100 Native American skeletons from this vicinity for the Smithsonian; John, his son, was instrumental in acquiring this property for a state park. From the overlook you can see the Illinois River and its bottomland and the unglaciated hills of Calhoun County.

Retrace your steps back to point [6] and go to your left, following Goat Cliff Trail (blazed in yellow) [8]. Immediately as you begin to descend, look to your right, where you will see loess. Take time to touch and feel this windblown silt. It is firm yet crumbly; it's easy to dig, yet it holds together. If you take a closer look, you'll notice that it has a uniform texture and is free from rocks.

The trail Ys at .85 mi.; go left [9], continuing to follow the yellow blazes. On your left is a loess hill prairie. The trail twists and turns uphill through an open forest. At 1.1 mi. the trail Vs. First take the spur to the overlook [10] (in the winter this is a good spot to look for wintering bald eagles); retrace your steps back to the intersection and go right, continuing to follow the yellow blazes.

As you navigate down, notice that the trail is lined with rocky outcrops and large oaks. Look on the left at the mortar- and bricklike precision of the rock strata, and on the right at the parklike forest. At 1.4 mi. [11], note a half-rock arch on the right. Look for columbine blooming in the cliff cracks during late April. You continue to head down through jumbles of rocks. By 1.75 mi. the outcrops and cliff are gone and you can hear highway noise, and by 1.85 mi. the trail skirts the highway [12]. In early spring this area is decorated with the blooms of redbud and dogwood trees. The trail soon ends at the north end of the parking lot.

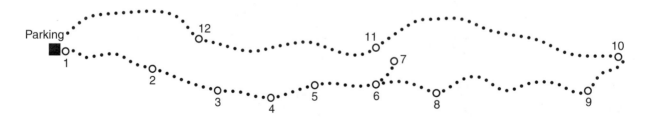

# Fern Hollow Trail

**Distance Round-Trip:** 3 miles
**Estimated Hiking Time:** 1.5 hours

*Hiking on this rolling woodland trail is not without peril. You will encounter wolves, rattlesnakes, and dragons—in this instance, a tree, a fern, and a flower. But like their real counterparts, they can be very difficult to find.*

**Caution:** Branches sometimes block the trail and roots are exposed. The trail is very slippery when wet.

**Trail Directions:** Park at the Flagpole Overlook, the second overlook parking area at the top of the bluff. It is on the right. Head south through the parking area; cross the park road, and the trail (Hickory North, marked with red-and-white-striped blazes) will appear a few feet down the road [1] (.05 mi.). Begin hiking through a maple woods along a deep ravine. On your left look for rattlesnake fern, with its lacy, bright-green, triangular leaves.

At .3 mi. [2] come to a trail intersection and go right. The trail is now marked with orange; you are on Fern Hollow Trail. For the next .1 mi. look for small limestone outcrops and fragile fern that line the trail. Keep an eye out for patches of doll's eye at .55 mi. [3] and throughout the hike. In the fall, the fruits of these plants are shiny white berries, each with a black dot that resembles the china eyes once used in dolls. These berries are very poisonous. Doll's eye is viewed by ecologists as an indicator of a good woods. Not far from the first patch of doll's eye, note a pair of large oaks on your left. From here the trail soon heads upward.

A bench is set at .8 mi. [4]. In the spring look here for large clumps of bellwort, wild ginger, and large patches of doll's eye, mixed with mayapples. As you cross the stream at .9 mi. [5] admire the ravine forest on the right. Here look for maidenhair ferns with feathery, flat fronds borne on glistening black stalks. The trail crosses the park road [6] (1.3 mi.) and reenters the woods on the other side. You are still following the orange marks as you hike in a mixed, second-growth woods. Note the clean understory on both sides.

At 1.4 mi. ignore a trail to the left and continue straight ahead [7]. You will enter an immature forest at 1.6 mi. [8]. The trail begins to head downward at 1.7 mi., and the forest also begins to improve [9]. Before you round the curve in the trail, look to your right for a large wolf tree [10] (1.75 mi.). (Wolf trees are usually oaks with wide-spreading canopies, indicating that at one time the area was more open.)

After sighting the wolf tree, again look for rattle-snake fern. If your visit is during the late spring, also

look for green dragons with their incomplete whorl of leaves and unique flower structure underneath (supposedly the dragon's tongue). Two miles brings a gully crossing, and for the next .25 mi. the trail is lined with Christmas ferns [11]. At 2.25 mi. [12] you leave the fern-lined hollow—the trail's namesake—and hike upward. On your left note a farm pasture as you hike through disturbed woods. A bench is provided for you to enjoy this pastoral setting.

At 2.7 mi. [13] you will head upward on an eroded path. Look on your right for another wolf tree as you climb steadily upward. Near the top is another trail going off to the right; take it [14] (2.9 mi.). (This is Hickory South Trail and is marked with red and white.) Within .05 mi. you will come to the park road [15]; go left back to the parking area, and enjoy the view from Flagpole Observation Area.

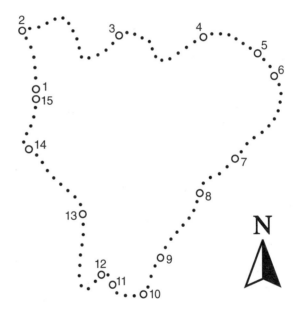

1. Start
2. Right turn
3. Doll's eye
4. Bench
5. Ravine forest
6. Road crossing
7. Go straight
8. Immature forest
9. Improving forest
10. Wolf tree
11. Christmas ferns
12. Uphill slope
13. Eroded path
14. Right turn
15. Park road

# 24. Forest Park Nature Preserve

- Enjoy spectacular views of the Illinois River Valley.
- Become a Hundred-Mile Hiker after reaching the century mark on the preserve's trails.
- Visit a woodland oasis located in the third-largest metropolitan area in Illinois.
- See wildflowers decorating the bluffs and ravines each spring and an unparalleled fall-color spectacle.

## Area Information

In 1839, J. Gould wrote of Peoria, "The bluff comes near to the river, and is covered, as is the narrow strip of bottom land, with a thick growth of timber." In Gould's time, the bluffs overlooking the Illinois River were a mix of oak woodlands and prairie openings that supported a diverse mix of wildlife and plant species. The bluffs at Forest Park Nature Preserve have similar rich woods and prairie openings, providing a window on that 1840s landscape.

Forest Park Nature Preserve was dedicated as the 13th nature preserve in Illinois. Although the entire area had been lumbered in the mid-19th century, the forest was allowed to grow back. A few of the old trees are still present in the preserve. Called wolf trees, these old specimens have the large, outstretched branches indicative of trees that grew in the open. This type of habitat doesn't maintain itself, however, and as you hike you might notice the telltale evidence of fire, used to keep the land open and healthy.

Gould concluded his visit by stating, "On the whole it is the finest site for a town that I ever saw." Forest Park, an oasis of woodland in a busy city and a small remnant of that fine site, today provides a glimpse of what Gould saw and the potential he envisioned.

**Directions:** From Peoria at the junction of Highways 29 and 150, take Highway 29 north for 3 miles; turn and go west on Gardner Lane .5 mi. to Forest Park Nature Center. The nature preserve is located to the west of the nature center.

**Hours Open:** The site is open year-round from dawn to dusk; it is closed on Thanksgiving, Christmas, and New Year's. The nature center and nature store are open Monday through Saturday 9:00 a.m. to 5:00 p.m. and Sunday from 1:00 p.m. to 5:00 p.m.

**Facilities:** The site maintains a nature center that houses displays, an area for programs and classes, a well-stocked gift shop, and mileage cards for participants in the hiker club. Water, restrooms, juice and soda machines, and trail maps are also found here. Picnic tables are outside the center.

**Permits and Rules:** Please leave your pets at home; they are not allowed on the trails or in the area. Dispose of litter properly. Stay on the trails—off-trail hiking only causes erosion and destroys plants. No biking or skiing is allowed.

**For Further Information:** Forest Park Nature Center, 5809 Forest Park Drive, Peoria Heights, IL 61614; 309-686-3360 or www.peoriaparks.org/fpnc.

## Park Trails

**Pimiteoui Trail (Forest Park Section)** (🥾🥾🥾🥾, 2.5 miles). This 1.25-mile linear trail begins south of the nature center. The trail hikes along the top of a bluff. Lots of wildflowers can be found along this trail during spring.

## Other Areas of Interest

North of I-74 in East Peoria, **Bennett's Terraqueous Gardens** is a small remnant of a seep, complete with spring runs. A boardwalk provides the opportunity for close views of marsh marigold and skunk cabbage. The area is maintained by the Fond du Lac Park District. For more information, call 309-699-3923.

Located in northeastern Peoria, **Detweiller Park** contains play areas, a golf course, BMX competition area, an archery range, and a nature preserve. The preserve has lush, spring-blooming wildflowers and two trails, the Ridgetop and Pimiteoui. The area is maintained by the Peoria Park District. For more information, call 309-682-1200.

**Wildlife Prairie Park,** 10 miles west of Peoria, is home to bison, bobcat, badger, and 30 other species of mammals that are or were native to Illinois. The grounds are a reclaimed strip mine; native vegetation is once again encouraged. The park includes a visitor center, restaurant, small railroad, and a gift shop. In 10 miles of trails, visit the animals and tour the park grounds. The longest trail is 4 miles. For more information, call 309-682-1200.

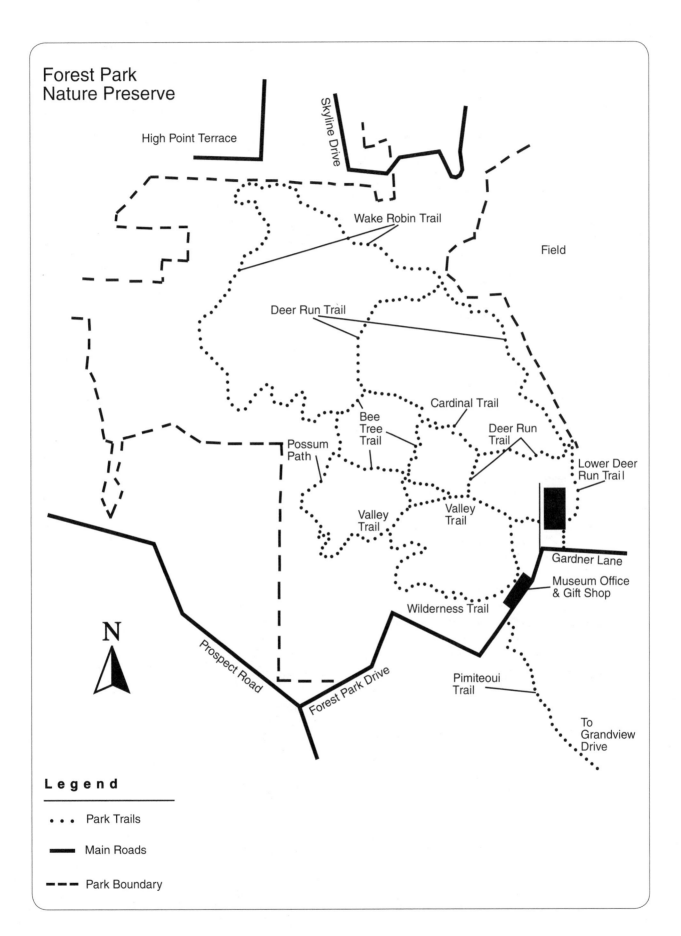

Forest Park
Nature Preserve

High Point Terrace

Skyline Drive

Wake Robin Trail

Field

Deer Run Trail

Cardinal Trail

Bee
Tree
Trail

Deer Run
Trail

Lower Deer
Run Trail

Possum
Path

Valley
Trail

Valley
Trail

Gardner Lane

Museum Office
& Gift Shop

Wilderness Trail

N

Prospect Road

Forest Park Drive

Pimiteoui
Trail

To
Grandview
Drive

**Legend**

. . . Park Trails

━━━ Main Roads

- - - Park Boundary

# Inside Trail
# (Several Combined)

 **Distance Round-Trip:** 1.75 miles
**Estimated Hiking Time:** 1 hour

*Hiking the trails at Forest Park is like riding a roller coaster—up one ridge, then down another, back up again, and around a switchback. All that's missing is an upside-down loop-the-loop!*

**Caution:** The trail can be very muddy. Logs sometimes block the trail and roots are exposed.

**Trail Directions:** The trail begins at the southwest corner of the parking lot. The first trail marker is for the Wilderness Trail [1]. Take advantage of several listening points along the trail, defined in the trail brochure as "places of quiet where the world can be contemplated with awe." At the start, before crossing a bridge, note a tree with three huge trunks on your right. At .15 mi. [2] begin an upward climb on a series of switchbacks (zigzag trails to help the climb). On the climb, enjoy the view of the valley below.

The trail emerges on a ridgetop, and you soon encounter the first listening point [3] (.3 mi.). The trail descends, intersecting at .4 mi. [4] with another; go left, winding along a creek on your left. The trail has changed names; it is now called Possum Path (.6 mi.). Along here note the large boulders in the forest understory [5]. Called glacial erratics, the boulders lie scattered where the glaciers left them.

At 1 mi. the trail becomes Bee Tree and forks to the right or straight; proceed straight ahead [6]. As you hike, look for familiar wildflowers, but notice the absence of ferns. This is a drier woods, and ferns in the understory have been replaced with woodland grasses and sedges. At 1.2 mi. [7] you will come to two more intersections. Bee Tree Trail intersects with Wake Robin; continue on Bee Tree, going straight. After a few yards the Bee Tree Trail intersects with Deer Run; go to your right and continue to hike on Bee Tree.

Pause at the River Outlook [8] (1.3 mi.) for a great view of the Illinois River Valley. From this vantage point the water is a deep blue and looks like a distant lake. The trail begins a descent and soon intersects with Cardinal Trail. Go straight on Cardinal Trail and continue to walk downward over a series of switchbacks.

While hiking, you'll pass several restoration areas. Although the hike appears to be only woods, on top of the south-facing ridges there used to be hill prairies. Fires are helping to bring the prairie plants back and restore this habitat. Cardinal Trail soon becomes Deer Run, and you have the option of going left or right. Go right [9] (1.5 mi.) and soon you'll enter a prairie restoration on the right.

At 1.6 mi. [10] Deer Run makes a T into Valley Trail; go left on Valley Trail and follow it back to the nature center where you can log in your miles as a new member of the Hundred-Mile Hikers.

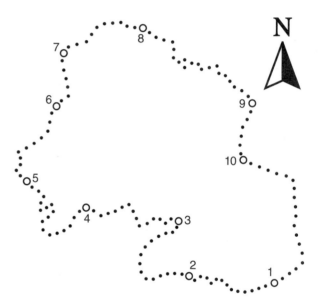

1. Start
2. Switchbacks
3. Listening point
4. Left turn
5. Large boulders
6. Go straight
7. Go straight
8. River Outlook
9. Right turn
10. Left turn

# Outside Trail
# (Several Combined)

**Distance Round-Trip:** 2.75 miles
**Estimated Hiking Time:**
1.25 hours

*The path is covered with an artist's palette of reds, yellows, oranges, and greens, creating a blanket of color throughout the trail.*

**Caution:** The trail can be very muddy. Logs sometimes block the trail and tree roots are exposed. Several stream crossings must be navigated on slippery rocks.

**Trail Directions:** Begin the trail behind the nature center [1]. Note the listening points scattered throughout the trail, usually adorned with a bench. The trail, marked with an occasional arrow and the trail's name, begins as a fairly wide path but soon narrows at the base of a bluff.

Before the first listening point, the trail intersects with the Valley Trail; take the Valley Trail. At .1 mi. [2] it intersects with Deer Run Trail. Continue straight on Valley Trail. On your right is a prairie restoration. Within .05 mi. Valley Trail and Valley Loop intersect; continue straight and head upward through a rolling oak, hickory, and maple forest.

At .25 mi. [3] cross a bridge and continue straight. You are now on Bee Tree Trail and are continuing the upward trek. Notice the restoration work in this area—the use of fire and selective plant removal—to bring the area back to original conditions. At the top of the climb [4] (.5 mi.), stay on Bee Tree and go to your right. Within a few steps the trail again intersects another one; this time go left on Wake Robin Trail.

Wildflowers are abundant here in the spring. Dutchman's breeches are everywhere; mayapple, bloodroot, and prairie trilliums (also called wake robins) are also fairly common.

As you begin the Wake Robin Trail, hike along the edge of a ridge. Note the shaggy bark of the shagbark hickory in this dry forest. Log steps lead down the ridge, and within .1 mi. you can cross a creek on a makeshift bridge of logs and stones [5] (.75 mi.). Scramble up the other side and go to the right, heading back uphill. At .9 mi. the trail is again on top of a ridge. Look off into the distance; when there are no leaves on the trees, you can see the Illinois River Valley far below [6]. You will also encounter a trail marker near here; go right.

At 1.4 mi. you reach the Wake Robin Listening Point [7]. On either side is an oak-hickory forest; straight ahead is a deep, cool ravine with sycamores and a creek. Begin the descent using steps and enter a ravine forest. Gone are the big oaks, and in their place are sycamores, cottonwoods, and maples. Look for the yellow blossoms of buttercup here in the spring and

in summer the flowers of blue lobelia. This is also a favorite area of wild turkeys.

Cross the creek [8] (1.5 mi.) and scramble up the other side. Note the row of large trees—perhaps part of the original forest. They stand out because the other trees are much smaller. In this section of the trail you can also see the many vines that use the trees for support as they reach for the sun. The vines provide food and cover for animals and enhance the habitat.

Cross another creek [9] (1.65 mi.), this time on stepping-stones. Within .1 mi. the trail intersects with Deer Run Trail; continue hiking straight and you'll reach a farmstead on the left. Remember that the preserve was grazed and is just now recovering. Within a few steps the trail curves to the right. The forest has given way to an old field that has grown up, and you are hiking through maple and elm. Soon the narrow path reenters the bluff forest.

At 2 mi., come upon another listening point [10], and a few yards away note a pair of large, open-grown oaks (wolf trees) on the left. One has a large hole that provides a nesting place for small mammals and a home for a species of mosquito.

Deer Run Trail divides [11] (2.25 mi.). Take the path to the right and climb uphill. Within .25 mi. you encounter another intersection [12]; proceed to your left, still on Deer Run Trail. At .1 mi. you are back to [2]; go left and retrace your steps back to the nature center. Just outside it, watch the antics of chipmunks as they steal seed from the numerous birdfeeders.

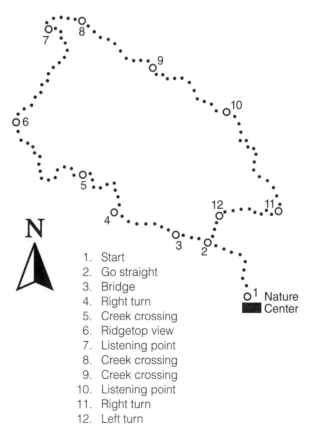

1. Start
2. Go straight
3. Bridge
4. Right turn
5. Creek crossing
6. Ridgetop view
7. Listening point
8. Creek crossing
9. Creek crossing
10. Listening point
11. Right turn
12. Left turn

# 25. Sand Ridge State Forest

- Climb a 60-foot-high sand dune in central Illinois.
- Bring your butterfly field guide for the hairstreaks, checkerspots, and fritillaries that crowd the summer blossoms.
- Relive a piece of botanical history and walk in the footsteps of the famous botanist Henry A. Gleason.
- Celebrate the beginning of summer with the waxy yellow blossoms of prickly pear cactus.
- Enjoy different types of fall colors—russet prairie grass, red-brown blackjack oak, and gray-green prickly pear.

## Area Information

The gently rolling sand dunes, expanses of oak-hickory forest, and stretches of sand prairie found at Sand Ridge State Forest contrast sharply with the black-soil landscape of central Illinois. The sand, deposited in the Illinois River Valley a few thousand years ago by the meltwaters of the Wisconsin glacier, creates a special home for a unique collection of plants and animals. The flora here is a combination of plants common to the tallgrass prairie of Illinois—little bluestem, butterfly weed, and rough blazing star—and Western plants usually associated with drier, open habitats—prickly pear cactus and silvery bladderpod.

The growing conditions here are strikingly different from those found on the black-soil prairies. Although the sandy areas receive the same amounts of heat, light, rainfall, and wind as the rest of the state, they experience larger variations in day-to-night and surface-to-subsoil temperatures. The water-holding capacity of the sandy soil is very low, and in open areas the surface sand is constantly shifting, sometimes forming dunes or blowouts (areas where the sand and vegetation are blown away by the wind).

Sand Ridge may be unique in its desertlike plant communities, but to an entomologist it is the butterflies that make it special, especially during mid- to late June. Butterfly weed is in full bloom and crowding the blossoms are hairstreaks, each small, gray-brown, and fast flying. Vying for space between the hairstreaks and checkerspots resides a treasure—regal fritillaries. As long as the sun is out, the regals "dance through the scrubby sand prairie vegetation; when the sun goes in, they magically disappear." All these contribute to the landscape that Gleason found so fascinating and explored for nearly 60 years.

**Directions:** Sand Ridge State Forest is located in Mason County, about 25 miles southwest of Peoria. Follow Illinois Route 136 to Mason County Road 2800 E and turn north. Continue in a straight line for about 6 miles, through the village of Forest City. This road turns west and becomes Mason County Road 2300 N and leads directly into the forest. The Henry Allan Gleason Nature Preserve is on the western edge of Sand Ridge State Forest.

**Hours Open:** The site is open year-round.

**Facilities:** A picnic area has grills, water, toilets, and a shelter. Campsites feature water, pit toilets, and a dump station. There is no electricity. Group camping and equestrian camping are also available. Hand trap range, hunting, horse trails, cross-country ski trails, and snowmobiling are also featured.

**Permits and Rules:** No horses or pets are allowed in Henry Allan Gleason Nature Preserve. In other areas of the forest pets must be leashed at all times.

**For Further Information:** Sand Ridge State Forest, P.O. Box 111, Forest City, IL 61532; 309-597-2212.

## Park Trails

Sand Ridge offers 44 miles of marked trails, ranging from 1.6 to 17 miles each, and 120 miles of fire lanes that offer plenty of hiking opportunities. The majority of the trails are on sand and are shared by horses.

## Other Areas of Interest

**Chautauqua National Wildlife Refuge** is located in Mason County; some of the greatest concentrations of wild ducks and geese along the Illinois River can be observed here each fall and winter. In addition to wildlife watching, the refuge offers fishing, mushroom and berry picking, boat access, and hunting. An interpretive hiking trail is located at the site headquarters and several trails are in development for this site. For more information, call 309-535-2290.

**Dickson Mounds Museum** is located between Lewistown and Havana. This museum is a center for study and interpretation of the prehistory of the Illinois River Valley. Here you can explore the world of native Americans that lived in the Illinois River Valley. For more information, call 309-547-3721.

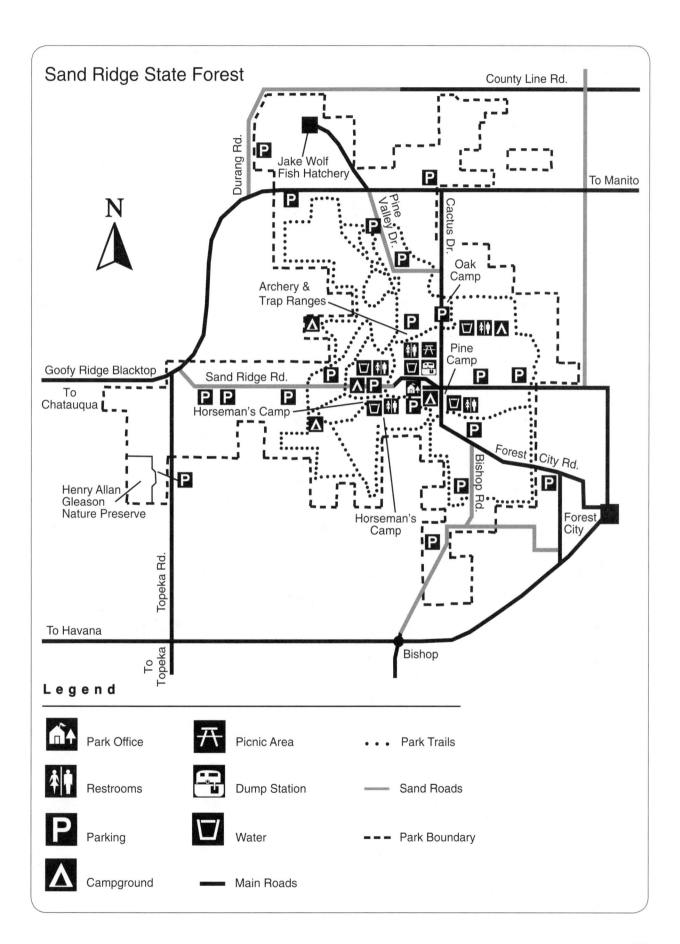

Sand Ridge State Forest

County Line Rd.

Durang Rd.

N

Jake Wolf
Fish Hatchery

To Manito

Pine Valley Dr.

Cactus Dr.

Oak
Camp

Archery &
Trap Ranges

Pine
Camp

Goofy Ridge Blacktop

Sand Ridge Rd.

To
Chatauqua

Horseman's Camp

Bishop Rd.

Forest City Rd.

Henry Allan
Gleason
Nature Preserve

Forest
City

Horseman's
Camp

Topeka Rd.

To Havana

Bishop

To Topeka

**Legend**

| | | | | |
|---|---|---|---|---|
| Park Office | | Picnic Area | | • • • Park Trails |
| Restrooms | | Dump Station | | —— Sand Roads |
| P Parking | | Water | | - - - Park Boundary |
| Campground | | —— Main Roads | | |

# Sand Ridge State Forest Sampler

**Distance Round-Trip:** 3.5 miles
**Estimated Hiking Time:** 1.5 hours

*A perfect late-fall hike, but not quite a blue-sky day, finds acorns and hickory nuts scattered along the trail. Bright orange bittersweet dangles from branches, and even a few turkey feathers litter the path. It puts one in a Thanksgiving kind of mood.*

**Caution:** The trail is sand and can sometimes be very hard to negotiate. Horses also use parts of the trail, so watch where you step. Take water on this hike!

**Trail Directions:** To reach the trailhead, take a right (north) on Cactus Drive 2600 E; drive past the archery ranges and oak camp. Take a left onto Pine Valley Drive; the trailhead is at the first parking area. Begin the trail at a brown post with an orange arrow and brown square (the first half of the hike will be marked with brown); skirt the road and within a few steps go left at a post with an arrow [1]. The trail is at first a grassy path but will soon become sand. The trail is crisscrossed with the mounds of pocket gophers. This is the only type of gopher that lives in Illinois. These underground-dwelling mammals live in areas where the soil is well drained, with an abundance of tuberous-rooted plants.

At .1 mi. the blue and brown trails intersect; continue straight on the brown trail [2]. The path has narrowed and you are heading up through an oak-hickory forest. Another marker appears at .2 mi.; continue straight. The oak forest is dominated by blackjack, black, and white oak. Take a few minutes to study these trees. Blackjack oak leaves are broadly triangular with three lobes (they resemble ducks' feet), and the acorns are often faintly striped with a cap of reddish-brown scales. White oak has seven to nine deep lobes on the leaves, and the acorns have knobby caps. Black oak has five to seven bristle-tipped lobes in the leaves, and the acorn caps have scales that form a slight fringe at the cup margin.

Notice how the non-native pines are beginning to colonize the oak forest. At the intersection at .4 mi. continue straight, passing a campsite on your left [3]. The trail descends and you are hiking down an old sand dune. The trail passes through the remnants of an old gate at .65 mi.; go right, still hiking on the brown trail [4]. The trail has widened and you are hiking through an old dune field.

At 1 mi. you will have a pine plantation on your left and an oak forest on your right [5]. The pines were planted to stabilize the dunes, but if you look to your right the native vegetation has stabilized this

area without the help of the non-native pines. At 1.3 mi. the blue and brown trails intersect again; go left, staying on the brown trail [6]. The trail emerges onto the road at 1.45 mi. [7]; go right and through the parking area and go back into the woods at the kiosk on the green trail [8]. The trail will now be marked with green arrows.

The green trail is for hikers only, and you will pass through an oak-pine forest with an understory of honeysuckle. At 1.7 mi. the trail winds through a Halloweenesque forest of tall cedar [9]. Within a few steps you will cross a fire lane; the green trail marker is on the opposite side. You will cross another fire lane at 2.1 mi. [10]; again, enter on the other side. The trail curves left as it winds through the pines.

At 2.25 mi. come to another fire lane and follow it for a few steps [11]; then enter the woods again, keeping with the green markers. You are soon hiking up a stabilized dune. A campsite appears on your right at 2.5 mi. [12]. The sand dunes are evident all around you as you hike on this rolling terrain. The trail curves left and begins to head down at 2.6 mi., and sand prairie soon becomes evident [13]. Look for switchgrass and round-headed bush clover. Patches of prickly pear cactus will soon be evident.

You will come to an intersection at 3.25 mi.; take the second left (sign), passing patches of cactus [14]. Another quarter of a mile and you are back to the parking area. Empty the sand from your shoes and you are finished.

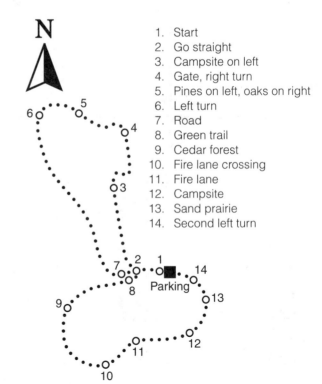

1. Start
2. Go straight
3. Campsite on left
4. Gate, right turn
5. Pines on left, oaks on right
6. Left turn
7. Road
8. Green trail
9. Cedar forest
10. Fire lane crossing
11. Fire lane
12. Campsite
13. Sand prairie
14. Second left turn

# Henry Allan Gleason Nature Preserve

  **Distance Round-Trip:** 1.15 miles
**Estimated Hiking Time:** .75 hour

*Botanist Henry A. Gleason, known worldwide for his publication* Gleason and Cronquist Manual of the Vascular Plants of Northeastern United States and Adjacent Canada, *explored the sand areas around Havana in the early 1900s while a student at the University of Illinois. Let's retrace his steps to discover and explore Devil's Neck.*

**Caution:** There is no formal trail, but the well-worn path is easy to follow. Stay on this trail because too many offshoots will damage the habitat.

**Trail Directions:** Park at the sign off Topeka Road for the Henry Allan Gleason Nature Preserve and begin the trail here [1]. At .1 mi. you should encounter a brown Illinois Nature Preserve sign. This will also be the first indication that you are about to explore an unusual area. A large dune, about 60 feet high and covered with prickly pear cactus and little bluestem, looms in front. Enter through the gate [2] and head up the well-worn path over the sand dune.

At .2 mi., enter a grove of blackjack oak. Take a look at their leaves, said to resemble ducks' feet. At .25 mi. you are high enough on the dune to enjoy a vista of the farmland far below. The vegetation around you consists of switchgrass, little bluestem, an occasional blackjack oak, and the ever-present cactus. Take an abrupt right [3] and continue to follow the faint trail.

You are skirting the large dune on your left. Along the trail during May, look for sand phlox and puccoon. By the end of summer these have been replaced by rough blazing star and round-headed bush clover. At .4 mi. you will come to a trail intersection; go left and up the dune [4]. Once you are on top, the trail disappears. Go to your right (gently) and explore Devil's Neck, the 60-foot-high dune overlooking the Illinois River Valley.

Gleason wrote about his first visit here on August 17, 1904: "By far the most interesting visit was to the Devil's Neck, a large wild expanse of blow sand, where we found many interesting things, especially unlimited quantities of *Cristatella jamesii* [a species of clammyweed] and a few plants of *Lesquerella spathulata* [silvery bladderpod] hitherto known only from Northwestern Nebraska and Montana."

Go right, walking along the top, and at .5 mi. go down into the blowout on the left, being careful not to disturb the sand [5]. If your visit happens to be in May, look for the silvery bladderpod—a yellow mustard. Although the plant is not the typical showy wildflower, it is important. This is its only location for hundreds of miles; the only other eastern site for this plant is in Minnesota. Head across the blowout to further explore the area. Go right again and begin to walk along the rim. Look for showy orange butterfly weed, listen for the call of the dickcissel, watch for the colorful wings of grasshoppers, and observe sulfur, buckeye, and monarch butterflies. Hike the perimeter of the blowout until you are near the point where you descended into it. From here take one final look at the impressive view and go left and back down the dune. Soon you will be back at [4].

Go left and continue on the original path. The trail ends at a fence [6] (.75 mi.). Climb over the chain and go right, walking on an old road that skirts the preserve. As you walk, look for another mustard, less rare and less welcome—garlic mustard—a non-native plant that is taking over many of Illinois' woodlands.

Shortly after receiving the news that the sand dune where he first saw *Lesquerella* in Illinois would be a nature preserve named after him, Gleason wrote to the chairman of the Nature Preserves Commission, "Sixty-seven years have rolled by since my first discovery of *Lesquerella* in Illinois. We had no cars in those days, and my trips entailed a four-mile walk out, another one back, and probably five or six hours work on those bare dunes of sun-burnt sand. But when I was last there, in 1966, *Lesquerella* was still growing on top of the highest dune as before, and doubtless has been growing since the Xerothermic Period, at least five thousand years ago."

At 1.05 mi. you are back at [2]; go left and retrace your steps to the parking area. Although this hike wasn't long in space, you hiked into a piece of the state's botanical history, back through the time of Gleason, and back at least 5,000 years.

1. Start
2. Gate
3. Right turn
4. Left turn up dune
5. Blowout
6. Fence

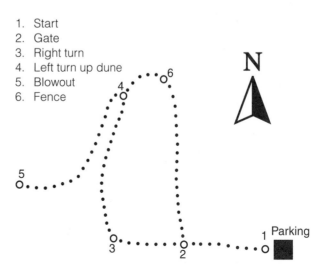

# 26. Starved Rock State Park

- For a challenge, in and out of canyons, up and down steps, and along ridgetops suitable for a mountain goat, the trails of Starved Rock State Park will test any hiker's nimbleness.

- During the winter, canyon trails lead to canyon waterfalls that have become icefalls—huge, statuesque, sculpted towers of ice.

- If you are satiated with the wide vistas of the Illinois landscape, the canyons and imposing walls of Starved Rock State Park afford welcome relief.

- Find harebell, reindeer lichen, yew, and mountain holly on the cool, craggy surfaces of the canyons. Called survivor species, these plants were left behind when the last glaciers receded.

## Area Information

Starved Rock and the adjacent canyons are eroded from porous St. Peter sandstone, laid down millions of years ago by a shallow inland sea. The sandstone was brought to the surface as a result of a huge upfold, known as the LaSalle Anticline. Streams have cut across the anticline and sunk their channels to considerable depth, giving rise to narrow, blind canyons and cliffs, surrounded by a closed canopy forest.

Waterfalls are found at most canyon heads. By summer these falls have slowed to a mere trickle or completely dried up. The waterfall at St. Louis Canyon is the exception. Fed by springs, this canyon stream never dries up, and in winter its fall is transformed into a column of ice, enhanced and constantly changed by water continuously trickling down the column and freezing.

Water falling on the porous sandstone rock quickly soaks in; thus, the sandy surface remains essentially dry. The plant communities found in the canyons are restricted to those species able to gain a foothold on the steep rock walls—usually lower forms of plant life—such as liverwort, grasping the canyon walls like moist fingers. At least one-third of all Illinois' fern species are part of the flora of Starved Rock.

Whether you want to hike the many trails, observe the waterfalls and unique flora, or simply enjoy the entertainment of chipmunks cavorting among the crevices and along the trails, Starved Rock State Park is a unique area of Illinois.

**Directions:** The park is located on the south bank of the Illinois River. From I-80 take Route 178 south to the entrance. From I-39 follow State Route 71 through Oglesby to the park entrance.

**Hours Open:** The site is open year-round from 5:00 a.m. to 9:00 p.m. except on Thanksgiving, Christmas Day, and New Year's Day. Trail parking lots are open from 8:00 a.m. to sunset. During deer season some park trails may be closed. The visitor center is open from 9:00 a.m. to 4:00 p.m. daily; it is closed during the aforementioned holidays.

**Facilities:** A visitor center, campground, lodge, and conference center are available, as well as boating and fishing activities.

**Permits and Rules:** Climbing, rappelling, and scrambling on the rocks are prohibited. Bicycles are not allowed on the hiking trails. Pets must be leashed at all times. Hikers must be off the trails by dark. Do not attempt to wade or swim in the river, in the canyon streams, or from any park shoreline.

**For Further Information:** Starved Rock State Park, P.O. Box 509, Utica, IL 61373; 815-667-4726.

## Tips on Interpreting Trail Signs

Trail maps are located at all trail access points, intersections, and points of interest to help keep you track. Colored dots and posts along the trails correspond to the colors found on the maps. (Brown dots or posts indicate bluff trails; red dots or posts are for river trails, and green dots or posts indicate interior canyons or connecting trails.) Finally, yellow dots on trees or posts show that you are moving away from the lodge or visitor center; white dots mean you are returning.

## Park Trails

**St. Louis Canyon** (🥾🥾🥾, 3 miles). If you begin at the visitor center, this 1.5-mile linear trail will take you though Aurora, Sac, Kickapoo, and St. Louis canyons. While the trail may be linear, it follows the twists and turns of the landscape. During the winter the frozen falls of St. Louis Canyon are spectacular and they are off limits to ice climbers. St. Louis Canyon can also be accessed off Route 178, where there is a parking area and trail.

## Other Areas of Interest

Starved Rock State Park is located adjacent to Matthiessen State Park.

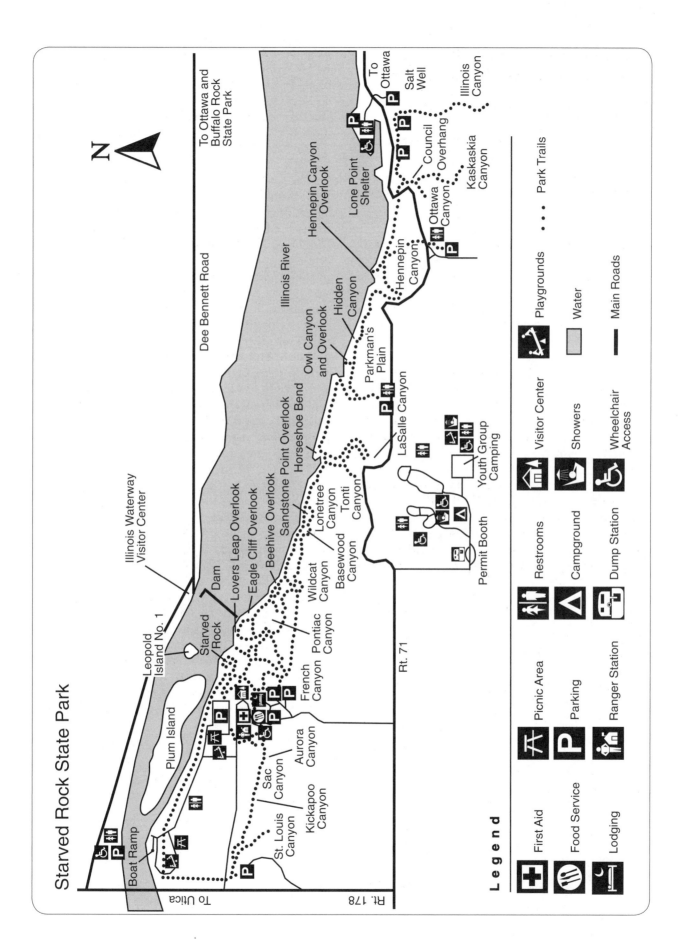

# Starved Rock State Park

N

To Ottawa and Buffalo Rock State Park

Dee Bennett Road

Illinois River

Illinois Waterway Visitor Center

Leopold Island No. 1

Starved Rock

Dam

Plum Island

Boat Ramp

To Utica

Rt. 178

Lovers Leap Overlook
Eagle Cliff Overlook
Beehive Overlook
Sandstone Point Overlook
Horseshoe Bend

Owl Canyon and Overlook
Hidden Canyon
Parkman's Plain

Hennepin Canyon Overlook
Lone Point Shelter

Hennepin Canyon
Ottawa Canyon
Council Overhang
Salt Well
To Ottawa

Kaskaskia Canyon
Illinois Canyon

LaSalle Canyon

Wildcat Canyon
Basewood Canyon
Lonetree Canyon
Tonti Canyon
Pontiac Canyon

French Canyon

Aurora Canyon
Sac Canyon
Kickapoo Canyon
St. Louis Canyon

Rt. 71

Youth Group Camping
Permit Booth

# Legend

| | | | | | |
|---|---|---|---|---|---|
| ✚ First Aid | 🅰 Picnic Area | 🚻 Restrooms | 🏚 Visitor Center | ⛷ Playgrounds | |
| 🍽 Food Service | 🅿 Parking | ⛺ Campground | 🚿 Showers | ▒ Water | |
| 🛏 Lodging | 🏚 Ranger Station | 🚽 Dump Station | ♿ Wheelchair Access | — Main Roads | |

··· Park Trails

# Starved Rock, Sandstone Point, and LaSalle Canyon

**Distance Round-Trip:**
5.5 miles
**Estimated Hiking Time:**
2.5 hours

*During a January thaw, the air smells of spring. A blanket of newly fallen snow covers the canyon floors, erasing any trace of previous visitors. You feel like an early traveler, discovering the canyons for the very first time.*

**Caution:** Use extreme caution on the steps during the winter; they can be very icy. During summer, moss growing on them can also cause slick conditions. Hike only where there are trails.

**Trail Directions:** Begin at the north entrance of the visitor center and go left on a paved path [1]. After a few steps, find a trail board (map). The trails are well marked, and maps of the area appear frequently at intersections. At .1 mi. [2] go left up steps and uphill to Starved Rock, a sandstone bluff that is 125 feet above the Illinois River. At the top [3] a boardwalk with signage explains the significance of this rock. After exploring the top, retrace your steps back to [2] and go left, following the path toward the canyons.

At .6 mi. [4] a trail map appears; go to the right and take a side trip to French's Canyon. This part of the hike will be marked with green poles. Proceed to the end of the canyon and enter it using steps carved into the sandstone. The trail is a narrow path that dead-ends at a waterfall. At the canyon's end [5] (.75 mi.) retrace your steps to the main trail and take a right to Lovers Leap and Eagle Cliff [6] (.9 mi.).

At 1.1 mi. go left [7]; the trail leads you through a barrens area. At 1.2 mi. the trail has reached Lovers

Leap [8] and the first of several overlooks of the river. Retrace your steps to the trail. Continue along the bluffs to Eagle Cliff. At 1.5 mi. the river (red) and a connecting trail (green) intersect [9]; go left, downhill, toward the river and hike along the riverbank. Cross a wooden bridge, come to a trail split, and go left, up the steps to Beehive Overlook [10] (1.7 mi.). Admire the view and descend on the opposite side. Soon you will cross a bridge over Wildcat Canyon.

At the intersection at 1.8 mi., continue on the path along the river [11]. Sandstone Point, where the river meets the bluff, is at 2.2 mi. [12]. A few steps past Sandstone Point, you will cross a bridge. Another bridge across an unnamed canyon will soon appear on your right at 2.4 mi.

At 2.5 mi. find a trail junction with a map [13]. Take the right fork and do not cross the arched bridge in front of you. At 2.65 mi. is another intersection; go right [14]; using a series of steps and bridges, the trail will dead-end into Tonti Canyon [15], the deepest canyon of the park. Retrace your steps to [14] (3 mi.) and go right to a trail that leads into LaSalle Canyon. The trail winds around a bluff and comes perilously close to the edge. At 3.2 mi. [16] you will come upon LaSalle Canyon and its falls. The trail skirts the overhang, enabling you to walk behind the falls. Soon the trail leads to the arched bridge that is now on your left [17] (3.6 mi.).

Cross the bridge and continue walking straight on the trail back to the Bluff Trail at 4 mi. Go left onto Bluff Trail and up 155 steps [18]. The trail will be marked with brown posts. From the top of Bluff Trail you are looking down into Lone Tree Canyon. A side spur to Sandstone Point Overlook will appear on your right. As you continue on the Bluff Trail, you will look into Basswood Canyon at 4.3 mi. [19].

At 4.5 mi., find a boardwalk; go right to view Wildcat Canyon [20], then retrace your steps back to the trail, which circles the canyon. The trail comes to a T at 4.6 mi.; go right [21]. At 5 mi. find a series of intersections; first go right and then, after a few steps, go left, and soon you are back at the visitor center.

1. Start
2. Stairs to Starved Rock
3. Starved Rock
4. Right turn
5. French's Canyon
6. Right turn
7. Left turn
8. Lovers Leap
9. Left turn
10. Beehive Overlook
11. Path along river
12. Sandstone Point
13. Right turn
14. Right turn
15. Tonti Canyon
16. LaSalle Canyon
17. Bridge
18. Left turn onto Bluff Trail
19. Basswood Canyon
20. Wildcat Canyon
21. Right turn

## Canyon Sampler— Owl to Illinois

 **Distance Round-Trip:** 6.8 miles
**Estimated Hiking Time:** 3 hours

*From my treetop viewpoint at an overlook, a bald eagle is almost eye to eye, and white pelicans floating down the Illinois River look like bathtub toys.*

**Caution:** The trail will cross a park entrance road, so watch for cars. There are several sections of the trail with tree roots.

**Trail Directions:** Take Route 71 and park at Parkman's Plain (restrooms open from May to October), and begin the trail at the trail board [1]. The trail starts out as gravel but will soon be either dirt or sand. You are hiking on a bluff but will soon descend into the canyons. Ignore several side trails as you start out.

After coming to a bridge and going down steps, you will come to a trail sign; go right and cross a stream (flowing in spring) [2] (.2 mi.). At .4 mi. go left to the overlook for Owl Canyon [3]; retrace your steps to the intersection and go left, continuing on the trail. As you undulate up and down the trail, you are able to peer into canyons and crevices. Through the trees on the left is a view of the river. At 1 mi. at an intersection, go right [4]. Hennepin Canyon will be on your left. Within .1 mi. is a bridge overlook into the canyon. Off the bridge, go left.

At 1.4 mi. you will cross a bridge; on your left are a series of "bathtubs" [5], which are circular pools eroded into the sandstone. Off the bridge, go up and left at the intersection to Hennepin Canyon Overlook; retrace your steps back to the intersection and go straight. An intersection with the Hennepin parking lot will appear at 1.5 mi.; continue straight along the

river. You will cross the road at 1.9 mi. [6] (don't forget to look both ways); go down on the other side.

A huge sandstone wall materializes on the right. This is Council Overhang. At the intersection (2 mi.), go right to a shelter cave, then take another right after descending the steps [7], and make one more right [8] as you hike to Ottawa Canyon. The trail will dead-end into the bowl of the canyon [9]. Retrace your steps to [8] and go right into Kaskaskia Canyon. The trail will dead-end in Kaskaskia Canyon with its small waterfall [10] (2.5 mi.). At one of the sand piles in the canyon, try to pick up a pinch of sand between your fingers. You cannot hang on to it because the grains are circular instead of angular. This is a characteristic of St. Peter sandstone.

Retrace your steps to [7], going right back up the stairs. At 2.9 mi. the trail Ys; go right [11] and over a bridge. At 3 mi. you will come to an intersection; go left [12] through a parking area. The trail will continue at the east end of the parking lot. You are walking through a floodplain forest. Within .25 mi. the trail comes out onto another parking lot [13]; cross it and rejoin the trail at the opposite end of the lot. You are now on the trail to Illinois Canyon.

You will cross a stream at least three times before finally ending at Illinois Canyon [14] (3.9 mi.). Now for the fun part, retrace your steps back to the parking area. After [12], continue to Ottawa Canyon and the overhang. At 5 mi. you will go up stairs, cross the road, and go up more stairs on the opposite side [6]. Continue straight past Hennepin Canyon parking. At 5.5 mi., go left at the Hennepin Canyon Overlook, bypassing the overlook this time. Have you noticed that even though you are retracing your steps, the scenery looks different? The final steps up and out of Owl Canyon are at 6.6 mi. Soon you are back at the trail board and parking lot.

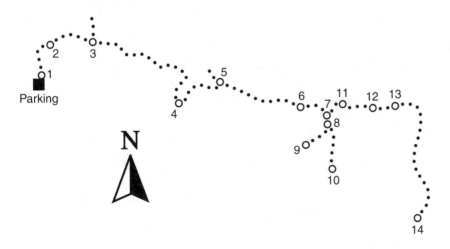

1. Start
2. Right turn, cross stream
3. Owl Canyon
4. Right turn
5. Bathtubs
6. Road crossing
7. Right turn, right turn
8. Right turn
9. Ottawa Canyon
10. Kaskaskia Canyon
11. Right turn
12. Left turn through parking lot
13. Parking lot
14. Illinois Canyon

# 27. Matthiessen State Park

- Revel in a geological paradise of sandstone canyons gracefully carved by flowing water.

- Discover Devil's Paint Box, Giant's Bathtub, and Cascade Falls.

- Enjoy the cool, moist canyons where mosses, ferns, and liverworts cover the walls and frogs, toads, and salamanders find refuge on the canyon floors.

- Relax in the park's serene beauty and solitude.

- Explore waterfalls that turn into icefalls each winter.

## Area Information

Formed by water erosion, the canyons of Matthiessen State Park (cut from St. Peter sandstone) consist of two levels, the Upper and Lower Dells. Water-based activity is constant in the canyon; as groundwater seeps from the canyon walls, it evaporates and deposits the minerals it carried to add color to the canyon walls.

Huge deer populations enjoyed these mineral deposits, called licks, and led to the park's first name—Deer Park. The original owner of the park was Frederick Matthiessen. With a large work crew, he oversaw the construction of the park's first bridges, trails, and stairways; some of these are still in use today.

Matthiessen State Park is just as spectacular as its sister park, Starved Rock, but less crowded. Here you can relax and enjoy the spring and summer wildflowers along the trails. During twilight hours, be on the lookout for flying squirrels.

**Directions:** Matthiessen State Park, located in central LaSalle County on State Route 178, can be easily reached from both Interstate 39 and 80.

**Hours Open:** The site is open year-round except on Christmas Day and New Year's Day. Trails cannot be accessed after dark and are closed during deer season.

**Facilities:** Picnic area, toilets, a restored fort, horseback riding, a field archery range, and a radio-controlled model airplane field are available. During winter weekends, cross-country skis may be rented.

**Permits and Rules:** No camping, rappelling, or rock or ice climbing are allowed. Do not remove any archeological material of Native American origin. All pets must be leashed. No off-trail hiking, and you must be off the trails by dark.

**For Further Information:** Matthiessen State Park, Box 509, Utica, IL 61373; 815-667-4868.

## Other Areas of Interest

Matthiessen State Park is located adjacent to Starved Rock State Park.

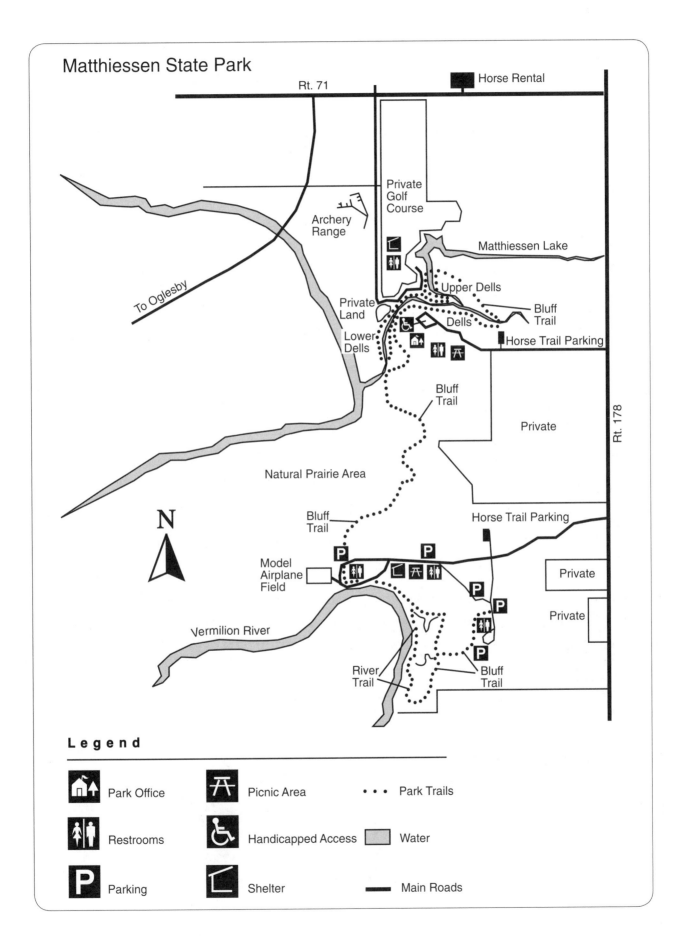

# Matthiessen State Park

Rt. 71

Horse Rental

Private Golf Course

Matthiessen Lake

Archery Range

To Oglesby

Upper Dells

Bluff Trail

Private Land

Dells

Lower Dells

Horse Trail Parking

Bluff Trail

Private

Natural Prairie Area

Bluff Trail

Horse Trail Parking

Rt. 178

N

Model Airplane Field

P

P

Private

P

Private

P

P

Vermilion River

P

River Trail

Bluff Trail

**Legend**

| | | |
|---|---|---|
| Park Office | Picnic Area | • • • Park Trails |
| Restrooms | Handicapped Access | Water |
| P Parking | Shelter | — Main Roads |

# Dells Trail

 **Distance Round-Trip:** 3 miles
**Estimated Hiking Time:** 1.5 hours

*Even though the Dells Trail of Matthiessen State Park
has icefalls in the winter, the water does not give up easily
and continues to flow, eroding the ice. As a result, huge
chunks of ice crack off and tumble into the canyon, leading
the imagination to places far away where pieces of glaciers
break off and tumble into the sea.*

**Caution:** The trails crisscross slippery streambeds,
giving a high probability of wet feet.

**Trail Directions:** The trail is marked with trail maps
at intersections. Begin the trail at the reconstructed
fort, northwest of the parking area. Descend a long
staircase to a bridge; a trail-map board is to your right
[1]. Cross the bridge and proceed to the right; ignore
the staircase going down on your far right.

At .25 mi. come to a trail junction [2]; go to your
right. The forest, which had been dominated by oaks,
is now a mixed woods with pines. The trail follows
a ridge between two deep canyons. At .4 mi. a series
of steps lead down. At the bottom a sign points right
to Cedar Point; go left [3], and soon you are hiking
through a narrow canyon, looking upward at the
sandstone bluffs.

The trail leads through a boulder-strewn streambed
to a waterfall. Climb a set of steps to the left and walk
into the streambed [4] (.55 mi.). You are now atop
Giant's Bathtub. Your feet are likely to get wet as you
cross the streambed; skirt it on the right. While you're
in the canyon, take a side trip to Lake Falls; in winter
marvel at the spectacular icefall. On your return from
the falls [5] (.6 mi.), cross the stepping-stones and go
up the staircase to your right. At the top of the steps
is a trail board; go right and cross
a large stone bridge over Lake
Falls [6] (.75 mi.). To the left
is Lake Matthiessen. After
crossing the bridge,

continue straight. The trail is now a sidewalk with
benches along the side and passes through an oak-
dominated mixed woods. In spring, check the woods
for wildflowers—hepatica and spring beauty.

At 1.05 mi. [7] round a point and go to the right; a
ski trail (marked with blue) goes off to your left. You
are hiking on a bluff top overlooking the canyon. By
1.55 mi. you have completed the first half of your
hike and are back at the original bridge [1]. Go down
the steps and recross the bridge, going left after the
crossing [8].

At 1.8 mi. [9] take a long series of steps to the left.
Cross a cement bridge and go to the left, down more
steps, at 2 mi. [10]. The bridge and steps are part of
the original trails that Matthiessen constructed, and
the steps lead to a side spur where you can explore
the interior of the canyon.

Go left and proceed down the canyon; off to your
right in a short box canyon is Devil's Paint Box. Here,
a seep has allowed dissolved minerals to precipitate,
leaving a palette of light-colored powders. The trail
skirts the bluff and enters a stream; cross over it using
the stones. Continue walking to the end of the canyon,
where the trail dead-ends in a huge bowl with another
waterfall [11] (2.15 mi.). Past water action has carved
out shelter and erosion caves, like catacombs, in the
canyon walls.

Retrace your steps to the cement staircase and
ascend. You are now back at the bridge and steps [10].
Go straight and climb a set of wooden stairs; at the
top go left. (The trail to the right continues and eventually becomes a horse trail.) At Strawberry Rock the
trail loops to the left. Along this section, look on both
sides of the trail for wafer ash, a favorite food plant
of giant swallowtail larvae. By late summer, look for
the 2.5-inch larvae, which look like a cross between
a bird dropping and a small alligator. At 2.7 mi. you
are back at the bridge [1] where you started the
hike. Go right and start the long climb back
to the fort.

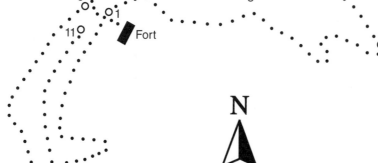

1. Start, bridge trail board
2. Right turn
3. Left turn
4. Giant's Bathtub
5. Stepping-stones
6. Bridge
7. Right turn
8. Left turn
9. Steps
10. Steps
11. Waterfall

# 28. Where Lincoln Walked

- Visit a settlement that shows what life on the prairie was like during Illinois' early days of statehood.

- See Lincoln depicted in statuary at various moments of his life.

- Tour the only home Lincoln ever owned and marvel at how Mary Lincoln was able to entertain from the smallest of kitchens.

- Become immersed in all things Lincoln at the Lincoln Presidential Museum.

- Even in the city you will find deer, although not necessarily in the conventional form.

## Area Information

**New Salem** was founded in 1828 on a ridge above the Sangamon River. Near the many streams in Sangamon County and in a rich mix of tallgrass prairie and timber, the town's location looked promising, situated as it was on an apparently navigable river and on a road connecting Springfield with Havana. Yet the village never prospered. The necessary improvements to make the river navigable never happened. At the village's peak, it had 25 buildings and 100 residents. By 1840, New Salem had ceased to exist.

The village's most famous resident was Abraham Lincoln. New Salem has been called his alma mater. Here he studied, worked at several trades, made his reputation for physical prowess and fairness, and began developing his talent for leadership. After six years in residence, he left the village to begin practicing law in Springfield.

**Springfield** has been called "the city Lincoln loved." He practiced law here and he delivered his famous "House Divided" speech in the Old State Capitol. Here he also made key decisions that affected his personal life; he fell in love, married, and bought a home.

Lincoln lived in Springfield for 24 years, and when he left he said, "To this place, and the kindness of these people, I owe everything." But Springfield is more than Lincoln. Government buildings, museums, statues, historic homes, and parks wait to be discovered and explored.

**Directions: New Salem** is 20 miles northwest of Springfield on Route 97. Take Route 125 out of Springfield for 5 miles until it joins Route 97. Turn north on Route 97 and travel north to the park entrance.

**Springfield** is located in the center of the state on both I-55 and I-72.

**Hours Open: New Salem** is open daily from 9:00 a.m. to 5:00 p.m. but closed on federal holidays. During the period of the Tuesday after Labor Day to April 15, the site is also closed on Mondays and Tuesdays. Most of the **Springfield** sites are also closed on holidays but open daily from 9:00 a.m. to 5:00 p.m. Check with the city's visitor center for individual site hours.

**Facilities: New Salem** has a visitor center, picnic area, restaurant, craft shop, and campground. The city of **Springfield** also has a visitor center. A National Park Service Visitors' Center is associated with Lincoln's Home. Free tickets may be obtained here for the home tour.

**Permits and Rules:** Put all litter in the nearest available trash container. No flowers, plants, shrubs, or trees may be removed or damaged. Children must be accompanied by adults.

**For Further Information:** Lincoln's New Salem, 15588 History Lane, Petersburg, IL 62675; 217-632-4000 or www.lincolnsnewsalem.com. Lincoln's Home National Historic Site, 413 S. Eighth Street, Springfield, IL 62701-1905; 217-492-4241. Springfield Convention & Visitors Bureau, 109 North Seventh Street, Springfield, IL 62701; 217-789-2360 or 800-545-7300 or www. visitspringfieldillinois.com.

## Other Areas of Interest

**Carpenter Park**, located 3 miles north of Springfield off Business 55, has 10 interconnecting trails. The 4.5 miles of trails travel through intermittent streams and floodplain forests dominated by large sycamore, silver maple, and box elder trees. Also find small seeps and sandstone outcrops. Parts of the park have been dedicated as an Illinois Nature Preserve. For more information, contact Springfield Park District, 2500 South 11th Street, P.O. Box 5052, Springfield, IL 62703; 217-522-8434.

**Lincoln Memorial Garden** is located on the southeast side of Lake Springfield in Springfield. Eighteen interconnecting trails total 5 miles and lead you on a journey through an Illinois landscape similar to what Lincoln experienced. The gardens, designed by the famed landscape architect Jens Jensen, are a living memorial to Abraham Lincoln. For more information, contact Lincoln Memorial Garden, 2301 East Lake Drive, Springfield, IL 62712-8908; 217-529-1111.

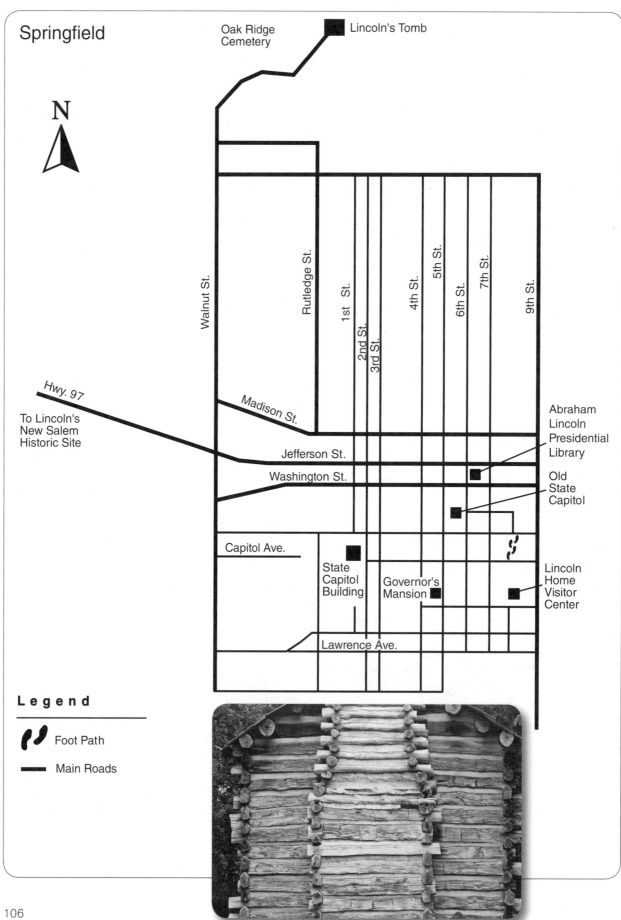

Springfield

N

Oak Ridge Cemetery

Lincoln's Tomb

Walnut St.

Rutledge St.

1st St.

2nd St.

3rd St.

4th St.

5th St.

6th St.

7th St.

9th St.

Hwy. 97

To Lincoln's New Salem Historic Site

Madison St.

Jefferson St.

Washington St.

Abraham Lincoln Presidential Library

Old State Capitol

Capitol Ave.

State Capitol Building

Governor's Mansion

Lincoln Home Visitor Center

Lawrence Ave.

**Legend**

Foot Path

Main Roads

# New Salem

 **Distance Round-Trip:** 3.5 miles
**Estimated Hiking Time:** 2 hours

*I wandered in the woods adjacent to the village, walked along the Sangamon River, and strolled the village streets. The only thought that came to mind was . . . from humble beginnings. . . .*

**Caution:** The trail crosses the highway; remember to look both ways. During periods of rain, the path will be muddy. Also be on the lookout for sticktights, plant seeds that attach to your clothing (especially sweaters) and won't let go.

**Trail Directions:** After an introduction to the area at the visitor center, begin at the south end of the parking lot near a trail board for Mentor Graham's Footsteps [1]. Mentor Graham, a self-educated man, taught school at New Salem for a nickel per pupil per day. He told Lincoln that he "most needed to study grammar." Later, Graham was to comment that Lincoln was the "most studious, diligent, strait forward [*sic*] young man in the pursuit of knowledge and literature than any among the five thousand I have taught in schools."

The trail is periodically marked and traverses second- and third-growth oak woods along a meandering stream. At .15 mi. [2] the trail crosses a bridge where the stream's bank is lined with Christmas ferns. Immediately after crossing the bridge, the trail splits; go uphill, following the blue trail marker.

At .35 mi. [3] you'll come upon the remnants of an old schoolhouse; on your left, surrounded by a split-rail fence, is an old cemetery. Buried here are members of the Bales family. As people moved away from the village, the Baleses bought their land and eventually owned the entire village site. The trail soon Ys; continue straight, and at .5 mi. you will cross another bridge and exit the woods near the main park entrance. Turn right and soon cross the road (Route 97) [4]; bear right at the culvert and go into the woods at a marker for Cardinal Ridge (.65 mi.).

Proceed up a steep hill; go right at the trail fork, and continue uphill. (The trees are numbered, in our case backward.) A sheet on this trail may be obtained at the visitor center. Note the large oak trees in the rolling, upland oak-hickory forest. For almost a mile the trail will wander through the woods. The villagers' hogs used to live in these woods, rooting in the dirt and feeding on the plentiful mast from the nut trees.

You will encounter a series of intersections [5] at 1.3 mi.; continue to the left. At 1.4 mi. continue to the left again, and at 1.5 mi. continue straight. The trail still follows the ridge. At 1.8 mi. the trail curves left and heads uphill, where you will soon go right [6] at the trail marker to Mentor Graham. You will wind your way down Cardinal Ridge, coming out where you went in. Cross Route 97 again, using caution [7] (2 mi.), and pass by a statue of Abraham Lincoln on horseback. A nearby log cabin structure has restrooms.

Walk through the picnic area and find a grassy path that parallels the park road. At 2.2 mi. you will go through a gate, cross a service road, and enter the village [8], where the path soon comes to a T; go right.

At the Denton Offutt Store, the trail Ys; go right [9] and down the steps, cross over the highway on the covered bridge, and visit the saw- and gristmill. The mill was the first structure in the village of New Salem. The big white oaks in this area were only saplings when Lincoln was here. Retrace your steps back to the village [9] and continue your tour of the village. (The visitor center has an excellent map explaining the structures.)

Take time to peer into or enter the houses of the pioneers and marvel at the historic breeds of livestock. Look at the detailed structure of the log houses. They were built with squared logs to better shed moisture, thus retarding rotting. They also allowed for more inside space that could be plastered. Your discovery of New Salem will end at the deputy statue of Abraham Lincoln [10]. Although the village has been restored as a memorial to Abraham Lincoln, it is also a memorial to our pioneer heritage—a typical settlement on the prairie in the early days of Illinois statehood.

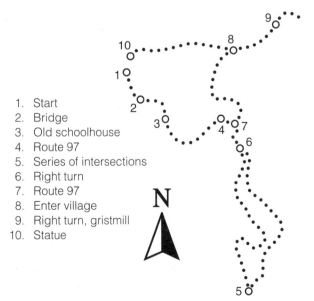

1. Start
2. Bridge
3. Old schoolhouse
4. Route 97
5. Series of intersections
6. Right turn
7. Route 97
8. Enter village
9. Right turn, gristmill
10. Statue

N

# Springfield's Lincoln

  **Distance Round-Trip:** 6.5 miles
**Estimated Hiking Time:** 4 hours

*While hiking, try to find the state's symbols—big bluestem, white oak, deer, cardinal, violet, and monarch. They were all present, but unrecognized, when Lincoln walked here. While the last three may be difficult to find, depending on the season, you will find huge specimens of white oak and even an urban deer might appear, although of the heavy-metal kind!*

**Caution:** The parking lot might be crowded during summer weekends. Use caution when crossing all streets.

**Trail Directions:** Park at Lincoln's Tomb, where there is free parking, restrooms, and water. Begin at the bust of Lincoln in front of his tomb [1]. Walk through the tomb and observe the various statues of Lincoln in the alcoves.

Exit the tomb and go left and down an asphalt path. Halfway around, take a staircase to the right for a side spur. Turn left at the bottom of the steps. Within a few feet you will encounter the public receiving vault for Abraham Lincoln. Retrace your steps to the tomb and continue circling it to the right.

Go to your right and through the parking lot [2] (.2 mi.); follow the cemetery road down the hill. Go right and follow the signs leading to the Illinois War Memorials. After visiting the memorials, exit the cemetery from the west gate onto North Walnut Street and go left [3] (.7 mi.). No sidewalk is present, so walk on the grassy border between the cemetery fence and the street. After one block turn left on Yates Street, again using the grassy strip. Follow Yates to Rutledge Street and turn right.

Stay on Rutledge for 1 mi. until it dead-ends into Madison; turn left on Madison [4] (2 mi.). Follow Madison to 1st Street and take a right. Follow 1st to Monroe Street. Cross Monroe Street and go right [5] (2.4 mi.), following Monroe to College Street. Go left on College, walk past the Illinois Visitor Center, and note the huge metal deer made from car bumpers.

Follow College Street to Edwards and turn left. On Edwards you will walk past the Illinois State Museum. Follow Edwards to 2nd Street and turn left [6] (3 mi.). Inside the State Capitol a block ahead you can obtain a brochure about the statues that line 2nd Street [7].

Follow the granite path into the Capitol. After you have finished exploring, exit the same way you entered and return to 2nd Street.

Cross the street and follow Capitol Street to 5th; go right [8] (3.4 mi.). After one block the Governor's Mansion is on your right. Take 5th Street to Edwards and turn right. (Edwards is not labeled; if you pass

the Vachel Lindsay Home, you have gone too far.) Walking on Edwards, you will pass the Governor's Mansion.

Follow Edwards to 4th Street and turn left on 4th. Follow 4th to Lawrence and take a side spur (right) to the Dana-Thomas House [9]. After viewing the house, retrace your steps to 4th and Lawrence (3.75 mi.) and continue east (straight) on Lawrence.

Follow Lawrence to 7th Street and turn left. Follow 7th to the Lincoln's Home Visitor Center [10] (4 mi.). At the center obtain a free ticket to tour the house.

From Lincoln's Home go left on 8th Street. (The home faces 8th Street.) Cross Capitol Street and walk through a complex of city buildings and a minipark. The street Ts into Adams, where you turn left [11] (4.6 mi.) and follow it to 6th. Turn right on 6th; the Old State Capitol is on the left [12] (4.7 mi.). In the rotunda of the Capitol is an original copy of the Gettysburg Address.

Follow 6th Street to Jefferson and turn right into the Abraham Lincoln Presidential Museum. There is an admission charge; take time to explore this fascinating look into the life of Lincoln [13]. After visiting the museum, go west on Jefferson (left) and continue to 2nd Street and turn right [14] (5.2 mi.). Follow 2nd for about a mile to North Grand Avenue. Go left on North Grand and follow it to Monument Avenue (less than a block) (6.2 mi.); go right [15].

Once you have arrived at the entrance to Oak Ridge Cemetery, continue straight on the cemetery road. You can see the tomb ahead. Before taking the asphalt trail to your right, look at the unique John Tanner monument on your left. An asphalt trail leads to the front of the tomb where you began the hike.

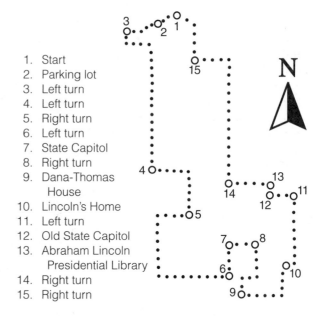

1. Start
2. Parking lot
3. Left turn
4. Left turn
5. Right turn
6. Left turn
7. State Capitol
8. Right turn
9. Dana-Thomas House
10. Lincoln's Home
11. Left turn
12. Old State Capitol
13. Abraham Lincoln Presidential Library
14. Right turn
15. Right turn

- Visit the largest prairie remnant in the state of Illinois—a place of grasses, wildflowers, and ceaseless prairie winds.

- Walk the trails in late summer to experience grasses taller than a person on horseback.

- Bring flower and grass field guides to help you identify more than 200 species found growing here.

- Discover how the prairie changes through the seasons—from the diminutive prairie violet on a gentle spring day to the reddish brown of big bluestem, harsh against the snow during an early February cold snap.

- Catch sight of deer, fox, grassland birds, and hawks.

## Area Information

Goose Lake Prairie is indeed a habitat of wildflowers, tall grasses, and relentless prairie winds—once home to the buffalo, wolf, prairie chicken, and otter. Today, abundant numbers of rabbits, muskrats, deer, and small rodents substitute for the fauna of old. Huge boulders scattered in the area are evidence of the geological history. These boulders were not formed in Illinois but were brought here more than 10,000 years ago by glaciers from the north.

Goose Lake itself no longer exists; it was drained before the turn of the century for farming and to mine the underlying clay. In its day, the lake that extended some 1,000 acres often was covered so thickly with geese and ducks that the water was not visible. Today, what remains is a series of ponds and marshes, outstanding examples of a once-common habitat—the prairie pothole. In 1840 Eliza Steele exclaimed, "I was in the midst of a prairie! A world of grass and flowers stretched around me, rising and falling in gentle undulations, as if an enchanter had struck the ocean swell, and it was at rest forever." This is Goose Lake.

**Directions:** From Morris, take Highway 47 south across the Illinois River (.7 mile) to the blacktop road known as Pine Bluff-Lorenzo Road. Turn left (east) and travel 6 miles to Jugtown Road; turn north to the park entrance.

**Hours Open:** The site is open year-round except on Christmas Day and New Year's Day. The visitor center is open from 10:00 a.m. to 4:00 p.m. During the winter (December to February) the visitor center is closed during the weekends, but the park is open.

**Facilities:** The site includes a visitor center with exhibits, a picnic area, cross-country ski trails, and restrooms.

**Permits and Rules:** Pets should be leashed and are not allowed in the nature preserve part of the park.

**For Further Information:** Goose Lake Prairie State Natural Area, 5010 N. Jugtown Road, Morris, IL 60450; 815-942-2899.

## Other Areas of Interest

**Heidecke State Fish and Wildlife Area** features Heidecke Lake (formerly called Collins Lake), which serves as a cooling lake for Commonwealth Edison. Only boats used for fishing and hunting are allowed on the lake. The fishing season opens April 1 and closes before waterfowl season; deer hunting and waterfowl hunting are allowed during season. For more information, call 815-942-6352.

The **National Heritage Corridor of the Illinois and Michigan Canal (I&M)** extends more than 100 miles, from Chicago to LaSalle/Peru. Within the National Heritage Corridor are 8 state parks or recreation areas and at least 39 significant natural areas. The 61-mile trail is multiuse and linear. The trail begins in Channahon and ends in LaSalle but can be accessed from many points. Fishing and canoe access are available. For more information call the Canal Corridor Association, 815-588-1100, or visit www.canalcor.org.

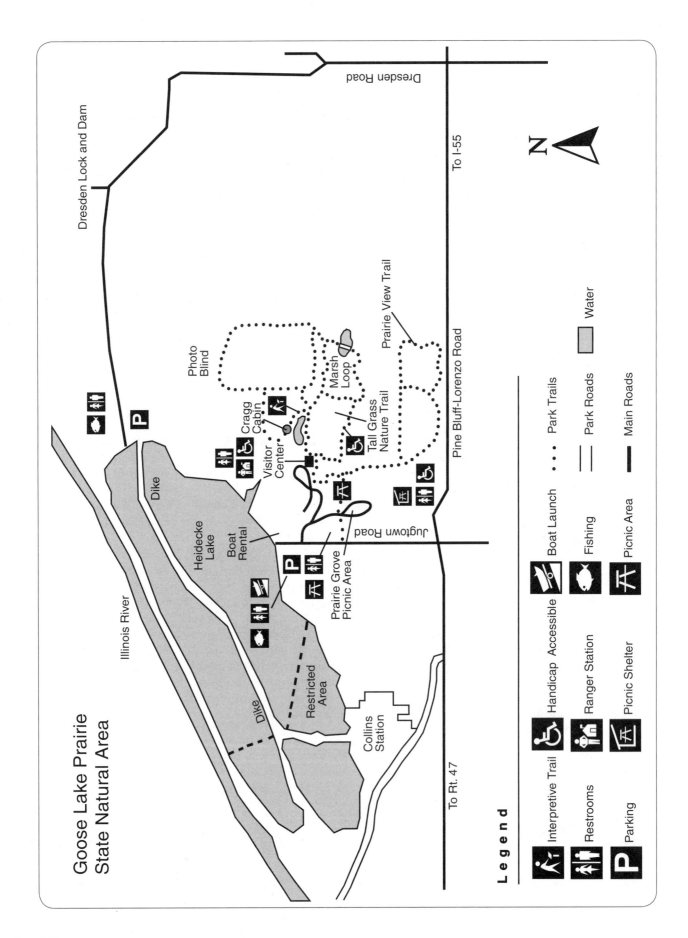

# Goose Lake Prairie
# State Natural Area

Dresden Road

Dresden Lock and Dam

To I-55

Pine Bluff-Lorenzo Road

Prairie View Trail

Photo Blind

Marsh Loop

Tall Grass Nature Trail

Cragg Cabin

Visitor Center

Illinois River

Dike

Heidecke Lake

Boat Rental

Dike

Restricted Area

Collins Station

Jugtown Road

Prairie Grove Picnic Area

To Rt. 47

**Legend**

Interpretive Trail · · · Park Trails

Handicap Accessible — Boat Launch

Restrooms — Park Roads

Ranger Station — Fishing

Parking — Main Roads

Picnic Shelter — Picnic Area

Water

# Tall Grass Nature Trail

🌿 **Distance Round-Trip:** 2.7 miles
🌿 **Estimated Hiking Time:** 1.1 hour

*Hiking this trail in late summer, with prairie grasses and forbs towering overhead, gives one the feeling of being lost in a sea of grass, a phenomenon undoubtedly similar to that experienced by early pioneers.*

**Caution:** The trail is a fairly level, mowed path with occasional slabs of bedrock embedded in it. The trails are also used by many mammals other than humans—watch for their scat.

**Trail Directions:** Segments of the trail have house-shaped signs with tidbits about the prairie landscape; take advantage of these to learn more about this vanishingly rare landscape. Begin the trail at the sign board directly behind the visitor center [1]. Take the trail to the right. The trail is a mown path, and by late summer you are hiking through acres of yellow sunflowers. At .4 mi. you have come to a wet prairie [2]; notice the cord grass and smartweed, two plants that don't mind wet feet. Along this section you will see cattails and depressions (dry prairie potholes); notice the large granite boulders embedded in the ground. These are called glacial erratics and are not from Illinois but were brought in from the north by the Wisconsin glacier.

A sign describing prairie potholes is at .5 mi. At the intersection at .6 mi., go right [3], and soon you will cross a bridge. During the summer look for the pink, spiky blooms of blazing star *(Liatris)* on either side of the trail. On the right is Goose Lake [4] (.81 mi.); unfortunately hikers no longer have access to this interesting prairie pothole, but take advantage of the picnic table for a few minutes of quiet observation. Who knows what might fly out of the pothole?

At the trail intersection at 1 mi., bear right (straight) [5]. The path looming ahead is arrow-straight and very quiet. Only whistling winds and rustling grasses can be heard. On the horizon are the towers of the Dresden Nuclear Power Plant and the General Electric Midwest Fuel Recovery Plant—sites early settlers would not have seen. This part of the trail is an excellent spot from which to view deer in a prairie. Other wildlife, although present and abundant, are usually in evidence only by their tracks, scats, or an occasional feather.

The path curves to the left at 1.4 mi., and a blind overlooking a water-filled pothole is on the right at 1.45 mi. [6]. Pause a few minutes in the blind to observe the pond in late fall; it may be filled with immature herons squawking and fishing. On other days all you might see is a lone mallard silently swimming along. The trail curves to the left again at 1.6 mi. [7] with another pothole on the right. Look for the pink blooms of false dragonhead or obedient plant, so called because when you move the flowers to the side they remain in that position.

All along this section are impressive expanses of prairie grasses. Unlike our popular lawn grasses, prairie grasses do not form carpets but grow in bunches. This is particularly visible if you hike in winter and spring.

A trail intersection appears at 1.95 mi.; go left and the trail is now packed limestone chat [8]. Take a right when the trail intersection appears at 2 mi. [9], and take another right within .1 mi. at the next intersection. You have now rejoined the interpretive trail with signage. Take a side spur at 2.3 mi. to the Craig Cabin [10]. This cabin is a replica of one of the first cabins in Grundy County and was nicknamed the "Palace" because of its two-story construction. Retrace your steps back to the trail and go right. End at the trail board behind the visitor center.

1. Start
2. Wet prairie
3. Right turn
4. Goose Lake
5. Go straight (bear right)
6. Blind
7. Curve left
8. Left turn
9. Right turn, right turn
10. Spur Craig Cabin

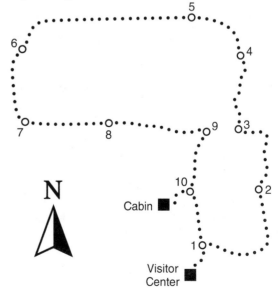

## Prairie View Trail

**Distance Round-Trip:** 3.3 miles
**Estimated Hiking Time:** 1.6 hours

*In the winter, the low sun gives the ubiquitous grasses a golden glow. The ice on the ponds is a bright, cold blue. Animal tracks are permanently embossed into the mud, at least until the next thaw.*

**Caution:** At the beginning of this trail, watch your step because there are culverts embedded in the path and part of the trail might be very wet or muddy during any season.

**Trail Directions:** The trail begins at the south side of the parking lot. Cross a concrete bridge and begin your hike **[1]**. The trail is a mowed swath through prairie grasses—Indian, big bluestem, and switch. During late summer the path is lined with gold—blooms of goldenrod and sunflowers—and during this time the trail is also an excellent site for viewing monarchs.

Ignore the trail coming in from the picnic area on the right and continue straight. If the path has been recently mown, look for glacial boulders embedded in the trail and also check the trail for scat or feathers from a predator's recent meal. In the winter, at about .35 mi. **[2]**, look on your left for the remnants of a stone fence, made with the many glacial boulders found as the land was cleared. Keep alert for hawks in this wide expanse of grassland; the occasional tree provides a perch from which they search for their next meal.

The trail forks at .6 mi. **[3]**; go left, following an old fence row. If you were hiking on a woodland trail, you would be looking for signs of wild turkeys, but along these grasslands look for pheasants, either calling, flushing up in front of you, or leaving the occasional feather on the trail. Straight ahead and to the right are the old spoil heaps of a strip mine.

A marsh filled with cattails appears on your left at .7 mi. **[4]**. Large expanses of common reed *(Phragmites)* interspersed with cattails are the dominant plants, and for the next .1 mi. the trail could be wet until it heads up. The trail forks at .85 mi.; note the sign explaining strip mines and the reclamation of the land. Go to the right **[5]** and pass small ponds on both your left and right. Begin a gradual ascent.

To your left, a short observation spur uphill at .95 mi. **[6]** leads to a great panorama of the spoil ponds and the prairie beyond. A bench at the top gives you a place for quiet observation. Continue back on the trail and walk by a series of spoil ponds. Contrast these ponds with the potholes on the prairies. The spoil ponds are lined with cattails and European weeds, while prairie potholes are lined with native reeds and grasses.

The trail forks at 1.1 mi. **[7]**; go left. During this part of the trail you are walking on top of spoil heaps. This part of the trail can be muddy, so check the ground for animal tracks. Once off the spoil heaps, the trail enters a mud flat **[8]** (1.6 mi.). A wooden boardwalk traverses the wettest area.

Soon you return to point **[5]**; take a left and retrace your steps to point **[7]** and go right (2 mi.). The trail parallels the road and will take you by the remnants of an old grove of trees. This is the shrubbiest part of the prairie. Prairies are sustained by fire, and with the suppression of fire, trees and shrubs begin to colonize, choking out the prairie vegetation. Removing trees and shrubs and beginning a fire regime will allow the prairie in this area to come back. Look for the weathered stumps and piles of wood chips on the right. At 2.45 mi. you have completed the loop and are back at point **[3]**. Continue straight, back to the visitor center and the parking lot, all the while watching the many butterflies—monarch, swallowtail, buckeye, or alfalfa—dancing, swirling, and rising against a blue sky.

1. Start
2. Stone fence
3. Left turn
4. Marsh
5. Right turn
6. Observation spur
7. Left turn
8. Mud flat

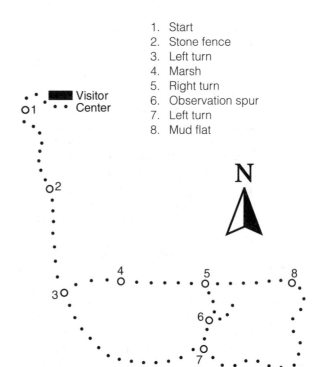

- Bring your binoculars because some of the state's rarest bird species are common here— bobolink, henslow's sparrow, loggerhead shrike, and dickcissel.

- Discover igloos (bunkers) even when it's not winter.

- Use your field guides because this site has 600 plant species, 100 species of breeding birds, 53 species of fish, and 25 species of reptiles and amphibians.

- Visit often, because this is a landscape in transition and you don't want to miss a single step!

## Area Information

Names are deceiving. Midewin National Tallgrass Prairie, a landscape of grassland birds and prairie restorations, was once the largest ammunition-production plant in the world—the Joliet Army Ammunition Plant. The plant was established in 1939 to produce ammunition and explosives for the military. At its peak during World War II, the plant employed more than 20,000 people and produced 5.5 million tons of TNT a week. Most operations of the plant ceased in the late 1970s.

A reuse plan for the area was adopted with the passage of the Illinois Land Conservation Act of 1995, and Midewin National Tallgrass Prairie was created. Over 19,000 acres are to be managed as open space for ecosystem restoration. The arsenal had almost 1,500 buildings on it, yet they were clustered. The majority of the land, while undeveloped, had been farmed or used for grazing cattle for years. Less than 3 percent of the land was in native vegetation. The area is a blank canvas for re-creating the first national tallgrass prairie east of the Mississippi River.

Cleanup of the contaminated areas is ongoing, and land restoration has begun. Native seed gardens have been established, over 85 species of prairie plants have been planted, pure fields of 5 species of prairie grasses have been established, and tree and brush removal is an ongoing project. The undeveloped, undisturbed land is a perfect habitat for grassland birds. Illinois' largest population of upland sandpipers is found here. The area supports 10 to 12 breeding pairs of loggerhead shrikes and 1,300 pairs of bobolinks. Midewin's name is the name of the Potawatomi healing society; it is appropriate, because the land has already begun the healing process.

**Directions:** Midewin National Tallgrass Prairie is located in Will County, south of Joliet. **Midewin Welcome Center** is located 2 miles north of Wilmington on State Route 53. **Hoff Road Trailhead** is located north of the welcome center. From the welcome center, turn right onto State Route 53 and travel approximately 4 miles to Hoff Road. Turn right and follow the road to the parking area. **Explosives Road Trailhead** is located approximately 2 miles north of the welcome center. Turn left off State Route 53 onto Explosive Road and follow the road to the trailhead.

**Hours Open:** The site is open year-round from one hour before sunrise to one hour after sunset. The welcome center is open 8:00 a.m. to 4:30 p.m. Monday through Friday. During the spring and summer, the center is open on Saturdays as well. The center is closed on Thanksgiving, Christmas, and New Year's.

**Facilities:** The welcome center has restrooms, water, displays, information, and a small bookstore. Rustic picnic areas and privy toilets are available at Turtle Pond, Hoff Road Trailhead, Explosives Road Trailhead, and P3 parking lot. At the trailheads, only privy toilets are provided.

**Permits and Rules:** Stay within the posted boundaries of the open areas. No motorized vehicles are allowed. All dogs must be leashed. No fishing or wading in streams.

**For Further Information:** Midewin National Tallgrass Prairie, 30239 S. State Route 53, Wilmington, IL 60481; 815-423-6370 or www.fs.fed.us/mntp.

## Other Areas of Interest

**Des Plaines Fish and Wildlife Area** is located 10 miles south of Joliet. Here the Des Plaines River joins the Kankakee River to form the Illinois River. The area offers picnicking, fishing, boating, camping, and hunting. The largest pheasant hunting site in the state is located here. Eighty acres of the area make up a dedicated nature preserve. For more information, call 815-423-5326.

## Other Trails

Eventually, a 48-mile trail system will be established at Midewin. In the meantime, nearly 20 miles of "interim" trails are available. Pick up a map at the welcome center for the current hiking trails and trailheads.

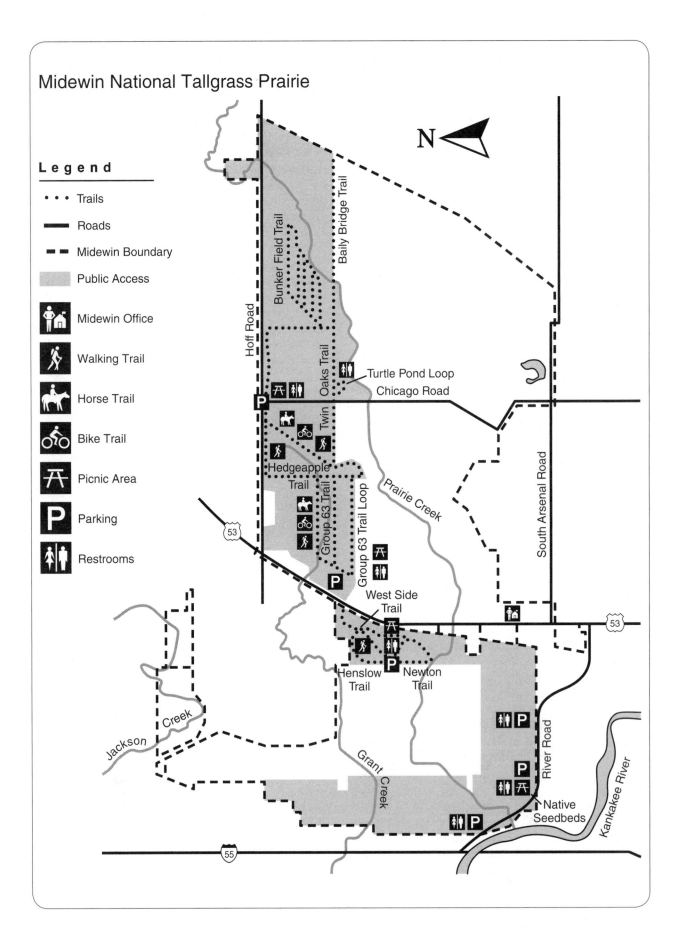

# Midewin National Tallgrass Prairie

**Legend**

- • • • Trails
- —— Roads
- – – Midewin Boundary
- Public Access
- Midewin Office
- Walking Trail
- Horse Trail
- Bike Trail
- Picnic Area
- P Parking
- Restrooms

N

Hoff Road

Bunker Field Trail

Baily Bridge Trail

Oaks Trail

Turtle Pond Loop
Chicago Road

Twin

Hedgeapple Trail

Group 63 Trail

Group 63 Trail Loop

Prairie Creek

South Arsenal Road

West Side Trail

Henslow Trail

Newton Trail

Jackson Creek

Creek

Grant Creek

Native Seedbeds

River Road

Kankakee River

53

53

55

# Hoff Road Trailhead–East Side Trails

 **Distance Round-Trip:** 4.5 miles
**Estimated Hiking Time:** 1.75 hours

*During early summer the trail is a symphony of birdsong, led by the ever-present dickcissel singing from the tops of shrubs, fence posts, or any other structure where they can project their song.*

**Caution:** The area is still under construction, so you may see heavy equipment on the roads working on demolition or restoration or in crop fields. Stay well away from this equipment; operators might not be able to hear or see you.

**Trail Directions:** The trail begins at the trail board at the Hoff Road Trailhead. Enter the area and go left on a wide, multiuse path that will be shared with bicycles [1]. At .35 mi. continue straight [2], ignoring the road to the right. It leads to an old skeleton of a building. Along the road are cottonwoods, sumacs, goldenrods, and Deptford pinks. The latter, although pretty, is a non-native plant.

Ignore the old roads coming in from the right and left and stay on the multipurpose trail. At 1 mi. is a trail marker; go right [3]. Large cottonwoods will be on your right. Within .25 mi. you will pass under some large electrical lines. You can hear the sizzling current. As you hike on this path, try not to step on the grasshoppers, which are the same color as the gravel. After you pass under the electrical lines, you will begin to see rounded humps on your left in the distance. These are storage bunkers or igloos. The bunkers were used for storing munitions manufactured at the Joliet Arsenal until they were shipped out for use by the army. The bunkers will remain as part of the history of Midewin.

At 1.75 mi. take a side spur to explore a bunker field [4]. Go right on the mown path; you are hiking on an old rail line that was used for transporting the munitions to the bunkers. The railroad line is now nothing but a grassy path. Take the first left and walk up and into a bunker. Discover the great acoustics of these bunkers as you sing or talk. Explore the bunker field as much as you like and then return to [4], where you will go left on Twin Oak Trail.

At the trail intersection at 2.25 mi., go right [5]. On your left is a true old field—land left fallow that is reverting back to whatever is in the seed bank. Along this section wild parsnip is abundant. It is an invasive plant that can cause severe skin blisters. Yet it is also a host plant for the black swallowtail butterfly.

At 2.75 mi. go left on a grassy trail to explore Turtle Pond [6]. Turtle Pond is manmade and fed by rainwater. It was originally used by employees of the arsenal for recreation. As you encircle the pond, look for bullfrogs, turtles, and dragonflies. You will come out on a grassy path near some prairie plant demonstration plots (these will be on your left). At 3.5 mi, go right [7], hiking on an old asphalt road with large, sandy ant mounds on either side. You will get a feel for "the mile" as you hike this mile-long stretch back to the trail board where you parked.

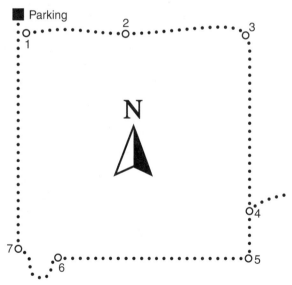

1. Start
2. Continue straight
3. Right turn
4. Bunker field, right turn
5. Right turn
6. Turtle Pond
7. Right turn

## Interim West Side Trails– Newton and Henslow

 **Distance Round-Trip:** 3 miles
**Estimated Hiking Time:** 1.5 hours

*For having such a warlike purpose in the past, this trail offers a very peaceful present. In early summer, when the daisies are in full bloom and small butterflies flit about, you might think you are hiking in an Andrew Wyeth painting.*

**Caution:** The area is still under construction, so you might see heavy equipment on the roads working on demolition or restoration or in crop fields. Stay well away from this equipment; operators might not be able to hear or see you.

**Trail Directions:** The trail begins at the information board at the Explosives Road Trailhead; go left on the mowed path [1]. The trail leads through a grassy meadow dotted with daisies and gives the impression of hiking through an Andrew Wyeth painting. If you hike in early summer, accompanying you will be hundreds of tiny, brown European skippers (a type of butterfly) and myriads of grasshoppers courting, mating, and always one step ahead of you.

At .3 mi. the grassy path gives way to gravel; go right through an old Osage orange hedgerow [2]. Osage orange trees, with their spiny branches, provided early farmers with a living fence. Here you are able to see how vast Midewin actually is. There are few manmade structures anywhere. Bear right at .65 mi. [3]; you are again hiking on a mowed path. The trail then curves right at .8 mi.; a fence with barbed wire will be on your left [4].

The Newton cemetery at 1 mi. contains only one grave—George Newton, who died in 1865 [5]. A large grove of ash trees grows nearby. At 1.15 mi. go left at the trail sign [6], and soon you are back at the information board. Cross the road and go left [7] (1.5 mi.). You are hiking through another grassy meadow. Be careful not to be mobbed by the red-winged blackbirds!

By 1.9 mi., in the distance on your left you can see bunkers [8] and a cottonwood copse. The bunkers, designed to store explosives, have concrete walls that are three to five feet thick. Their earthen covering camouflaged them from aerial view and helped keep the TNT inside at a stable temperature.

During early summer, look for a flash of black, white, and yellow; these are bobolinks. You might also notice that this area lacks any type of structure (small trees and shrubs) for the birds to perch on, so they are using the trail markers! The trail curves to the right at .2.2 mi. [9], and within a few steps you will cross a gravel path. Stay on the grassy path, and cross another gravel path at 2.6 mi. [10]. Stay on the grassy path. Those gravel pathways are part of a new trail under construction. At 3 mi. you are back at [7]. Cross the road to the parking area.

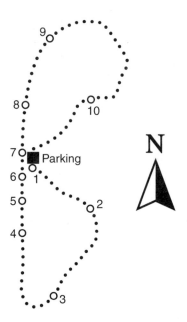

1. Start
2. Right turn, hedgerow
3. Bear right
4. Curve right
5. Newton grave
6. Left turn
7. Road crossing, enter Henslow Trail
8. Bunkers
9. Curve right
10. Gravel path crossing

# 31. Spitler Woods State Natural Area

- Enjoy New England–style fall colors.
- Don't forget your spring wildflower field guide, because parts of the park are carpets of wildflowers.
- Discover an east-central Illinois prairie grove.
- Warm up before the hike at the park's exercise stations.

## Area Information

When Europeans began to settle the Illinois country, what is now central Illinois was largely prairie, interrupted by forests only on floodplains, on slopes bordering streams, and in isolated prairie groves. Many of these groves were miles apart, completely surrounded by prairie. The typical prairie grove consisted of oak-hickory and maple-basswood forests that supported an understory of small shrubs—redbud, pawpaw, and sassafras—and showy wildflower displays. Today these groves, if they haven't been altered by logging, grazing, or clearing, are still ecologically resilient islands of life in the midst of Illinois' cornbelt.

When what is now Spitler Woods was first surveyed in April 1821, it was described as "gently rolling woods composed mainly of oak, hickory, walnut, and maple trees." For many years Mrs. Ida Spitler owned the forest. She would not allow hunting, timber removal, or grazing. As a result of Mrs. Spitler's stewardship, the woods was able to retain most of its original prairie grove species. Some of the trees range from 30 to 40 inches at breast height, and over 225 plant species may be found here.

In 1937, Mrs. Spitler donated the forest to the State of Illinois for the purpose of preserving for posterity the high-quality forest and its associated wildlife. In 1982, the forest was dedicated as an Illinois Nature Preserve, citing that "it contained one of the largest acreages of old-growth woods in central Illinois."

**Directions:** Spitler Woods State Natural Area is 8 miles southeast of Decatur and .5 mile east of Mount Zion. In Mount Zion, take Highway 121 to Spitler Park Drive, turn east, and go .5 mile to the entrance.

**Hours Open:** The site is open year-round.

**Facilities:** This is a day-use park with many picnic areas. Available are both large and small picnic shelters, restrooms, drinking water, horseshoe pits, volleyball and basketball courts, a soccer field, and playgrounds.

**Permits and Rules:** The trail is part of an Illinois Nature Preserve, so pets must be leashed. No collecting of plants or animals. No bicycles.

**For Further Information:** Spitler Woods State Natural Area, 705 Spitler Park Drive, Mount Zion, IL 62549; 217-864-3121.

## Other Park Trails

The site offers a .5-mile fitness trail with 11 exercise stations. The Red Oak Ramble Trail is also .5 mile and is designed for those with physical limitations.

## Other Areas of Interest

Located on the western edge of Decatur, **Rock Springs Conservation Area** offers more than 1,300 acres of forest, prairie, and wetlands. The area offers an interactive nature center, picnicking, Homestead Prairie Farm, and a nature reference library. There are 8.5 miles of hiking trails and 2 miles of the Rock Springs/Fairview Park bike trail through the area. For more information, call 217-423-7708.

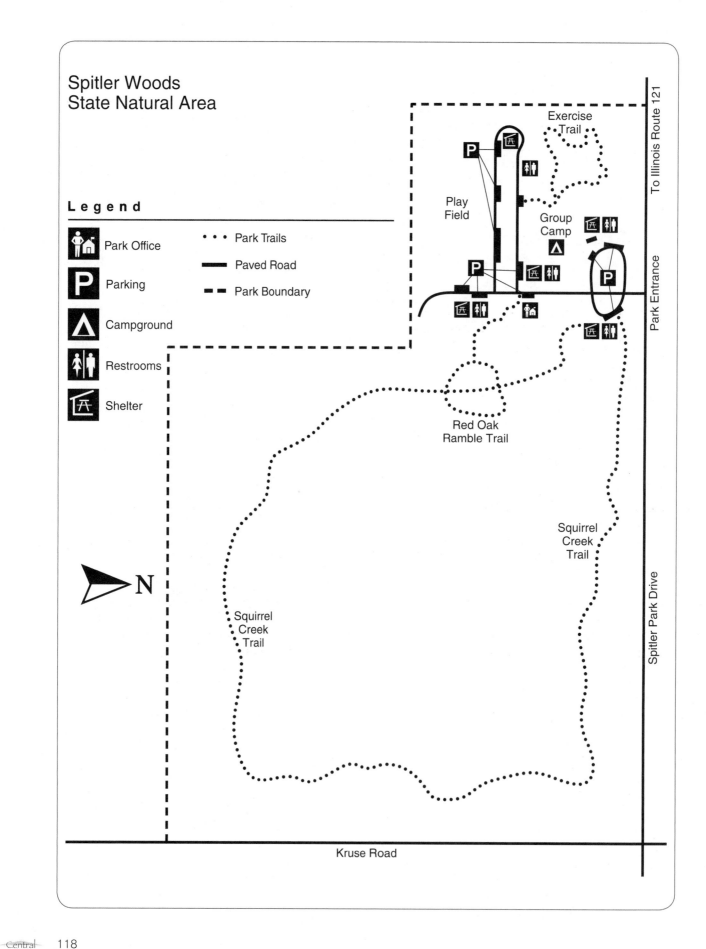

Spitler Woods
State Natural Area

**L e g e n d**

Park Office

Parking

Campground

Restrooms

Shelter

Park Trails

Paved Road

Park Boundary

To Illinois Route 121

Exercise
Trail

Play
Field

Group
Camp

Park Entrance

Red Oak
Ramble Trail

Squirrel
Creek
Trail

N

Squirrel
Creek
Trail

Spitler Park Drive

Kruse Road

# Squirrel Creek Trail

 **Distance Round-Trip:** 2 miles
**Estimated Hiking Time:** 1 hour

*A late-summer exploration revealed several treasures of the woods: Ebony pelecinid wasps, with their long, threadlike abdomens, would suddenly fly by while scorpion flies, with their mottled brown wings, rested on the stinging nettle. As for bird life, a persistent wood peewee sang throughout the hike.*

**Caution:** Watch your step because roots are growing within the path.

**Trail Directions:** Park in the Long Creek Pavilion area; the trail begins at the sign on the left [1]. Immediately note the large bur oak on your left. Within a few steps you will come to a boardwalk; use that, not the eroding dirt path. At .15 mi. you will cross the first of several bridges throughout the hike [2]. When you cross a second bridge at .2 mi., note the large sycamore tree on the right, and in spring look for Virginia bluebells here [3].

The trail soon heads up, leaving the floodplain forest, and travels past an arching white oak. The undulating trail will take you by several large white and red oaks; look closely at the trees in this section; many support scars of past lightning strikes. At .75 mi., note a particularly large lightning-damaged oak on the right [4]. At 1 mi. you will cross a bridge over Squirrel Creek [5]; pause for a few minutes to watch the activity up and down the stream. Whether it's water striders skating across the surface or migrating warblers above your head, there always seems to be something going on.

From the bridge the trail soon heads up. Look for the scaly bark of sugar maples in this area. In the spring, patches of *Uvularia* (bellwort), a yellow,

dangling flower, are found here. At 1.3 mi., find a boardwalk across the creek [6]. The woods here were cut at one time (the trees are smaller and the understory shows disturbance). The trail intersects with Red Oak Ramble's paved path at 1.7 mi. [7]; continue on Squirrel Creek Trail. Just before the intersection, did you see the gnarled and twisted remnants of an Osage orange hedgerow?

The trail intersects again with Red Oak Ramble within a few steps. Zigzag to Squirrel Creek Trail on the right. Just before the picnic area, go left, and soon you are back at the parking area.

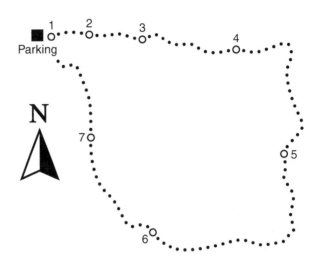

1. Start
2. First bridge
3. Large sycamore
4. Lightning-damaged oak
5. Bridge over Squirrel Creek
6. Boardwalk
7. Intersection with Red Oak Ramble

# 32. Ballard Nature Center

- Look a larger-than-life praying mantis in the eye.
- Discover the Southern Till Plain.
- Bring your field guides; this site boasts 50 species of butterflies and skippers, 22 species of dragonflies, and 21 species of reptiles and amphibians.
- See what a dream, hard work, and restoration savvy can accomplish.

## Area Information

Ballard Nature Center, south of Effingham, is in the middle of the Southern Till Plain. This area was glaciated not by the Wisconsin but the earlier Illinoisan glacial episode. The soils are thin with poor drainage, and many of the soils have a high clay content, leading to a claypan subsoil. Also in this isolated area is a gem of a nature center.

Ernie Ballard had a dream, a nature center where everyone could learn about nature and have a good time. He deeded 210 acres of land to the Soil and Water Conservation District of Effingham County for this purpose. Some of the land had been in field crops, while another piece was timber. The Conservation District soon realized that maybe an independent board of directors would be the proper route for this project. Several members of the board are biologists and conservationists. They remembered how much fun it was for them as kids to spy a frog in a pond or chase butterflies along the trail.

From the original corn, beans, and timber to the present 104 acres of woodlands, 56 acres of restored prairie, 29 acres of savanna restorations, and 20 acres of restored shallow water wetlands, the area is abuzz with activity. During the spring and summer at any one time, over 12 species of dragonflies may be seen, bullfrogs glare at you just above the water's edge, and a female mallard waddles down the path followed by ducklings in her wake. Ernie Ballard's dream has come true.

**Directions:** From Altamont, take US Highway 40 east, approximately 2.25 miles to the entrance on the right. From Effingham, take US Highway 40 west approximately 8.75 miles to the entrance on the left. The nature center's sign is next to the entrance road.

**Hours Open:** The site is open year-round from dawn to dusk. The nature center is open from 8:00 a.m. to 4:00 p.m. Monday through Friday, noon to 4:00 p.m. on Saturday, and 1:00 p.m. to 4:00 p.m. on Sunday (April through October).

**Facilities:** The nature center includes educational and interactive displays, meeting rooms, restrooms, and water. On-site find pavilions, picnic facilities, and a kids' fishing pond.

**Permits and Rules:** No bikes, horses, ATVs, or vehicles are allowed on the trails. All plants and animals are protected. Pets must be leashed at all times.

**For Further Information:** Ballard Nature Center, 5253 E. US Highway 40, Altamont, IL 62411; 618-483-6856 or www.ballardnaturecenter.org.

## Other Areas of Interest

Located 14 miles northeast of Salem, Illinois, **Stephen A. Forbes State Recreation Area** was originally 20 acres with a 2-acre pond. Today the area is over 3,100 acres and has a lake with 18 miles of shoreline. Picnicking, fishing, and boating are popular activities at this site. There are four hiking trails ranging in length from .25 mile to 2.5 miles. For more information, call 618-547-3381.

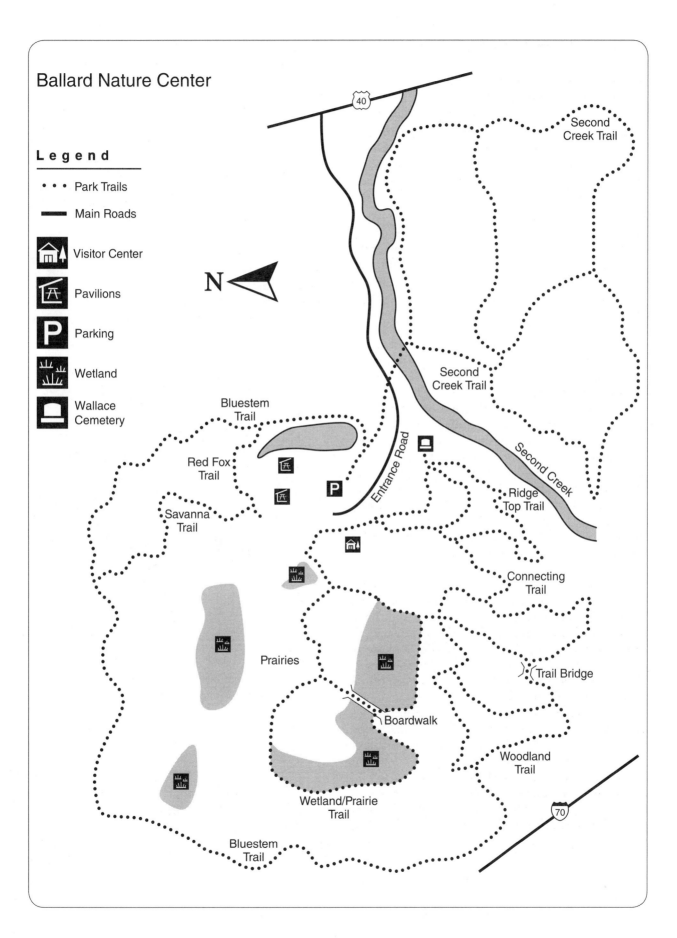

# Ballard Nature Center

**Legend**

- • • • Park Trails
- ▬▬ Main Roads
- 🏠 Visitor Center
- ⛺ Pavilions
- 🅿 Parking
- 🌾 Wetland
- ⬛ Wallace Cemetery

N

40

Second Creek Trail

Second Creek Trail

Second Creek

Bluestem Trail

Red Fox Trail

Entrance Road

Ridge Top Trail

P

Savanna Trail

Connecting Trail

Prairies

Trail Bridge

Boardwalk

Woodland Trail

Wetland/Prairie Trail

70

Bluestem Trail

# Wetland and Prairie Trails

 **Distance Round-Trip:** 1.75 miles
**Estimated Hiking Time:** 1 hour

*It's a hot July day, yet I am unaware of any heat and humidity; the trail's activity holds my attention. A ruby-throated hummingbird is feeding at scarlet cardinal flowers, clouds of damselflies dance over the wetlands, a red-winged blackbird dive-bombs me as I hike too close, and in the distance I hear a bobwhite quail.*

**Caution:** Watch for dive-bombing red-winged blackbirds.

**Trail Directions:** Begin at the trail map in front of the nature center and go left on the gravel path through a prairie restoration [1]. You will soon pass a spur to your right with a bench under a hackberry tree. Stay on the main trail. At .1 mi. go right on the Wetland Trail [2]; along the path enjoy the seasonal blooms of the prairie restoration—bergamot, gray-headed coneflower, and black-eyed Susan are just a few of the many blooms. Carolina grasshoppers will always be one step ahead of you!

At .15 mi. go left on the Wetland Boardwalk [3]. Make sure you have your dragonfly field guide with you. Pause for a few minutes to watch these sky predators defend territories, mate, lay eggs, or just soak up the sunshine (thermoregulate). At the end of the boardwalk, go right [4]. On your right will be a wetland and to your left an oak-hickory forest. The wetland finally gives way to all prairie at .4 mi. [5]. See if you can find Illinois bundle flower—it has mimosa-like leaves and its seed heads look like small pinecones.

At .5 mi. you have looped around the wetland and are back at [3]. Retrace your steps back across the boardwalk (who knows what you might have missed?), and this time go left off the boardwalk [4]. Frogs will plop in the water ahead of you. Look along the edges for turtles sunning on logs. At the intersection (before the grove of shagbark hickories) [6] (.6 mi.), go left and continue around the wetland.

You will soon leave the wetland behind and retrace your steps back to the trail map (.7 mi.). Walk across the parking area to the kids' fishing pond platform and go right, skirting the fishing pond [7]. On your right is a trail intersection for the Bluestem Trail; go left [8] on the mowed wood-chip trail through a shagbark hickory grove. At .9 mi. go right onto the Bluestem Trail (there is a trail sign) [9]. The trail is a mowed path

through a prairie restoration in progress. Look for the trail's namesake grass as you hike. Big bluestem will be the tallest grass; its seed head has three awns that resemble a turkey foot (the other name of the grass).

At 1.15 mi. locate an ephemeral pond on your left (by summer it has dried up) [10]. While you hike this section, you can contrast what the area used to look like—corn—and what it is reverting to—prairie (original landscape). The trail soon winds away from the adjacent cornfield through nice patches of big bluestem. If you are silent along this segment, you might hear bobwhites call their names.

At the trail intersection at 1.25 mi., go left on Savanna Trail [11], and at the intersection at 1.5 mi. go right on Fox Trail [12]. Along both of these segments you will pass ephemeral ponds; these fishless ponds are important for amphibian conservation. Go right at the end of Red Fox Trail, and soon you are back to the parking area.

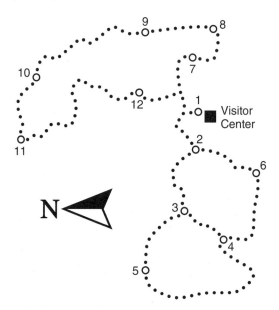

1.  Start
2.  Right turn onto Wetland Trail
3.  Left turn onto Wetland Boardwalk
4.  Turn off boardwalk (right first time, left second time)
5.  Prairie
6.  Left turn
7.  Skirt fishing pond
8.  Left turn
9.  Right turn onto Bluestem Trail
10. Ephemeral pond
11. Left turn onto Savanna Trail
12. Right turn onto Red Fox Trail

# Second Creek Trail

 **Distance Round Trip:** 1.4 miles
**Estimated Hiking Time:** 1 hour

*As I hiked, I interrupted a gathering of dainty sulfur butterflies puddle-clubbing (gathering moisture and nutrients from a wet spot on the ground). They fluttered around my head like a golden halo.*

**Caution:** Look both ways when you cross the park road.

**Trail Directions:** Begin at the nature center and cross the parking area and road, heading to the kids' fishing pond [1]. Within .1 mi. a trail intersection will appear; go right onto Second Creek Nature Trail [2] and head downhill. You will cross a footbridge at .15 mi.; cross the road and cross a second bridge within a few steps [3]. Follow the trail signs. As you explore this trail of forest, prairie, and stream, who knows what you will discover?

You soon come to a trail T; go left [4] to hike the outside loop. The trail is through a prairie restoration on the right and a woods on your left; look for woodland sunflower and goldenrod. Mole trails (nature's underground excavator) will crisscross the path. The trail heads into a mixed woods at .25 mi. [5]. Take advantage of the signage; many of the trees are labeled.

The trail crosses a bridge at .35 mi., winds through a large sycamore grove [6], and then skirts the creek. Once out of the woods, the trail heads up through a prairie restoration. At the trail intersection at .5 mi., continue following the Outside Loop Trail [7]. You will be walking on a grassy mowed path where you can see adjacent farm fields. The trail curves through prairie and heads into an oak-hickory woodland.

At .75 mi. cross a bridge and head up; at the top of the intersection, continue on the Outside Loop [8]. The trail leads you through recovering woodlands. The trail emerges from the woods at .9 mi. into a gooseneck wetland [9]. Goosenecks are where streams or rivers meander; they're so tight that their channels

nearly meet one another. Here at Ballard the stream has formed an oxbow wetland (a meander cut off from the stream). By summer this wetland appears as nothing more than a grassy depression with cottonwood seedlings.

Back down and away from the oxbow, you will cross a bridge and go left. At 1.15 mi. you are back at [4]. Go left, retracing your steps as you cross the two bridges and the park road. Head up the trail to the fishing pond and finally back to the parking area. What new discoveries did you make while you hiked Second Creek?

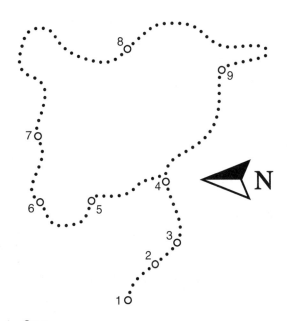

1. Start
2. Right turn
3. Footbridge, road, footbridge
4. Left turn
5. Woods
6. Sycamore grove
7. Continue on Outside Loop Trail
8. Continue on Outside Loop Trail
9. Gooseneck wetland

# 33. Iroquois County State Wildlife Area

- Hike along the floor of an ancient bog while you look for carnivorous plants.
- Discover some of Illinois' unusual habitats—sand savanna, shrub prairie, wet sand prairie, and an old bog.
- Bring your butterfly field guide to differentiate between the fritillaries found here—great spangled, meadow, variegated, Aphrodite, and the elusive regal.
- Visit an area of unusual crops—turf on one side of the highway, potatoes on the other side, and a flower farm down the road.

## Area Information

Ferns on the prairie! It doesn't seem possible, but many things about Iroquois County State Wildlife Area don't seem as they should. Iroquois County State Wildlife Area is situated in a low, glacial outwash plain that consists of marshlands, sand ridges, and dunes. The area was initially set aside in 1944 to protect the declining prairie chicken population. Unfortunately, the prairie chickens did not survive. What was protected instead is one of the best remaining sedge meadow, wet prairie, sand savanna, and marsh complexes left in the state.

Found here are plants more common in the east, especially the Atlantic Coastal Plain. In the spring, in addition to the common blue violet, you can find the arrow-leaved, lance-leaved bird's foot, sand violets, and the rare primrose violet (found only in Iroquois and Kankakee counties). Yellow star grass grows in profusion, as do several ferns—cinnamon, sensitive, royal, and marsh. A diligent search of the remnant bog will yield a low, wet area carpeted with sphagnum moss and drying peat. Viewed from ground level, the round, sticky-leaved, carnivorous sundews glisten in the sun. Across the way in the adjacent wet sand prairie, clumps of cinnamon fern are interspersed with pink blazing star.

While the majority of the area is open to public hunting, the 480-acre Hooper Branch Savanna Nature

Preserve is set aside for nature study and hiking, awaiting interesting discoveries by all who visit.

**Directions:** Iroquois County State Wildlife Area is located 2 miles north and 3 miles east of Beaverville in the extreme northeast corner of Iroquois County. From St. Anne take Highway 1 south 2 miles, and then turn left (east) on County Road 3300 for 9 miles to the nature preserve parking lot.

**Hours Open:** The site is open year-round from sunrise to sunset. Hooper Branch Savanna Nature Preserve is open year-round, but during hunting season there is limited access to the conservation area. The dog exercise area is closed from April to August for the protection of breeding wildlife.

**Facilities:** Picnicking, archery, a hand trap range, a dog exercise area, a seasonal concession in operation during hunting season, hunting, snowmobiling, and privy toilets are all available.

**Permits and Rules:** Pets must be leashed in the nature preserve. No collecting of plants or animals.

**For Further Information:** Iroquois County State Wildlife Area, R.R. 1, 2803 E. 3300 N. Road, Beaverville, IL 60912; 815-435-2218.

## Park Trails

Several miles of fire lanes (unmarked trails) may be explored. A 1.2-mile trail, of which .3 mile is handicap accessible, is located at parking area 2.

## Other Areas of Interest

Called "wonderful land" by the Potawatomi, the area that was to become **Kankakee River State Park** has been popular since the late 1700s. Today, people come to enjoy the many water activities (fishing, canoeing, and boating), seek the quiet beauty of Rock Creek (a 3-mile hike leads to a waterfall and limestone canyons), or just relax (there are over 250 campsites and also cabins). In addition, there are several miles of horse trails and a 10.5-mile bicycle trail along the river. For more information, call 815-933-1383.

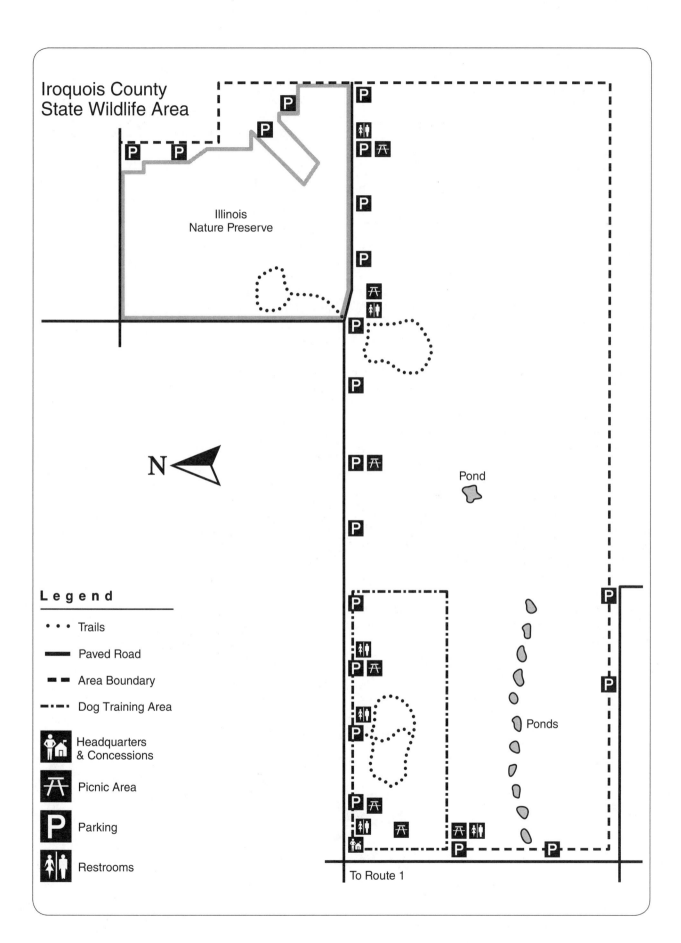

Iroquois County
State Wildlife Area

Illinois
Nature Preserve

N

Pond

Ponds

**Legend**

• • • Trails

——— Paved Road

– – – Area Boundary

–·–·– Dog Training Area

Headquarters
& Concessions

Picnic Area

P Parking

Restrooms

To Route 1

# Hooper Branch Savanna

 **Distance Round-Trip:** 2.5 miles
**Estimated Hiking Time:** 1.3 hours

*During a recent Fourth of July hike, the patriotic colors were supplied by red-headed woodpeckers, white-tailed deer, and eastern bluebirds. Fireworks were provided by the sparkling globules of sundew and the orange and black insects—net-winged beetles and three species of fritillary butterflies.*

**Caution:** Prepare for wet feet in the prairie-bog area.

**Trail Directions:** Park in Parking Area 8 and begin the trail at the nature preserve sign across the road [1]. The trail is a wide, sandy path, and on either side of the trail are sumacs and oaks. This is one of the better spots in the state to look for red-headed woodpeckers flitting between the dead snags. You will see many mounds caused by Illinois' only gopher—the plains pocket gopher—so named for the fur-lined pockets, one under each jawbone, that carry food and nest materials.

At .25 mi. you will emerge into an oak savanna [2]. Hooper Branch Savanna is the largest single tract of native savanna remaining in Illinois. Savannas are a mix of trees and prairie plants and usually have a parklike appearance. Black oak is the dominant savanna tree at Hooper Branch. The trail soon curves left through an assortment of oaks—white, pin, black, and blackjack.

A trail intersection appears at .45 mi.; go straight (to the left) [3]. The trail now passes along the edge of an old field, which soon gives way to oaks. Don't forget to look down; you are treading on some interesting cushions of moss. You have completed the loop at .8 mi. and are back at [3]. Retrace your steps back to [1].

Cross the road and go straight on the sandy path [4]. You are now hiking in the wet prairie and shrub prairie portion of the preserve. Ignore the fire break and the trail to the right at 1.35 mi. [5]. Look for royal, cinnamon, and lady fern in this area. At 1.5 mi., at an intersection, continue straight [6]. The bracken fern in this section is waist high and the oaks have given way to prairie. Underfoot the sandy soil has become peaty sphagnum. The open areas on the left are wet sand prairie. In late July look for pink blazing stars here and oftentimes a sport (which has white flower spikes as well).

On your left at 1.7 mi. is a remnant of an old bog [7]. You are welcome to explore it, but beware of wet feet. Here you might find sundew, sphagnum moss, and dwarf blueberry. To your right is a wet shrub prairie with islands and thickets of cinnamon fern. Walk to the end of the wet prairie on your left (east) and then turn around and retrace your steps to [5] (1.9 mi.) and go left.

On your left will be the tangled edge of the shrub prairie. At 2.1 mi. go right [8]; on either side of the trail is a degraded savanna with various ages of oaks. You will soon pass a grove of quaking aspen on the left; among the aspen are two oak wolf trees (outspread branches, indicating they were open-grown). The dying pines on both sides of the trail seem out of place here (and are, because they were planted).

A small sand dune appears on your right at 2.35 mi. [9]. Within .1 mi. come to a trail intersection; go left and you are soon back where you started.

1. Start
2. Savanna
3. Go straight (to the left)
4. Road crossing, go straight
5. Ignore fire break and trail to right
6. Crossroads, go straight
7. Bog
8. Right turn
9. Sand dune

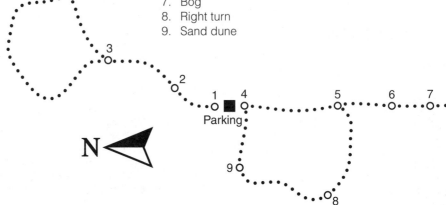

# 34. Forest Glen Preserve

- Journey to where north meets south and east meets west, at least botanically.

- Climb a 72-foot tower for a panoramic view of the Vermilion River Valley.

- Discover seeps—but stay on the trail, lest the water in the supersaturated soil seep into and fill up your shoes.

- Hike along wooded ravines, the Vermilion River, a tallgrass prairie, grassy meadows, and quiet ponds.

- The sugar maples and beeches, framing a brilliant blue fall sky, provide an unforgetable fall color show.

## Area Information

Forest Glen Preserve, dedicated in 1968, is located in the Vermilion River Basin, with the river forming its eastern boundary. Some of its unusual features are calcareous seep springs, with their own unique vegetation; tulip trees growing in the beech-maple forests of the ravines and adjacent uplands; and occasional hill prairies on west-facing bluff tops. These diverse features result from the Vermilion River lying in a tension or transition zone between the beech-maple forests of the east and the prairie peninsula and oak-hickory vegetation to the west.

The area's seeps are a type of wetland (often at the base of a hill) in which groundwater flows down through a porous material until it reaches an impermeable layer, such as clay, that channels it to the surface. The seeps of Forest Glen support skunk cabbage—the state's earliest flowering plant, and one that makes its own heat to protect its precious bud and warm the winter ground around it. Marsh marigold, sweet flag, and bog twayblade orchids are also found here. Two of the seeps at Forest Glen are Illinois Nature Preserves—Forest Glen Seep and Howard's Hollow Seep.

The beech-maple woods are more typical of forests in the eastern United States and reach only a few miles into Illinois. American beech and tulip trees are not found in the central and western parts of Illinois. Take advantage of the Beech Grove and Big Tree trails and the Russell Duffin Nature Preserve to see these stately giants, especially the beeches with their smooth, gray bark. These two plant communities, and many others, make Forest Glen a natural jewel to be discovered and rediscovered on a regular basis.

**Directions:** Forest Glen is located in southern Vermilion County and is 7 miles northeast of Georgetown. From the junction of Highway 1 and Blacktop Road 1200 N in Westville, turn east and follow the blacktop road east and south 5 miles; then turn and go east 1.8 miles to the entrance of the preserve.

**Hours Open:** The site is open year-round. The observation tower closes at dark.

**Facilities:** Shelter houses are available for picnicking, plus each picnic site is furnished with a charcoal grill. Tent, RV, and group camping sites are available, and some of the sites have electricity. There is also a central water supply, restrooms, and a dump station. Fishing in two stocked ponds is allowed. In addition, the park has an arboretum, a tree and shiitake mushroom research area, a pioneer homestead, and an education campus. Below Hawk Hill Trail is an access point for canoeing.

**Permits and Rules:** No bicycles, horses, snowmobiles, or motorcycles are allowed on the trails. No collecting of plant, animal, or mineral specimens is allowed (although you may collect leaves, nuts, fruits, and mushrooms). All pets must be leashed. Park only in the lots. No swimming is allowed in the park.

**For Further Information:** Forest Glen Preserve, 20301 E. 900 North Road, Westville, IL 61883; 217-662-2142 or www.vccd.org.

## Park Trails

**Hawk Hill Trail** (🥾🥾🥾, less than 1 mile). The trail begins at the observation tower and ends at the Vermilion River. It follows a ridge, edged by deep ravines on each side, and heads down a steep hill to the river valley.

**Hickory Ridge Trail** (🥾🥾, 1.5 miles). This trail is accessible only from other trails—Hawk Hill or Tall Tree Trail—and passes through open fields and woods with two stream crossings.

**Spring Crest Trail** (🥾, .33 mile). Exceptional spring wildflowers highlight this trail as you walk through woods and skirt the edge of several ravines.

**Crab Tree Trail** (🥾🥾, 1.5 miles). The trail passes through open woods, successional fields, beech woods, and deep ravines. During wet weather, parts of the trail might require boots. This is an excellent trail for wildlife observation.

**River Ridge Backpack Trail** (🥾🥾🥾🥾, 11 miles). You must preregister at the park office before hiking here. The trail takes in a variety of habitats (including a restored tallgrass prairie, wooded ravines, beech forests, several ponds, and seeps) and interesting terrain (steep climbs and descents and many stream crossings).

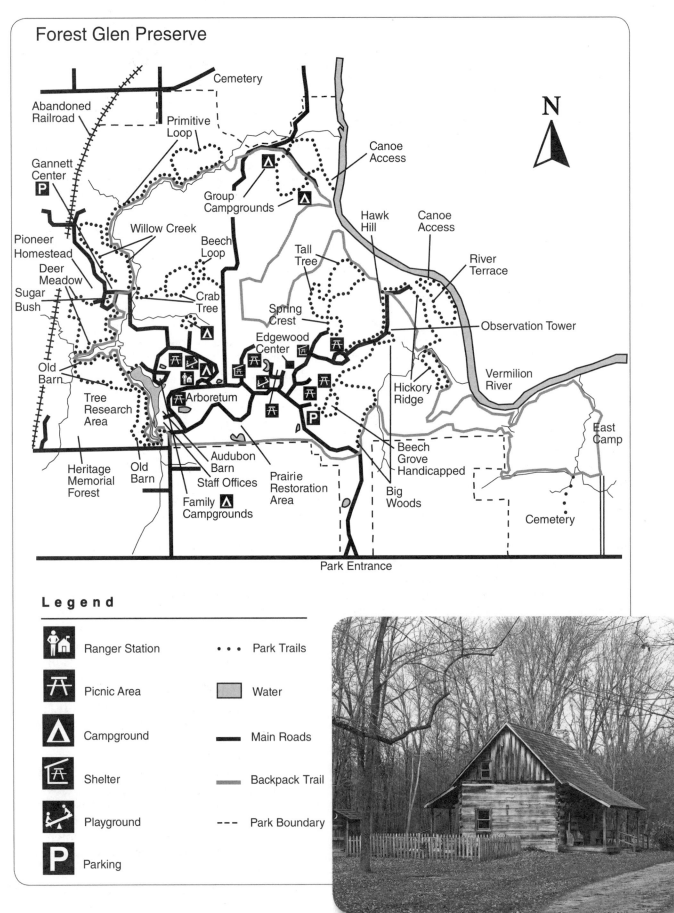

## Forest Glen Preserve

N

Cemetery

Abandoned Railroad

Primitive Loop

Gannett Center
P

Canoe Access

Willow Creek

Group Campgrounds

Hawk Hill

Canoe Access

Pioneer Homestead

Beech Loop

Tall Tree

River Terrace

Deer Meadow

Sugar Bush

Crab Tree

Spring Crest

Observation Tower

Edgewood Center

Vermilion River

Old Barn

Hickory Ridge

Tree Research Area

Arboretum

East Camp

Heritage Memorial Forest

Old Barn

Audubon Barn

Staff Offices

Family Campgrounds

Prairie Restoration Area

Beech Grove Handicapped

Big Woods

Cemetery

Park Entrance

## Legend

| | | | |
|---|---|---|---|
| 👷 Ranger Station | • • • Park Trails | | |
| 🏕 Picnic Area | ▢ Water | | |
| △ Campground | ━ Main Roads | | |
| 🏕 Shelter | ━ Backpack Trail | | |
| 🛝 Playground | --- Park Boundary | | |
| P Parking | | | |

# Willow Creek, Deer Meadow, and Old Barn Trails

 **Distance Round-Trip:** 3.75 miles
**Estimated Hiking Time:** 2 hours

*While walking I saw deer, rabbits, fox squirrels, and chipmunks and stepped on mole tunnels. But the best by far were the skunks scurrying toward the stream—skunk cabbages, that is.*

**Caution:** The trail can be very muddy and is very narrow in a couple of places, so watch your step.

**Trail Directions:** Park at Sycamore Hollow Campus at the Gannett Center parking area and head east (downhill) on the road. Once down, find a large open area on your left. Willow Creek Trail starts on the northeast corner [1]. Begin at the trail sign and pick up a trail guide to enhance your hiking experience. If you hike in the spring, enjoy the chorus of wood frogs in the adjacent pond. You are hiking along a ridge above the stream. Head into woods filled with large sugar maples. On the left you will begin to see the large, caladium-like leaves of skunk cabbage.

At .25 mi. take a short spur on your right to view a coal deposit and get a close look at Willow Creek [2]. Back on the main trail, look left and you will see the nature preserve sign for Howard's Hollow Seep, a one-acre wetland within the forested hills. Look for skunk cabbage, marsh marigold, and lots of jewelweed here. At .3 mi. the trail intersects with the primitive loop [3]. Continue to the left on Willow Creek. At .35 mi. you will see a large white oak on your right; on your left a few steps farther is the opening to old Dog Mine, a one-person coal mine. The trail curves left and passes through a grassy area and back through the woods.

At .75 mi. come to a trail intersection; go left and head toward the campus area [4]. As you round a bend, you are struck by a sinuous line of sassafras. The trail comes out at the back of the Gannett Center [5] (.85 mi.). Cross the park road and enter Deer Meadow Trail on the right at .9 mi. [6].

At 1.05 mi. cross the road; the trail is off to the right [7]. Within a few yards, go left and pass between the house and barn of the original settlers of the area, James and Anna Ogden. From the homestead the trail goes left on a wide, grassy path. While walking between the woods and old field, look for goldenrod galls. A trail comes in from the left at 1.40 mi. [8]; continue straight and look for large white oaks on both the right and left. After walking under the branches of a large oak, you will encounter a stream on the right that is lined with scouring rush—nature's pop beads.

At 1.5 mi. you will come to a trail intersection; go right and cross the creek [9]. Black-winged damselflies skirt the edge, and the water is so clear you can see small minnows along the sandy bottom. Once uphill, go right and discover a seep (not a bog, as the sign says), where skunk cabbage literally runs down the slope. From the seep, continue through oak woods that have many maple seedlings (maple takeover). Since oak woods need fire to help maintain their composition, maples will dominate the oaks if fire is suppressed. The trail comes out into a large open area at 1.85 mi. [10]; go left. The trail Ys at 2.3 mi.; go left and soon you will cross a bridge.

A wetland appears on the right at 2.35 mi. [11]. Take advantage of the bench to observe any animal interactions. Soon you will cross a bridge, and the woods will conceal the lake on your right. On your left is an open meadow. At 2.65 mi. the trail curves away from the lake, and soon a deep ravine appears on your right.

At 2.85 mi. the trail Ts; go left [12] and though a woods littered with maples. You will soon head down into the ravine (a railing is provided), cross a bridge, and head back up the other side. At 3.1 mi. you have completed the loop and are back at [9]; go right and recross the plank bridge. After the bridge, go right again. The trail comes out at the creek and heads left on a narrow path that is precariously close to the edge. At 3.4 mi. the trail curves left and then heads up and away from the stream [13]. An overlook will appear on the left at 3.60 mi. [14]. Admire the view, then go right and down, but do not cross the creek. The trail now forks, but continue heading up (to the left), following a red arrow. Once up, go right, skirting the edge of the woods; an exhibit of rocks and birds of prey is located at the education center near where you parked.

1. Start
2. Coal deposit
3. Trail intersection
4. Left turn
5. Back of Gannett Center
6. Deer Meadow Trail
7. Road crossing
8. Go straight
9. Right turn
10. Left turn
11. Wetland
12. Left turn
13. Moving away from stream
14. Overlook

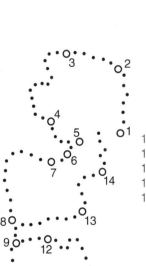

# Big Woods Trail

 **Distance Round-Trip:** 2.5 miles
**Estimated Hiking Time:**
1.33 hours

*Instead of a Stairmaster, try this trail that goes up and down the rolling terrain, climbs the many steps of the observation tower, and then heads back along the rolling terrain. When you hit that final downhill climb, you'll feel the burn!*

**Caution:** Roots are exposed on the trail. Watch your step as you climb the observation tower; some of the boards are loose.

**Trail Directions:** Park at the Beech Grove parking area and begin the trail at the board [1] on an asphalt path. The many downed trees are the result of a tornado. At .05 mi. you will begin to see the smooth, gray bark of large beeches and a trail fork; go right [2]. Look for tiny, gray tree frogs the size of a nickel on the foliage along here, find daddy longlegs under the leaves, and don't forget to look down at your feet. You just might see a bright brown and yellow millipede saunter by. An overlook for the ravine is at .1 mi. [3]. At .2 mi. admire the large tulip tree just before the trail intersection for Big Woods Trail, where you go right [4].

On your right is a black oak and a white oak; the two trees have literally grown together. Note the different-colored barks. On your right, as you walk on a narrow ridge, are ravines cloaked with Christmas fern, maidenhair fern, and wild ginger. At .40 mi. come to another trail intersection [5]; go left and up, and examine the bluff on your left for hepatica (which blooms in March). By .5 mi. you are in an open woods where many of the trees have double or triple trunks. A bench appears at .6 mi., and if you use it and are quiet, you should be rewarded with a visit from the resident chipmunks. The trail now heads down into the ravine.

From the bridge crossing at .7 mi. the trail undulates and is lined with numerous beech trees [6]. This may be one of the prettiest woods in Illinois. At .95 mi. the trail emerges in an open area and the observation tower is on your right [7]. If it is open, climb up, take time to catch your breath, and enjoy the view. If you're lucky, you may be eye to eye with

a turkey vulture! Head back down and retrace your steps to [7]. Return on the Big Tree Trail and catch up on things you missed the first time. Watch your step along here, at least until you get your land legs after your trek up the tower.

Retrace your steps to point [5] (1.7 mi.) and go left. You will immediately come to a signpost (number 7) that points out the large beech tree on the left (at least 100 years old). This tree is now dying. Notice how it decays differently from other tree species. At 1.75 mi. go down the steps, cross the creek on a log bridge, and head up the steps and to the right [8]. It appears that the uplands took the brunt of the tornado damage, as the ravine forest is fine. As you walk on a narrow ridge between two ravines, look for the long, oval leaves of pawpaw, a shrub in the understory. The trail now heads up more steps. Look at the bluffs on both sides; they're covered with hepatica and wild ginger.

At the top, you are walking in an open woods with a fairly clean understory. Look for a row of tall, straight tulip trees and take a final glance at the smooth, gray bark of the beech trees. At 2.05 mi. pass the trailhead for Big Tree Trail and go right, walking along the road [9]. It has nice, wide shoulders. By 2.35 mi. the woods have disappeared and you are now walking through old field and planted trees, but still next to the road. At 2.5 mi. go right and you are back at the Beech Grove parking area.

1. Start
2. Right turn
3. Overlook
4. Right turn
5. Left turn
6. Beeches
7. Open area
8. Creek crossing
9. Road

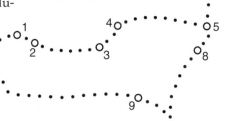

# 35. Robert Allerton Park

- Discover wonderful sculptures as you walk through the woods and gardens.

- Enjoy not only a profusion of spring wildflowers but also well-manicured gardens.

- Take peaceful, pleasant hikes and encounter birds, butterflies, wildflowers, and wildlife.

- Gaze upward at the 15-foot *Sunsinger* as he embraces the morning sky.

- Visit one of the official Seven Wonders of Illinois.

## Area Information

Allerton Park, located near Monticello, began as a series of landholdings along the Sangamon River, purchased in 1863 by Samuel Allerton. The land, known then as "The Farms," was a model production livestock and crop farm. In 1946 this land was given to the University of Illinois for research and educational purposes. In addition to the farmland, the grounds contained landscaped gardens and more than 100 sculptures.

The Sangamon River divides the park into two sections. The north contains the gardens and sculptures, whereas the south is a relatively undisturbed example of an Illinois stream valley ecosystem. The southern section supports a 600-acre floodplain that includes a nearly primeval forest and has been declared a national natural landmark. River bluffs are dominated by red and bur oak, and some 75 acres of reclaimed prairie (complete with prairie rattlesnakes) are there for exploring. The park is a sanctuary for plants and animals: 1,090 species of plants, 60 species of breeding birds, 30 species of animals, and 28 species of reptiles and amphibians.

**Directions:** Robert Allerton Park is located off I-72 near Monticello. To the **North Entrance (North River Trail)** from I-72: Take exit 164 (Monticello/Bridge Street); turn south toward Monticello; turn right (west) at the first intersection (Old Route 47); drive 2 miles, then turn left on County Road 625 East; drive 1 mile to a T, then turn right onto County Farm Road. After .5 mile turn left into the Allerton Park entrance through brick columns. Follow the signs to the visitor center. To the **South Entrance (Buck Schroth Trail):** Take exit 164 (Monticello/Bridge Street); turn south into Monticello; continue straight into town to the first stoplight and turn right onto Market Street (ignore the brown Allerton Park signs). At the four-way stop sign, turn right onto Marion Street, drive to the T at the stop sign, and turn left onto Allerton Road. Continue for 3.5 miles, turning right at the sign for the Schroth Trail parking lot.

**Hours Open:** The site is open year-round from 8:00 a.m. to dusk, except Thanksgiving, Christmas Day, and New Year's Day.

**Facilities:** A visitor center has snacks, restrooms, and information about the park and the Allerton family. Picnicking is permitted. The hiking trails may be used for cross-country skiing during the winter. Allerton House, the family mansion, is used as a conference center and is usually not open to the general public.

**Permits and Rules:** All dogs and other animals must be leashed. No alcoholic beverages or firearms are allowed. No fishing, hunting, or camping is permitted. Nothing is to be removed from the park. (Picking flowers, either wild or cultivated, is prohibited.) Do not swim or wade in the river or ponds.

**For Further Information:** Allerton Park and Retreat Center, 515 Old Timber Road, Monticello, IL 61856; 217-333-3287 or www.allerton.uiuc.edu.

## Park Trails

**North Side Trails** ( 🥾 🥾 , total 6 miles). Two out of the four north side trails circulate around the landscape gardens. The park's sculptures can be seen on Orange Trail (*Fu Dogs*) at .8 mi., Yellow Trail (the Chinese musicians and *Centaur*) at 2.3 mi., Brown Trail (Pioneer Cemetery) at 2.2 mi., and Purple Trail (*Sunsinger*) at .7 mi.

**South Side Trails** ( 🥾 🥾 , total 7.5 miles). Experience a near-primeval central Illinois forest, prairie, and profuse spring wildflowers by taking one of these trails: Red Trail (3.1 mi.), Blue Trail (2.4 mi.), or Green Trail (2 mi.).

## Other Areas of Interest

Located near Monticello, **Lodge Park—Piatt County Forest Preserve,** offers camping, primitive toilets, fishing, and hiking. In the spring a veritable artist's palette of color awaits you in the form of wildflowers along the banks of the Sangamon. For more information, call 800-952-3396.

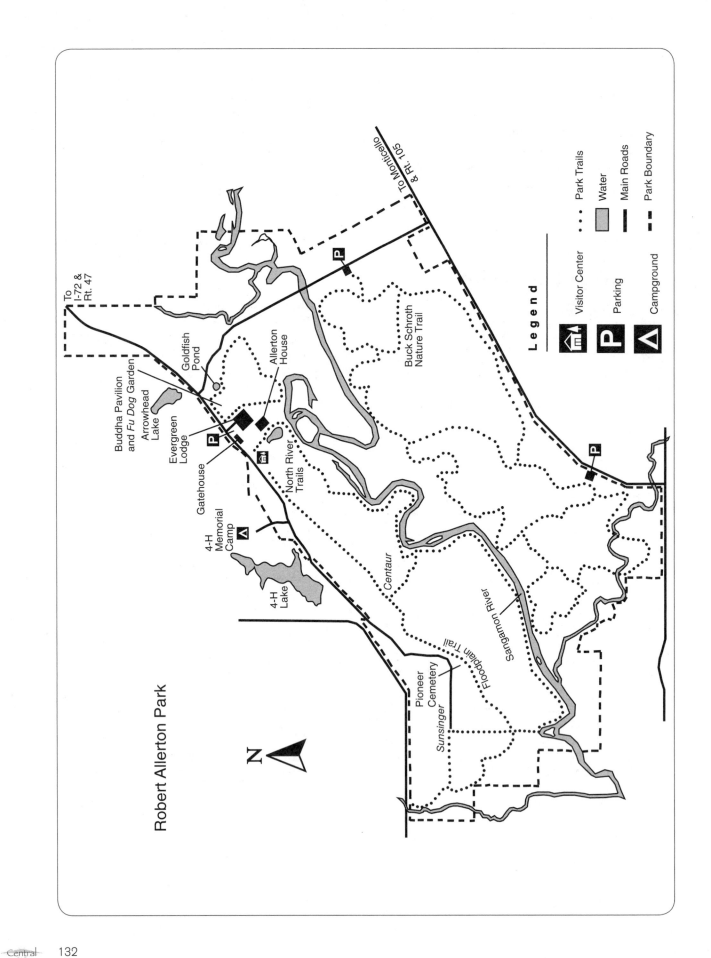

Robert Allerton Park

N

Legend

Visitor Center · · · · Park Trails
P  Parking     Water
▲  Campground ── Main Roads
         – – Park Boundary

To Monticello & Rt. 105

To I-72 & Rt. 47

Goldfish Pond

Allerton House

Buck Schroth Nature Trail

Buddha Pavilion and *Fu Dog* Garden

Arrowhead Lake

Evergreen Lodge

Gatehouse

North River Trails

4-H Memorial Camp

4-H Lake

*Centaur*

Sangamon River

Pioneer Cemetery

*Sunsinger*

Floodplain Trail

# North River Trails

**Distance Round-Trip:** 5.25 miles
**Estimated Hiking Time:** 2.5 hours

*Hiking these pieces of several trails allows one to discover some of the many treasures of the park—the bottomland forest of the Sangamon, a larger-than-life Apollo, acres of wildflowers, finely manicured gardens, and blue* Fu Dogs.

**Caution:** The trail can be very muddy near the river. Poison ivy and stinging nettle are everywhere.

**Trail Directions:** From the main parking lot near Allerton House, walk back to the parking-lot entrance, but go right just before the road and walk down a vine-lined allée [1]. Straight ahead is the *House of the Golden Buddhas.* From here go right and through the *Fu Dog* Garden [2] (.15 mi.). From the *Fu Dog* Garden enter the woods and continue on the trail. On your left is a seep.

At .35 mi. the trail curves right and heads toward the river [3]. Floodplain forest will be on your left. At the trail intersection at .85 mi., keep straight and head uphill [4]. Soon the back of Allerton House comes into view. At .9 mi. the trail Ys; go left, crossing stones. Head up the steps [5]. Once at the top, follow the trail to the left. The Sangamon River is on the left; to the right is a small patch of woods, backed by Allerton's open vista of grass. The trail is now part of a river terrace, 10 to 12 feet above the river.

Continue straight at 1.25 mi. (another trail comes in from the right) [6], and within .5 mi. the trail Ts; go left, skirting the river. During the summer look for tiny toads traversing the trail and note the tall, straight sycamores. Bright yellow sneezeweed carpets the area. At 2 mi. go left [7]; you are hiking through an excellent example of a bottomland forest, where you can marvel at leaning maples, large oaks, and linear sycamores. At 2.9 mi. note an island in the Sangamon [8], and the trail soon curves right.

At 3.3 mi. the trail goes right, heading away from the river [9]. During late summer look for bright red cardinal flower amidst the stinging nettle and ruby-throated hummingbirds dancing above them. Straight ahead, in the distance, you may get a glimpse of the famous *Sunsinger.* You are now walking on the remnants of an old road. Another trail intersects your path [10] (3.4 mi.), but continue straight and uphill to the statue. The trail emerges on a road that circles the statue [11] (3.5 mi.). Go right, walking along the wide, grassy shoulder. Few can resist a side spur to take a closer look at the *Sunsinger.*

The *Sunsinger* is actually Apollo greeting the morning sky with song

and extended arms. Continue to walk on the grassy shoulder, away from the *Sunsinger,* and follow the park road. At 3.75 mi. take a side spur on your right to explore the Pioneer Cemetery [12]; retrace your steps back to the park road. Within a few steps is a narrow footpath off to the right; take this.

This short trail soon comes to a T; go left and hike between upland forest on the left and floodplain forest on the right [13] (3.95 mi.). Soon the *Death of the Last Centaur* appears in the distance; head uphill to enjoy this unusual depiction [14] (4.25 mi.). Continue northeast (straight) on the rolling trail, which is lined with tall oaks that arch over the path. At 4.45 mi. you will pass a trail to the House in the Woods, but continue straight and into an allée of spruce trees [15]. The natural portion of the hike has ended.

At 4.9 mi. you will enter the sunken gardens, marked with fish-topped pillars [16]. Cross the garden and go up the steps on the other side along a path lined with statuary of Chinese musicians. You may now navigate the hedge maze and pass through a cedar allée with the statue *Adam* in the center. At the statue of *Girl With a Scarf,* take a right [17] (5.15 mi.). You will soon pass through a brick-wall gate, topped with baskets of stone fruit and the bronze figures *Sea Maidens;* go left [18], following the paved path back to the parking area.

1. Start
2. *Fu Dog* Garden
3. Right turn
4. Go straight
5. Steps
6. Go straight
7. Left turn
8. Island in river
9. Right turn
10. Trail intersection
11. *Sunsinger*
12. Cemetery
13. Left turn
14. *Death of the Last Centaur*
15. Spruce trees
16. Sunken gardens
17. Right turn
18. Left turn

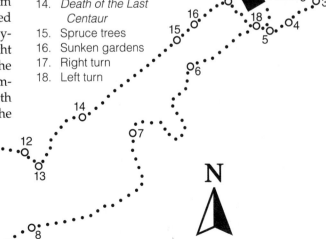

# Buck Schroth Nature Trail

  **Distance Round-Trip:** 2.1 miles
**Estimated Hiking Time:** 1 hour

*Although Buck is no longer around to guide you on his popular nature walks through the park, his legacy lives on with interpretive signs, and his presence is still felt.*

**Caution:** During late spring and summer, the mosquitoes can be very pesky. Don't forget to wear repellent.

**Trail Directions:** Begin the trail at the parking area just south of the Sangamon River [1] and hike through a recovering woods. Cross the bridge and head uphill. Parts of the trail are old asphalt, remnants of a trail laid out by the Allertons. The trail comes to a T at .1 mi. [2]; go right. A sign explains who Buck Schroth was and the purpose of his trail. Eugene "Buck" Schroth, biology teacher, former director of Allerton House, and Allerton volunteer extraordinaire, was attracted to the park's diversity. He spent more than 50 years here walking, studying, learning, and imparting this knowledge through popular wildflower talks and tours of the nature trails. This trail is a fitting memorial to him.

At .2 mi. you enter the floodplain forest. The first station is at .25 mi. [3] and concerns fungi (mushrooms). Here you can learn more about morels (mushroom hunting is not allowed in the park) and the other numerous species of fungi that thrive here. The Sangamon River soon comes into view on the right. At .35 mi. you have arrived at the Sangamon River station [4]. The Sangamon remains a natural stream; stop here to learn more about the ecology of the river and its floodplain.

The floodplain forest is soon replaced by more upland species; look for wolf trees on the right. (Wolf trees are usually oaks with large outspread branches, indicating they grew in the open.)

You will soon pass a small, temporary pool on the right, but it isn't what it appears to be. In reality, at least when the Allertons were here, this was a hog wallow (.4 mi.). A station on tracking Allerton mammals is near the wallow. The wildflower station appears at .6 mi. [5]. April through May is a wonderful time to visit the park and walk among the profusion of spring flowers. Virginia bluebell, blue-eyed Marys, violet, and phlox carpet parts of the park. Here Buck reaches forth from the past and tells you what will be blooming and when. At .7 mi., come to a trail intersection [6]; go left. Look for deer as you hike this stretch. Exit the woods at .8 mi. and encounter the savanna station [7]. Learn more about savannas and the clues used to identify this habitat in the park and elsewhere. Now go left and skirt the prairie.

As you walk by the prairie, feel the leaves of the compass plant. At one time pioneers used it to tell direction; luckily, you have a nice wide trail. Like the woods in progress you have just passed through, this is a prairie in progress. Another station at .95 mi. [8] provides information on the importance of Allerton Park for migrating songbirds. Come to a trail intersection at 1.05 mi. [9] and go right, but not before studying the station about a group of beasts undoubtedly encountered on the trail—the insects. As you continue to skirt the prairie, note examples of ongoing restoration.

At 1.25 mi. go right and take the short path to discover the prairie—a landscape that once covered 60 percent of the state [10]. Return to the trail and continue on, eventually heading into the woods to discover why Allerton Park may be the ultimate butterfly garden, and explore butterfly alley [11] (1.3 mi.). One-third of the state's butterfly species can be found in the park. From butterfly alley, retrace your steps and look for deer, admire the prairie flowers, watch dragonflies sun themselves, and if you are really lucky, encounter a prairie rattlesnake. (It belongs here, so admire it but leave it alone!)

Back at [9] (1.65 mi.), continue straight and through the woods. At 1.75 mi. you will pass the station on exotic plants [12]. Isn't it ironic that in the exotic landscape of Allerton, exotics should be a problem? By 1.95 mi. you are back at [2]. In the words of Buck, hopefully you learned not only about the "various and sundry plants, but [also about] trees, birds, and nature." Go right and retrace your steps to the parking area. Whether or not you saw any of the things highlighted by the interpretative signs, you certainly feel that you have. If you come to Allerton Park often enough, though, it is a foregone conclusion that eventually you will see everything that Buck saw.

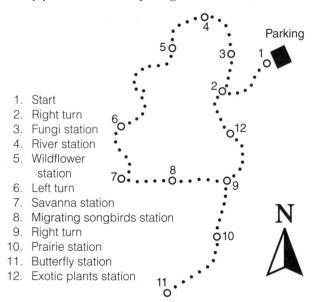

1. Start
2. Right turn
3. Fungi station
4. River station
5. Wildflower station
6. Left turn
7. Savanna station
8. Migrating songbirds station
9. Right turn
10. Prairie station
11. Butterfly station
12. Exotic plants station

- Hike through a sculpture garden.
- Compare a prairie grove of the past to one of the present.
- Take advantage of an urban nature oasis.
- Herald spring with the call and sightings of the American woodcock.

## Area Information

When settlers first came to Champaign County, they found huge expanses of prairie with forest growing along rivers and streams. Near what was to become Urbana grew the "Big Woods" or "Big Grove," a 10-square-mile area of timberland along the Salt Fork River. Settlers throughout Illinois preferred to clear trees from the woods to create farmland instead of breaking the tough prairie sod; this area was no exception. A cabin was built on the edge of the Big Grove in 1822, and the town that grew up was named Urbana by Sen. John Vance, who represented Vermilion County. Urbana was the name of his boyhood home in Ohio.

Busey Woods is one of three surviving parcels of the Big Grove. During 1909 the Saline Branch, which flowed through Busey Woods, was channeled, creating a seasonal oxbow pond. From 1910 to 1970 the south half of the woods was used as pasture. That use can still be seen in the difference in vegetation between the north and south parts of the woods. In the 1960s the owners made plans to develop the woods, and as a result large amounts of rubble and debris were dumped in low spots. Fortunately, local citizens worked to save the woods, and in 1971 the woods were donated by the Busey family to the University of Illinois Foundation. Twenty years later, Busey Woods became the property of the Urbana Park District.

As a typical prairie grove, Busey Woods consists of oak-hickory and maple-basswood forests that support an undergrowth of redbud, pawpaw, and prickly ash. The understory vegetation includes spring wildflower displays. Beginning as early as March, the floor is carpeted with wave after wave of showy wildflowers. As summer approaches, the canopy closes and the woods become dark, and by late summer only jewelweed is found blooming in the dense shade.

Meadowbrook Park was formerly the McCullough farmstead. Today, it is a 130-acre park that includes paved and unpaved paths, PrariePlay playground,

organic garden plots, Walker Grove, 60 acres of prairie, and several gardens. These gardens include the Windmill Garden, which features one of the first Fairbanks Windmills. Around the windmill are patches of heirloom annuals that central Illinois farmsteads would have planted. The Celia and Willet Wandell Sculpture Garden was established in 1998 and is an ever-changing outdoor sculpture gallery. The Timpone Family Tree Grove allows visitors to look closely at small trees and shrubs and imagine how to use them in their gardens. Meadowbrook is an urban oasis to be visited often.

**Directions: Busey Woods** is located in northwest Urbana. Exit I-74 at Lincoln Avenue. Head south on Lincoln Avenue to University Avenue (about 1 mile). Turn left onto University Avenue; after passing the Carle Hospital complex, turn left onto Broadway Avenue, and finally take a left onto Thompson and into the parking lot.

**Meadowbrook Park** is located in southeast Urbana. Exit I-74 at Lincoln Avenue and head south, following Lincoln Avenue until it Ts into Windsor Road. Take a left onto Windsor Road and at the first four-way stop sign turn right onto Race Street. The entrance and parking area will be on your left.

**Hours Open:** Both sites are open year-round from dawn to dusk. The Anita Purves Nature Center near Busey Woods is open Monday through Friday, 8:00 a.m. to 6:00 p.m., and Saturdays from 9:00 a.m. to 4:00 p.m. It is closed on Sundays.

**Facilities:** Busey Woods and the adjacent Crystal Lake Park have an accessible playground, ball fields, seasonal boating, picnic tables, ice skating, fishing, restrooms, horseshoes, shuffleboard, a swimming pool, pavilions, a boat house, and the Anita Purves Nature Center. Meadowbrook Park offers pavilions, an accessible playground, open fields, and seasonal restrooms (April 15-October 15).

**Permits and Rules:** At Busey Woods, collecting items, walking pets, and bicycling are not permitted. At Meadowbrook Park, dogs, bicycles, in-line skates, and skateboards are allowed on paved paths only. Dogs must be leashed at all times and their waste removed. Picnicking is allowed in the shelters only. Removal of park property or natural materials is prohibited.

**For Further Information:** Urbana Park District, 505 W. Stoughton, Urbana, IL 61801; 217-367-1544; www.urbanaparks.org. Anita Purves Nature Center, 1505 N. Broadway, Urbana, IL 61801; 217-384-4062.

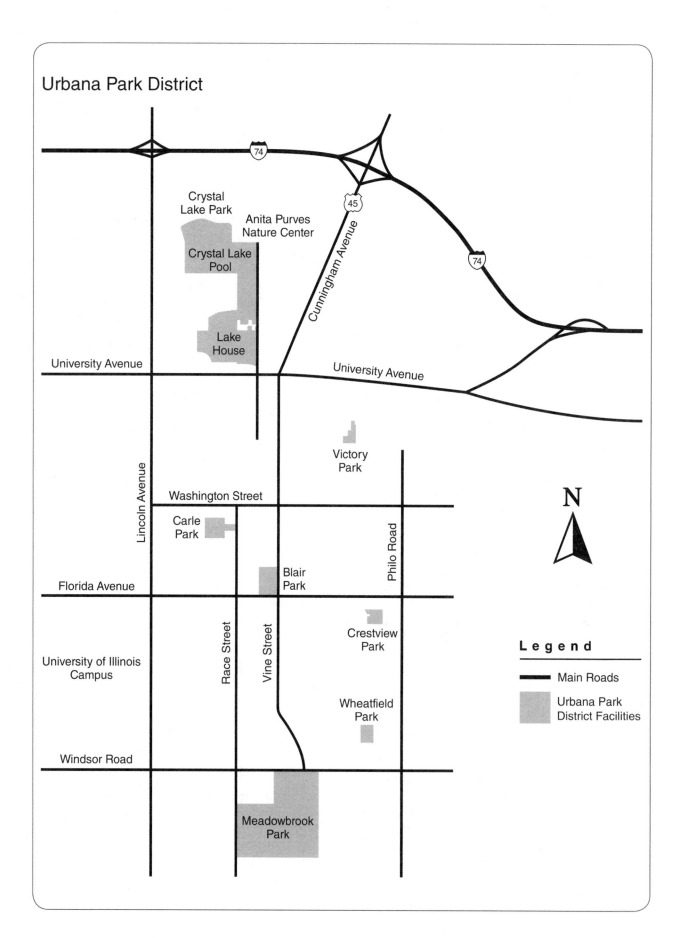

Urbana Park District

Crystal
Lake Park

Anita Purves
Nature Center

Crystal Lake
Pool

Lake
House

University Avenue

University Avenue

Cunningham Avenue

Victory
Park

Lincoln Avenue

Washington Street

Carle
Park

Philo Road

Blair
Park

Florida Avenue

Race Street

Vine Street

Crestview
Park

University of Illinois
Campus

Wheatfield
Park

Windsor Road

Meadowbrook
Park

N

Legend

Main Roads

Urbana Park
District Facilities

# Meadowbrook Park

 **Distance Round-Trip:** 2 miles
**Estimated Hiking Time:** 1 hour

*This is a trail where culture and nature intermingle. Where else can you see a sculpture of a sinewy nude against a backdrop of a prairie, hear the peents of the American woodcock while admiring a larger-than-life stone rabbit, or watch dancing green darner dragonflies swirl above a primary-colored humanoid dragon?*

**Caution:** This trail is very popular with skaters, joggers, dog walkers, and bicyclists—be aware.

**Trail Directions:** Start at the map near the Race Street parking area [1]. The trail is a concrete path with mile and kilometer markings. Within a few steps the organic garden plots and Windmill Garden are on your left, while a sensory garden is on your right. The windmill is original to the property and the small garden is modeled after a kitchen garden you might find at a farmstead. For a short side spur, wander the sensory garden path and then continue on the trail. A picnic shelter and walnut grove are on the right. During spring the grove attracts migrating warblers and during summer the grove has an understory of coneflowers.

At .25 mi. is an intersection; go left [2]. Prior to the intersection, note a catalpa tree and notice its large, heart-shaped leaves and bean-like seedpods. If you are lucky, it might be a year when catalpa sphinx caterpillars are abundant. These black caterpillars with yellow racing stripes can, if numerous enough, defoliate this tree.

Soon on your right will be a prairie restoration and on your left an open grassy area which gives way to a dogwood thicket. As you walk don't forget to look at the labeled sculptures; along this section of trail the trees are also named. The trail Ts at .5 mi.; go right [3]. On your left will be Windsor Road; prairie will be on your right. During the late winter and early spring, this is a good place to look and listen for pheasants.

Turn right at the sculpture garden sign and the colorful *Fathers and Sons* sculpture [4]. Within a few steps, turn left and cross a bridge over McCullough Creek. You will find a park map here as well. The trail soon Ts; go right toward the play area and past the red hammer sculpture labeled *Minimal Response III*. Wind your way around the play area. Another intersection appears at .8 mi., go right [5], where you will soon pass by a primary-colored sculpture. During weekends the large expanse of grass showcases the talents of local flying-disc dogs and the arial antics of the model airplane club.

At .95 mi. prairie encompasses the trail. During the spring listen and look for red-winged blackbirds and common yellowthroats; by summer, goldfinches are common in this area. During early fall look for woolly bear caterpillars crossing the path. Folk wisdom suggests that the color and thickness of the caterpillar's coat are predictors of the length and severity of winter. Why do they cross the road? Unlike most moths, woolly bears spend the winter as a caterpillar, so they are crossing the path seeking a suitable hiding place to spend the cold months.

A prairie viewing platform (Freyfogle Overlook) appears at 1.15 mi. [6]. Take advantage of this viewpoint, looking at the prairie and its various inhabitants. In the fall, right in front of the platform is a large clump of cream gentians. Satiated with the view, continue on. The trail curves right at 1.3 mi. During March at dusk this is a good section to listen and look for the American woodcock's courtship dance. The woodcock is a small, mottled brown, rotund shorebird. It utters a nasal "peent," and as the bird spirals skyward its wings make a whirring twitter.

At 1.5 mi. another map appears as the trail curves left over a bridge [7]. Stay on the cement path. Once over the bridge you enter the Denise and Ernest Grove, a savanna restoration on your left. On the right is a willow- and cottonwood-lined stream. At dusk this is a popular area for white-tailed deer. At 1.75 mi. the trail curves right and you cross another bridge. On the other side you are greeted by a larger-than-life rabbit [8].

Check the power lines on the left for ruby-throated hummingbirds during the summer. The orange, tubular flower underneath the power lines is trumpet vine. It belongs to the same plant family as the catalpa tree. The trail winds by the Timpone Ornamental Tree Grove where all the trees are labeled. The final trail intersection appears at 2 mi.; go right back to the map where you began.

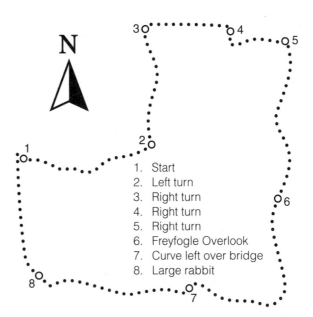

1. Start
2. Left turn
3. Right turn
4. Right turn
5. Right turn
6. Freyfogle Overlook
7. Curve left over bridge
8. Large rabbit

# Busey Woods and Crystal Lake Park

  **Distance Round-Trip:** 3.35 miles
**Estimated Hiking Time:** 1.15 hours

*As I wandered the remnants of the Big Grove, twins came to mind: one well-groomed and wide-pathed, with a few robins, geese, and squirrels; the other rugged, with a narrow path and full of nature's possibilities.*

**Caution:** Watch for exposed roots and goose droppings on the trial. You will cross the park road so use caution.

**Trail Directions:** Start at the Anita Purves Nature Center at the sign labeled "trails" and go left on an asphalt path [1]. As you head down the steps and angle left, check out the bird feeders. Cross the bridge over the Saline Ditch and turn right. After a few steps turn right again. The trail Ys; go right again and you are now hiking on a boardwalk through a piece of the Big Grove, an oak-hickory and maple woods with a pawpaw understory. Take advantage of the signage and benches along the boardwalk.

As you round the corner, notice the osage orange trees. Jonathan B. Turner, an early professor at the University of Illinois, was an advocate of this living hedgerow. At .2 mi. is a bench and signage describing shifting views [2]. Look for a large chinquapin oak and large cottonwoods. Stumps throughout the woods are evidence of past giants. At .25 mi. ignore the right trail; stay on the boardwalk as you pass signage describing restoration and a large bur oak with lobed leaves on the right. Under the power line, go right onto a narrow path that will soon widen.

Three trails come in at .45 mi.; go right through the maples [3]. The cement slabs you pass by are reminders of the past as the owners were trying to fill in low spots to develop the area. An ephemeral pond (an old channel of the Saline Branch) is on the right with a large oak alongside it. Pawpaws, which have large, oval leaves that are commonly over a foot long, are prolific in this area. In the winter, pawpaw can be recognized by its alternate branches and the feathery appearance of its hairy, brownish terminal buds. The pawpaw is the food plant of zebra swallowtail larvae.

At .6 mi. swing right along a large bur oak and over a wooden footbridge; the trail then curves right. At .7 mi. is an intersection; go left [4], cross a bridge, and go left again past two large shagbark hickories. You pass an observation deck over a small pool before the trail curves left and heads up and you find yourself at the rear entrance to the woods. Go left [5]; you are soon walking under power lines with an understory of goldenrod.

An intersection appears at 1.2 mi.; go right [6] into a maple grove where the trail subtly Vs; go right into a recovering woods. The trail Ts at 1.4 mi.; go right and then bear left (do not go down into the slough). Continue to bear left, with another left taking you to the edge of the Saline Ditch. You are walking on top of a spoil heap that was created when the ditch was dug. The trail comes to another T at 1.65 mi.; go right, back over the bridge. Once over the bridge take another right and walk through a picnic area and past a large frog sculpture [7]. Walk along the road and parking area.

At 1.8 mi. take the sidewalk path heading south [8]. A swimming pool will be on your left, while a hedge is on your right. Take a right over a bridge and you have entered Crystal Lake Park [9], a manicured section of the old Big Grove. A huge sugar maple will be on your right; notice the old, flaky bark. At the corner of the fence, the road curves right; go left and cross the road [10] (2.1 mi.). You will pass a fountain on your right and should also begin to encounter the resident flock of Canada geese. At 2.4 mi. go left; do not cross the bridge as you continue to walk along the lake. The sidewalk has given way to grass. From the lake angle toward a narrow dirt path that eventually heads to the street. The Saline Ditch will be on your left and a grassy knoll on the right.

The path dead-ends into Broadway Avenue [11]; go left and cross over the Saline Ditch. At 2.6 mi. go left and reenter the park [12]. Walk along the edge of the park road past a double-trunked red oak and large sycamores. You will hear the fountain that you passed earlier as you hike through a grove of white oaks. Ignore the bridge on your left and continue to follow the park road. Walk through a parking lot at 3.15 mi. and continue straight. You will soon be back at [9]. Go right and retrace your steps past the swimming pool and to the parking area.

1. Start
2. Bench
3. Three-trail intersection, right turn
4. Left turn
5. Left turn
6. Right turn into maple grove
7. Large frog
8. Swimming pool on left
9. Enter Crystal Lake Park
10. Left turn, cross road
11. Broadway Avenue, left turn
12. Left turn, reenter park

# 37. Fox Ridge State Park

- Bring your insect field guide and practice your entomological skills in summer.
- Hike on ridges with clean understories and descend into valleys where you are engulfed by vegetation.
- Develop an appreciation for the diversity of daddy longlegs.
- Among an overabundance of maples, enjoy the park's fall colors.

## Area Information

Nestled along the Embarras River, Fox Ridge State Park belies its prairie heritage. It is a series of ravines along a glacial moraine. Simply translated, this area is very hilly! The Embarras forms the western boundary of the park. In historic times it provided early settlers with food, water, and transportation. Flatboats carried the settlers' goods to the Wabash River, and from there to points beyond. This small parcel of land was taken over by the state during the late 1930s.

The park is used not only for recreation but also for research. The Illinois Natural History Survey maintains a laboratory here with scientists studying the lake, streams, and ponds in order to improve fishing. Ridge Lake was the first lake where scientists were able to control the water level. They have studied the effect drawdowns have on fish, whether supplemental feeding of the lake's fish is helpful, and what happens with the introduction of predators, such as walleye and muskellunge. These fishery studies are some of the longest and most continuous in the country.

Civic pride is strong locally. The Fox Ridge Foundation is very active in promoting and improving the park so that visitors will have a good time and return often.

**Directions:** Fox Ridge State Park is located 8 miles south of Charleston, off Route 130.

**Hours Open:** The site is open year-round.

**Facilities:** These include camping (which includes a rent-a-camp), five reservable picnic shelters, two baseball diamonds, sand volleyball courts, and fishing by reservation only due to the research on the lake (call 217-345-6490). Fishing and canoeing in the Embarras are open to all.

**Permits and Rules:** No bicycles are allowed on the trails.

**For Further Information:** Fox Ridge State Park, 18175 State Park Road, Charleston, IL 61920; 217-345-6416.

## Park Trails

**Wilderness and Family** (👣👣👣, .25 mile). Both of these trails are .25-mile linear trails through oak, hickory, and maple woods. Both are lined with mayapples and jack-in-the-pulpits in the understory and provide good views into the ravines.

## Other Areas of Interest

Located 20 miles northeast of Charleston, **Walnut Point State Park** offers fishing, camping, hunting, and picnicking. Take advantage of a tree-lined drive to learn your native Illinois trees and to enjoy the spring wildflowers. Two trails total 2.25 miles. For more information, call 217-346-3336.

**Lincoln Log Cabin State Historic Site** was the 1840s farm and home of Thomas and Sarah Lincoln, Abraham Lincoln's parents. From May through October the farm comes to life with crops, livestock, and costumed living-history interpreters. Located south of Charleston, the site is open year-round from 8:30 a.m. until dusk Wednesday through Sunday. For more information, call 217-345-1845 or visit www.lincolnlogcabin.org.

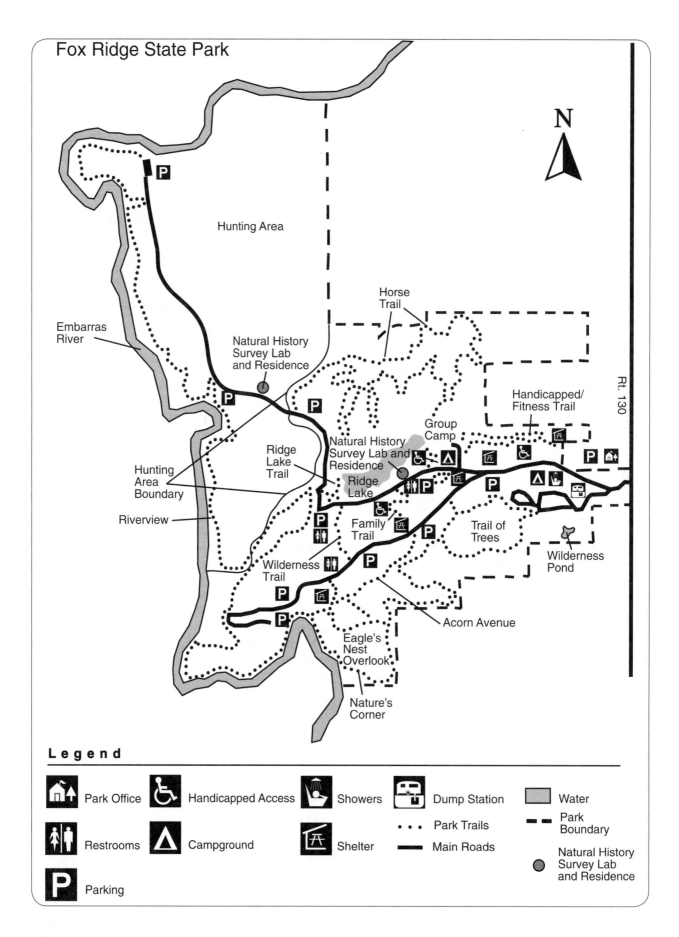

# Fox Ridge State Park

Hunting Area

Horse Trail

Embarras River

Natural History Survey Lab and Residence

Handicapped/ Fitness Trail

Rt. 130

Group Camp

Natural History Survey Lab and Residence

Ridge Lake Trail

Hunting Area Boundary

Ridge Lake

Riverview

Family Trail

Trail of Trees

Wilderness Pond

Wilderness Trail

Acorn Avenue

Eagle's Nest Overlook

Nature's Corner

## Legend

| | | | | |
|---|---|---|---|---|
| Park Office | Handicapped Access | Showers | Dump Station | Water |
| Restrooms | Campground | Shelter | ••• Park Trails | − − Park Boundary |
| Parking | | | — Main Roads | Natural History Survey Lab and Residence |

# Riverview Sampler

 **Distance Round-Trip:** 1.5 miles
**Estimated Hiking Time:** 1 hour

*During the summer this is a place to practice your ento-mological skills. Dragonflies and damselflies flit about on vegetation along the river, crane flies hang motionless on stinging nettle, butterflies form puddle clubs on the trail in front of you, and all are accompanied by the inevitable drone of mosquitoes.*

**Caution:** The trail can be very muddy. Logs sometimes block the trail and roots are everywhere.

**Trail Directions:** Park your vehicle at Shady Ridge Shelter and begin the trail at the far-east end of the parking lot at an old trail board [1]. Head down on a gravel path. Look on either side of the trail at the veg-etation and the insects it conceals. Look for hanging crane flies, green katydids, and daddy longlegs. As you continue down, look for the large, oblong leaves of pawpaw. Pawpaw is the larval food of the zebra swallowtail, so look for this showy butterfly during spring and summer.

Once you're down, a trail intersection appears (.15 mi.); go right on Riverview Trail [2]. The trail is on the edge of the floodplain and upland forest. On the left is a bottomland forest of cottonwoods, while on the right is an upland forest of maple, oak, and hickory. At .2 mi. go left for a side spur to see the great bend in the Embarras River [3]. Eventually the river will cut across the neck of the bend and shorten its course. The former channel now cut off will fill with groundwater and an oxbow lake will form. Retrace your steps back to the trail.

At .25 mi. the trail will Y; go left [4], keeping the Embarras River on your left. Notice the riprap along the edges; this is done in order to keep the river from eroding its banks. Within a few steps an intersection will appear; continue straight on a narrow path through a floodplain forest dominated by cottonwoods, silver maples, and stinging nettle. The white fuzz that litters the trail during the early summer is seed from the cottonwood tree. Don't get too close to the stinging nettle because any contact will cause some of its hairs to break off and embed in your skin. An

irritating acid that fills the hollow of each hair will make this a memorable, if painful, experience. Luckily, the discomfort is short-lived.

As you hike along this section you are able to catch glimpses of the river; notice how the river is full of mud and silt bars and that you are hiking faster than the current. You can tell this is the river's floodplain because sometimes the trail is pure sand. The trail will follow the meandering of the river. At .85 mi. you will come out into a grassy field and young forest [5]; go left. The trail is lined with goldenrod. Check the stems of these plants for oblong growths. These growths are called galls and are formed by a fly when she lays her eggs in the stem. Don't forget to look overhead; during late summer over a dozen green darner dragonflies may be circling, hawking the insects you stir up as you hike.

The trail circles a wetland with ironweed and wil-lows before coming out onto the park road at 1.1 mi. [6]; go right. At 1.25 mi. you will pass a boat launch area; go left into the woods on Riverview Trail [7]. Along this section, look for bluebirds and eastern king-birds as they hawk for insects. Within a few steps you will have completed the loop and are back at [2]; go left, back up the hill to the Shady Rest Picnic Area.

1. Start
2. Right turn onto Riverview Trail
3. Great bend
4. Y in trail, left turn
5. Left turn
6. Right turn
7. Left turn

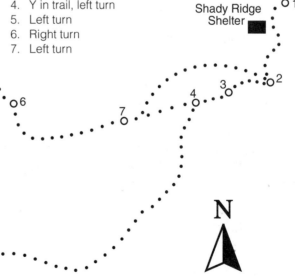

# Acorn Avenue
# and Trail of Trees

**Distance Round-Trip:** 2.75 miles
**Estimated Hiking Time:** 1.4 hours

*This is a hike that provides a complete workout—large and small steps, twisting switchbacks, and flat stretches. Even your neck gets a workout as you strain to look up at the lofty trees.*

**Caution:** Logs are sometimes blocking the trail and roots protrude from the trail. Respect all signs telling you to stay off an area due to erosion.

**Trail Directions:** The Acorn Avenue Trail starts across the road from the Brick Shelter. Begin at the trail board and go right and down the gravel steps [1]. At the bottom, go left and cross a bridge (the first of many crossings). At .1 mi. [2] you will come to a trail intersection; go right and cross another bridge. Look for an unusual multitrunked sycamore on the right as well as fragile and Christmas ferns and the heart-shaped leaves of wild ginger.

At .25 mi. [3] note a pair of cottonwoods and a huge, leaning sycamore on your left, and walk under the arch of a bending buckeye. At the trail intersection at .35 mi., continue straight [4], following the signage for Eagle's Nest. On both sides of the trail are large multitrunked sycamores. This species, recognized by its peeling scaly bark, has the largest single-blade leaf of any North American tree. Sycamore leaves can be up to 10 inches long. The trail forms a T at .4 mi. [5]; go left and follow the sign to Eagle's Nest.

Head up a series of steep steps. At the top is an overlook for Gobbler's Knob. From here continue uphill along a narrow path on top of a ridge. Ravines are on either side. The trail comes to a T at .65 mi.; go right [6]. As you hike along this segment of the trail, take notice of all the maple seedlings and saplings. These woods were once dominated by oaks, evidenced by the large examples that remain. Oak seedlings cannot tolerate shade as well as maple seedlings can, so the once-stately oak forest is being taken over by maples.

The trail forks at .7 mi. [7]; go left. Look for brown tiger beetles with white markings that are always one step ahead of you. The trail begins to head down on a switchback (ignore the cutoffs and stay on the trail) and a bridge crossing. After the bridge [8] (.85 mi.), look to your right for hydrangea and pawpaw trees before heading up and hiking on another ridge.

The trail now heads down with the help of a switchback at 1 mi. [9]. Once on level ground, note the towering pawpaw and ostrich ferns. You will cross three bridges before coming to a trail intersection [10] (1.4 mi.). Go right, and within a few feet the trail will fork; go right again. Along this connecting trail note the fern-covered ridges. At 1.45 mi. the trail forks again; go right and up the stairs [11]. Along the stairs, note the profusion of hepatica and bloodroot; both bloom in very early spring. The wooden steps soon become dirt steps and require a giant's stride to reach them.

At the top, the trail is now on a ridge dominated by oaks and maples. Did you notice the large oak with four trunks? Look and listen for pileated woodpeckers here and don't miss the impressive ravine on the right. By 1.75 mi. the solitude of the hike and the open understory of the woods are both gone. The trail is near the campground [12] where the woods have been disturbed. The trail forks again at 1.9 mi.; go left and skirt the campground [13].

Once you are away from the campground, the openness of the woods returns. The trail heads down with the help of switchbacks. While going down, look at decaying branches and logs for brightly colored mushrooms. At 2.35 mi. cross the bridge and go left [14]; soon you will cross another bridge and the trail will fork. You are back at [11]; bear right, retracing your steps. The trail comes to a T at 2.5 mi. [2]; go right, cross the creek, and head up the numerous steps to your vehicle.

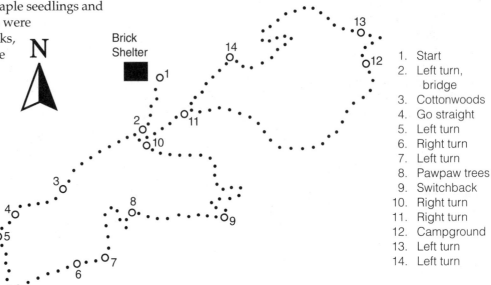

1. Start
2. Left turn, bridge
3. Cottonwoods
4. Go straight
5. Left turn
6. Right turn
7. Left turn
8. Pawpaw trees
9. Switchback
10. Right turn
11. Right turn
12. Campground
13. Left turn
14. Left turn

- Hike through both natural and archeological history.

- Traverse a trail that will give you a workout worthy of a mountain goat.

- Bring your field guides to discover the park's 400 species of plants, 200 species of birds, and a myriad of insects.

- Tour the Bunker Hill Historic Area.

- For a true entomological spectacle, visit the park in the year 2021 to view the next generation of the periodical cicadas.

## Area Information

Kennekuk Cove County Park, dedicated in 1975, is more than 3,000 acres in size. The state's only National Wild and Scenic River, the Middle Fork, borders the park on the west, as does the Middle Fork State Wildlife Area. Kickapoo State Park is 3 miles to the south. Kennekuk consists of oak-hickory wooded ravines, successional fields and meadows, prairie patches, and marshes. Three Illinois Nature Preserves are located within the park's boundaries.

Windfall Prairie is one of those nature preserves. It is a gravel bluff prairie with a seep spring at the base of its bluff. During 1973, Robert Evers, a botanist with the Illinois Natural History Survey, recorded more than 125 plant species from this prairie. The dominant species were little bluestem, Indian grass, and prairie dock. In his field notes he wrote, "In May, Indian paintbrush clothed the prairie with a scarlet hue. Scattered throughout were stems of blue-eyed grass, downy phlox, stargrass, puccoon, and meadow parsnip. In June, the few stalks of leadplant showed their dense spikes of purple flowers . . . In late summer and early autumn, blazing star, partridge pea, tall tickseed, stiff gentian, goldenrod, and gerardias added their colors to the bluff. Seven plants of the hill prairie variant of the ladies'-tresses, an orchid, grew in this prairie."

The Middle Fork, a winding river with rocky bluffs, steep banks, and clear pools over sand and silt, might have been called Kickapoo Fork, as the river rises in the morainal prairie near the site of the Grand Village of the Kickapoo Indians. For centuries the waters of the Middle Fork served as a forest-shaded canoe path; an ancient route, known as the "Sauk and Kickapoo Trace," paralleled its course.

Kennekuk is not only a park of natural history, but also one of human history. The Collins Site was a platform mound covering 42 acres, situated on a Middle Fork River terrace remnant. The area has been identified as a major Late Woodland and Mississippian ceremonial complex. It is unusual to find Mississippian components this far north. No structural elements can be seen today; the Collins Site is a mown field with markings indicating where certain features were located. Bunker Hill Historic Area is an area of restored buildings, a Pullman dining car, and a gazebo. While Vermilion Chapel, the oldest church in Vermilion County, is original to the site, the other buildings have been relocated from other areas and restored.

**Directions:** Kennekuk Cove County Park is located five miles west of Danville. From I-74 take the Martin Luther King exit (210) and go east on Route 150 for less than a mile to the first stop light at Henning Road. Turn left on Henning Road and go north for 4.5 miles, following the signs to the park.

**Hours Open:** The site is open year-round. Check the park's Web site for hours, as they vary with the season.

**Facilities:** Rental buildings and shelters are available for picnicking. Each picnic site is furnished with a charcoal grill and fire ring and has playground equipment and horseshoe courts. There are six ponds and lakes, as well as the Middle Fork River for fishing, canoeing, boating, wildlife hunting (archery deer, turkey, waterfowl, and upland game), cross-country skiing, and mushroom hunting. Boat, canoe, and paddleboat rentals and concessions are available in season. A visitor center is open daily, except in winter months, and includes a natural history museum, 1,000-gallon aquarium, and Native American display. There are no campground facilities. Bunker Hill Historic Area buildings are open 1:00 to 4:00 pm Saturday and Sunday, Memorial Day through Labor Day.

**Permits and Rules:** No bicycles, horses, snowmobiles, or motorcycles are allowed on the trails. No collecting of plant, animal, or mineral specimens is allowed (although you may collect leaves, nuts, fruits, and mushrooms). All pets must be leashed. Park only in the lots.

**For Further Information:** Kennekuk Cove County Park, 22296-A Henning Road, Danville, IL 61834; 217-442-1691; www.vccd.org.

## Park Trails

**Lookout Point Trail** ( , 1 mile). This trail crosses one of the highest points in Vermilion County (700 feet above sea level) as it traverses a deep, wooded ravine and provides a nice view of the Middle Fork River Valley.

**Raccoon Run Trail** ( , 20 minutes). The easy trail is for the young and even is accessible to strollers.

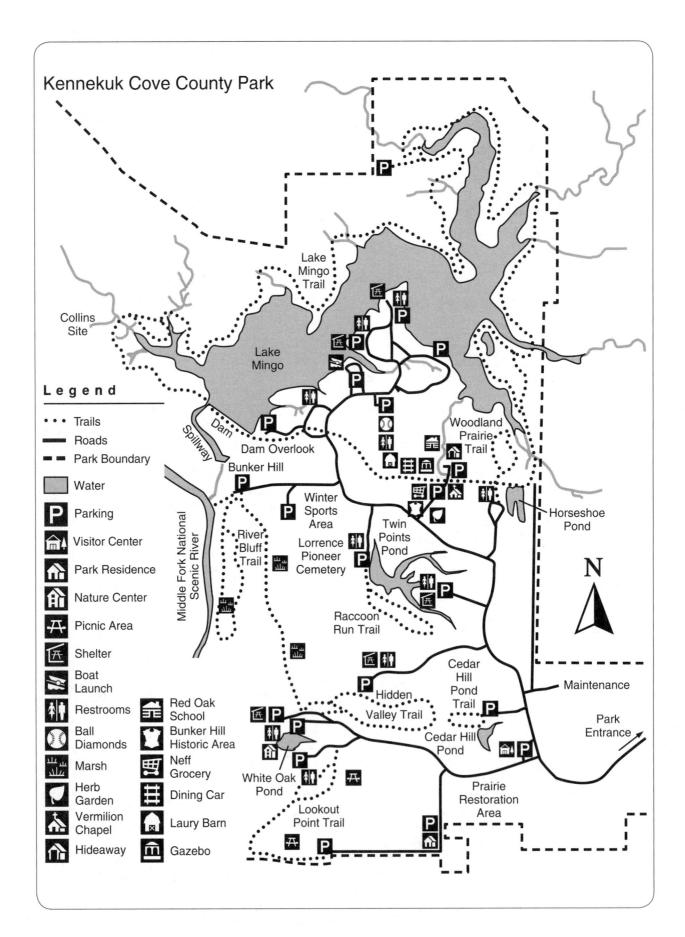

# Kennekuk Cove County Park

Collins Site

Lake Mingo Trail

Lake Mingo

**Legend**

- • • • Trails
- —— Roads
- – – Park Boundary
- Water
- **P** Parking
- Visitor Center
- Park Residence
- Nature Center
- Picnic Area
- Shelter
- Boat Launch
- Restrooms
- Ball Diamonds
- Marsh
- Herb Garden
- Vermilion Chapel
- Hideaway

- Red Oak School
- Bunker Hill Historic Area
- Neff Grocery
- Dining Car
- Laury Barn
- Gazebo

Spillway

Dam

Dam Overlook

Bunker Hill

Middle Fork National Scenic River

River Bluff Trail

Winter Sports Area

Lorrence Pioneer Cemetery

Twin Points Pond

Woodland Prairie Trail

Horseshoe Pond

Raccoon Run Trail

Maintenance

Cedar Hill Pond Trail

Hidden Valley Trail

Cedar Hill Pond

Park Entrance

White Oak Pond

Lookout Point Trail

Prairie Restoration Area

**N**

# Windfall Prairie and Collins Site

 **Distance Round-Trip:** 2.25 miles
**Estimated Hiking Time:** 1.5 hours

*One May day I had the privilege to hike this trail with an area naturalist. He showed us pottery shards found at the site and how to make a fire using flint and a friction technique. Instead of being a simple mown area, the Collins Site came alive. At Windfall Prairie nothing escaped his notice, whether it was the buzzy call of a blue-winged warbler or diminutive yellow star grass.*

**Caution:** Watch for roots in the trail. The trail is very narrow in a couple of places, so watch your step.

**Trail Directions:** Wind through the park following the signs. Park in parking area E, which is the dam overlook. Don't forget to bring your binoculars, not only for the birds but to survey the fragile prairie plants as well. (The numbers found along this trail do not correspond to the mileage points in this book.)

The trail begins beyond the red gate [1]. Note the large rock on the right. This was in the valley before it was flooded by the dam. Within a few steps you are hiking over the dam. Note the depth of the lake by looking to the left. Also look for fishermen, both human and avian (great blue and little green herons and kingfishers), as this area appears to be a popular spot. Once you cross the dam you will head up. As you cross under the power lines look up at the poles, which are often capped not with gargoyles but with turkey vultures.

You are hiking in a recovering oak-hickory and walnut woods. Notice the occasional large specimen, such as the large white oak on your left at .5 mi. [2]. This tree is at least 200 years old. The mown path has given way to dirt, but is still easy to follow. The Lake Mingo Trail comes in on your right [3] (.75 mi.); ignore this trail. Within a few steps the trail for Windfall Prairie and Collins Site appears; take it [4].

At .8 mi. the trail splits; go right to first explore Windfall Prairie Nature Preserve [5]. You are walking on a ridge through an oak-hickory forest, and at 1 mi. you will pass by two large oak trees. At 1.05 mi. take the path to the right for a short side spur and a vista of Middle Fork River [6]. Look for extensive raceways of gravel and sand and clear pools, both qualities that contributed to this stream being named a National Wild and Scenic River. On the opposite banks look for nesting northern rough-winged swallows. These mouse-colored aerial acrobats possess a small beak and a big mouth as they glide and glean insects from

the air. Off to your left of the vista is Windfall Prairie Nature Preserve. Use your binoculars to look for the plants Robert Evers saw in the 1970s; many of them are still present in this fragile area.

Retrace your steps back to the trail and continue on the path; the prairie will be on your right. At 1.1 mi. take a right and retrace your steps back to [5]. Go right (straight) onto the Collins Trail (1.25 mi.) and head downhill. The trail is a narrow, dirt path and offers glimpses of the Middle Fork through the trees. The understory is black snakeroot and poison ivy, so do not stray from the trail. Go left [7] at the intersection at 1.35 mi. You will soon (1.4 mi.) come into a clearing; this is the Collins Site [8], named after the last private owner, Andy Collins. The Collins Site is circular; it marks the spot where evidence of a hut was found. Dark stains in the soil, found during excavation, were the remnants of poles set in the ground. Flakes of flint and pottery shards were also found during excavation. Once you have completed the circle retrace your steps back to [5] (1.5 mi.). From [5] retrace your steps back across the dam and then to the parking area.

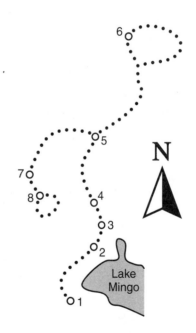

1. Start
2. Large white oak on left
3. Lake Mingo Trail on right
4. Trail for Windfall Prairie and Collins Site
5. Right turn
6. Middle Fork River vista
7. Left turn
8. Collins Site

# Lake Mingo Trail

**Distance Round-Trip:** 7.3 miles
**Estimated Hiking Time:** 3 hours

*This trail was a treat not only for my feet as I traversed over hill and dale, but also for my senses. I saw a newly molted plains garter snake, so cryptically one with the grass and leaves of the trail; I heard the scream of a red-tailed hawk as it took off; I took time to smell the asters along the way.*

**Caution:** Roots are exposed on the trail; sometimes they are helpful as steps on the hills, but many times they are trail obstacles. There is also the possibility of wet feet.

**Trail Directions:** Wind through the park following the signs. Park in parking area E, which is the dam overlook. Begin the trail at the red fence **[1]**. The first .75 mile of the hike is the same as the Windfall Prairie and Collins Site (page 145). As you cross the dam don't forget to look for butterflies, as the dam is always a great viewing spot. At .75 mi. a path leads to the right; take it **[2]**. You will be walking the trail backward, so you will not be able to see the signage. The trail heads down, crosses the first of several footbridges, and climbs back up. It then winds along a creek through second- and third-growth oak-hickory woods.

At 1 mi. Lake Mingo is finally visible. The name Mingo means "treacherous" or "his highness," and is also referred to as Chief's Lake. As you wind in and out of coves, the lake will always be on your right. Look for the flat leaves of pondweed on the quiet water. Illinois has 23 different kinds of pondweed and all are valuable sources of food for waterfowl. A large white oak appears at 1.2 mi. **[3]**, and within a few steps a shortcut trail appears on your left; ignore it. Instead, head down and over a footbridge and then up.

The trail Ys at 1.4 mi.; go right and an inlet soon appears. Look for red-eared slider turtles sunning on the exposed logs **[4]**. The first of several power line cuts is at 1.6 mi. **[5]**, but within a few steps you are back in the woods. During the next mile you will cross two more footbridges as you traverse up and down through a recovering woods. Another power line cut appears at 2.5 mi.; there is then a steep downhill descent using tree roots as steps **[6]**. Cross a footbridge and go up to another power line cut. An open area with a picnic table by the lake appears at 2.7 mi.; take a side spur to enjoy the water and take a break **[7]**. The trail follows the power lines, but soon curves back into the woods.

The trail forks at 3 mi. Go right, and within a few steps there is another fork; go left. (The trail here is like a Z and bends back on itself.) Remember that Lake Mingo is always on your right **[8]**. You will soon head down and within .25 mi. you will cross another footbridge and head into a shrubby old field. A sign for Bethel Road Access is at 3.4 mi.; go right and downhill **[9]**. Note the clusters of wild ginger on both sides of the trail. You will cross a bridge over water at 3.55 mi. **[10]**. Look for green herons lurking along the sides and frogs hidden by the carpet of duckweed covering the water.

The trail splits at 3.75 mi.; go right and down, past a small bald cypress with knees **[11]**, and then back up. At 4.4 mi. you will cross another footbridge; go up the trail and encounter an open field on your left **[12]**. The trail skirts the field and immediately heads back into the woods. A large white oak appears on the left. There is a steep downhill descent at 4.6 mi. **[13]** where you will cross a bridge and then head up. At 4.8 mi. go left and down **[14]**. During the next .5 mi. you will cross four more bridges; as you cross the last one look for ancient beaver gnawings on the trees.

At 5.5 mi. go right (there is also a mile marker sign here) **[15]**. Ignore the trail on your left at 6 mi.; stay on the 6-foot-wide path that soon enters a lowland forest along a stream. Dodsen Cemetery will appear on your left at 6.35 mi. **[16]**. Continue straight on the trail, passing a pond on your left, through a picnic area and past the Lake Mingo Trail "start here" sign.

Bunker Hill Village is at 6.6 mi. **[17]**. Walk straight across Sycamore Street onto a mown path. Take time for a short side spur and wander the village if you like. Once past the village go right at the pole with the arrows at 6.9 mi. The trail arrows now correspond to the direction you are hiking. The grassy field soon gives way to a honeysuckle- and autumn olive-lined trail. Cross the road (7.1 mi.) and soon take the left fork back to parking area E.

**N**

1. Start
2. Right turn
3. Large white oak
4. Right turn
5. Power line cut
6. Steep downhill descent
7. Picnic table/side spur
8. Trail Zs
9. Right turn, downhill
10. Bridge over water
11. Small bald cypress
12. Open field on left
13. Downhill descent
14. Left turn and down
15. Right turn
16. Dodsen Cemetery
17. Bunker Hill Village

# South

Southern Illinois is defined as the area south of Interstate 70.

## Topography

The terrain in the south is dictated by glaciation, either as an earlier presence or by its total absence. Parts of the region were glaciated not by the most recent Wisconsin glacial episode, but by the earlier Illinoian glacial episode some 200,000 years ago. South of a line from Fountain Bluff on the Mississippi River to the Shawneetown Hills, near the mouth of the Wabash River, rise the Shawnee Hills, a landscape untouched by glacial ice.

North of the Shawnee Hills the topography is gently rolling, with steep bluffs rising along the Mississippi. As the river nears Illinois' southern border, however, it grades into a broad floodplain with oxbow lakes. The Shawnee Hills feature east-to-west sandstone escarpments with bluffs, ravines, overhangs, cliffs, and canyons. South of the Shawnee Hills the land is a broad plain, once the northernmost extension of the Gulf of Mexico. Today, it is occupied by the Cache River.

## Major Rivers and Lakes

The Mississippi River forms the western boundary; the eastern and southern boundaries are completed by the Wabash and Ohio rivers. The Wabash forms the boundary of Illinois and Indiana for nearly 200 miles. It is the second-largest tributary of the Ohio and one of the first routes the early French used in settling here. The Ohio, which serves as the boundary between western Kentucky and southernmost Illinois, was at one time a shallow, free-flowing river. Today, it

is a series of deep navigational pools maintained by 20 locks and dams.

Interior rivers are numerous. The Big Muddy has a series of impoundments along its course—Rend Lake (the second-largest manmade lake in the state), Crab Orchard Lake, Kinkaid Lake, and Lake Murphysboro. The Saline River flows into the Ohio, whereas the Little Wabash contributes water to its larger cousin, the Wabash. Among southern Illinois streams are Bay, Lusk, Hayes, Big, and Big Grand Pierre creeks, which are small in length and drainage area but flow through scenic areas and are clear and mostly spring fed. These are perhaps the most aesthetically pleasing streams in Illinois.

The Cache River Basin, referred to by early settlers as "inaccessible and a drowned land," marks the geographical point where the last invasion of the sea into the Midwest reached its northernmost limit. It lies a few miles from the southernmost extent of the continental glaciers. This basin has been designated a wetland of international importance. Horseshoe Lake, a former bend of the Mississippi River, is located in the Lower Cache Basin and is the largest natural lake in the southern part of the state.

## Common Plant Life

Just as forests were few and far between in the central part of Illinois, prairies were mostly absent from the south. If prairie did occur, it was given special names—Fults Hill Prairie, Looking-Glass Prairie, and Twelve-Mile Prairie. In the north, it was the woodlands that stood out on the landscape (Funk's Grove,

Big Grove, Ten-Mile Grove) and received special nomenclatural attention. The prairies here are similar to those found in the central part of the state. Loess hill prairies occur along the bluffs of the Mississippi River and are dominated by side oats grama, little bluestem, vervain, and leadplant.

Along the Wabash grows the last stronghold of the eastern deciduous forest. In the lowlands are beech, sweet gum, and tulip trees. The floodplains are characterized by oaks—shumard, pin, overcup, swamp white, and bur. Along the stream banks are silver maple and sycamore. The understory consists of large colonies of larkspur, mayapple, bloodroot, and blue-eyed Mary.

In the upland forests of the Shawnee Hills, white and black oak and shagbark hickory flourish. Drier areas have post, blackjack, and scarlet oaks. Beech, tulip tree, and sugar maple prefer the ravines; the floodplains support sycamore and Kentucky coffee tree. Interesting wildflowers include French's shooting star, white trillium, celandine poppy, phacelia, squirrel corn, and yellow trout lily. On the dry escarpments a variety of lichens and mosses grow, along with yellow stargrass and bluets.

The cypress swamps have vegetation more typical of Louisiana. They hold extensive tracts of bald cypress (some of the oldest trees east of the Mississippi), tupelo gum, and pumpkin ash. Buttonbush and lizard's-tail ring most of the swamps and wet areas. Red iris, the former state flower of Louisiana, is found here, as is spider lily (a mid-August bloomer). Duckweed covers the swamp surfaces, whereas yellow pond lily and American lotus blanket large portions of shallow lakes.

## Common Birds and Mammals

Any remaining large tract of old forest is the home of the barred owl and pileated woodpecker. Both are more often heard than seen, their calls echoing through the woods. Red-headed woodpeckers are numerous, and near wet areas look for prothonotary warblers; coots; great, little blue, and green-backed herons; great egrets; yellow warblers; and the common yellowthroat. The impoundments of Rend Lake and Crab Orchard Lake are home to thousands of Canada and snow geese each winter.

The area's most notorious reptile may be the cottonmouth. Other notable herpetofauna include the loud-voiced green tree frog, innumerable tiny toads, skinks sunning on the sandstone, frogs covered with duckweed, rustling box turtles, and hundreds of red-eared slider turtles basking on logs in the swamps and lakes.

Mammals to look for are white-tailed deer, raccoons, gray squirrels, white squirrels (in Olney), coyotes, beaver, otter, woodchucks, and the elusive bobcat. Many interesting and unusual insects, besides the pesky mosquito, include tiger and zebra swallowtails, lichen grasshoppers, and large walking sticks.

## Climate

The mean average temperature is 35 degrees F in January and 79 degrees F in July. Rainfall averages 45 inches per year; the highest totals are in May (4.6 inches). The mean average snowfall is 9 to 15 inches; fewer than 10 days a year have 3 or more inches of snow on the ground. Some years no snow is recorded. The land along the Ohio and lower Mississippi rivers has the warmest and wettest climate in Illinois.

## Best Features

- Size and species diversity of trees
- Shawnee National Forest
- Sandstone escarpments and related formations
- Swamps of the Cache
- Spring wildflowers with a southern flavor
- Biennial migration of the herpetofauna
- Ravines, shelter caves, cliffs, and canyons
- Clear, rock-bottom spring-fed streams

- Enjoy spectacular views of the Mississippi River floodplain and Missouri hills.
- Discover a hill prairie and its unique combination of vegetation.
- Look for the splendid tiger beetle during summer and fall.
- From a bird's-eye perch, look for bald eagles during the winter and turkey vultures and hawks year-round.
- Hike through a storm of butterflies during late summer.

## Area Information

To most people, prairies are flat grasslands. It is not the topography, however, that distinguishes a prairie, but the vegetation. Prairies growing on pronounced slopes are called hill prairies. Located high on a west-facing bluff overlooking the Mississippi River, Fults Hill Prairie is one of those special prairies. John Marks, a Wisconsin botanist, dubbed hill prairies "goat prairies" because of their location on slopes so "steep that only a nibble goat could graze them." This attitude and inaccessibility helped hill prairies survive. They were too difficult to farm, and very few animals had the dexterity to graze them. Thus, by the 1950s hill prairies were the largest remnants of virgin prairie left in Illinois.

With the cessation of fire, however, many hill prairie landscapes have been taken over by trees and shrubs from adjacent woodlands. Only the occasional

prairie plant gives any indication of the area's former glory. If your visit to Fults Hill Prairie occurs just after a burn has taken place, do not despair for the land; volunteer stewards are managing this grassland to keep a piece of vegetation history in Illinois alive and well. Fults Hill Prairie was dedicated as the state's 30th nature preserve in 1970. In 1986, the preserve was designated a national natural landmark by the U.S. Department of the Interior.

**Directions:** Fults Hill Prairie is located along the Mississippi River bluffs near the town of Fults, about 25 miles south of Belleville. You can reach it from Bluff Road (a blacktop road), which joins Maeystown Road northwest of the area, and finally Illinois 3. From the south end of Fults, take Bluff Road southeast 1.6 miles to a small parking area and a preserve sign.

**Hours Open:** The site is open year-round.

**Facilities:** A picnic table and garbage can are found in the small parking area.

**Permits and Rules:** The trails are located in a dedicated Illinois Nature Preserve. Because of its status, no pets are allowed on the trails. Do not disturb or remove anything from the preserve.

**For Further Information:** Fults Hill Prairie Nature Preserve, 4301 S. Lake Drive, Chester, IL 62233; 618-826-2706.

## Other Areas of Interest

Located in Monroe County, **Illinois Caverns** was originally called Mammoth Cave of Illinois. The caverns' 6 miles of passages are open to the public for exploration (Thursday to Saturday), but there are several requirements for entry: You must have a permit, a group of at least four, and three sources of light; you must also be prepared to get wet. For more information, contact Illinois Caverns, Site Interpreter, 4369 G Road, Waterloo, IL 62298; 618-458-6699.

Listed on the National Register of Historic Places, **Maeystown** is mostly populated by direct descendants of its first inhabitants, immigrants from Germany. Following an old German custom, many of the homes are built directly into the hillsides and with locally quarried limestone. For hungry, hot hikers there is a general store with drinks and ice cream.

# Fults Hill Prairie Trail

**Distance Round-Trip:** 1.6 miles
**Estimated Hiking Time:** 1 hour

*No longer do you need to be as nimble as a goat to hike this goat prairie! The 200 steps have made the hike upward a little less challenging but no less steep. Even with the steps, take advantage of the resting spots along the way to take in the view and catch your breath.*

**Caution:** The trail is very steep with no guardrails near the bluff edge. Use common sense and do not get too close to the edge.

**Trail Directions:** Begin the trail at the bottom of the steps. There are approximately 200 steps through a hardwood forest [1]. In the spring, find an abundance of larkspur and phlox carpeting the hill. At the top [2] (.25 mi.), take advantage of the overlook for a great view of the Missouri hills across the way (Mississippi River Valley). Another overlook within a few yards provides a bird's-eye view of Kidd Lake Marsh (the irregular-shaped body of water), a small remnant—dominated by cattails and cordgrass—of the huge wetlands that used to occupy the bottomlands. The area supports a small population of venomous cottonmouth snakes and is the northernmost occurrence of the species in Illinois. Don't forget to retrace your steps back to the trail.

The woods have changed from mixed hardwoods to a dry oak-hickory forest with some red cedars. To your right is a glimpse of the hill prairie before the trail heads back into the woods. Soon you are walking along the top of the bluff surrounded by dogwoods and, unfortunately, poison ivy. As you hike the ridge, zebra swallowtails or buckeye butterflies might keep you company.

At .5 mi. [3] go left, following a path through saplings with a fern understory. In the spring, look for the solitary stems of bellwort; gaze upward to see great blue herons flying to the adjacent marsh or turkey vultures gliding on the thermals. The trail now begins to head uphill at .9 mi. [4] and will soon curve to the left. Enjoy a fabulous view once you exit the woods (1 mi.). You are now in the midst of a hill prairie [5].

Little bluestem, Indian grass, and big bluestem are the dominant grasses. The purples of leadplant, purple prairie clover, purple coneflower, and vervain and the yellows of puccoon and coreopsis break up the green carpet, depending on the season.

The trail splits within a few yards—go right for a short side spur to explore the prairie. Continue to the right to explore a long finger of prairie on a narrow goat trail. In the spring, look for white blue-eyed grass, a diminutive relative of the iris. In the fall, the pink blossoms of autumn wild onion grace the path. Don't forget to look down to discover a tiger beetle with a green head and a red-brown body. These are called splendid tiger beetles and occur only along Illinois' western edge and in far southern Illinois. At 1.15 mi. you will come to an overlook [6]. Before you are the hills of Missouri and a quilt pattern of farm fields. Once you have taken in the view, retrace your steps back up to [5] (1.25 mi.); go right down the steps and back into the woods. At 1.45 mi. [7] the trail comes out into an open rocky area called a glade. This sunny area is a great gathering place for nectaring butterflies, and if the season is right you could be hiking through a small storm of them. Watch your step as you continue to hike downhill and cross a footbridge. Around the bridge each spring is a profusion of phacelia, a plant often encountered in the Great Smoky Mountains. After crossing the bridge, you have completed the loop and are back at the parking area.

## Fults Hill Prairie

Parking

Bluff Rd.

Fults Hill Prairie Trail

N

1. Start
2. Overlook at top
3. Left turn
4. Uphill, curve left
5. Hill prairie
6. Overlook
7. Glade

- Discover sandstone bluffs, clear streams, and waterfalls.

- Bring a plant identification guide to help you identify over 440 plants that grow in the preserve; several species are more at home in Missouri than in Illinois.

- Hike through a native shortleaf pine forest. This is one of only two places where shortleaf pine is found in Illinois.

- View the largest display of prehistoric petroglyphs and pictographs in Illinois.

- Explore perhaps the most beautiful ravine in Illinois.

## Area Information

At first glance, Piney Creek Ravine may appear indistinguishable from the sandstone ravines of the Shawnee National Forest, yet there is a major difference. This area underwent the scraping and grinding of the glaciers many years ago; the ravines of the Shawnee Forest were spared such icy depredations. Piney Creek Ravine was created in a relatively short time, carved by glacial meltwaters eating their way through the soft sandstone.

Sandstone cliffs enclose both sides of Piney Creek, and its bottom is a solid layer of sandstone, not the more familiar cobbles, sand, or mixture of both found in most area streams. In addition, the sandstone bottom is marked by long, deep grooves. Occasionally, Piney Creek drops off into small, clear pools. In other places, the creek is so close to the sandstone walls that it splashes against the vertical surfaces, providing a constantly moist habitat for ferns in cracks and crevices. As abruptly as the sandstone cliffs begin, they soon taper off; after a short distance they disappear entirely, replaced by a flat floodplain woods.

There are almost 200 prehistoric rock art designs in Piney Creek Ravine, left by Native Americans that lived in the area from A.D. 500 to 1550. The art was created by either pecking or grinding (petroglyph) or painting (pictograph) designs on rock surfaces. The designs include humans, deer, birds, and crosses. On May 31, 2001, the rock art of Piney Creek Ravine was placed on the National Register of Historic Places.

A major portion of the trail skirts Piney Creek. Take time to discover its bottom, waterfalls, and undercuts; although the stream appears tame, use extreme caution. Its rocks are quite beautiful yet very slippery and totally unforgiving to the careless hiker.

**Directions:** From Highway 4 at the northwest end of Campbell Hill, take Rock Crusher Road 6.5 miles west to Piney Creek Road. Turn right and go 1.5 miles to the preserve's parking area.

**Hours Open:** The ravine is open year-round. It closes at dusk.

**Facilities:** The site has a picnic table with a trash receptacle.

**Permits and Rules:** This trail is in a dedicated Illinois Nature Preserve; pets must be leashed. Remove nothing from the preserve. Do not deface or disturb the rock art or any rock surface within the ravine.

**For Further Information:** Piney Creek Ravine Nature Preserve, 4301 South Lakeside Drive, Chester, IL 62233; 618-826-2706.

## Other Areas of Interest

**Randolph State Fish and Wildlife Area,** located 5 miles northeast of Chester, provides numerous outdoor recreational activities. These include picnicking, boating, hunting, fishing, and camping. The area features several short hikes, including an interpretive nature trail designed by a local Boy Scout troop. For more information, contact Site Superintendent, Randolph County Conservation Area, 4301 S. Lake Dr., Chester, IL 62233; 618-826-2706.

The creator of Popeye the Sailorman, Elize Segar, was born in Chester, Illinois. Many of the cartoon's characters were modeled after residents of Chester. A six-foot **bronze statue of Popeye** is located in Segar Memorial Park, near the Chester Bridge.

# Piney Creet Trail

 **Distance Round-Trip:** 2.5 miles
**Estimated Hiking Time:** 1.5 hours

*Although there is plenty to see at any time of the year, during the early spring this trail is subtly beautiful—the gray rocks are covered with green circular lichens and buried in the burnished leaves of past autumns.*

**Caution:** The rocks are extremely slippery when wet! Use common sense and respect the trail.

**Trail Directions:** Begin the trail at the sign for Piney Creek Nature Preserve and go through the gate [1] along a wide undulating grass swath between two fencerows. At .25 mi. [2] the trail curves right, and within a few steps you encounter a trail board. Follow the mown path into the preserve. You will also find a plaque on a large stone commemorating the placement of the preserve on the National Register of Historic Places. The trail will be marked with green trail markers.

At .35 mi. [3] cross a footbridge; within a few steps you encounter an overgrown glade community on your right. A glade is an opening in the woods with an expanse of sandstone. The exposed rocks are covered with mosses and lichens, and cedars are the dominant tree. On your left is a dry oak-hickory forest. During spring, look for pussytoes along this segment of the trail. These flowers have a woolly stem and a cluster of white fuzzy flowers that resemble a cat's paw.

The trail heads downward and crosses a stream with a bedrock streambed. Rejoin the trail on the opposite side and head uphill. Soon the trail will fork [4] (.5 mi.); go right and continue uphill. Look left across the ravine; those pine trees are the shortleaf pine, found in only two locations in Illinois. As you hike along the ridgetop, look left (especially in winter and spring) for a great view of a waterfall [5] (.65 mi.). You will hear the waterfall before it comes into view. In the valley below, admire the gray rocks covered with green lichens. Just past the view of the waterfall, cross a stream on rock stepping-stones.

A trail intersection appears at .85 mi. [6]; go left and downward, pausing to look into the ravine below. After a small descent, the trail curves left and down. Cross the stream on the giant slabs of bedrock, looking to your left and right for waterfalls. (You are walking over one!) Join the trail on the other side at the green trail marker.

As the trail heads upward, glance at the stream and its narrow channel cut through the rock [7] (.95 mi.). The trail will proceed through a grove of shortleaf pines. The trees have slender, drooping branches and trunks covered by a light, cinnamon-red bark that is

broken into large, scaly plates. Away from the creek, you are hiking through a dry oak-hickory forest. Sightings of Piney Creek are infrequent, with only glimpses of the bluff through the trees.

At 1.3 mi. head downhill into another stream valley [8]. The spring flora that was absent on the dry upper ridgetop are now present—spring beauty, trout lily, and prairie trillium. You are hiking in a cool, deep Ozark ravine with a fern understory as the trail skirts Piney Creek. The trail begins to head upward [9] (1.5 mi.) and skirts a sandstone bluff. In less than .1 mi. [10] go left at an intersection to explore the area's rock art. An interpretive sign explains the rock art and what you will see. In addition to the art, note the mud dauber tubes that are nests for the wasp larvae that have been provisioned with paralyzed spiders. Also look for the name Blanche Malone, speculating on who she might have been. The trail soon fades into the creek. Retrace your steps back to the intersection [10] (1.7 mi.) and go left, crossing the stream up the other side. The trail curves right and goes up. At 1.85 mi. you are back at [4]. Retrace your steps out of the preserve, through the grassy area, and back to your vehicle. Don't forget to keep an eye on the fencerows. As I headed back to the parking area, a sharp-shinned hawk swept over my head while chasing one of the small birds in the fencerow.

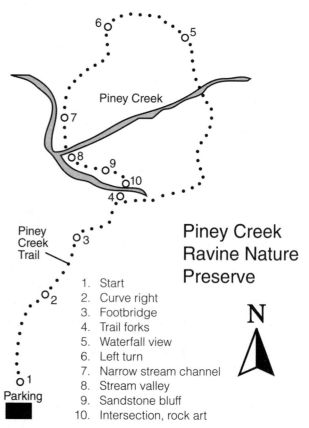

**Piney Creek Ravine Nature Preserve**

**N**

1. Start
2. Curve right
3. Footbridge
4. Trail forks
5. Waterfall view
6. Left turn
7. Narrow stream channel
8. Stream valley
9. Sandstone bluff
10. Intersection, rock art

- Why does the snake cross the road? Find out by hiking the road along the base of the bluff.

- Enjoy spectacular views from Inspiration Point.

- Bring your reptile and amphibian guides to help you identify the 59 species of snakes, salamanders, turtles, frogs, lizards, and skinks that live here.

- Discover a beautiful winding forest road and forested cove carpeted with wildflowers.

- Enjoy some of the best fall colors in Illinois, set against the backdrop of white limestone cliffs.

## Area Information

LaRue-Pine Hills is a 5-by-2-mile strip of land running north to south in the Shawnee National Forest. Designated in 1970 as the National Forest Service's first ecological area, and in 1991 as a National Research Natural Area by the Department of the Interior, LaRue-Pine Hills is a fascinating melting pot of widely varying habitats. Limestone cliffs like those in the Missouri Ozarks, swampland reminiscent of Louisiana, and densely wooded coves like those of the Appalachians coexist here.

In a 4-square-mile area, 1,200 plant species are found—35 percent of all plant species known from Illinois. Ninety percent of the state's known mammal species occur here, including the elusive bobcat, which routinely ranges over the rugged forest ridges. The rare eastern wood rat, a type of pack rat, lives at the base of the bluffs.

For two months each spring and fall, the road at the base of the bluffs is closed to vehicular traffic to allow the many species of reptiles and amphibians that hibernate among the rocks along the bluff a safe route for migration into and out of the swamp. LaRue-Pine Hills is the most diverse natural area of its size in the Midwest—an Illinois biological Garden of Eden.

**Directions:** LaRue-Pine Hills is 3 miles north of the small town of Wolf Lake and is best reached from Illinois Route 3. Of the three entrances to the area, the easiest is the Big Muddy River Levee Road. When you round a large curve in the road, the bluffs of LaRue-Pine Hills literally spring into view. At the intersection, go right to the base of the Bluff Trail (Forest Road 345) or left to Inspiration Point Trail.

**Hours Open:** The site is open year-round. One of the best times to hike and visit is when Forest Road 345 (road at the base of the bluffs) is closed for the herptile migration—March 15 to May 15 and September 1 to October 30.

**Facilities:** Picnic areas are available, although pit toilets are found only at Pine Hills campground, located on Forest Road 236, 1 mile east of Wolf Lake.

**Permits and Rules:** Collecting of any kind is prohibited.

**For Further Information:** Mississippi Bluffs Ranger Station, 521 N. Main, Jonesboro, IL 62952; 618-833-8576.

## Park Trails

**Observation Overlook Trails** (👣👣, .2 to .75 miles). Forest Road 236, along the bluff top of Pine Hills, gives access to a series of overlook trails. Ranging in length from .2 mile to .75 mile and offering stunning vistas of the area, these trails afford views of the shortleaf pines that the park is named after (a species found in only one other location in the state).

**Godwin Trail** (👣👣👣, 6 miles one way). The west trailhead is located about .04 mile south of the Inspiration Point parking area. The trail extends 6 miles one way. The trail crosses both Clear Springs and Bald Knob Wilderness areas, meandering along ridgetops, descending into Hutchens Creek, and passing through cane thickets.

## Other Areas of Interest

Located west of Route 127, the famous **Bald Knob Cross** was built as a monument for peace. This is the highest landmark in Union County.

**Devil's Backbone Park,** on the Mississippi River in Grand Tower, is quite scenic and boasts a sandbar beach and several rock formations: Devil's Backbone, Devil's Bake Oven, and Tower Rock. A .5-mile linear trail traverses the Backbone. For more information, call 618-565-2454.

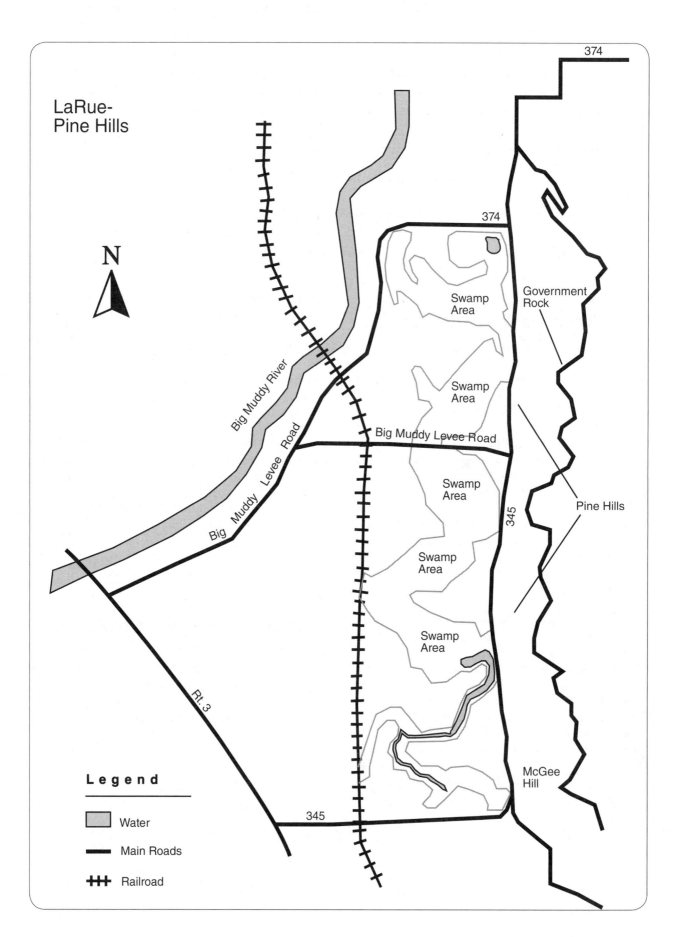

LaRue-
Pine Hills

N

Big Muddy River

Big Muddy Levee Road

Big Muddy Levee Road

Big Muddy Levee Road

374

374

Swamp
Area

Swamp
Area

Swamp
Area

Swamp
Area

Swamp
Area

Government
Rock

Pine Hills

345

McGee
Hill

Rt 3

345

**Legend**

Water

Main Roads

Railroad

# Snake Road
# (Base of the Bluff Road)

🐾  **Distance Round-Trip:** 5 miles
🐾  **Estimated Hiking Time:** 3 hours

*Whether the trail is so flooded or muddy that you walk it in hip boots, or so dusty your shoes kick up miniature dust devils, hundreds of tiny frogs will celebrate your presence. They hop along in front of you. Remember why the road is closed, and watch where you step!*

**Caution:** Poisonous snakes may be encountered; take care and leave them alone. Collecting or disturbing them is prohibited! Three species of poisonous snakes inhabit LaRue-Pine Hills: copperhead, timber rattlesnake, and cottonmouth. The best times to hike the road are two months in the spring and again in the fall when the profusion of wildflowers or fall colors are at their best and the road is closed for the herptile migration. At other times you might be sharing the road with the occasional car.

**Trail Directions:** The Big Muddy Levee Road comes to a T at the bluffs of LaRue-Pine Hills; go right and park in the Winters Pond Picnic Area. Before beginning the hike, observe the birdlife of Winters Pond (which is actually a borrow pit for the levee road). From Winters Pond, head through the picnic area and turn right onto the road at the base of the bluffs [1]. It will be gated when the road is closed. This is a linear hike, so concentrate on the swamp going out and the cliffs coming back.

The forest to the right is a floodplain woods with water-tolerant trees. At .3 mi. [2] the swamp first comes into view and will soon be at the edge of the road, if not over the edge! Take time to study the green carpet of duckweed covering the water.

By .5 mi. [3] the swamp has receded from the road, leaving small, vine-entangled trees in its place. These single trees soon become an impenetrable, vine-covered thicket. Throughout this hike, the swamp's edge will mimic an ocean tide. At one point it will be close to the road and then slowly recede from sight into a tangle of shrubs and vines, only to return again farther down the road.

During the spring the path is lined with larkspur, phlox, and prairie trillium. Look for hummingbird sphinx moths nectaring at the phlox. At .8 mi. [4] look for large patches of trout lily. The spots on the leaves are said to resemble those on a trout—unfortunately, the only type of trout you will find here.

Although the imposing bluffs are on the left and precariously close to the path, continue viewing the swamp and walking on the right [5] (1.25 mi.). At 1.75 mi. you might encounter southern leopard or green tree frogs. Farther down the road, note the large trees [6]. A gate that closes the road for migration is the turnaround point at 2.5 mi. [7]. During the hike back, study the right side again; this time it will feature rocky bluffs and a sea of flowers.

As soon as you turn around to head back, you can see the imposing white bluffs. Just like the swamp, the bluffs come and go from view. Springs are in evidence by the small streams coming from the bluffs. Look for chipmunks taking advantage of these springs for a cool drink. The upland forest on top of the bluffs is as dry and green or brown as the swamp is green and lush [8] (2.75).

You come close up with the limestone bluffs at 3 mi. [9] and can actually touch the rocks. At 3.35 mi. [10] you'll see the first of several small ponds along the base of the bluffs. Look closely at the sticks lying in the road near these ponds (especially those that weren't there on the trip out). They might not be sticks at all but migrating cottonmouths, copperheads, or yellow-bellied water snakes!

For the next mile look for snakes on the road, for bright yellow tiger swallowtails, or for black-and-white-striped zebra swallowtails. The latter two will be flitting in front of you or imbibing nutrients from a moist spot on the road. On the right at 4.75 mi. you encounter the last of the ponds [11]. As you continue to hike, listen to the noisy symphony of sounds around you. Five miles finds you back at Winters Pond Picnic Area, likely with several memorable herp encounters to add to your life list.

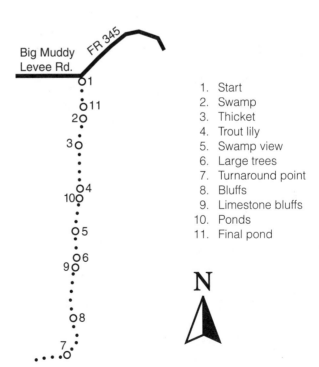

1. Start
2. Swamp
3. Thicket
4. Trout lily
5. Swamp view
6. Large trees
7. Turnaround point
8. Bluffs
9. Limestone bluffs
10. Ponds
11. Final pond

## Inspiration Point Trail

 **Distance Round-Trip:** 2 miles
**Estimated Hiking Time:** 1 hour

*Like the snakes that bask on LaRue-Pine Hills Road, this trail slithers up the side of the cliff like one long S-shaped serpent.*

**Caution:** You might have to navigate downed trees. At the top of the bluff the fence is there for a reason; do not go too near the edge.

**Trail Directions:** Big Muddy Levee Road dead-ends into the bluffs; turn left and soon turn right. Park on the right at the McCann Springs Picnic Ground. The trail begins by crossing a narrow footbridge; go left off the bridge [1]. During the spring the area immediately after the bridge supports a lush flora. Look here for your favorite spring wildflowers.

Within the first .1 mi. note the large gray beeches and straight-trunked tulip trees. These trees indicate an old-growth forest—centuries of undisturbed growth. At .3 mi. [2] the trail begins to climb upward with a series of switchbacks. The upward trek yields close-up views of the abundant mayapples. As you climb, note which mayapple stems have two leaves. Only those stems with two leaves will flower this year.

The lush green understory is left behind as you head upward into a dry oak-hickory forest [3] (.5 mi.). Look down into the ancient valley as you hike upward. Stay on the main trail, ignoring the many "unofficial" side trails. The .6 mi. mark yields the first of two fenced overlooks [4]. What a view! From here you can see the old channel of the Big Muddy River and an aerial view of the swamp. Continue the upward climb.

The second fenced overlook [5] (.65 mi.) provides a better-than-treetop view. At the end of the railing the trail forks—go right for yet another spectacular view,

and then circle back down and rejoin the main trail. Note the carpets of cleft phlox in spring. The trail ends at a parking area 1 mi. from the start [6]. Retrace your steps back to McCann Springs Picnic Ground.

During the hike back, while still among the treetops, look for chickadees as they scold from the cedars, or watch as they build nests and forage for food. Use caution while snaking your way back down into the palette of green, where the chickadees' chirps will be replaced by chorusing frogs.

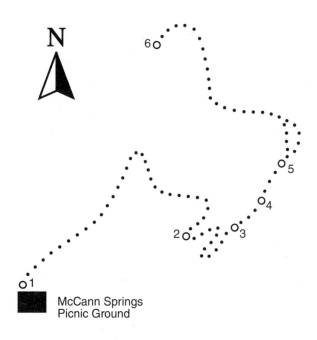

1. Start
2. Upward slope
3. Oak-hickory forest
4. Overlook
5. Overlook
6. Parking area

- Walk through the narrow, echoing aisles of Giant City.

- Look for the names of Union and Confederate soldiers carved into the sandstone walls of Giant City.

- View Devil's Standtable, a Native American stone fort, and a unique water tower with a 50-foot observation deck.

- Bring a plant guide to help identify the park's 800 species of flowering plants and 30 kinds of ferns. The best place for plant identification is Fern Rocks Nature Preserve.

- Hike the Trillium Trail in the evening and discover why a nearby town has a vulture fest.

## Area Information

At one time, this region was under a warm inland sea that reached as far as the Gulf of Mexico. Slowly the sea receded, landforms emerged, streams began to cut deep valleys, and, over the millennia, striking sandstone formations were created. Faulting and folding of the sandstone formed structures unique to the park with names like Whale's Mouth and Devil's Standtable. Perhaps the most unique feature, however, is Giant City—the park's namesake.

In Giant City the massive rock formations create walls so perfect they appear to be manmade. The sections of rock form cool, shaded streets and alleys, thus resembling a giant city. During the Civil War, the cliffs and canyons became a haven for soldiers of both Union and Confederate armies; their names are still visible in the soft sandstone walls.

Perhaps the crown jewel of the park is Fern Rocks Nature Preserve. Fern Rocks is named for the abundant ferns that adorn its sandstone walls. These sandstone escarpments continuously drip water and leave driplines on the valley floor, the habitat for French's shooting star. Also found at Fern Rocks is a profusion of blue-eyed Marys, and its gentle slopes are carpeted with white trillium and celandine poppy.

Whether you seek to climb trails to high places, stand and marvel at a precariously balanced rock, or try your luck at locating some of the 800 species of flowering plants, Giant City State Park offers many wonders and can provide many weekends of eventful exploration.

**Directions:** Giant City State Park is located 12 miles south of Carbondale. From Carbondale take US 51 south to Makanda Road; go left (east) and follow the signs to the park.

**Hours Open:** The site is open year-round except on Christmas Day and New Year's Day. The trails close at dusk. The visitor center is open 8:00 a.m. to 4:00 p.m. daily, closing only on major holidays.

**Facilities:** The site offers fishing, boating, horseback riding, swimming, rappelling, camping, picnicking (both tables and shelters), children's playgrounds, limited hunting, a visitor center, and a lodge with a dining room.

**Permits and Rules:** Trillium Trail in Fern Rocks is in a dedicated Illinois Nature Preserve. Because of its status, no pets are allowed on the trail. In the rest of the park, pets must be leashed at all times.

**For Further Information:** Site Superintendent, Giant City State Park, 235 Giant City Road, Makanda, IL 62958; 618-457-4836. For information about the lodge or for reservations, call 618-457-4921.

## Park Trails

**Stone Fort Trail** (👣👣, .4 mile). This is a loop trail that explores a remnant Native American stone fort. The view from the bluff provides a great overview of the north end of the park. The trail goes uphill, adjacent to a small flowing stream—a good place to birdwatch (look for summer tanagers).

**Indian Creek Shelter Nature Trail** (👣👣, .75 mile). Hike along Indian Creek and explore a virgin forest and a shelter bluff (cave) that was used by Native Americans from A.D. 400 to 1100.

**Post Oak Trail** (👣, .33 mile). Along this wheelchair-accessible trail you will discover Makanda sandstone and its corresponding bluffs, moist to dry upland forests, and a good population of prickly pear cactus.

**Red Cedar Hiking Trail** (👣👣👣, 16 miles). The trail may be covered in a day. If you are taking two days to hike the trail, however, you must be on the trail by noon of the first day and obtain a camping permit. The trail traverses the perimeter of the park. Some of its highlights include Indian Creek, Stonefort Cemetery, drift coal mines, Old Makanda, sandstone bluffs lining the stream valleys, a small waterfall, and numerous rock outcrops.

## Other Areas of Interest

**Southern Illinois University,** located in Carbondale, offers cultural activities and museums. In the center of campus is a mature black oak forest given to the university by a former Civil War veteran with the condition that the grove be preserved. For more information, call 618-453-2121.

**Touch of Nature Outdoor Education Center,** located in the Shawnee Forest near Giant City State Park, is an outdoor environmental and experiential learning facility. Courses offered include canoeing, rappelling, and backpacking. For more information, call 618-453-1121.

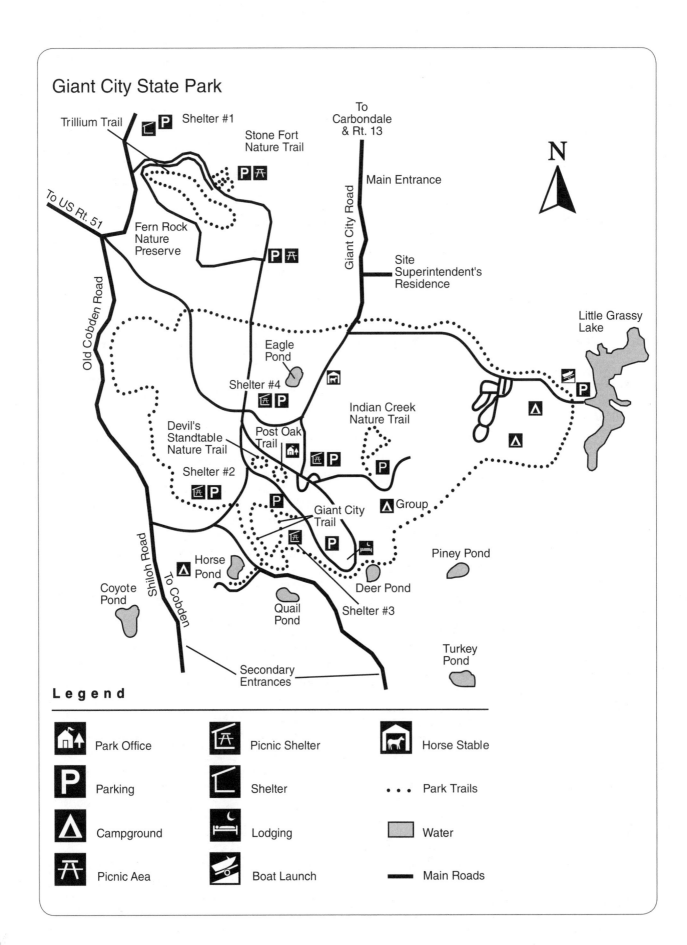

# Giant City State Park

Trillium Trail

Shelter #1

Stone Fort
Nature Trail

To Carbondale
& Rt. 13

Main Entrance

N

To US Rt. 51

Fern Rock
Nature
Preserve

Giant City Road

Site
Superintendent's
Residence

Little Grassy
Lake

Old Cobden Road

Eagle
Pond

Shelter #4

Indian Creek
Nature Trail

Devil's
Standtable
Nature Trail

Post Oak
Trail

Shelter #2

Giant City
Trail

Group

Shiloh Road

To Cobden

Horse
Pond

Piney Pond

Coyote
Pond

Quail
Pond

Deer Pond

Shelter #3

Turkey
Pond

Secondary
Entrances

## Legend

| | | |
|---|---|---|
| Park Office | Picnic Shelter | Horse Stable |
| Parking | Shelter | • • • Park Trails |
| Campground | Lodging | Water |
| Picnic Aea | Boat Launch | —— Main Roads |

# Giant City Trail

 **Distance Round-Trip:** 2.25 miles
**Estimated Hiking Time:**
1.33 hours

*It is little wonder that early visitors, likely accustomed to only isolated one-room log cabins, found these rock formations singularly frightening and mysterious and dubbed them a "giant city." Even for eyes accustomed to imposing skyscrapers, this landscape is still impressive.*

**Caution:** Many tree roots and large rocks have eroded from the trail—watch your step. The trail also crosses a park road, so watch for cars.

**Trail Directions:** Park at the Giant City Trail parking area and begin at the trail board. You will immediately cross a bridge over Giant City Creek [1]. The trail is marked with yellow markers and an occasional white arrow. At .1 mi. the trail forks [2]; go right and begin to head upward. Just ahead sandstone bluffs form a stone wall.

Near the top of the bluff, continue right and pass blocks of rock that have broken off from the bluff. To whet your appetite for what is to come, leave the trail that skirts the bluff. You are now walking through the outskirts of Giant City, a veritable sandstone suburbia [3] (.3 mi.). Pass through an alleyway of rocks and go straight [4] for a side spur to Devil's Standtable, where you are walking downhill on a limestone path that soon comes to Shelter 2 [5] (.45 mi.) and a grassy play area. Walk by the shelter and the swings and cross the stream on the second bridge on your right. From here you will come into a parking area; walk left until you see the sign for Devil's Standtable Trail across the road. Begin the trail [6] at .6 mi.

After a short uphill climb, you will again come to the familiar sandstone bluffs. A shelter bluff soon comes into view, formed because the softer sandstone in the lower part of the bluffs eroded faster than the upper layer (permeated with iron ore) [7] (.75 mi.). Continue onward to a large, freestanding pillar called Devil's Standtable or Mushroom Rock (on your left). This was once a large block of the bluff that separated during some earlier geological event. The softer areas of the sandstone have eroded, leaving the large base and the iron-embedded cap [8] (.8 mi.). At Devil's Standtable the trail forks; go right, and soon you are back at the road. Cross the road and head back into the parking area, recrossing the bridge and skirting the play area and Shelter 2 [5]. Go right and head back up the hill, rejoining the Giant City Trail [4] (1.2 mi.) and going right.

At 1.4 mi. the trail forks again; go left near a shelter bluff, and soon you will come out near a wooden boardwalk that will lead you through the city [9] (1.5 mi.). Soon you will "hit the wall" and encounter what looks like a dead end. You are in downtown Giant City. Take care walking the streets of Giant City; follow all directional arrows. During a hot summer, the cool walls offer a welcome relief. In lieu of billboards, this city has names and dates carved into the sandstone walls. Many were the pioneer residents of the area. Seek out the oldest name and date you can find, but please refrain from adding yours to the walls. You leave the city, fittingly, by walking under a delicately balanced rock [10]. Be sure to consider that it weighs several tons!

From the balanced rock, go down wooden steps and stroll through giant, lichen-covered rocks, following these until they fade into the hillside. At 1.8 mi. [11] the trail curves left and soon you enter the drier side of the bluff. At 1.9 mi. [12] the trail heads upward with steps fit for giants. Continue upward on the chiseled flagstone steps, compliments of the Civilian Conservation Corps in the mid-1930s. One final push upward and soon the trail curves to the right and downward, back to the trail board and parking.

1. Start
2. Right turn
3. Suburbs
4. Spur to Devil's Standtable
5. Shelter 2
6. Devil's Standtable Trail
7. Shelter bluff
8. Devil's Standtable
9. Downtown
10. Balanced rock
11. Drier side of bluff
12. Giant steps

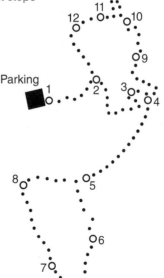

# Trillium Trail

**Distance Round-Trip:** 1.5 miles
**Estimated Hiking Time:** 1 hour

*In the spring, Trillium Trail lives up to its name. In the first few steps appear not only the familiar prairie trillium but graceful, arching white trillium that lines the path and mingles with the abundant spring flora.*

**Caution:** During the wet season the rocks can be very slippery, so watch your step.

**Trail Directions:** Begin the trail to the left of the signboard for Fern Rocks Nature Preserve and start the trek upward [1]. The trail is a well-worn path, occasionally marked by a black post with white arrows. Note the huge chunks of sandstone ahead of you and to the right. The vertical separations in the rock were caused by glacial meltwaters. In the spring, within the first .1 mi. your senses are inundated with flowers of every hue. The familiar and unfamiliar grow together—squirrel corn, celandine poppies, white trilliums, mayapples, and spring beauties [2]. Search the rock ledges for precariously perched yellow trout lilies.

At .2 mi. the trail crosses a bridge [3] and passes by blocks of sandstone that have broken off from the main bluff. The bluffs are layered; the lower part is Makanda sandstone and the top is Drury shale. A fine layer of loess rests on top of the shale. The blocks break off because of erosion of the underlying softer layer. Note the different shapes the boulders take—from ultrathin to large and square. After crossing the bridge, look to the right to see how an intermittent waterfall has smoothed the surface of the rock and created stairsteps.

The trail passes very close to the road and appears to fork at .25 mi.; stay to the right [4]. Pass between the bluff and a large broken chunk of sandstone and come to a series of rock steps leading upward. Along here each spring look for both Dutchman's breeches and squirrel corn growing in the protected corners of the bluff. Be alert for bumblebees and bumblebee sphinx moths, a harmless look-alike (mimic) of the bumblebee. They can be seen pollinating the same plant.

Another bridge crossing is at .6 mi. [5], but before crossing, admire the profuse spring flowers. From here the trail begins an upward climb, first over stone chunks and finally on wooden steps; go right at the top of the steps.

On top of the bluffs the lush spring understory has disappeared. Around you is a dry forest dominated by red and white oaks and hickory. Along the bluff top look for the metallic green of tiger beetles. They will always manage to stay one step ahead. Also look for small white butterflies with orange-tipped wings. Appropriately called orange-tips, they are more typical of the Southwest than Illinois.

As you cross the bridge at 1.15 mi., peer into the crevice below [6], created when a section of bluff split apart. If you are hiking in the fall, you might notice that many of the leaves are coated with a whitewash. The whitewash is from the many vultures (both turkey and black) that roost at the top and in the trees across from the bluff. The top of the trail at dusk is a great vantage point for viewing these silent scavengers. From the bridge the trail descends, back into the lush, green ravine forest. As you hike here, look for some of the 30 species of ferns that reside in the park. Most of these fern species are located in the preserve—hence the name *Fern Rocks*. By 1.5 mi. the trail has wound back down, returning you to the trail board.

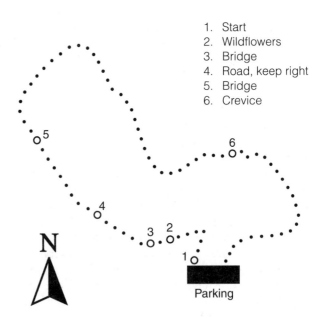

1. Start
2. Wildflowers
3. Bridge
4. Road, keep right
5. Bridge
6. Crevice

N

Parking

# 43. Little Grand Canyon

- Discover sheer cliffs, deep canyons, and moist ravines.
- Experience a unique canyon that opens onto the Mississippi River floodplain.
- Watch where you step—spring wildflowers literally carpet the canyon floor.
- Revel in scenic vistas provided by trail overlooks.
- Bring a fern field guide to aid in identification of the area's 27 species of ferns.

## Area Information

Three sides of Little Grand Canyon are made up of the cliffs and bluffs known as Hickory Ridge, bordering the Mississippi River Valley. On its western side, the canyon ends at the Big Muddy River, a tributary of the Mississippi. From the river's floodplain the canyon bluffs rise over 300 feet.

During the 1930s the area was known as the Hanging Gardens of Egypt or Rattlesnake Den. The *Gardens* nickname referred to the abundance of wildflowers found on the canyon floor; the *Rattlesnake* moniker noted the snake den that was once among the best in the eastern United States. Snake collectors from around the country came here for choice reptiles. Too much collecting and people's intolerance of the remaining few have greatly reduced the reptile population.

The best way to view Little Grand Canyon, which is a national natural landmark, is from the Loop Trail. The trail encompasses every inch of the rise from the valley floor to the top of Hickory Ridge. Traverse the canyon through steep sandstone creek beds using subtle stone steps carved by the Civilian Conservation Corps (CCC), and encounter wildflowers and wildlife all along the trail.

**Directions:** Little Grand Canyon is 8 miles southwest of Murphysboro, between Illinois 127 and Illinois 3. From Murphysboro go south on Route 127 for 5 miles. Turn right at Etherton Road and travel 3 miles to Poplar Ridge Road (the last mile is gravel), then turn right onto Little Grand Canyon Road and follow it to the entrance. The routes are marked with brown directional signs.

**Hours Open:** The site is open year-round from 6:00 a.m. to 10:00 p.m.

**Facilities:** The site offers a picnic area and toilets.

**Permits and Rules:** Be careful with fire. Pack all trash and remove it. It is illegal to take or kill any snake in the Little Grand Canyon area.

**For Further Information:** Shawnee National Forest, Mississippi Bluffs Ranger Station, 521 N. Main, Jonesboro, IL 62952; 618-833-8576.

## Other Areas of Interest

Located 1 mile west of Murphysboro, **Lake Murphysboro State Park** is situated among wooded, rolling hills. The well-stocked, star-shaped lake is but one draw of the park. A 3-mile trail explores part of the lake, a ravine, and a ridge. You may wander some of the many unofficial paths looking for patches of native orchids—yellow lady's slipper, showy orchis, purple fringeless, twayblade, coral root, and ladies' tresses. For more information, contact the Lake Murphysboro State Park at 618-684-2867.

**Pomona Natural Bridge,** near the small town of Pomona, spans 90 feet across a ravine and is one of the few natural bridges east of the Mississippi River. Take time to traverse the .3-mile loop trail to view the rock formation and ravine. For more information contact the Mississippi Bluffs Ranger Station at 618-833-8576.

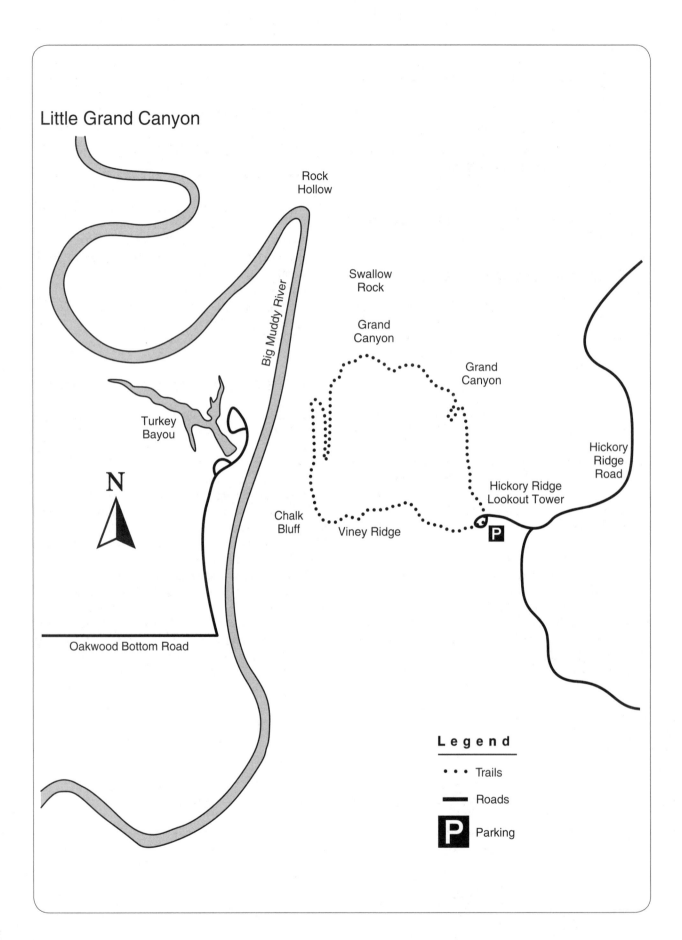

Little Grand Canyon

Rock
Hollow

Swallow
Rock

Grand
Canyon

Grand
Canyon

Big Muddy River

Turkey
Bayou

Hickory
Ridge
Road

N

Hickory Ridge
Lookout Tower

Chalk
Bluff

P

Viney Ridge

Oakwood Bottom Road

**Legend**

• • •   Trails

——   Roads

P   Parking

# Loop Trail

**Distance Round-Trip:**
3.6 miles
**Estimated Hiking Time:**
2 hours

*This trail follows a valley and becomes so steep that you must descend (and climb out) via a series of stone steps carved not by the ancients but by the CCC.*

**Caution:** You will be climbing on wet sandstone, so use extreme caution because it is very slippery. Even the moss is slick! The trail also passes along the top of some very imposing cliffs. Stay on the trail!

**Trail Directions:** In the center of the parking area, note the concrete blocks, all that remains of the Hickory Ridge Lookout Tower. Begin the hike to the right of the tower remains [1] and descend a series of steps. The trail is marked with white blazes on trees. Continue downhill; the woods on either side are mixed hardwoods dominated by oak and beech. At .35 mi. [2] find an overlook from which you can see the tops of trees (sycamore and beech) growing in the ravine forest below. On the opposite bluff is a habitat called a barrens (basically exposed rock with scrubby, gnarled cedar trees and a few prairie grasses).

When you have passed the overlook and headed left on the trail, note a cleft in the rock below and to the right. This cleft is actually the trail into the canyon! You are soon descending 200 feet down a rocky defile (a narrow passage), aided by the occasional steps cut into the sandstone [3] (.5 mi.). You go right and then left, looking for the easiest path down—the steps were carved by the CCC in the 1930s. Don't forget to notice the pothole waterfalls near the bottom.

From the defile you enter a deep, green valley (Little Grand Canyon). Go left and cross a creek using stepping-stones [4] (.55 mi.). You have entered a ravine forest dominated by giant beech trees. Each spring the understory is a carpet of spring wildflowers—phlox, trillium, squirrel corn, and many others—and butterflies hover around the flowers. On the left is a meandering stream that is backed by interesting colorful bluffs. You'll be crossing the stream at least four more times, using rocks as bridges. After the final crossing, the path leads away from the stream and you should begin to notice that many of the large trees are dead [5] (1 mi.).

The trail begins to head uphill and to the left (1.25 mi.), away from the devastated trees. On your right note the Big Muddy River [6] and the mouth of the canyon. The tree deaths were caused by the flood of 1993. The trees that stood away from the flood's reach did fine, but an estimated 18 to 37 percent of the mature trees near the Mississippi River were killed during the flood.

At 1.45 mi. [7] the trail enters a valley with bluffs on both sides. From here you soon cross two small streams and head up another rocky defile. Use a similar set of cryptic stairs carved into the sandstone [8] (1.6 mi.). A few steps might require giant strides. Cross the canyon and head up on the opposite side. You will be walking upward along a ridge, with the valley below on your right.

Take advantage of the view (and catch your breath) at River Bottom Overlook at 2.15 mi. [9]. From this bird's-eye vantage you can see where the Mississippi River Valley meets the Shawnee Hills. Look for the old channel of the Big Muddy River (a channelized stream) that is now an oxbow lake.

From the overlook, continue upward as you hike along Viney Ridge, on top of the Chalk Bluffs. Once again note the magnificent rugged valley to your left, full of wildflowers each spring and great colors each fall. In the valley below, all the species coexist in a colorful mosaic; here on the ridge look for small, isolated patches of single species—cushions of Dutchman's breeches, mayapples tumbling into the valley, or small groupings of toothwort.

You reach the top of the ridge at 2.6 mi. [10], where a bench is provided before you begin the undulating trek along a series of ridges. As you hike the remaining mile, look into the forest below, which is reminiscent of the cove forests of the Appalachians. The hike ends at the remnants of the old fire tower.

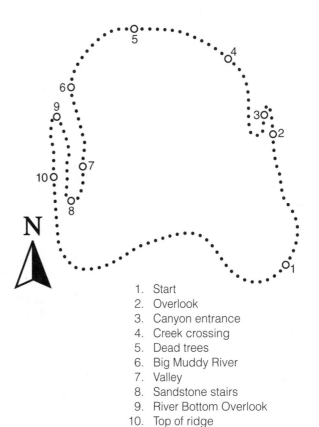

1. Start
2. Overlook
3. Canyon entrance
4. Creek crossing
5. Dead trees
6. Big Muddy River
7. Valley
8. Sandstone stairs
9. River Bottom Overlook
10. Top of ridge

# 44. Cedar Lake

- Visit an Appalachian cove forest in the Shawnee.

- Look for sunning skinks and cavorting chipmunks.

- Hike through a sandstone glade.

- Discover that manmade lakes aren't just for fishing.

- Bring a mushroom guide to help you identify all of the colorful fungi encountered along the trail.

## Area Information

Although many lakes exist (and most of them have intriguing names) in the Shawnee Hills of southern Illinois, none are natural. All were created by humans for one purpose or another. The Civilian Conservation Corps built Crab Orchard Lake; Lake of Egypt is a power-plant lake built to cool a steam-generating plant. Kinkaid, Cedar, Devil's Kitchen, and Little Grassy were constructed as water supplies and for recreation. These lakes offer more, however, than muskie, trout, walleye, bluegill, or a constant supply of drinking water. Many have excellent hiking trails, not just paths whose only claim to fame is that they allow you to hike around something. They offer fascinating and rugged opportunities to interact with some of nature's finest.

Cedar Lake and Little Cedar Lake are deep, clear lakes, perfect for canoeing, boating, and fishing. Cedar Lake was constructed in 1973 and stocked with fish in 1974. While private lands border the northern portion of the lake, the southern half is surrounded by the Shawnee National Forest, Illinois' only national forest. Along this southern half, hardwood forests and sandstone bluffs line the lake's shores.

**Directions: Cedar Lake** is located 11 miles south of Murphysboro. Take Route 127 for 9 miles south of Murphysboro. Turn east (left) onto Dutch Ridge Road. After 1.2 miles turn right onto Cove Hollow Road, which dead-ends at the parking area and trailhead.

**Little Cedar Lake** is south of Cedar Lake. Take Route 127 about 11 miles south of Murphysboro. Turn east (left) onto Landreth Road and travel about a mile. The last half mile is over a steep, deeply rutted road, so proceed with caution or park here unless you have a high-clearance vehicle.

**Hours Open:** Both sites are open year-round.

**Facilities:** Boating and fishing are offered. No toilet facilities are available.

**Permits and Rules:** The trails at Cedar Lake skirt private property; please respect their land. Hikers should yield to equestrians.

**For Further Information:** Mississippi Bluffs Ranger District, 521 N. Main Street, Jonesboro, IL 62952; 618-833-8576 or 618-687-1731 or www.fs.fed.us/r9/forests/shawnee.

## Other Areas of Interest

Located northwest of Murphysboro, **Kinkaid Lake** offers the only muskie fishing in southern Illinois. In addition to various water activities, Kinkaid Lake features a 15-mile (one way) linear hiking trail. The trail skirts the south side of the lake, investigating finger coves and passing between the lake and exposed sandstone outcrops. A 3-mile loop trail has been developed within Johnson Creek Recreation Area. For more information, contact Mississippi Bluffs Ranger District, Murphysboro Work Center, 2221 Walnut Street, Murphysboro, IL 62966; 618-687-1731.

Located along many of the popular hiking trails of the Shawnee National Forest are vineyards. Nine wineries dot a 30-mile **Shawnee Hills Wine Trail** through the rugged hills and forests. These wineries offer tours and tastings. For more information, go to www.shawneewinetrail.com.

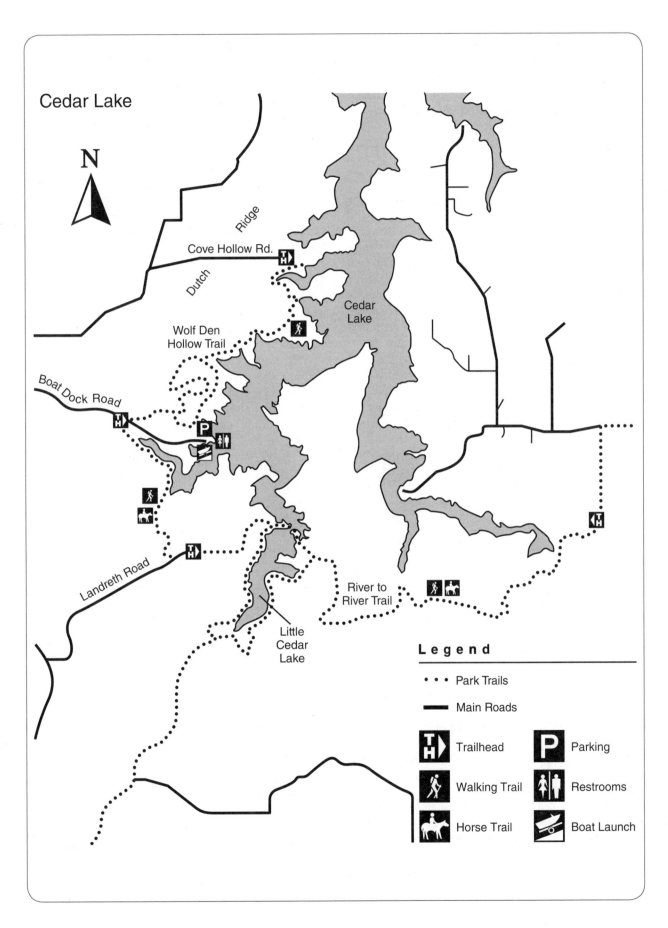

Cedar Lake

N

Ridge

Cove Hollow Rd.

Dutch

Wolf Den
Hollow Trail

Cedar
Lake

Boat Dock Road

P

Landreth Road

River to
River Trail

Little
Cedar
Lake

**Legend**

• • •  Park Trails

──  Main Roads

**TH** Trailhead

**P** Parking

Walking Trail

Restrooms

Horse Trail

Boat Launch

# Cove Hollow Trail—
# Cedar Lake

**Distance Round-Trip:** 6 miles
**Estimated Hiking Time:**
3 hours

*Hike between large, sliding slabs of sandstone while seeking sunning skinks! Enjoy views of a lake more reminiscent of the north woods than an Illinois impoundment.*

**Caution:** The trail skirts private land; stay on the well-marked trail. Several areas are steep, rocky, and slippery when wet.

**Trail Directions:** Take the farthest right trail; a signboard should mark Cove Hollow Trail [1]. The trail is at first marked by blue arrows and immediately descends on sandstone steps. Cedar Lake soon comes into view. Go between the bluffs and chunks of broken sandstone to another set of sandstone steps and descend into the valley. The trail angles right.

Cove Hollow, a shelter cave, is on your right at .25 mi. [2]. During the rainy season, it is topped with a small waterfall. While hiking in this ravine, look for jack-in-the-pulpit, which blooms during the spring. By late summer all that is left are clusters of fiery-red berries. The trail is now marked with white diamonds on trees. Cross the small stream using rocks as stepping-stones [3] (.35 mi.). Look for a large beech tree to the right of the stream and, during early spring, note the yellow trout lilies growing in pockets on the side of the bluff.

The lake is on the left as you hike on an undulating trail through sandstone outcrops. Soon the bluffs and the lake are no longer in sight, hidden by cedar, pine, and honeysuckle. At .95 mi. [4] the trail heads up and angles right. The bluffs, however, soon come into view; nearby, look for a large tulip tree with a white diamond. Also look for orange-tip butterflies, a species that might be mistaken for cabbage butterflies, except the males are adorned with brilliant orange wingtips. Females, alas, are somewhat duller in color. As larvae, the orange-tips feed on toothwort and other mustards.

The looming bluff on the right at 1.2 mi. [5] has several nearby signs indicating private land. For the next .75 mi. the trail will pass by the bluffs and large chunks of broken sandstone. In the jumbled rocks, look for skinks basking in the sun and chipmunks scurrying, squeaking, and otherwise cavorting about. Look at the understory for pawpaw trees with large, tropical-looking leaves, and for goldenseal, a type of buttercup.

At 2.1 mi. you will come to a trail intersection [6] with plenty of signage (trail names and mileage points); go right and head upward. You are now hiking along the ridge above Wolf Den Hollow and through a very dry oak-hickory forest. As you walk up, the hollow becomes narrower. Cross a stream [7] (2.4 mi.) and try the other side of the hollow, again heading upward. At 2.5 mi. [8] go to the right, following the white diamonds. Once up, go left; you are now walking along the opposite ridgetop. Cedar Lake will soon come into view on your right.

At 2.8 mi. [9] you will begin to descend from the ridge and will be hiking along the edge of a bluff. Within .2 mi. you will pass through the first of a series of sandstone glades, open expanses of exposed sandstone covered with lichens and moss. These hot, dry exposures support short, gnarly blackjack oak, prickly pear cactus, bluets, and false garlic. After the second glade, the trail continues downward on a slippery switchback.

Level ground and another trail intersection are at 3.3 mi. [10]. Go left, skirting the bluff you just hiked on. Through the trees you are able to catch glimpses of Cedar Lake on your right. As you hike along, look for faces sculpted in the bluff knobs. At 3.6 mi. you will hike under a shelter bluff [11]; from here look to your left for a small natural arch. Under the shelter bluffs during spring, look for clumps of French's shooting star, a rarely occurring relative of the prairie shooting star with a fondness for growing under the driplines of bluff overhangs.

From the overhang, hike through a field of sandstone boulders, up and then down (be careful not to turn an ankle!). Cross a stream at 4 mi. and you are back at an earlier intersection [6]. Retrace your steps to the parking area. While hiking back, enjoy the serenity of Cedar Lake on the right and look for any missed skinks, chipmunks, interesting erosional patterns on the sandstone (Liesegang rings), and wildflowers.

1. Start
2. Cove Hollow
3. Stream crossing
4. Angle right
5. Bluff
6. Right turn
7. Stream crossing
8. Right turn
9. Bluff edge
10. Left turn
11. Shelter bluff

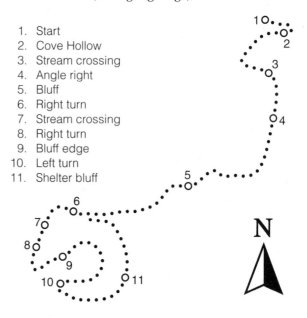

# Little Cedar Lake

*(If you are hiking in the dry days of summer, it's a 3-booter. But after a rain, give yourself an extra boot because the trail turns into slippery clay. Also prepare to cross a natural-looking but manmade dam.)*

**Distance Round-Trip:** 5.75 miles *(If you do not have a high-clearance vehicle, you will need to park .7 mile from the trailhead and walk the extra distance, making the total distance 7.15 miles.)*

**Estimated Hiking Time:** 4 hours

*I was expecting only things lake-related on this hike—not arachnids! I encountered two spiders; one was broad-leaved spiderwort with pale purple blooms, the last of the spiderworts to bloom. The other was black, hairy, and tarantula-sized. I still haven't figured out what kind of spider it was.*

**Caution:** Use caution when crossing the causeway—it is slippery. Beware of poison ivy and poisonous snakes. Watch for roots and rocks in the trail. Hikers should yield to equestrians.

**Trail Directions:** If Landreth Road is too rutted, park on the right where the road forks (left is a gate and private property) and walk the final .7 mi. to the trailhead. There is a circular drive where the trail begins. Begin hiking at the trail marker, which is adjacent to an ancient sugar maple [1]. You are hiking through tall, straight tulip trees and sycamores on a rolling path. Periodically you will pass trees with dark twisted limbs; these are sassafras. The trail will be marked with white diamonds. Be sure to watch your step as tiny toads cross your path.

A trail intersection appears at .8 mi.; go right [2] to begin encircling the lake, which will be on your left. A mixed oak and maple woods is on either side of the narrow, undulating path with an understory of

1. Start
2. Right turn
3. Up rocky spur
4. Forest
5. Creek crossing
6. Honey locust, creek crossing
7. Curve left, pines
8. Trail Ts
9. Left turn, River to River Trail
10. View of lake
11. Spillway

pawpaw, wild ginger, and fern. The trail will either be marked with white diamonds or white diamonds with a blue I (River to River Trail).

Head up a rocky spur [3] at 1.45 mi., where the trail will pass a large tulip tree. A balanced rock and a shelter bluff will appear on your right. Don't forget to look at the cross bedding in the cliff face. Look for broad-leaved spiderwort along this section. Within .1 mi. you will cross a rocky stream and hike through a cove forest reminiscent of the Smokies.

There is poison ivy along the trail, but also note the other leaves of three—tick trefoil. The tick refers to its sticky seed pods, which detach and cling like ticks. At 1.9 mi. the trail goes off into the forest, leaving the lake views behind [4]. While you still will encounter rock outcrops, a thick understory cloaks both sides. You are at the lower end of the lake, crossing the creek that was dammed to create the lake at 2.15 mi. [5]. Go left; the trail has become a wide grassy path and there is a wetland on your left. You will soon take a right, away from the lake and up.

At 2.4 mi. locate a big honey locust on your left and then cross a creek [6]. The trail now heads back through mixed hardwoods and up. You will also pass through the occasional pine plantation. The trail along this section is an old road (there are bits of asphalt in the trail). The trail will curve to the left [7] at 2.75 mi. through a grove of pines and then cross a creek with more pines on the left.

The pines will soon give way to tulip trees and oaks. After you hike uphill, the trail will come to a T [8] (3.15 mi.). Go left; an orchard will be on the right. Within .05 mi. the trail will come to a Y; go left again on a gravel path with pines on both sides. When in doubt, go left; there are several trails in this area made by horses.

You are now hiking on a grassy path, first through a tulip tree plantation on the left that will give way to white pines. Go left again [9] at 3.45 mi. and you are now hiking on the River to River Trail. Finally, the pines give way to rolling woods with small ravines and an oak-hickory upland forest. The lake comes into view again at 4.15 mi. [10].

Cross the lake on a natural rock shelf (4.35 mi.), and in the summer look for puddling swallowtails—tiger, spicebush, and zebra—drinking in the moist areas on the rock. The rock shelf gives way to a grassy spillway [11] and dam. You are back at intersection [2] at 4.45 mi. and have completed the loop around the lake. Retrace your steps back to the trailhead at the large maple.

If you were able to drive your vehicle to the trailhead, you are finished; otherwise you have .7 mi. before you are back at your vehicle.

Landreth Road (rutted)
Trailhead
N

# 45. Trail of Tears State Forest

- Bring a plant identification guide to help you identify over 620 species of flowering plants and ferns. The main picnic area has one of the best displays of squirrel corn and celandine poppy in the state.
- Listen for the call of the pileated woodpecker and look for these large birds throughout the park.
- See one of the last remaining fire towers in southern Illinois.
- Appreciate the hard work of the Civilian Conservation Corps (CCC) as you use one of their log and stone shelters or walk past a stonework stabilization wall.
- Contemplate Robert Frost's poem, "The Road Not Taken," as you pass many fire trails heading off into the distant forest.

## Area Information

Southern Illinois has more kinds of trees than all of Europe. You can get a glimpse of this arboreal variety at Trail of Tears State Forest—huge beeches in ravine forests, dry hilltop forests of black and white oak, and isolated clumps of the uncommon red buckeye in the adjoining nature preserve. Nearly all species of trees found in southern Illinois occur at Trail of Tears.

Originally known as the Turkey Farm, Trail of Tears was established in 1929 as the Kohn–Jackson Forest. The purpose of the forest was to set aside lands for the growing of timber for forest products, watershed protection, and outdoor recreation. Union State Tree Nursery, which produces up to 3 million seedlings a year, is located here. More than 40 fire trails are open for hiking and exploration of this 5,100-acre forest.

The forest's present name memorializes the tragic time when Native Americans from the Cherokee, Creek, and Chickasaw nations were displaced from their reservations in the southeastern United States and forced to move to Oklahoma. They overwintered in makeshift camps 4 miles south of the forest's southern boundary. Hundreds died, and their trek became known as the Trail of Tears.

**Directions:** Trail of Tears State Forest lies in western Union County, 5 miles northwest of Jonesboro. Access to the forest is from Illinois Route 127 on the east and Route 3 from the west. Take Trail of Tears Blacktop off either of these highways to reach the forest.

**Hours Open:** The site is open year-round. During turkey hunting season, it is closed to all other activities.

**Facilities:** Picnic areas, which include two large and two small shelters, camping (both tent and backpack), horseback riding, and hunting are available.

**Permits and Rules:** No pets are allowed on the trail in Ozark Hills Nature Preserve. Otherwise, pets must be leashed at all times. Motorized vehicles and bicycles are not allowed off paved or gravel roads. All-terrain vehicles are prohibited. Because of narrow gravel roads, large recreational vehicles are discouraged. Indiscriminate killing of snakes is prohibited.

**For Further Information:** Trail of Tears State Forest, 3240 State Forest Road, Jonesboro, IL 62952; 618-833-4910.

## Other Areas of Interest

**Lincoln Memorial Picnic Grounds** is located in Jonesboro, the only town in the North to be occupied by the Union troops during the Civil War. It is a monument that commemorates the site of the third senate debate between Lincoln and Douglas (held in 1858). A half-mile loop trail is also at the site. For more information, call 618-833-8576.

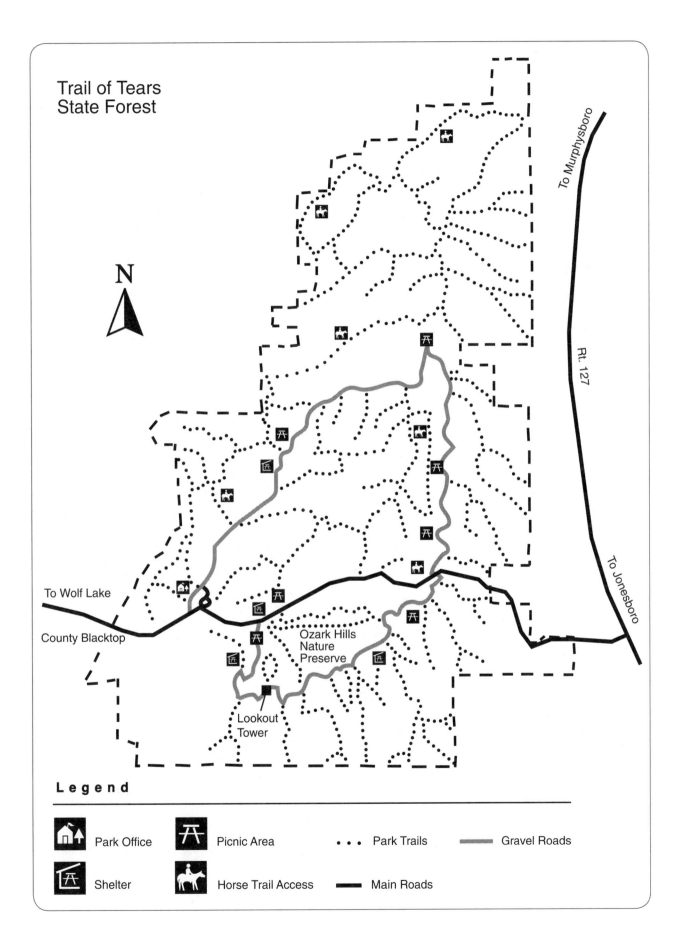

Trail of Tears
State Forest

N

To Murphysboro

Rt. 127

To Jonesboro

To Wolf Lake

County Blacktop

Ozark Hills
Nature
Preserve

Lookout
Tower

**Legend**

Park Office

Shelter

Picnic Area

Horse Trail Access

Park Trails

Main Roads

Gravel Roads

## Fire Trails 21 to 29

 **Distance Round-Trip:**
4.1 miles
**Estimated Hiking Time:**
2 hours

*This trail is a treat for the eyes and a challenge for legs and feet as you climb many hills through one of the state's best forests. Listen to the screech (no, those aren't your calves) of a pileated woodpecker. All the while take time to ponder about that mysterious fire trail not taken.*

**Caution:** The road to the trailhead is closed from December 25 to April 30; an extra 1.7 miles each way is then required to reach the start. Look out for fallen branches and tree roots on the trail; these could lead to an unexpected stumble on a steep slope.

**Trail Directions:** Traveling east on the county road through the forest, you will pass a horse camp area on the left. The road then curves; look to the left for a paved road that could be closed, depending on the time of year. As you drive to the trailhead you will pass several campsites and fire trails. Fire trails are maintained for access to the inner forest. The road dead-ends at a large picnic area. Begin the trail on the right of the information board [1] and join fire trails 21 to 29. This part of the hike is also a horse trail, so watch your step!

You will be hiking through a dry oak-hickory woods with an occasional smooth, gray-bark beech. Along the trail look for a crow-sized black bird with a bright, poppy-red crest. This is the pileated wood-pecker, a common resident of Trail of Tears State Forest. Shortly after fire trail 29, fire trail 21 appears at .35 mi. [2]. Go up a short rise, come to a T, and go left. Fire trail 22 will be on your right as the trail curves left. If hiking in the early spring, look for a large patch of yellow-flowered bellwort. A major fire trail intersection appears at .65 mi. [3]. Continue straight ahead, ignoring the trails to the right and left. Be sure to look to your left into the deep, forested ravine below.

After a stimulating uphill climb, fire trail 24 will be on your right at .9 mi. [4]; at the intersection go left (fire trail 25 will be on your right). From this vantage point, when the leaves are off the trees, you can see Bald Knob Cross. At 1.1 mi. you will come upon an unmarked fork in the trail [5]. Follow the horse trail signs to the right. Look along the trail for clumps of rue anemone, called windflower because it is always in motion even in the slightest breeze.

Fire trail 26B is to the right as you continue along a narrow path on top of a ridge. Admire the incredible oaks. By 1.55 mi. [6] the trail forks; curve to the left. If there are no leaves on the trees, take advantage of the great view to the right. Prepare for a climb up and down a hill. The narrow foot trail you are now on could be compared to walking on the back of a giant sinuous snake.

At 1.7 mi. [7] you will come to an intersection. Continue straight; the trail is now labeled Hickory Hill. Begin a steep descent in a deeply rutted path at 2 mi. [8], passing from the realm of the oaks to that of the beeches. Once into the beech grove, note the exposed and eroded bluffs of chert (flint). Here the bedrock is limestone, not sandstone as in other parts of the Shawnee. After crossing the stream, the trail goes to the left of a large beech.

Cross the stream again and look to your right for some great examples of beeches with their exposed gray roots gripping the hillside. During the summer the stream may be nothing more than a few wet pools.

This area has not been heavily traveled (no names are carved into the beeches). Instead of following the stream, it is time to head back up. At 2.4 mi. come to an intersection and go left and up [9]. You do not want the Red Shale Hill Spur. You will be climbing up a knuckle that has been reinforced with four-by-sixes. This is a narrow trough of a trail and one very steep climb.

At the top at 2.6 mi. [10] pause to catch your breath and then go left. Fire trail 27A appears on your right at 3 mi. [11]. Continue on and you will have come full circle when you come out on fire trail 27 [12] (3.35 mi.). Go right and hike past fire trails 23, 28, 22, 21, and 29. A final uphill climb will put you back at the beginning trail board (4.1 mi.). Pause here to remember Robert Frost, and perhaps one day you will return to explore those many other paths not taken.

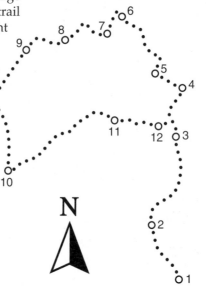

1. Start
2. Trail 21
3. Go straight
4. Left turn
5. Right turn
6. Good view
7. Intersection, go straight
8. Steep descent
9. Left turn and ascend
10. Left turn
11. Trail 27A
12. Right turn

# Ozark Hills Nature Preserve

 **Distance Round-Trip:** 3.5 miles
**Estimated Hiking Time:**
1.75 hours

*Hiking this trail in the spring allows you to enjoy great spring flora. Hiking in the fall allows you to admire the leafless trees and enjoy one of the best forests in the state.*

**Caution:** From May 1 to December 25 the road you will be hiking on is open to traffic. Sticks, branches, and limbs may litter the trail.

**Trail Directions:** Park at the main day-use area across from the white barn. Begin the hike at the yellow gate by the large red buckeye tree. The road is closed to vehicle traffic from December 26 to April 30 [1]. Note the cherty slopes with large beech trees and a rich spring understory. Celandine poppy and squirrel corn are especially abundant.

Part of the hike is on a one-lane road. At .125 mi. [2] you will cross a series of bridges built by the CCC. After the fourth bridge, the trail begins an uphill climb. As you labor upward, note the ridge on your left. You are passing through a mature second-growth forest. As the climb continues, the rich flora at the bottom gives way to scattered patches of understory plants. At an intersection at .4 mi. [3], go left and continue uphill. On the right is a campsite. Within .2 mi. fire trail 2 will appear on your right.

The forest's fire tower (no longer used) appears at .9 mi. [4]. Look left to see down into the valley and the rugged forest. Continue upward from the fire tower, passing fire trails 3 and 4. On your left a sign appears indicating the boundary of the nature preserve and

fire trail 5 [5] (1.3 mi.). Go left, taking fire trail 5, and explore the nature preserve. You are now hiking on a ridge within the forest you admired from the entrance road. Look up at the fan-shaped canopy of the oaks and look down for Y-shaped turkey scratchings in the oak leaves. At 1.6 mi. the trail angles left and heads down [6]. Use caution as you come down the slippery ridge.

Once at the bottom, go right [7], cross a bridge, and curve right, passing a ball field and Shelter 2. Ozark Hills Nature Preserve is straight ahead; go through the split-rail fence. At the kiosk take the right trail (2 mi.). This area is geologically similar to the Ozark region of Missouri, thus the name of the preserve. At first you are hiking through a pure stand of tulip trees but will soon cross a footbridge as the trail curves left. At 2.2 mi. [8], cross another bridge and immediately go right; the trail begins to curve uphill. You will then cross a series of footbridges. At the final bridge (this one has a railing) at 2.4 mi. [9] (you knew this was coming), begin the climb up. Once you have reached fire trail 12, go left and continue uphill. Soon the trail levels off.

At 2.9 mi. [10] the trail begins to head downward and there are no switchbacks. As you descend, don't forget to look in the woods for red buckeyes. These red flowering shrubs are fairly rare in Illinois and inhabit the rich woodlands of a few southern areas. At 3 mi. the trail curves left and continues down. At the bottom cross the bridge and go right, retracing your steps to [7]. Once you recross the bridge, follow the gravel road back to where you began the trail at the large red buckeye, enjoying the spring wildflowers along the way.

**N**

1. Start
2. Bridges
3. Campsite
4. Fire tower
5. Left turn, fire trail 5
6. Left turn and descend
7. Right turn
8. Bridge
9. Uphill climb
10. Descend

South

# 46. Horseshoe Lake Conservation Area

- Hike amidst a honking flurry of activity in the goose capital of the world.

- Enjoy a forest more reminiscent of the South—bald cypress, water tupelo, and red buckeye.

- Beginning in late June, revel in a profusion of American lotus blooms.

- Bring your binoculars to look for Mississippi kites, little blue herons, red-shouldered hawks, and prothonotary warblers.

## Area Information

Horseshoe Lake Conservation Area is known nationally as the the goose capital of the world. Situated adjacent to the Mississippi River and the Shawnee National Forest, it is in the southernmost tip of Illinois. The conservation area consists of an island, a nature preserve, lowland forests of bald cypress, tupelo gum and swamp cottonwood, and Horseshoe Lake. It is a haven for thousands of ducks and geese during migration and throughout the winter.

Horseshoe Lake is a long, narrow horseshoe-shaped lake that was originally an old bend of the Mississippi River—a crescent of still water in an abandoned loop of river channel. An oxbow forms when a river cuts across the neck of a meander and shortens its course. The former channel then fills with river overflow or groundwater seepage to form an oxbow. The lake, having no inlet or outlet, went partially dry during the months of July and August until 1930, when a fixed concrete spillway was constructed. Today, Horseshoe

Lake is a 2,400-acre lake with a 30-mile shoreline and a constant four-foot depth. It was designated a national natural landmark in 1974.

This area has been part of one of the greatest concentrations of wintering waterfowl in the Mississippi Flyway. The state of Illinois first purchased 49 acres in 1927 to develop as a Canada goose sanctuary.

Before the establishment of the refuge, most of the geese wintered along the Mississippi River between Cape Girardeau, Missouri, and Baton Rouge, Louisiana. Canada geese have wintered at Horseshoe Lake since 1928, when the first 1,000 birds arrived. By the late 1960s over 300,000 geese would winter there. Recently, due to changes in land-use patterns and winter temperatures, the count has been reduced to 50,000 birds.

**Directions:** The trail is located on Island Road in Alexander County, just east of Illinois Route 3 and 7 miles north of Cairo. From Route 3, turn on Miller Road; go 1.2 miles and turn on Island Road, which dead-ends into a parking area.

**Hours Open:** The site is open year-round except on Christmas Day and New Year's Day.

**Facilities:** Picnicking, a playground, camping (electricity and showers), shallow-water fishing, boating, and hunting are all available.

**Permits and Rules:** The trail may be closed during the hunting season, so call ahead. Pets must be leashed at all times.

**For Further Information:** Horseshoe Lake Conservation Area, P.O. Box 85, Miller City, IL 62962; 618-776-5689 or 618-776-5215.

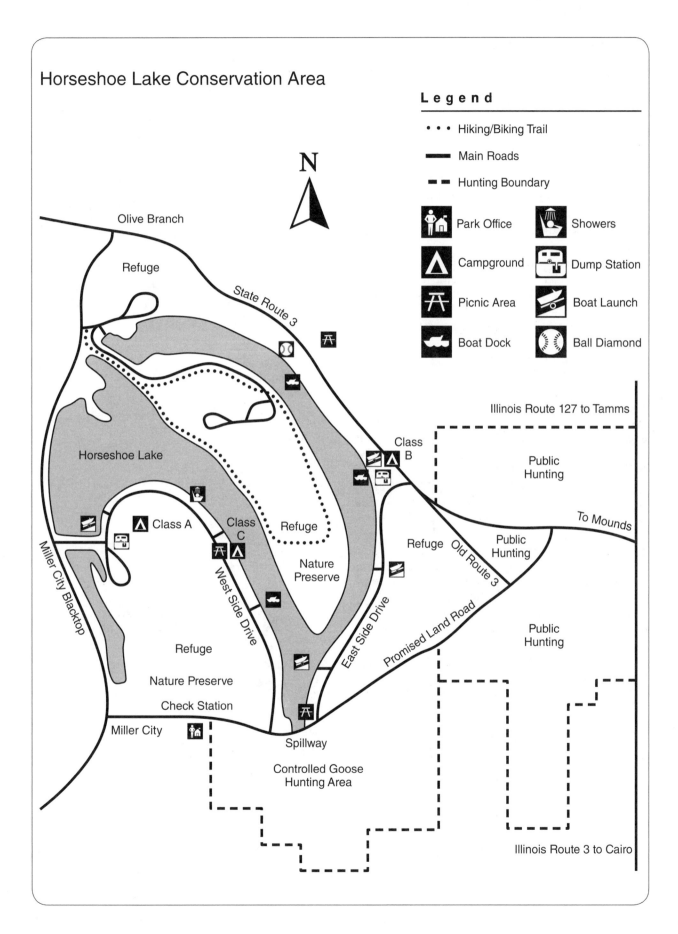

# Horseshoe Lake Conservation Area

## Legend

• • • Hiking/Biking Trail

── Main Roads

─ ─ Hunting Boundary

Park Office

Showers

Campground

Dump Station

Picnic Area

Boat Launch

Boat Dock

Ball Diamond

N

Olive Branch

Refuge

State Route 3

Horseshoe Lake

Class A

Class C

Refuge

Nature Preserve

Class B

Illinois Route 127 to Tamms

Public Hunting

To Mounds

Public Hunting

Refuge

Old Route 3

Miller City Blacktop

West Side Drive

Refuge

Nature Preserve

Check Station

Miller City

East Side Drive

Promised Land Road

Public Hunting

Spillway

Controlled Goose Hunting Area

Illinois Route 3 to Cairo

# Horseshoe Lake

 **Distance Round-Trip:** 5.75 miles
**Estimated Hiking Time:** 2.5 hours

*While I was hiking on a ducky day (gray, misting rain), waterfowl were all around. Several hundred mallards rose from the swamp; their rush of wings sounded like thunderous applause. Wary snow geese circled above me, looking to land and trying to determine if I was friend or foe. And, of course, the ever-present Canada geese paid no attention to me in my bright red raincoat.*

**Caution:** You will be sharing the trail with bicyclists.

**Trail Directions:** Begin at the metal gate [1], where you will be hiking on a levee road with the lake on either side. Sparrows, woodpeckers, and wrens are busy in the shrubs and trees adjacent to the levee. In summer lotus beds surround you, and by late fall waterfowl are everywhere.

An intersection appears at .45 mi.; go right [2]. A wildlife planting will be on your left, and on your right is the edge of the lake—cypress and tupelo trees. You get only glimpses of the edge through the viney tangles. During most of the hike, food plots will be on your left. As you pass under the limbs of a white oak, an unobstructed view of the lake and its bottomland forest appears at 1.25 mi. [3].

The trail curves right at 1.5 mi. [4]. The "swamp" is closer here, with more gaps and better views. Oak hardwoods will be on the left. Along this stretch of the trail note the large, straight cypress. At 2.2 mi. go left, away from the water, where there is a sign indicating no bicycles [5]. On your right is Horseshoe Lake Nature Preserve. The woods in the preserve are a near-virgin forest of American beech, sugar maple, and swamp chestnut oak growing on loamy soils. In the spring, look for the scarlet flowers of red buckeye, a southern understory tree.

For the next three-quarters of a mile, the nature preserve and its buffer will be on your right. On your left will be an "old field" and food plots. Watch for deer (they might bound across the path in front of you) and woodpeckers (they crisscross from swamp to preserve). At 3 mi. go left, leaving the preserve behind [6]; the lake has returned on the right. Along this section of the trail you are walking under the branches and limbs of huge pin oaks. Pin oaks are a wet-site species that are heavy acorn producers, a characteristic that allows them to be used in green tree reservoir management for waterfowl development.

At 4 mi. you will come to a stop sign; stop and go right [7]. For the next mile you will be hiking under pin oaks with food plots on your left and glimpses of the lake and its aquatic life on your right. You will pass by one or two large cypresses as well. Food plots will appear on both sides of the trail at around 5 mi., and along this straightaway you will have almost completed the loop. At 5.35 mi. you are back at [2]; go right, hiking on the levee road again and observing lake life. All too soon you are back at the parking area.

1. Start
2. Intersection
3. View
4. Curve right
5. Left turn
6. Left turn
7. Stop, right turn

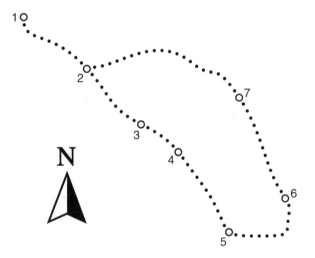

- Visit an Illinois Native Plant Society–recommended super site for spring wildflowers.

- See the dramatic effects of groundwater in the form of collapsed coves and Liesegang rings.

- Explore a rockbound valley with slot canyons, shelter caves, and a tunnel cave.

- Drive the roads of the refuge where Canada geese, wild turkeys, and white-tailed deer are common and bobcats have been known to cross your path.

- Enjoy a profusion of waterfowl and eagles during the winter.

## Area Information

Crab Orchard National Wildlife Refuge, with its three manmade lakes, is a fishing and recreational water sport enthusiast's dream. With so many recreational opportunities, it is one of the few national wildlife refuges where wildlife observation is not the main activity.

The refuge lies on the northern edge of the Shawnee National Forest and is located in the center of the Mississippi River Flyway. The refuge was created not only to reclaim land that had been farmed to death and deforested in the 1930s but also to provide winter feeding and resting for Canada geese.

Within the refuge's 44,000 acres are 700 species of plants, 245 species of birds, 33 mammals, and 44 species of reptiles and amphibians. Perhaps some of the best areas to look for the refuge's diversity are south of Crab Orchard Lake. Devil's Kitchen Lake is clear, clean, and cold. It is so deep that rainbow trout thrive in its depths. Yet this area supports one of the best wildflower spectacles in the state. Farther to the south find Crab Orchard Wilderness and Panther Den Wilderness, rugged terrain where who knows what might cross your path.

**Directions: Crab Orchard National Wildlife Refuge** is located near Marion. From the junction of I-57 and Route 13, drive 3 miles west on Route 13 to Route 148. Turn south and drive 2.5 miles to the visitor center.

**Devil's Kitchen Lake** is located southwest of Carbondale. Take Route 13 east from Carbondale to Refuge/Spillway Road and wind around Crab Orchard Lake for several miles. A park sign will direct you to Devil's Kitchen Lake. Once there, go straight on the road that skirts the lake. The parking area for the trail will be on your left.

**Panther Den Wilderness** is located south of Devil's Kitchen Lake. From Devil's Kitchen Lake take Grassy Road south to Rocky Comfort Road. Turn right and follow the signs to Blue Sky Vineyards. Just past the vineyards, turn left on Panther Den Road and follow it to Panther Den Lane. Go left and the road will dead-end in the parking area.

**Hours Open:** The visitor center is open daily from 8:00 a.m. to 4:30 p.m., except on major holidays. All other areas are open year-round.

**Facilities:** The refuge has a visitor center, three campgrounds, several marinas, boat ramps, swimming, and hunting (during season).

**Permits and Rules:** Contact the visitor center before your visit to become familiar with regulations. Public access to some areas is restricted. User fees are required for all vehicles and boats on the refuge; this includes Rocky Branch Trail. Pets must be leashed.

**For Further Information:** Crab Orchard National Wildlife Refuge, 8588 Route 148, Marion, IL 62959; 618-997-3344 or www.fws.gov. Panther Den Wilderness, Mississippi Bluffs Ranger District, Murphysboro Work Center, 2221 Walnut St., Murphysboro, IL 62966; 618-687-1731.

## Park Trails

**Woodland Loop Trail** (🥾, 1 mile). The trail begins at the northeast area of the visitor center parking lot and travels through a flatwoods and to a pond with platform overlooks.

**Wild Turkey Trail** (🥾, 3 miles). This 1.5-mile linear trail follows a fire lane through a pine plantation and deciduous forest.

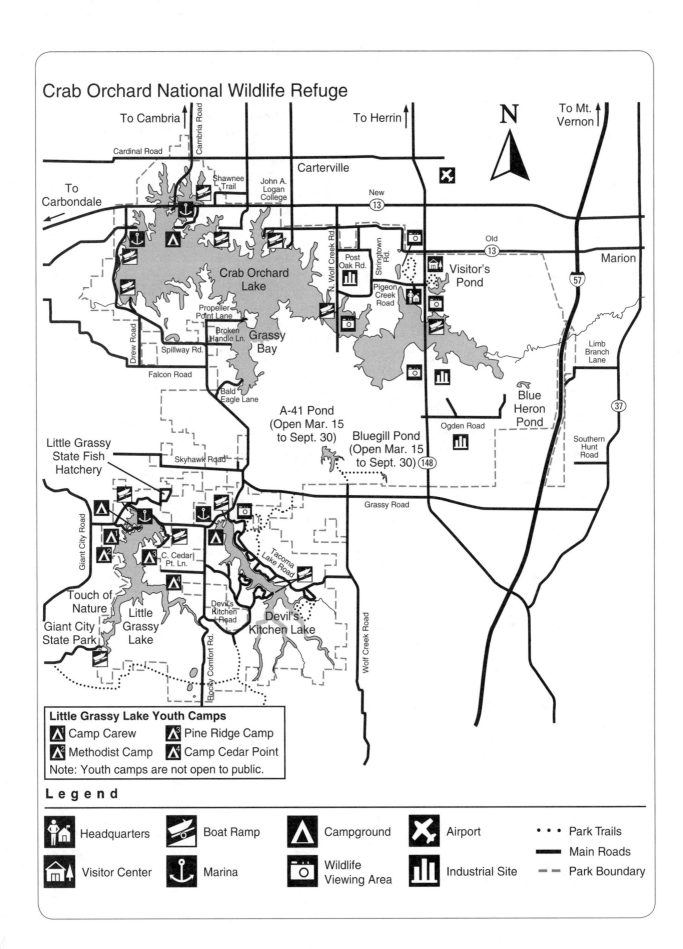

# Crab Orchard National Wildlife Refuge

To Cambria

To Herrin

To Mt. Vernon

N

Cardinal Road

Cambria Road

Carterville

To Carbondale

Shawnee Trail

John A. Logan College

New (13)

Old (13)

Marion

Crab Orchard Lake

N. Wolf Creek Rd.

Post Oak Rd.

Stringtown Rd.

Pigeon Creek Road

Visitor's Pond

(57)

Propeller Point Lane

Broken Handle Ln.

Grassy Bay

Limb Branch Lane

Drew Road

Spillway Rd.

Falcon Road

Bald Eagle Lane

Blue Heron Pond

(37)

A-41 Pond
(Open Mar. 15 to Sept. 30)

Bluegill Pond
(Open Mar. 15 to Sept. 30)

Ogden Road

Southern Hunt Road

Little Grassy State Fish Hatchery

Skyhawk Road

(148)

Grassy Road

Giant City Road

C. Cedar Pt. Ln.

Tacoma Lake Road

Touch of Nature

Little Grassy Lake

Devil's Kitchen Road

Devil's Kitchen Lake

Giant City State Park

Wolf Creek Road

Rocky Comfort Rd.

## Little Grassy Lake Youth Camps

- 🔺¹ Camp Carew
- 🔺³ Pine Ridge Camp
- 🔺² Methodist Camp
- 🔺⁴ Camp Cedar Point

Note: Youth camps are not open to public.

## Legend

| | | |
|---|---|---|
| 🏠 Headquarters | 🚤 Boat Ramp | 🔺 Campground |
| 🏚 Visitor Center | ⚓ Marina | 📷 Wildlife Viewing Area |
| ✈ Airport | • • • Park Trails | |
| ▬ Main Roads | ▦ Industrial Site | - - - Park Boundary |

## Panther Den Wilderness

  **Distance Round-Trip:** 2.6 miles *(does not include exploration of rock-bound valley)*
**Estimated Hiking Time:** 1.2 hours

*While I didn't hear the scream of a panther, I did hear the loud tapping and rattle of a pileated woodpecker, a denizen of ancient woods. I also experienced one of the most beautiful valleys in Illinois.*

**Caution:** Horses also use this trail. Use caution during hunting season; wear orange. Note several stream crossings; during the wet season you could get wet feet.

**Trail Directions:** The trail begins at the parking area; take the trail to the right of the information board [1]. The trail is marked with white diamonds. You are hiking through a recovering forest that, as you descend, becomes oak and hickory. At .15 mi. you will be hiking along a creek [2]; note the large sandstone slabs in the creek bed. This stream flows over pure sandstone in spots. You will cross the stream at .3 mi. [3]. Observe the undercutting on the left; outcrops will soon start to appear.

At .5 mi. there is another stream crossing, and the River to River Trail (marked with white diamonds and a blue *I*) comes in on the right [4]. You will be hiking on the River to River Trail for a portion of the hike. Rock outcrops are on both sides of the trail now, and at .75 mi. the sandstone walls are huge, imposing, and very close to the trail. The trail forks here; take a side spur to the right and explore this interesting area [5].

Here you will encounter vertical sandstone walls, slot canyons, shelter bluffs, a tunnel cave through the rock, and the rock formation called Panther Den. Don't forget to look for red oxide streaking or honeycombing on the walls. Once your curiosity has been satisfied, return to [5] and continue right on the River to River Trail.

You are still hiking amidst sandstone outcrops, just not so imposing. In the spring, look for wildflowers—Jacob's ladder, waterleaf, and fumitory. In the fall, putty root orchid leaves litter the ground. After 1 mi. you will have four stream crossings [6]; don't forget to look for shelter bluffs as you cross. After the fourth crossing, the trail heads up [7] (1.2 mi.) and you are soon hiking in Crab Orchard Wilderness; the trail curves left and you are hiking on top of a bluff through cedar and second-growth woods. Trail markings are infrequent along this section.

At 1.6 mi. you will cross a wet area [8], still hiking on the River to River Trail. Soon you will come to a pine plantation [9] (1.8 mi.); for the next .4 mi. you will be in and out of the pines. While hiking through the pines, look for turkey scratchings in the pine needles (a V- or Y-shaped area). A trail comes in from the right at 2.15 mi. [10]; stay left on the River to River Trail, skirting a pine plantation on the right.

The trail forks at 2.3 mi. [11]; go left and downhill. **Do not** follow the River to River Trail's white diamonds with blue *I*s. You are now hiking on what appears to an old county road that will lead you back to the parking area.

1. Start
2. Creek along trail
3. Stream crossing
4. River to River Trail
5. Side spur
6. Four stream crossings
7. Trail ascends, Crab Orchard Wilderness
8. Wet area
9. Pine plantation
10. Trail junction
11. Y in trail

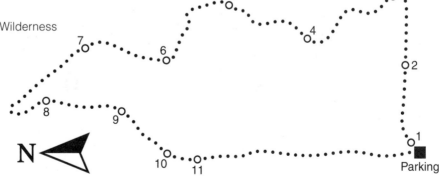

# Rocky Bluff Trail–
# Devil's Kitchen Lake

 **Distance Round-Trip:** 2 miles
**Estimated Hiking Time:** 1.1 hours

*Like someone who likes to eat dessert before dinner, I did the sweetest part of the trail first. I couldn't wait for the colorful wildflowers or the mouthwatering waterfall!*

**Caution:** The trail can be very muddy. Fallen saplings often block the way, and roots are exposed. Some of the rocks can be very slippery. In the fall, leaves might obscure parts of the path. During deer season use caution and wear bright orange.

**Trail Directions:** Park on the left side of the road and begin at the trail board [1]. Trail intersection points will be marked with a trail map. Go left and head downward, using the steps and metal handrail to aid with the steep descent. Within 100 feet look to your right for a great waterfall, especially if a heavy downpour has occurred before your visit. Continue down small stone steps with another handrail to aid in a stream crossing.

Again look to your right at the small canyon and waterfall. Note a large alcove and a collapsed smaller alcove above at its head [2] (.1 mi.). The waterfall helps to remove debris. The alcove was formed by a process called groundwater sapping—when groundwater seeps out from a cliff's face and undermines the cliff. Erosion at the seepage face creates an alcove and, as the back of the alcove retreats, the overhanging rock is undermined and eventually collapses in an interesting geological formation. In the spring the ground here is carpeted with wildflowers of every imaginable hue. This might just be the best wildflower display in the state!

A trail intersection is at .2 mi.; go left [3]. On your left in the spring are acres of blue-eyed Marys along Grassy Creek. These relatives of snapdragons are one of the few spring wildflowers that must come up each year from seed (annuals). The trail skirts Grassy Creek [4] (.3 mi.). On the left look for signs of nature's engineer: downed trees and muddy slides made by beavers. At .5 mi. [5] the trail skirts a sandstone bluff on the right. Try to spot small circular depressions in the sand caused by antlion larvae. These effective snares trap all manner of small insects for prey. An antlion waits with open jaws for hapless victims at the bottom of the pit. Also notice the dark, concentric rings on the bluffs; called Liesegang rings, they are caused by groundwater flowing through the sandstone, eroding it and leaving behind mineral deposits.

As you skirt the bluff, you will walk under a shelter cave and soon step onto a point overlooking Grassy

Creek. Enjoy the view before heading uphill. At .7 mi. [6] head up using the steps; you will be hiking through an oak-hickory forest on a ridge overlooking Grassy Creek.

All too soon the views of sandstone, Grassy Creek, and wildflowers are gone. At 1 mi. [7] cross a bridge before heading upward into an oak-hickory forest. You are hiking on a ridge between two ravines. Look to your right for a great view of the ravine. The trail intersects [8] with Wild Turkey Trail at 1.25 mi.; go right and hike on a wide path.

Another intersection appears at 1.5 mi.; go right [9] and back into the woods. The grassy path soon becomes a narrow trail through the woods. Don't forget to look to your right to marvel at the ravine woods as soon as the trail descends [10] (1.8 mi.). You will soon cross a stream; use caution because the stream is running across sandstone slabs [11] (1.85 mi.). The trail continues straight ahead with another stream crossing at 2 mi., this time over a wooden bridge [12].

From here the trail soon ends, completing the loop. If visiting in the spring, have a second helping of dessert—take the few extra steps to enjoy the waterfall, collapsed alcove, and profusion of wildflowers once again.

1. Start
2. Waterfall
3. Intersection, left turn
4. Skirt creek
5. Sandstone bluff
6. Ascend steps
7. Bridge
8. Right turn
9. Right turn
10. Descend
11. Sandstone
12. Wooden bridge

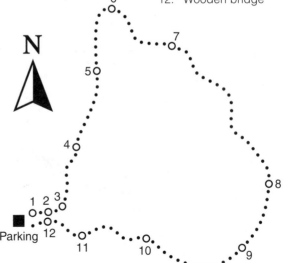

# 48. Ferne Clyffe State Park

- View sandstone canyons, deep gorges, shady dells, shelter caves, unique rock formations, and intermittent (seasonal) waterfalls.
- Discover Hawk's Cave, the largest of the park's shelter caves. This structure is an immense undercut in the sandstone with a large overhanging ledge that forms a natural amphitheater.
- Look for the circular depressions of antlion pits and the sinuous patterns of snakes in the dust under the vast overhang of Hawk's Cave.
- Explore Round Bluff Nature Preserve and discover many of the park's 700 species of plants.
- Experience alleyways between large boulders carpeted with spring wildflowers.

## Area Information

Ferne Clyffe State Park lies just south of where the Illinoisan glacier stopped its southward advance. The park's massive sandstone outcroppings, although untouched by the ice, were not unaffected. Glacial meltwaters from the receding ice widened and deepened canyons and carved terraces, steps, and shelter bluffs in the canyon walls. Round Bluff, a massive sandstone outlier, stands alone, an island separated from the other bluffs in the park. Hawk's Cave, a shelter cave hewn by wind and water, is a vast overhang 150 feet long and nearly as high.

In the spring, assemblages of wildflowers and ferns line the trails, descending into and traversing the ravines—mayapple, yellow trout lily, Dutchman's breeches, and squirrel corn. The latter species covers the valley floor with lush, feathery foliage. Large sandstone blocks have separated from the canyon walls and created blind alleys and narrow passages within the forest. On top of these blocks are isolated islands of wildflowers, many never experiencing human footprints.

In the 1920s Ferne Clyffe State Park was considered the most beautiful spot in Illinois. Today, it is still an area not to be missed during a visit to southern Illinois.

**Directions:** Located on Illinois 37, 1 mile south of Goreville and 12 miles south of Marion, the park is easily accessible from both I-57 and I-24. Take exit 7 from I-24 and head west to Route 37. The park entrance is a short distance south on Route 37. From I-57 take exit 40, then drive east to Route 37 and south to the entrance.

**Hours Open:** The park is open year-round. It is closed on Christmas Day and New Year's Day.

**Facilities:** Picnicking, RV and tent camping, fishing, and horseback riding are available.

**Permits and Rules:** Round Bluff is a dedicated Illinois Nature Preserve. No pets are allowed on the trail or in the nature preserve. Also within the nature preserve, no hunting, camping, fires, picnicking, or rock climbing is allowed. Dogs must be kept on a leash no longer than 10 feet. Bicycles and ATVs are prohibited on park trails.

**For Further Information:** Ferne Clyffe State Park, Route 37 South, P.O. Box 10, Goreville, IL 62939; 618-995-2411.

## Park Trails

**Rebman Trail** (.25 mile). A level loop trail dedicated to the area's former owner leads by a small waterfall. A marker dedicated to Miss Rebman marks the beginning of the trail.

**Goreville Boy Scout Trail** (.5 mile). This linear trail connects the park to the town of Goreville.

**Blackjack Oak Trail** (1 mile). This linear trail with two steep climbs traverses Deer Ridge. Impressive vistas and blackjack oaks among the dry bluff tops are worth the climb.

**Ferne Clyffe Trail** (1 mile). An easy loop circles the lake's shoreline, giving anglers ample opportunity to cast their lines.

**Happy Hollow Trail** (5 miles). This trail (for both horses and hikers) winds through woods and wildlife food plantings, and it has several creek crossings.

**Happy Hollow Backpack Trail** (5 miles). A linear trail leads campers to a primitive camping area.

**Happy Hollow Horse Trail** (8 miles). This horse trail leads from the horseback camping area to the Happy Hollow Trail.

**Cedar Bluff Trail** (2 miles). This linear trail leads to a scenic vista atop Cedar Bluff, proceeds along a ridgetop, and soon descends the bluff.

**Bobcat Loop** (1 mile). This loop trail is in the heart of Cedar Bluff. It provides a link with Cedar Bluff and Big Buck Creek trails.

## Other Areas of Interest

**Dutchman Lake,** near Vienna, was constructed during the early 1970s. The main recreational activities are fishing and boating, with some primitive camping. A faint, unmaintained 2-mile trail follows the northeast shoreline and the sandstone bluff tops. Highlights of the trail include seasonal waterfalls and vistas of Dutchman Lake. For more information, call 800-699-6637.

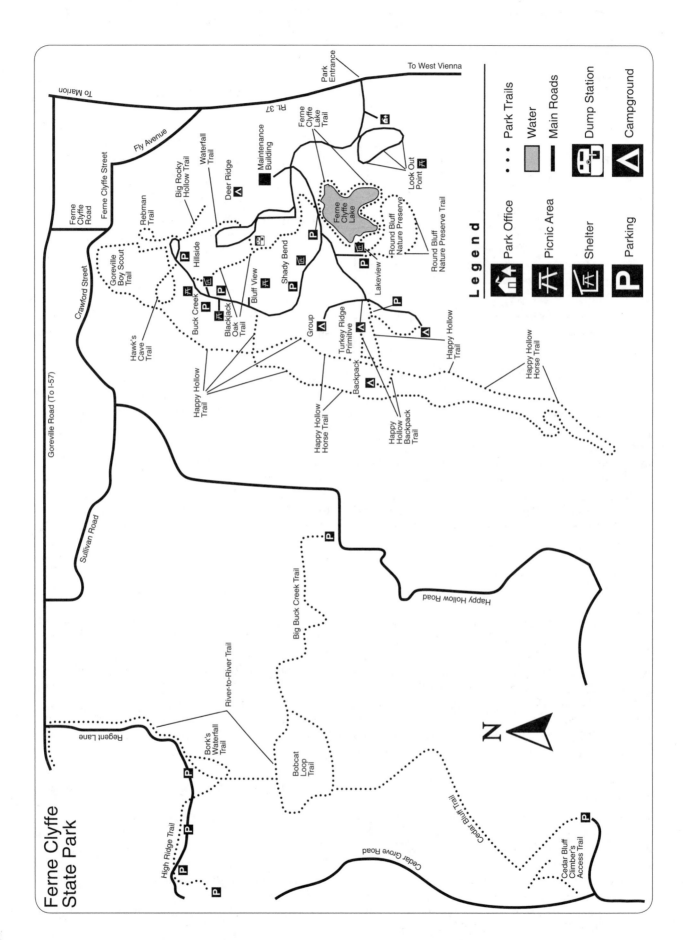

# Ferne Clyffe State Park

**Legend**

Park Office | Park Trails
Picnic Area | Water
Shelter | Main Roads
Parking | Dump Station
| Campground

**Roads and Streets:**
To Marion
To West Vienna
Park Entrance
Rt. 37
Fly Avenue
Ferne Clyffe Street
Ferne Clyffe Road
Crawford Street
Goreville Road (To I-57)
Sullivan Road
Regent Lane
Happy Hollow Road
Cedar Grove Road

**Trails and Features:**
Big Rocky Hollow Trail
Waterfall Trail
Deer Ridge
Maintenance Building
Ferne Clyffe Lake Trail
Look Out Point
Round Bluff Nature Preserve
Round Bluff Nature Preserve Trail
Rebman Trail
Hillside
Goreville Boy Scout Trail
Shady Bend
Bluff View
Lakeview
Buck Creek
Blackjack Oak Trail
Hawk's Cave Trail
Happy Hollow Trail
Group
Turkey Ridge Primitive
Backpack
Happy Hollow Horse Trail
Happy Hollow Backpack Trail
Ferne Clyffe Lake
Big Buck Creek Trail
River-to-River Trail
Bork's Waterfall Trail
Bobcat Loop Trail
High Ridge Trail
Cedar Bluff Trail
Cedar Bluff Climber's Access Trail

N

# Hawk's Cave, Blackjack Oak, and Waterfall Trails

 **Distance Round-Trip:** 3 miles
**Estimated Hiking Time:** 2 hours

*An overweight dog joined us for part of the trail and soon was wheezing and puffing; he turned back. What a shame—he missed the bird's-eye view of Round Bluff from the overlook, the antlion pits of Hawk's Cave, and a beautiful multilevel waterfall.*

**Caution:** Watch your step on the trail: Tree roots and rocks have eroded from the soil of the path. A couple of stream crossings provide the possibility of wet feet.

**Trail Directions:** Park at Boat Rock Picnic Area. The trailhead is off the parking area. Cross Buck Creek using the ford [1], and look on your left for a trail board pointing to Hawk's Cave. The gravel trail begins with a bridge crossing and heads uphill. In the spring, pause at the bridge to look for migrating songbirds.

At .1 mi. [2] the trail forks; go to the right. After hiking through a mixed-hardwood forest for .3 mi., you'll encounter Hawk's Cave [3], a huge shelter cave. In the spring, look under the dripline for French's shooting star, a wildflower once thought to grow only in Illinois. If visitors have been few, check the dust for the dendritic patterns of snakes or for antlion pits. Antlions are immature insects that dig pits to trap prey. Each pit has a voracious larva waiting with open jaws at the bottom for its next meal!

After exploring the cave, continue on the rocky trail. At .35 mi. a giant boulder resides near the path [4]. During wet weather look for slimy salamanders slithering across the trail. By .5 mi. you have finished the loop of Hawk's Cave Trail [2]. Retrace your steps to the trailhead.

Recross Buck's Creek and walk on the road along the parking and picnic area [5] for a short distance. Go past a large chunk of sandstone and observe the top. In spring it will be carpeted with wildflowers. You will soon see a sign for Blackjack Oak Trail on the left [6].

The trail immediately begins an uphill climb on a gravel path. You will skirt a huge sandstone bluff with saxifrage on its shelves. At .85 mi. the trail forks; stay left (the right leads to a picnic area). Within a few steps (eight or nine) the trail forks again [7]. (Pay attention—this is very faint and the trail marker had been knocked down.) Go left and uphill, where you will skirt a boulder and soon come upon mini-shelter bluffs. For the next .25 mi. you will be hiking uphill. On top, the trail crosses rock outcroppings interspersed with gravel. At 1 mi. [8] follow the trail to your right to a Blackjack Oak Trail sign. Immedi-

ately after the trail sign is an overlook to your right, complete with a park bench for enjoying the forest panorama below.

Continue on the path along a ridge. At 1.4 mi. [9] the trail emerges from the forest with an impressive view of the lake and Round Bluff Nature Preserve. Within less than .1 mi. follow a sign leading left to Deer Ridge Campground [10] (1.5 mi.).

Soon the paved road of the campground (1.6 mi.) will appear [11]. Take a left and follow the road to an intersection by the sanitary dump; take the middle road and follow the right arm of the campground loop road. By 1.9 mi. see a marker leading to the Waterfall Trail [12] on your right—hike in.

The rocky dirt trail descends through a dry oak-hickory forest. Giant boulders have eroded away from the cliff and are slowly working their way downhill. At one such boulder (2.1 mi.) the trail veers right [13]. Within a few steps the trail comes to a V; go right at a huge moss-covered block of sandstone, passing by a huge beech, first on the right and then on the left.

At 2.3 mi. [14] the trail comes to an intersection; go right on the Waterfall Trail. It soon passes through a deep, cool ravine. The tree in the center of the trail is a blue beech. The trail crosses an iron bridge with a boardwalk to the box canyon, complete with a waterfall [15] (2.6 mi.). In autumn, however, all that will be found is a wet cliff face footed by a small, still pool. Hike out on the same trail you entered, but do not turn at [14]—continue straight. The trail will lead to the parking area on the loop road, and at 3 mi. you should be at your vehicle.

1. Start
2. Right turn
3. Hawk's Cave
4. Large boulder
5. Picnic area
6. Blackjack Oak Trail
7. Two trail forks
8. Right turn
9. Overlook
10. Left turn
11. Campground
12. Waterfall Trail
13. Veer right
14. Right turn
15. Waterfall

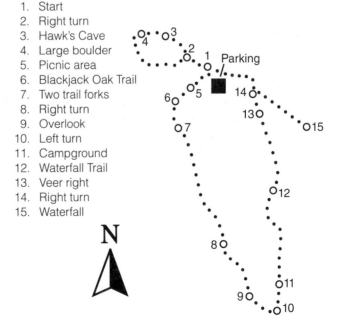

# Round Bluff Nature Preserve Trail

   **Distance Round-Trip:** 1 mile
**Estimated Hiking Time:** 1 hour

*This is a trail for all seasons. In the fall box turtles rustle in the fallen leaves. In the winter the mobbing calls of crows alert you to a nearby owl. Summer mosses and ferns give the bluff a luxuriant coat of green. Yet spring is perhaps best, with a profusion of wildflowers arranged in an artist's palette of colors.*

**Caution:** Watch your step on the trail and steep, slippery stairs; tree roots and rocks have eroded from the soil of the path.

**Trail Directions:** The trail begins near the Lakeview Picnic Shelter and parking area. Start your hike at the large nature preserve sign [1]. The trail begins as a mowed path but soon becomes hard-packed dirt. A hiker silhouette on a brown post marks the trail. Round Bluff, a 300-million-year-old sandstone knob, is immediately visible on your left. The roots of several red cedars have eroded out of the soil and crisscross the path. At .1 mi. [2] the bluff is at the trail edge. At this point find a series of steps. Look up and observe that the cedars have branches only on the side away from the cliff face. This is the portion of the tree that receives sunlight.

A side spur appears on the left at .3 mi. [3]. Take the short trail and examine the champion winged elm of Illinois. Back on the trail you'll encounter another side spur at .4 mi. [4] that leads to a glade community (a dry bedrock opening in the forest). If you decide to explore this area, take care: Trampling can be harmful to the vegetation. Look for bright red fire pinks along this section of the trail in April. Beyond the spur the trail descends with a series of wooden erosion-control steps. You are now on the northern side of the bluff; here during the spring are the best displays of wildflowers.

At .5 mi. [5] cross a spring, the only one in the nature preserve. Here the trail traverses up and down. Take time to look left at the interesting cracks and crevices in the sandstone. Hike under an overhang at .7 mi. [6], which might be wet during spring. Facing you is a steep set of steps. Before going down them,

note a crack in the sandstone that is cloaked with ferns, lush and green even in dry summers.

Beginning at .8 mi. [7], note the impressive sandstone bluff and the erosional patterns etched into the rock. Close observation may yield a skull or a monkey face. From this point on appear spectacular assemblages of spring wildflowers. Stay on the trail to avoid stepping on a trout lily, spring beauty, jack-in-the-pulpit, or hay-scented fern. At .85 mi. [8] cross a bridge over a small stream. The area in front of you is a carpet of Dutchman's breeches, squirrel corn, waterleaf, and pale corydalis in early April.

At 1 mi. [9] you encounter the Lakeview Picnic Shelter and parking lot. The area has picnic facilities, a water fountain, and pit toilets.

1. Start
2. Bluff
3. Champion winged elm
4. Glade
5. Spring crossing
6. Overhang
7. Sandstone bluff
8. Bridge
9. Picnic shelter

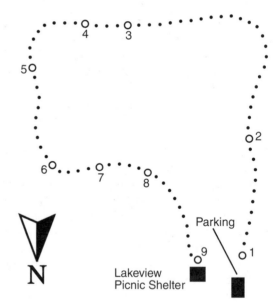

# Big Buck Creek Trail

 **Distance Round-Trip:** 3.8 miles
**Estimated Hiking Time:**
1.75 hours

*Navigate your way through floodplain and upland forests, crisscrossing Big Buck Creek several times. Here, you can experience everything from pine plantations to relatively pristine forest.*

**Caution:** In the spring the stream crossings are likely to result in wet feet.

**Trail Directions:** The parking area and the trailhead are part of Ferne Clyffe State Park West and are located on Happy Hollow Road. Begin the trail [1] at the trailhead and head north on a fairly wide but undulating gravel path through mixed hardwoods. At .1 mi. [2] the trail curves left and ascends. At this point the trail is marked by a horse and white diamonds. In the spring you will pass a small waterfall.

By .5 mi. the trail veers to the left [3] and narrows to become a dirt path. Rock outcrops are soon passed on the left, and soon you are in the floodplain of Buck Creek. Note the tall sycamores, smartweed, and viney tangles. Cross a stream [4] at .65 mi. with rock outcrops on your right and a large sugar maple on your left. Follow Buck Creek on your left. Another stream crossing is at .9 mi. [5] with a large rock outcrop on the right. Note the floodplain woods on the left and a mixed-hardwood forest on the right. Don't forget to look down—this area is a favorite for turkey dust baths. Look for oval depressions, Y-shaped scratchings, and the occasional feather.

At 1.15 mi. you will come to a trail junction [6]; go right on a deeply worn path. The creek will be on your left and outcrops on the right. A large, double-trunked river birch [7] (1.3 mi.) marks the next stream crossing. At 1.45 mi. is the widest stream crossing [8], likely to result in wet feet in spring. Once across, you will encounter a grove of tulip trees on the left and lofty oaks on the right. Go left and uphill at the intersection at 1.55 mi. [9]. You are hiking along the side of a ridge with rocky outcrops on the left and ferns in the understory. These will soon give way to a pine plantation on both sides.

As you begin to descend, the trail will T; go left [10]. The creek will be on your right (2.15). As you hike this section, look for a large sugar maple and a bur oak. You will also encounter a river oats thicket. River oats are an inland relative of sea oats that help stabilize sand dunes along the East Coast. This attractive grass grows best in areas that are prone to flooding.

At 2.35 you will come to the final three stream crossings [11]. As you cross, take time to look in the drying pools for large, black tadpoles. After the final crossing the trail ascends and you are back at the trail junction [6]; go right, retracing your steps back to the parking area.

1. Start
2. Curve left, ascend
3. Left turn, trail narrows
4. Stream crossing
5. Stream crossing
6. Junction
7. River birch
8. Major stream crossing
9. Intersection
10. Trail Ts, left turn
11. Stream crossings

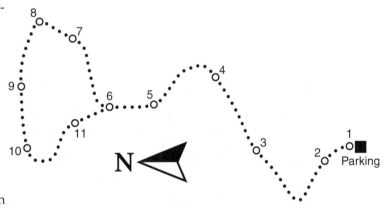

South

# Borks Waterfall Trail

**Distance Round-Trip:** 1.25 miles
**Estimated Hiking Time:** 1 hour

*How often do you get to drive over a waterfall before you actually see it? After admiring the waterfall from the top, hike down to the bottom to discover beech trees that have become one with the sandstone.*

**Caution:** Rocks and roots litter the first segment of the trail. If you're hiking in the fall, leaves might conceal the path.

**Trail Directions:** From Goreville Road turn south onto Regent Road. After a mile cross Rocky Ford. The parking area (pull in) will be on the left, along with a white diamond trail marker. Begin the trail [1] hiking on a ridge with a deep ravine on the left. At .1 mi. go left [2] and downhill; note the huge beech tree on the right as well as rocky outcrops on both sides. You are hiking on an undulating path where the beeches and rocky outcrops often merge into a gray rugged cliff face.

At .3 mi. the trail comes out into a grassy area with a buried pipeline running through it; go left and, before the orange poles, go left again [3], following a trail into the woods where a large rock outcrop dwarfs you on the left. The trail follows a stream to your right. Cross this stream at .45 mi. [4]. Notice how the valley is closing in. Within .05 mi. the trail goes up and you begin to skirt a sandstone outcrop [5]. In the fall you will be walking on a crunchy carpet of American beech leaves.

Continue straight, and at .6 mi. you have come to a box canyon and waterfall [6]. In the winter the waterfall becomes an icefall, with the rim of the canyon etched in icicles. Box canyons are three-sided and resemble an open-ended box. The pool at the base is called a plunge pool and is home to water striders and tadpoles. Take a few moments to study the canyon with its steep sides before retracing your steps back to the parking area. Don't miss your two right turns at the grassy area [3], and take time to admire the large gray beech trees as you wind your way uphill, remembering that the waterfall is not just a destination but a journey.

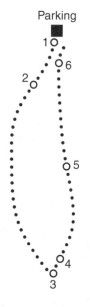

1. Start
2. Left turn, downhill
3. Grassy area, left turn, left turn
4. Stream crossing
5. Ascend, skirt outcrop
6. Box canyon and waterfall

# 49. Tunnel Hill State Trail

- Discover the light at the end of the tunnel as you hike through a 543-foot railroad tunnel that was built in the 1870s.
- Enjoy the view into the valley from your perch atop a long railroad trestle.
- Discover almost everything that makes a railroad a railroad—a tunnel, road cuts, a trestle—but no rails!
- Instead of a train whistle, listen for the whistle of chipmunks, letting you know you are getting too close.
- Look for beavers, otters, herons, and frogs as you walk one of the state's best wildlife-viewing areas.

## Area Information

At one time traffic on the Tunnel Hill State Trail was the rumble of freight and Pullman cars as coal, salt, orchard-grown peaches, and apples were transported cross country. The railroad line was developed in 1872 as part of a federal program where land was made available to the states for cross-country railroad development. Ambrose Burnside, a Civil War general, took advantage of the program and began the Vincennes and Cairo Railroad, so named because the termini were Vincennes, Indiana, and Cairo, Illinois.

The railroad changed hands many times. The last owners were Norfolk and Southern Railroad. In 1991, they gave Illinois the railroad right of way between Harrisburg and Karnak. A trail for hikers and cyclists was developed on the line, stretching for 45 miles from Harrisburg to Karnak, passing through flat farm country and the hills of the Shawnee National Forest, through wetlands, and along meandering creeks and bluffs.

The trail has 23 trestles ranging in length from 34 to 450 feet. The highest point along the trail is Tunnel Hill at 680 feet. The railway decided that rather than go over it they would go through it, resulting in a 543-foot tunnel. Although you can see the light at the end, somewhere in the middle the darkness and perspective merge, surprising you. But this is just one of the many surprises the trail holds. Whether you're viewing a partially albino otter in the winter or a signature from the distant past, this is one of the premier trails in the state.

**Directions:** The visitor center for the Tunnel Hill State Trail is located on State Highway 146 in the community park in Vienna. The center is in an old railroad depot. Parking and trail access are in the towns of Harrisburg, Carrier Mills, Stonefort, New Burnside, Tunnel Hill, and Karnak.

**Hours Open:** The trail is open year-round. The visitor center is open 8:00 a.m. to 4:00 p.m. seven days a week but staffed only on Saturdays and Sundays.

**Facilities:** The access areas offer drinking water, parking, and toilets.

**Permits and Rules:** Motorized vehicles, horses, and hunting are not allowed on the trail. Pets must be leashed.

**For Further Information:** Tunnel Hill State Trail, Highway 146 East, P.O. Box 671, Vienna, IL 62995; 618-658-2168.

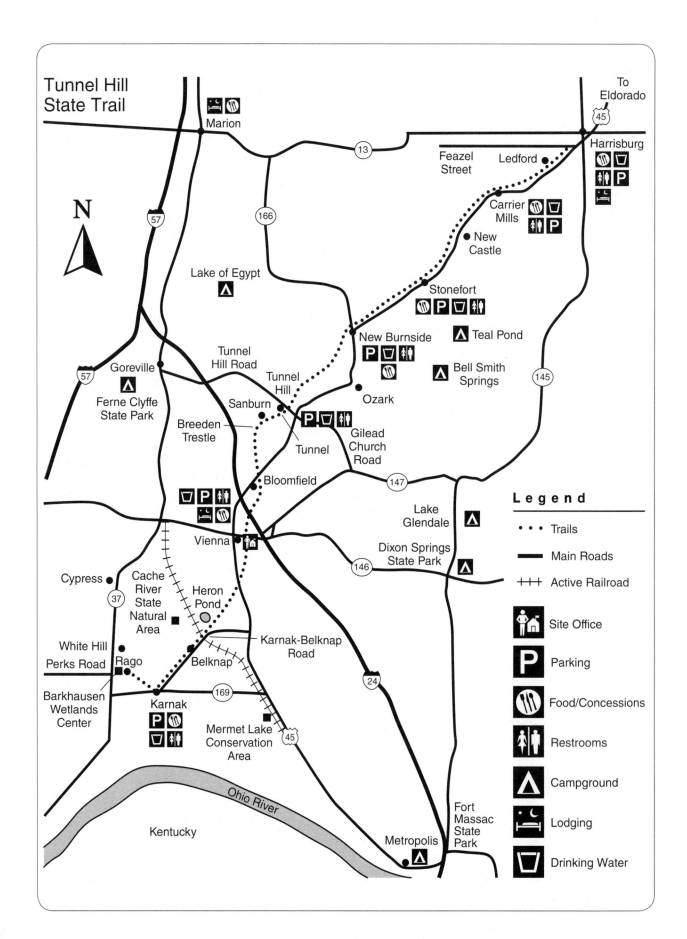

# Tunnel Hill State Trail

**Legend**

· · · Trails

━━━ Main Roads

+++ Active Railroad

Site Office

P Parking

Food/Concessions

Restrooms

Campground

Lodging

Drinking Water

# Tunnel Hill

 **Distance Round-Trip:** 5.2 miles
**Estimated Hiking Time:** 2.5 hours

*While hiking on this past transportation artery, I encountered another type of transport—a dung beetle carrying a piece of raccoon dung to who knows where! Also, hiking the tunnel at dusk gives an eerie sensation as your arms and legs disappear into the tunnel's historic gloom.*

**Caution:** You will be sharing the trail with bicyclists and joggers.

**Trail Directions:** Park in the Tunnel Hill parking area, located between routes 37 and 45 on Tunnel Hill Road, and begin at the kiosk; go left (south) **[1]**, hiking on a crushed-gravel trail. Look to your left and right for shale outcrops. At .25 mi. you will come to the tunnel **[2]**; note how it is wider at the top than at the bottom. After emerging from the tunnel you will notice the shale has been replaced by sandstone. A hardwood forest is on both sides. Mile marker 215 appears **[3]** (.4 mi.); this remnant from the railroad days denotes the distance from Danville, Illinois.

As you hike, observe how the outcrops and walls generally recede, and soon you are hiking on top of a ridge. An intersection with a stop sign appears at .95 mi. **[4]**; continue straight. By 1.25 mi. **[5]** you have gone from the elevated bed to a railroad cut and the temperature is slightly cooler. Railroad marker 216 soon appears and the roadbed is built up again. The landscape will undulate around you as you hike. Keep a lookout for large oak and sycamore trees. Chipmunks will squeal a warning that you are too close while spooked white-tailed deer leap across the path.

The trail makes a gradual left at 1.9 mi. **[6]**. Just after railroad marker 217 you will find a bench on the right **[7]** (2.4 mi.). The Breeden Trestle, which is the trail's highest elevation at 90 feet, is at 2.5 mi. **[8]**. Walk across the trestle and enjoy your treetop view of the landscape. Who knows what birds you might come eye to eye with? At the end of the trestle, turn around and retrace your steps.

Once off the trestle, notice the outcropping on your right **[9]** (2.85 mi.). Look closely for dates carved in the stone—1890 and 1953. Continue to retrace your steps back to the tunnel, looking for wildlife and admiring the pastoral setting.

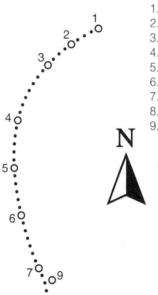

1. Start
2. Tunnel
3. Marker 215
4. Intersection with stop sign
5. Railroad cut
6. Gradual left
7. Bench
8. Breeden Trestle
9. Rock outcrop with dates

**N**

# Barkhausen Wetlands Center

**Distance Round-Trip:** 5.6 miles
**Estimated Hiking Time:** 2.5 hours

*Whether it's slatey skimmer dragonflies that dance one step ahead of you, a bald eagle on its distant perch, or otters wrestling and sliding in a slough, this is one of the state's best wildlife-viewing trails, and a silent hiker will be rewarded.*

**Caution:** You will be sharing the trail with bicyclists and joggers. The wetlands center locks its gate at 4:30 p.m.

**Trail Directions:** Begin at the partners' kiosk [1] south of the visitor center, and go right on the wide, paved path. A prairie restoration is on either side and common milkweed is abundant, so look for the life stages of the monarch. A sign marks the spot where the town of Rago once stood. The path is now crushed limestone [2] (.2 mi.), and a regenerating forest replaces the prairie. The dead snag on your far left is a favorite perch of a bald eagle.

At .4 mi. cross a bridge [3], go through the green gate, and go right. Within a tenth of a mile you will cross a larger bridge over the Cache River [4]. Pause and look for red-eared slider turtles, gar, water snakes, great blue herons, and patterns in the duckweed. In the winter flocks of blue-winged teal fly overhead. Off the bridge you are hiking through the eastern edge of Section 8 Woods, a cypress tupelo swamp and floodplain forest and an Illinois Nature Preserve that contains the state champion water tupelo. This section of the trail will be accompanied by the plinks of turtles sliding into the water on either side of you. Look here for otter slides.

Railroad mile marker 350 [5] and a bench appear at 1.4 mi. This is a remnant from the railroad days denoting the distance from Chicago. On your left at 1.8 mi. is a seasonal wet area; the large oaks are from the red oak group [6]. In the summer this section is a good dragonfly hike; several species bask on the trail in front of you. Another bench [7] appears on your left at 2 mi.; look in this area for vandalized turtle nests—their broken shells will be strewn about.

A stop sign and road crossing appear at 2.8 mi. [8]. This is a good point to turn around and retrace your steps, listening for several species of frogs—cricket, bird-voiced tree, and bull—and also birds—red-shouldered hawk, fish crow, and barred owl. Once you have recrossed both bridges and the Wetlands Center is in sight, go right on the Eagle Slough Trail [9] (5.2 mi.). This is a paved path with trail signage made by a group of volunteers called the Cache Corps of Discovery. Take advantage of the signs to learn about the area's organisms.

In the summer each segment of the sidewalk has an eastern pondhawk dragonfly, and no matter the season, there is always coyote scat. This path might even give you a closer look at a bald eagle. By now you have completed the journey and should have added a wildlife sighting, or two, to your life's list.

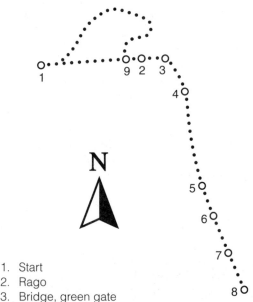

1. Start
2. Rago
3. Bridge, green gate
4. Cache River crossing
5. Marker 350
6. Red oaks
7. Bench
8. Stop sign, turn around
9. Eagle Slough Trail

- Visit the watery home of bald cypress and water tupelo trees.
- Walk into the heart of a swamp on a floating boardwalk.
- View a landscape more typically associated with the bayous of Louisiana.
- Listen for a prothonotary warbler chortling as it feeds its young, the hammering of a pileated woodpecker on a long-dead snag, or the startled cry of a wood duck fleeing through the drowned forest.

## Area Information

"This river is hidden," said a French adventurer credited with naming the Cache River when he spotted its log-jammed mouth on the Ohio in 1702. His words are still true: The Cache must be actively sought to be experienced. The Cache River watershed, a result of thousands of years of geologic action, is divided into the Upper Cache River and the Lower Cache River. The Cache River Basin marks the geographical point where the last invasion of the sea (some 30 million years ago) reached its northernmost limit. In the original United States Land Survey, this area was referred to as "inaccessible, a drowned land." Because of the efforts of conservation groups and concerned citizens, the area is today protected and no longer inaccessible.

The Cache River has three dedicated nature preserves and two national natural landmarks along it. Some of the oldest and largest trees in Illinois and the United States occur in its floodplain. This distinguished group includes one of the largest trees in Illinois (a bald cypress) and the oldest living stand of trees east of the Mississippi River.

From Little Black Slough and Heron Pond (examples of southern swamps at the northernmost limits of their range) to the southern exposure of Wildcat Bluff, where a hill prairie looks onto the floodplain forests and upland woods, the area is truly unique. Eighteen miles of hiking trails offer a sample of the diverse wetlands, grasslands, and forests that make up the Cache River State Natural Area.

**Directions:** The Cache River State Natural Area has several parcels and covers over 10,000 acres. The **Henry N. Barkhausen Cache River Wetlands Center** is located south of Cypress, 2 miles north of the intersection of Highways 169 and 37, or 9 miles south of the intersection of Highways 146 and 37.

To reach the **site headquarters** from Vienna, Illinois, at the junction of Highways 45 and 146, take Highway 45 south 5 miles to Belknap Road; turn right (west) and go to the town of Belknap. Turn right onto 300 N. (the Dongola-Belknap Road). In the town turn right (north) at a large white church on the right side of the road. Follow the gravel road .9 mile to the park office. To reach the trailhead parking area (Tupelo Trail and others), follow a gravel road through a gate on the north side of the office for .6 mile. To reach **Heron Pond** from Vienna at the junction of Highways 45 and 146, take Highway 45 south 5 miles to Belknap Road, turn right (west), and go 1.5 miles to a gravel road (Heron Pond Lane); turn right onto Heron Pond Lane and go north .5 mile to a large parking area.

**Hours Open:** The Wetland Center is open Wednesday through Sunday from 9:00 a.m. to 4:00 p.m. year-round with the exception of major holidays. The site office is open weekdays from 8:00 a.m. to 4:00 p.m. year-round.

**Facilities:** The Wetland Center offers maps, informational exhibits, audiovisual presentations, and a computer touch-screen virtual tour of the Cache. Canoe access and privy toilets are available at some access points.

**Permits and Rules:** Several areas within the Cache River State Natural Area are state nature preserves: Heron Pond–Wildcat Bluff, Little Black Slough, and Section 8 Woods. Pets are not allowed in nature preserves. Hunting, trapping, fires, camping, picnicking, and rock climbing also are not allowed in nature preserves.

**For Further Information:** Cache River State Natural Area, Site Superintendent, 930 Sunflower Lane, Belknap, IL 62908; 618-634-9678. Henry N. Barkhausen Cache River Wetlands Center, 8885 State Route 37 South, Cypress, IL 62923; 618-657-2064.

## Other Areas of Interest

**Lower Cache River Canoe Trail** is a 3- to 6-mile canoe route that winds through backwater sloughs to the state champion bald cypress tree. For information on accessing the site, call 618-634-9678.

Walk among some of the area's largest cypress and tupelo trees in **Big Cypress Tree Access**, a lowland wooded area. The access is located on the west edge of Karnack. Go 2.25 miles west of Belknap on the Dongola-Belknap Road, then south on the gravel road for 1.25 miles. The access is on the east (left) side of the road. A short trail leads you to the trees. For more information, call 618-634-9678.

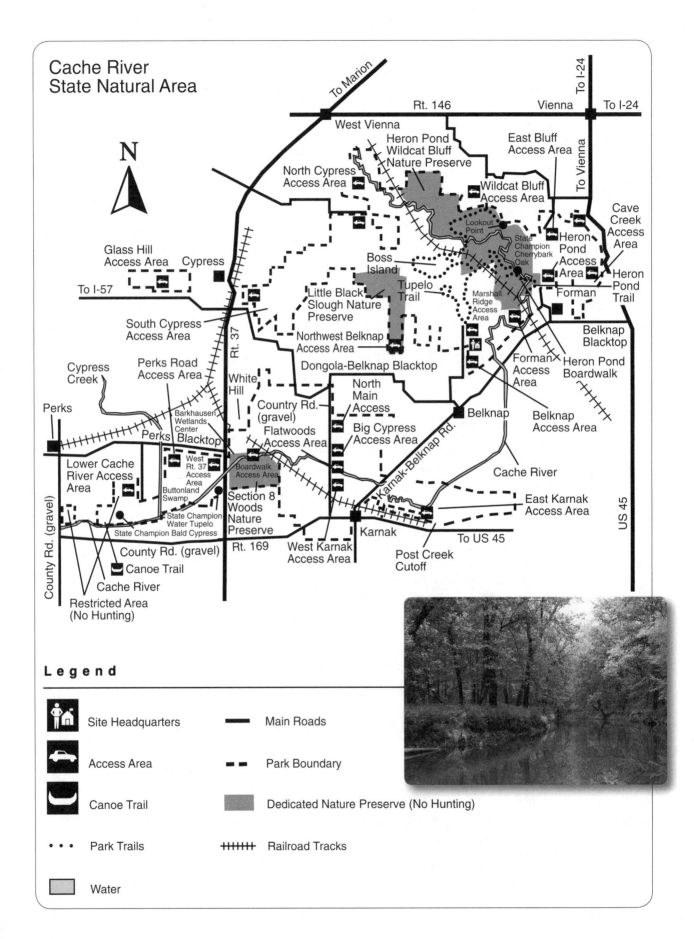

# Cache River
# State Natural Area

**N**

To Marion

Rt. 146    Vienna    To I-24

To I-24

West Vienna

Heron Pond Wildcat Bluff Nature Preserve

East Bluff Access Area

North Cypress Access Area

Wildcat Bluff Access Area

To Vienna

Cave Creek Access Area

Glass Hill Access Area

Cypress

Lookout Point

State Champion Cherrybark Oak

Heron Pond Access Area

Heron Pond Trail

To I-57

Boss Island

Tupelo Trail

Forman

South Cypress Access Area

Little Black Slough Nature Preserve

Marshall Ridge Access Area

Rt. 37

Belknap Blacktop

Cypress Creek

Perks Road Access Area

Northwest Belknap Access Area

White Hill

Dongola-Belknap Blacktop

North Main Access

Forman Access Area

Heron Pond Boardwalk

Perks

Barkhausen Wetlands Center

Country Rd. (gravel)

Flatwoods Access Area

Big Cypress Access Area

Belknap

Belknap Access Area

Perks Blacktop

West Rt. 37 Access Area

Boardwalk Access Area

Karnak-Belknap Rd.

Cache River

Lower Cache River Access Area

Buttonland Swamp

Section 8 Woods Nature Preserve

East Karnak Access Area

State Champion Water Tupelo

US 45

State Champion Bald Cypress

County Rd. (gravel)

Canoe Trail

Rt. 169

West Karnak Access Area

Karnak

To US 45

Cache River

Post Creek Cutoff

Restricted Area (No Hunting)

## Legend

| | | | |
|---|---|---|---|
| 🚹 Site Headquarters | — Main Roads | | |
| 🚗 Access Area | - - Park Boundary | | |
| 🛶 Canoe Trail | ▓ Dedicated Nature Preserve (No Hunting) | | |
| ••• Park Trails | ┼┼┼┼ Railroad Tracks | | |
| ▓ Water | | | |

# Heron Pond Trail

 **Distance Round-Trip:** 2.5 miles
**Estimated Hiking Time:** 1.25 hours

*With the aid of a boardwalk, you can experience the strange, silent, primeval world of a southern Illinois swamp. Early visitors, who lacked the luxury of a boardwalk, described this swamp as a "cheerless miserable place," or more simply "the pit of hell." Your experience is sure to be much more enjoyable.*

**Caution:** This area is one of the few places in Illinois where, if you see a snake in the water, it is probably a poisonous cottonmouth! Cottonmouths are especially fond of basking on the trail during summer. In the spring, several water crossings along the trail will likely soak your feet.

**Trail Directions:** From the parking area the trail begins at the brown park information board [1]. Here a large map shows the extent of the Cache River State Natural Area. Don't forget to read the interpretive panels along the trail. Blue blazes and occasional metal posts with hiker symbols mark the trail.

The hike begins on a limestone path that winds its way downhill. At .05 mi. [2] note a large boulder with a plaque dedicating this area as a national landmark. A suspension bridge crosses the junction of the Cache River and Dutchman's Creek. After crossing the bridge, follow the trail through a floodplain forest of large maples, oaks, and sycamores. In the spring look for shows of blue phlox; in summer seek out the long, swordlike leaves of spider lilies and spectacular white flowers (blooms are found in mid-August). In fall, Christmas ferns are one of the few plants that remain green.

From .3 to .5 mi. you will encounter a series of large stepping-stone bridges [3]. In dry weather these help prevent the swamp (on your left) from draining into the channelized Cache River on your right. During wet springs this area is sometimes underwater and the rocks are slippery, so use caution. Soon, fingers of the swamp are visible from the trail on your left. As you hike this section, look to the Cache for glimpses of soft-shell turtles, hooded mergansers, or mink.

At .55 mi. the trail forks [4]; go left to the boardwalk and enter the realm of a cypress-tupelo swamp. All around are cypress trees with their knobby knees supporting small islands of plants. Cypress trees are one of the few evergreens that lose their needles in fall. Water tupelos are rounder at the base and have oval, deciduous-looking leaves. The green carpet on the swamp is duckweed. Take a close look at it for any small or large frogs camouflaged by a mantle of duckweed. In spring, bright yellow prothonotary warblers nest overhead. Before turning around at the end of the boardwalk, take time to listen and look through the trees. Herons have returned to Heron Pond and a rookery is located beyond the boardwalk. In the evening this is also a good spot for viewing vultures (both black and turkey) coming in to roost. Retrace your steps to the trail and proceed to the left.

At .7 mi. the trail forms a V and a park sign lists trail options [5]. Take the left fork, following the edge of Heron Pond (the swamp). Along this often muddy trail, cypress knees offer a close inspection and female wood ducks will sound an alarm, accompanied by their whirring wing beats. Heron Pond soon ends and the trail curves to the right [6]. The trail goes uphill and winds its way through a regenerating woods.

At 1.35 mi. a metal trail marker gives you several hiking options [7]. A short side trip left (200 feet) leads to the state champion cherrybark oak tree [8]. Walk around the tree, which takes at least 20 kindergartners to encircle. From here you have the option of taking the Linkage Trail that will lead you to the site office and to Little Black Slough, or backtracking 200 feet and rejoining the Heron Pond Trail and eventually the parking area.

Backtrack to the first junction [7], continue straight, and return along the wide trail through hardwood forest. Look for camouflaged green tree frogs along here. After a few steps a trail to the river appears on your left; continue straight. At 1.85 mi. you will rejoin the main trail [4]. You have just completed the loop and will hike back along the Cache, keeping an eye out for redheaded woodpeckers. More redheaded woodpeckers occur in the Cache than in any other place in the state. Soon you will recross the series of stepping-stone bridges, cross the suspension bridge, and finally climb uphill to the parking area.

1. Start
2. Large boulder
3. Stepping-stone bridges
4. Intersection
5. Left turn
6. Curve right
7. Left turn
8. Cherrybark oak tree

N

South

# Tupelo Trail

  **Distance Round-Trip:** 2.5 miles
**Estimated Hiking Time:** 1.5 hours

*Hike to Little Black Slough for great wildlife viewing. The leaves of tall trees glisten against the backdrop of an incredibly blue sky. A bluebird fusses in a dead tupelo tree, woodpeckers fly from treehole to treehole, a hawk screams overhead, a young raccoon yawns and stretches in a feathery cypress tree, and an elusive wild turkey skitters across the trail. All this happens along the Tupelo Trail each autumn.*

**Cautions:** During a wet year, portions of the trail may be underwater, so come prepared in the spring. Be warned that this part of southern Illinois has poisonous snakes: copperhead, timber rattlesnake, and water moccasin.

**Trail Directions:** Park your vehicle at the Marshall Ridge Access Area and begin the trail in the northwest corner of the parking area [1]. The trail will have brown metal markers with the white silhouette of a hiker. Your hike begins on a crushed-rock road with a rolling, pastoral scene to the left and woods to the right. You should take a short side trip across the road to the created Michael Wolfe Memorial Wetlands. Here look for waterfowl and a variety of wildlife. The trail is easy and has an informational kiosk about the site. Return to the main trail.

After .25 mi. the trail forks and the crushed rock ends [2]. A sign points left for the Tupelo Trail. Begin hiking down an old dirt forest road that passes through a dry oak-hickory forest. During an excellent nut-crop year, walking on this stretch of trail is like walking on ball bearings! Check the woods for large tulip and sweet gum trees with multiple trunks. The understory is largely pawpaw. At .75 mi., the trail forks and heads straight or to the left [3]. Continue straight ahead and veer to the right, skirting an old field that soon changes to woods.

At 1 mi. the trail heads downhill [4]. Watch your step—the leaf-covered trail hides treacherous, rocky outcroppings. In the spring many of these outcrops are covered with pale yellow corydalis. Look for puttyroot orchid leaves along this section. Although these orchids bloom during the early summer, they produce a single basal leaf in the autumn. Bear to the left after a large rock outcropping and cross a very small creek. The woods are now dominated by maple and sweet gum. Beware of the large cablelike vines going up the trees—these are poison ivy!

Straight ahead at 1.1 mi. you see the swamp edge [5], now a floodplain forest of dead trees killed by flooding when a beaver family dammed the area during the late 1980s. In the fall this area may be ablaze not with fire but with the yellow nodding bur marigold, a fall-blooming annual that can carpet the area under the dead trees. This is certainly one of the most dramatic and unusual wildflower displays in Illinois. Look for woodpeckers among the dead snags and for tiny frogs along the water's edge. For the next half mile the trail will skirt the edge of this swamp dominated by water tupelo. A few cypress trees soon begin to appear along with live tupelo trees. Although the swamp on your right receives much of your viewing attention, the woods to the left are impressive too, having many large, straight-trunked oak and tulip trees.

Take time to stop and view the swamp. This is one of the truly primeval landscapes found in Illinois. At 1.4 mi. the trail begins an ascent, although still skirting the swamp on your right [6]. The path becomes narrow and rocky. On the left are large patches of Christmas fern on a hill covered with rock outcroppings.

The trail now goes up [7] (1.5 mi.), leaving the swamp behind. At the crest of a small hill is an intersection with two hiking signs. Go to the right. At 1.65 mi. [3] you will come to another intersection. You have just completed a short loop, discovering the watery world of a tupelo swamp. Hike to the right on the same trail you entered on, through the dry oak-hickory forest. A .5 mi. walk brings you back to point [2] and the Tupelo Trail sign. Take a right on the crushed-rock path that leads back to the parking area.

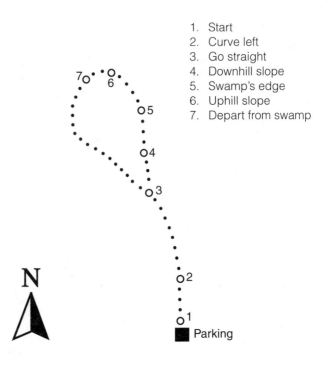

1. Start
2. Curve left
3. Go straight
4. Downhill slope
5. Swamp's edge
6. Uphill slope
7. Depart from swamp

# Little Black Slough and Wildcat Bluff Trails

 **Distance Round-Trip:** 6.4 miles
**Estimated Hiking Time:** 3.2 hours

*As I rounded the corner and Little Black Slough came into view, it was as if the ground were on fire and every available woody surface were being consumed by the bright yellow flames. It was fall and the nodding bur marigolds were blooming!*

**Caution:** This area is one of the few places in Illinois where if you see a snake in the water, it is probably a poisonous water moccasin or cottonmouth! Cottonmouths are especially fond of basking on the trail during summer. Do not disturb the cabin, and use caution crossing the railroad because it is an active line. During times of rain, portions of the trail could be wet.

**Trail Directions:** From Vienna turn onto Highway 45 south for 2.8 miles; turn west onto Ballowe Church Road, and after 1.8 miles turn left onto Wildcat Bluff Road. The road will dead-end into the parking lot. From the parking lot go downhill to a kiosk **[1]** where you will begin the trail by taking a right onto the Little Black Slough Trail.

The trail begins as an old country road with a ravine forest on the left and an old field on the right. Periodically, pieces of the bedrock will show through. The old field on the right gives way to an oak-hickory forest, with occasional hillside prairie barrens. At 1.2 mi. the trail begins to descend **[2]** and will soon curve left. A lowland bottomland forest of mixed hardwoods is on either side. A tulip tree plantation, planted by the Main brothers in 1924, is on your right **[3]**. Compare these trees to the natural forest on the left (1.4 mi.).

The Cache River will be forded **[4]** at 1.6 mi. on a crossing made by the Main brothers after the original bridge washed out. As you cross, look for whirligig beetles and cricket frogs. You are now on Boss Island, which was originally called Bost Island, and hiking through sycamore and tulip trees. The Bost cabin **[5]** is on your right at 1.75 mi. Take time to walk around the cabin that was built in 1853 from hand-hewn cypress. Eight children were raised in the cabin, which is now home to a colony of big-eared bats and a black vulture.

Within a few steps you will cross a railroad. Use caution because it is an active line! Come to an intersection **[6]** at 1.9 mi. and go left. Another intersection

**[7]** is at 2.2 mi. This is the linkage trail to Heron Pond; go right. Your first views of Little Black Slough are at 2.35 mi. **[8]**. Some of the finest timber in the state was once found here. Forested areas were cut in the 1870s and the wood was shipped to Chicago to help rebuild the city after the great fire. From this point on, limestone and sandstone bluffs rise with the elevation as you hike west on the island. Take advantage of the bench and enjoy the view, especially if it is fall and the burr marigolds are in bloom. For the next mile Little Black Slough will be on your left, and even with leaves on the trees you are offered some great views of this high-quality swamp.

At 2.8 mi. the trail curves right **[9]** and ascends through a pine plantation on your right. The swamp is finally left behind **[10]** when the trail curves right again at 3.25 mi. A large red oak **[11]** will be on your right at 3.65 mi. Tree plantations are on either side. These trees were planted over 50 years ago, and their small size indicates how spent the soil is. You are back at an intersection **[6]** at 4.45 mi. Continue straight, retracing your steps, crossing the railroad and the Cache, leaving the island behind, and finally returning to the trail kiosk.

1. Start at kiosk
2. Trail descends
3. Tulip plantation
4. Cache crossing
5. Bost cabin
6. Intersection
7. Intersection
8. View Little Black Slough
9. Trail ascends, curve right
10. No longer view the swamp
11. Large red oak

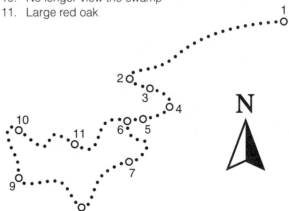

# Lower Cache Access

 **Distance Round-Trip:** 3.2 miles
**Estimated Hiking Time:** 1.6 hours

*The Lower Cache Access is one of the few places you can put your canoe in, yet this trail allows you to explore both the front and back sides of the swamp without ever getting in the water. Even though I didn't get wet in the traditional sense, I did sweat through my clothes while hiking in this hot, humid landscape.*

**Caution:** Once again, poisonous cottonmouths are common here and are especially fond of basking on the trail during summer. Watch out for cypress knees and holes in the trail. During times of rain, portions of the trail might be flooded.

**Trail Directions:** The Lower Cache Access Area is located west of the Barkhausen Wetlands Center. Go west on Perks Road for 1.5 miles and turn south (left) onto South Quarry Road. The parking area is in 1 mile. Begin the trail [1] at the information board and go right on the paved path. At .2 mi. [2] the trail curves left onto a viewing platform. From the platform look to the southeast to see the second-largest tree in the state—a giant bald cypress. Take a good look here; soon you will see the backside of this swamp while hiking in the treeline across the way.

After enjoying the sights and sounds, retrace your steps back to the parking area and head east on the Swamp Trail [3] (.45 mi.). On your left is a restoration area; the swamp is just visible on the right. The impenetrable wall of green on the right consists of giant cane and is called a canebrake. Giant cane is the only bamboo native to Illinois. In the early 1800s canebrakes were over a mile wide along the Cache River!

By .8 mi. cane is on both sides of the path as the trail curves right [4]. A bench is on your left as you enter a lowland forest of sugarberry, silver maple, bald cypress, and water tupelo of the Lower Cache. Within a tenth of a mile duckweed-covered Cypress Creek appears on the left. Listen for the plops of turtles going in the water ahead of you and look on the sides of the trail for scavenged turtle eggs. Note that the creek is straight, channelized early in the 20th century. In the forest on the right notice the high waterlines on the stands of young tupelo trees.

The trail curves to the right at 1.2 mi. [5]. This is the junction of Cypress Creek and the Cache River. At 1.4 mi. you are on the backside of the Lower Cache Swamp [6]. Fresh beaver chewings and trails from the swamp to the river, as well as buttonbush, are found on this portion of the trail. Buttonbush is a large, spreading shrub whose flowers appear as white globular balls. At 1.7 mi. you can hike no farther; the trail dead-ends [7] into a cypress grove with the Cache River on the left and the swamp on the right.

Retrace your steps, enjoying the swamp and the river. Tread lightly: Who knows what you might see? In the duckweed look for sinuous paths caused by snakes; they could be basking in the branches of a buttonbush. The milk cartons on some of the trees are nest boxes for a long-term prothonotary warbler study. Turkeys may forage in the path ahead of you, quickly disappearing into the wall of cane. Upon returning to the parking area, walk down the boat ramp for a great front-side view of the swamp.

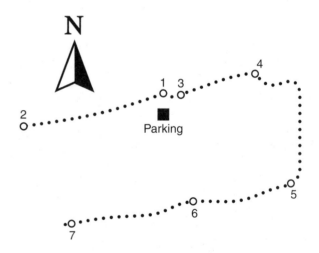

1. Start
2. Viewing platform
3. Swamp Trail
4. Curve right
5. Junction, Cypress Creek and Cache River
6. Backside of Lower Cache Swamp
7. Trail dead-ends

- Visit a wetland complex of international importance.
- Observe large numbers of herons, egrets, and waterfowl.
- View the underground infrastructure of a cypress while you discover Cypress Creek.
- Hike through a primeval forest, little changed since John James Audubon first visited the area.

## Area Information

Cypress Creek National Wildlife Refuge, nestled between the Ohio and Mississippi rivers in the Cache River Watershed, is relatively new. It was established in 1990 with an emphasis on land acquisition, habitat restoration, and education. With 80 percent of the original forest gone, restoration is a primary goal, and over 1.2 million native hardwood seedlings have been planted on over 3,000 acres.

Over the last 100 years more than half of the former wetlands in the Cache Watershed have been lost to land clearing and drainage projects. With this loss of habitat the health of the Cache River Wetlands was in critical condition. Local citizens took to the cause and in 1990 the refuge was established, along with the Cache River Joint Venture. The Joint Venture is a partnership with the Refuge, the Illinois Department of Natural Resources, the Nature Conservancy, and Ducks Unlimited. Their goal is not only to restore 60,000 acres along the Cache Watershed but also to protect it.

The Frank Bellrose Wildlife Viewing Area was established to honor one of the state's pioneer waterfowl biologists. It is a great example of the adage, "If you build it, they will come." A visit to the Bellrose Preserve one winter evening was like a living snow globe of activity. The sunset was a palette of reds, pinks, and oranges swirled together; white-tailed deer bounded in front of us; hundreds of mallards and pintails tried to settle for the evening under the watchful eye of two bald eagles; and thousands of snow geese swirled above corn stubble like darkened ashes from a dying fire. The refuge and surrounding area are like a fine wine, improving each year.

**Directions:** The refuge headquarters is located on the campus of Shawnee Community College. Take exit 18 on I-57 and drive east 6 miles on Shawnee College Road. Turn right at Shawnee College and Rustic Campus Drive. To reach **Limekiln Slough,** turn left onto Cache Chapel Road (before headquarters). The parking area is within a mile. To reach **Hickory Bottoms,** travel north on Duckworth Road (in the town of Perks) and proceed for 2.5 miles. Turn right on 50 N. (Bailey Road, which is gravel) and follow it to the parking area.

**Hours:** The sites are open daily, with the exception of the Bellrose Preserve, which is open from 7:30 a.m. to 3:30 p.m. Monday through Friday. The trails are closed during the hunting season.

**Facilities:** Parking and toilets are at some sites.

**For Further Information:** Cypress Creek Wildlife Refuge, 0137 Rustic Campus Drive, Ullin, IL 62992; 618-634-2231, http://midwest.fws.gov/cypresscreek.

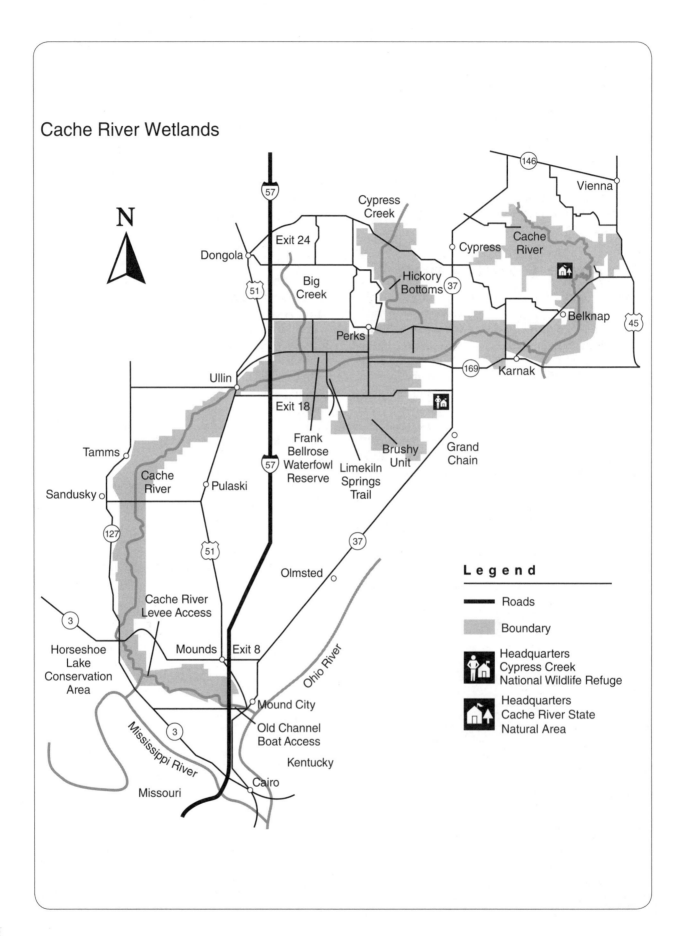

Cache River Wetlands

Legend

Roads

Boundary

Headquarters
Cypress Creek
National Wildlife Refuge

Headquarters
Cache River State
Natural Area

# Limekiln Slough

  **Distance Round-Trip:** 2.4 miles
  **Estimated Hiking Time:** 1.4 hours

*The trail has a tropical jungle feel to it with the large leaves of the pawpaw and viney tangles of grapevines draped over the branches of the trees.*

**Caution:** Poisonous snakes, such as the cottonmouth (water moccasin), are possibilities. Look out for tree roots across the trail.

**Trail Directions:** Begin the trail at the large red oak tree in the parking lot [1]. Although the trail is not marked, it is easy to follow, and you may get the feeling of being one of the first people to explore the area. The trail begins as a grassy path; on your left is a lowland or floodplain forest. These are forests along streams and rivers that have poor soil drainage and low permeability. Because they are flooded frequently, they have a lower diversity of tree species than forests on higher ground. At .25 mi. a sugarberry tree [2] is on your right. These trees have silver-gray bark with corky warts and are a southern relative of hackberry.

Don't forget to look down as you hike; segments of the trail are favorite areas for turkey dust baths. Look for oval depressions with Y-shaped scratchings in the leaves. A pair of American beeches [3], resembling large elephant legs, will materialize on your left at .4 mi. This area has a nice display of spring wildflowers in April. You will come to a boardwalk at .5 mi. [4]. As you cross it, look to your left for large American lotus beds. These will begin to bloom in early summer.

Another boardwalk will appear at .65 mi. This one traverses a slough [5], in this case a stretch of soft, muddy, waterlogged ground. Look for the uncommon pumpkin ash as you cross. Its seeds have broad, elliptical wings and litter the boardwalk by fall. Coming off the boardwalk, you will encounter several small cane thickets and wind your way past two large oaks. At 1 mi. as you walk over the roots of a large, hollow leaning red oak [6], you should see the swamp on your left. The trail dead-ends into the swamp at 1.2 mi. and you have reached the Limekiln Springs [7], which feed Limekiln Slough. Notice the limestone bedrock that juts into the swamp. While most of the sites in the Cache are underlain with gravels, this is one of the few with a limestone outcrop. Note one of the springs on your left.

As you retrace your steps back to the large red oak and the parking area, look for Illinois mud turtles and listen to the many calls of birds. The Cache is one of the remotest and quietest areas in the state.

1. Start
2. Sugarberry
3. Beeches
4. Boardwalk
5. Slough
6. Red oak
7. Limekiln Springs

**N**

South

# Hickory Bottoms

**Distance Round-Trip:** 2.45 miles
**Estimated Hiking Time:** 1.2 hours

*This trail offers large, pillarlike trees and a multitude of cypress knees, but it's the little things, from southern leopard frogs and creole pearly-eye butterflies to velvet ants and stinging rose caterpillars, that will keep you coming back.*

**Caution:** Poisonous snakes, such as cottonmouth (water moccasin), are possibilities. Look out for tree roots in the trail.

**Trail Directions:** Begin the trail at the large hackberry tree [1] and head down the gravel path. Within a few steps a cypress tree is on your right and cane is on your left. You will cross a bridge at .1 mi. [2] and go left. A trail marker will appear at .15 mi. Go left [3] into the woods and immediately note two large, pillarlike oaks. You are now hiking in a mixed hardwood forest dominated by lofty oaks, hickories, and tulip trees. The gravel path will follow Cypress Creek.

At .2 mi. the trail emerges from the woods [4]; go left and within a few steps take another left and head back into the woods. (A trail sign is there to direct you.) For the next .3 mi. the trail will skirt Cypress Creek and you will have to decide whether to look right at the lofty oak and tulip trees or left at the cypress and their many knees on the edge of Cypress Creek. If the creek is low, you will be able to see the exposed underground infrastructure of a cypress.

The trail Ts at .65 mi. [5]. Go left for a short spur across the bridge. The trail then curves right and crosses a short boardwalk for a view of a swamp in the making. Note the small cypress and buttonbush. Retrace your steps back to [5] and continue straight, winding through the woods. The trail curves right at 1.1 mi. [6], but stay on the gravel path. In less than .1 mi. the trail curves left and comes to an intersection [7]. Go left, walking on an old forest road that is lined with an even-age stand of saplings. The saplings on the left soon become a mature hardwood forest.

At the intersection [8] go straight and then left (1.5 mi.). The tract of forest on your right was known as the Big Woods at one time. Continue straight and then curve right; you should have saplings on your left. At 1.65 mi. you will come to a large cypress with a tupelo gum and sycamore in the background. This is a good place to turn around [9]. Don't forget to look for large, straight oaks as you hike out of the Big Woods and bear right, retracing your steps. At [7] continue straight, walking on a wide, grassy path. Finally, you will recross the bridge [2] and soon return to the large hackberry.

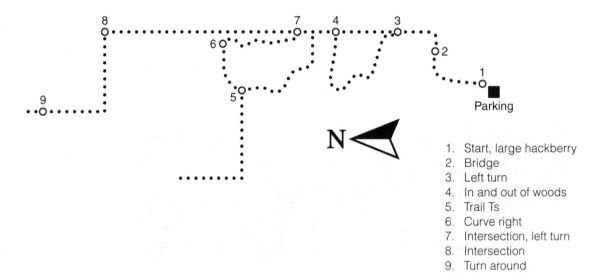

1. Start, large hackberry
2. Bridge
3. Left turn
4. In and out of woods
5. Trail Ts
6. Curve right
7. Intersection, left turn
8. Intersection
9. Turn around

- Look for dozens of red-eared slider turtles basking on every available log.

- Imagine you are in Florida with views of double-crested cormorants, great white egrets, great blue herons, and osprey.

- Brush up on your herpetofauna: Banded water snakes sun in the shrubs; snapping, slider, soft-shell, or box turtles cross the paths; and frogs and toads keep up an endless serenade.

- Enjoy unfamiliar wildflowers, such as copper iris, American lotus, and lizard's-tail.

- Visit one of Illinois' best wildlife viewing areas.

## Area Information

Mermet Lake Conservation Area was at one time a cypress swamp, referred to as the Mermet Bottoms. Attempts were made to drain the lowlands, but the Mermet Bottoms remained low and swampy. Remnants of the swamp can be seen in a few old cypress trees standing in the middle of the lake. During 1962, a system of levees was constructed, creating a lake for duck hunting. Each fall the lake's level is dropped 2 inches to accommodate hunters. After the hunting season, the level is restored. The area has over 200 acres of grains planted in the open fields to attract waterfowl. Even though Mermet is a hunter's lake, over 90 percent of the visitors are fishermen casting for largemouth bass, channel catfish, or sunfish.

Although managed for waterfowl, other types of wildlife are abundant. On any warm, sunny day—spring, summer, or fall—every available log is crammed with turtles, their necks outstretched as they bask. Snakes entwine themselves in the branches of shrubs to catch the sun's warming rays. Mink may be seen running along the downed logs in the wet woods, and great blue herons lurk in the shadows for unsuspecting fish.

**Directions:** Mermet Lake is just off US 45 in Massac County, 14 miles northwest of Paducah, Kentucky.

From the north, take exit 16 off I-24 onto Illinois 146. Illinois 146 quickly intersects with US 45. Go south (left) on US 45 for 9 miles to Mermet Lake. From the south, take I-24 to the Metropolis exit at US 45. Take US 45 north for 11 miles to the lake.

**Hours Open:** The site is open year-round. During duck season the site is open for hunting only, and all trails and the road are closed.

**Facilities:** Picnicking, toilets, fishing, boating, and hunting are included. There is no drinking water on the premises.

**Permits and Rules:** Pets must be leashed at all times.

**For Further Information:** Mermet Lake Conservation Area, 1812 Grinnell Road, Belknap, IL 62908; 618-524-5577.

## Other Areas of Interest

For a glimpse of a bottomland forest and forested swamp that mirrors the wilderness documented by public land surveyors in 1807, visit **Sielbeck Forest State Natural Area.** This island of timber was once part of the Big Black Slough, a wetland-rich floodplain that once covered thousands of acres. There are no official hiking trails or amenities, but you are welcome to explore the area and encounter some of the enormous trees. For more information, call 618-524-5577.

Located near Metropolis, **Fort Massac State Park,** overlooking the Ohio River, was the first state park in Illinois. The annual Fort Massac Encampment (October) and several living-history weekends bring the past to life. The park features a fort and museum complex as well as camping, picnic areas, and a boat ramp. A 1-mile loop trail, also designated as a forest watch tree identification trail, begins and ends near the fort. For more information, call 618-524-4712.

Visit **Metropolis** (the only city in the United States with this name), the official home of Superman. Tour the largest collection of the superhero's memorabilia at the Super Museum. For more information, call 618-524-5518 or 800-949-5740 (Metropolis Chamber of Commerce).

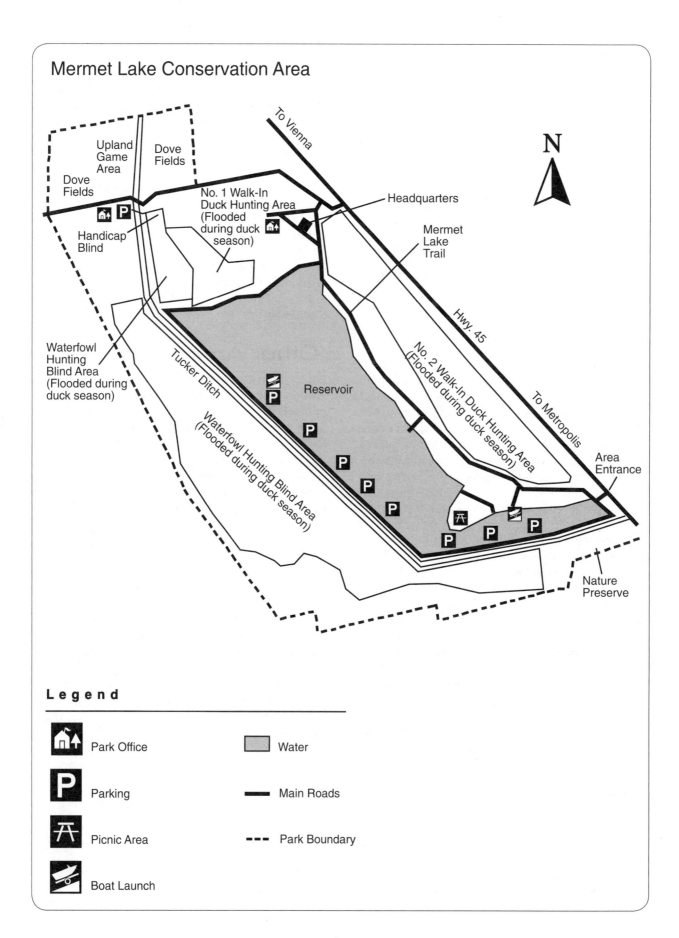

# Mermet Lake Conservation Area

To Vienna

N

Upland Game Area

Dove Fields

Dove Fields

Dove Fields

Headquarters

Mermet Lake Trail

No. 1 Walk-In Duck Hunting Area (Flooded during duck season)

Handicap Blind

Hwy. 45

To Metropolis

Waterfowl Hunting Blind Area (Flooded during duck season)

Tucker Ditch

Reservoir

No. 2 Walk-In Duck Hunting Area (Flooded during duck season)

Waterfowl Hunting Blind Area (Flooded during duck season)

Area Entrance

Nature Preserve

## Legend

Park Office

Parking

Picnic Area

Boat Launch

Water

Main Roads

Park Boundary

# Mermet Lake Trail

 **Distance Round-Trip:** 5 miles
**Estimated Hiking Time:** 3 hours

*Near dusk a great blue heron is camouflaged by the lengthening shadows of the dying cattails as it fishes in an open pool. Scaups and redheads swim nearby, while geese fly overhead, looking for a safe haven to land. A bald eagle surveys the activity from a leafless bald cypress.*

**Caution:** This is a one-way, multipurpose trail that you will share with bicyclists, cars, geese, snakes, and turtles—keep alert.

**Trail Directions:** While driving into Mermet, don't forget to check the open, grassy area near the park office for wild turkeys. Park either at the restroom or the Bluebird Trail near the lake. Take a right onto Levee Road and begin the trail [1]. You will be hiking with the traffic, following the road around the lake. Immediately on your left you will notice the large American lotus beds, which begin to bloom in late June. Even in winter, when they are arched over and create abstract designs in the ice, they are interesting to observe. Scan the lotus with your binoculars; who knows what lurks under those large leaves?

The first of many pull-offs begins at .3 mi. [2]. Look for red-eared sliders shingled on submerged logs like an ancient slate roof. In the ditch on the right, red iris blooms in May. At the second pull-off [3] (.5 mi.) you see a remnant cypress from the Mermet Bottoms. This is a favorite perch for tree swallows, bald eagles, and cormorants. As you curve left at .8 mi. you will pass a boat dock [4] and restrooms. Look for osprey in this area as they nest in the trees across from the dock.

For the next mile [5] you will parallel a levee borrow ditch on your right. This area is a good place to look for muskrat and beavers, and you should see remnants of beaver lodges. Geese with goslings are abundant here in the late spring. On your left is the lake; look for rafts of coots, whirligig beetles spinning out of control along the water's edge, and steely-gray great blue herons always just ahead of you. At 1.9 mi. find a levee on the right [6] where you can take a short hike. Explore this area, looking for shorebirds, waterfowl, and deer; then return to the main trail.

Continue to hike around the lake. On your right, when the area is dry, is a favorite haunt of deer. Don't forget to look up; the trees are favorite perches for red-shouldered and red-tailed hawks. In the lake are more cypress trees, which during the spring may be leafed out with dozens of cormorants.

At 2.6 mi., Mermet Swamp Nature Preserve, a bottomland swamp, comes into view [7]. Listen for the high-pitched squeal of the female wood duck as she and her colorful partner flee through the tupelo. Wood ducks are tree-cavity nesters, and the habitat on the right is perfect for them. The trail curves left at 2.8 mi. [8]; this area is one of the best places in Illinois to view a sunset. Look across the road on your right for lizard's-tail and copper iris.

Borrow Pond is on your right at 3.1 mi. [9]. Look for turtle snouts encased in bubbles early in the morning and geese families in late spring. Within a tenth of a mile you will come to a fishing pier and picnic area. Note the traffic is now two-way. Go left to check out the area [10]. It's a good place to get close to the lotus in summer. Retrace your steps back to Levee Road.

As you hike this section notice the forest, or what is left of it, on your right. A devastating tornado struck here in 2003. The force broke off the trees and twisted their trunks. What was left was unsalvageable for lumber. Look for raccoons and woodpeckers here. At 4 mi. is another side spur [11]. Off the boat dock look for arrowhead, little green herons, and tiny toads. Retrace your steps back to Levee Road.

The area on your left is a transition zone of swamp and cattails. Check the shrubs for basking snakes; on the right is a food plot area that usually has deer and turkeys at dusk. By 4.6 mi. you enter the cattail zone [12], announced by a chorus of red-winged blackbirds. Scan the edges as bitterns lurk along this section in late spring. Here also are the largest lotus beds. You are almost back to [1]; before you exit look for kingfishers on the snags. Kingfishers are excitable birds that express their displeasure by giving a call that has been compared to a New Year's Eve noisemaker.

No matter what the season or time of day, there is always something interesting going on at Mermet, even if it's only chatting with the locals (fishing along the lake) about the size of the one that got away.

1. Start
2. First of many pull-offs
3. Cypress
4. Boat dock
5. Parallel the levee
6. Side spur to levee
7. Nature preserve
8. Sunset
9. Borrow Pond
10. Fishing/picnic area
11. Spur
12. Cattail zone

N

South

# 53. Max Creek

- Hike to the heart of scenic Johnson County.
- Take the vortex challenge.
- Experience the silence of sandstone.
- Look for spring wildflowers and enjoy fall colors.

## Area Information

Max Creek is in the eastern portion of the Shawnee National Forest. It lies in Johnson County and is a tributary to Bay Creek, which eventually empties into the Ohio River, and appears to be just another picturesque creek in the Shawnee. Yet a local legend envelops Max Creek.

Max Creek flows between two bluffs on each side of the hollow that jut out like triangular fingers. The jagged shapes of the walls likely indicate there is a fault, a breach of the earth's crust where rocks have been displaced along a plane. These separated to form the hollow. It is believed that Max Creek is located on such a fault line.

Some believe that a vortex is located in Max Creek. A vortex has to do with conflicts in the earth's magnetic fields, and these are usually found next to and above a fault. In the 1930s five families lived in the area. They told stories of colored mineral lights dancing across Max Creek and gold coins glittering in the water. Present-day hikers have experienced the vortex with feelings of being thrown off balance, seeing optical illusions, or just experiencing a great pressure, as if being pulled toward the creek.

While some claim a vortex disorients and disrupts people's sense of balance and direction, others say a vortex heals the body and spirit. If the latter is true, I did encounter the vortex during this hike. The silence and beauty of Max Creek healed both body and spirit after a very hectic workweek.

**Directions:** From I-24 take Highway 45 north 3.25 miles to Taylor Ridge Lane. (There will be a trail crossing sign near the turnoff.) Turn right onto a gravel road and travel 1.6 miles, where the road dead-ends into the parking area and trailhead.

**Hours Open:** The site is open year-round.

**Facilities:** None. The town of Vienna is about 5 miles from the trailhead.

**Permits and Rules:** None.

**For Further Information:** Hidden Springs Ranger Station, 602 N. First Street, Route 45 North, Vienna, IL 62995; 618-658-2111.

## Park Trails

**River to River Trail** (🥾🥾🥾🥾🥾, 148 miles). The River to River Trail is an east-to-west trail that honors the routes of the pioneers, beginning at Battery Rock on the Ohio River and ending at Devil's Backbone Park on the Mississippi. The Max Creek Trail is on the River to River Trail. The River to River Trail is marked with white diamonds with a blue *I*. For further information, contact the River to River Trail Society at 618-252-6789 or www.rivertorivertrail.org.

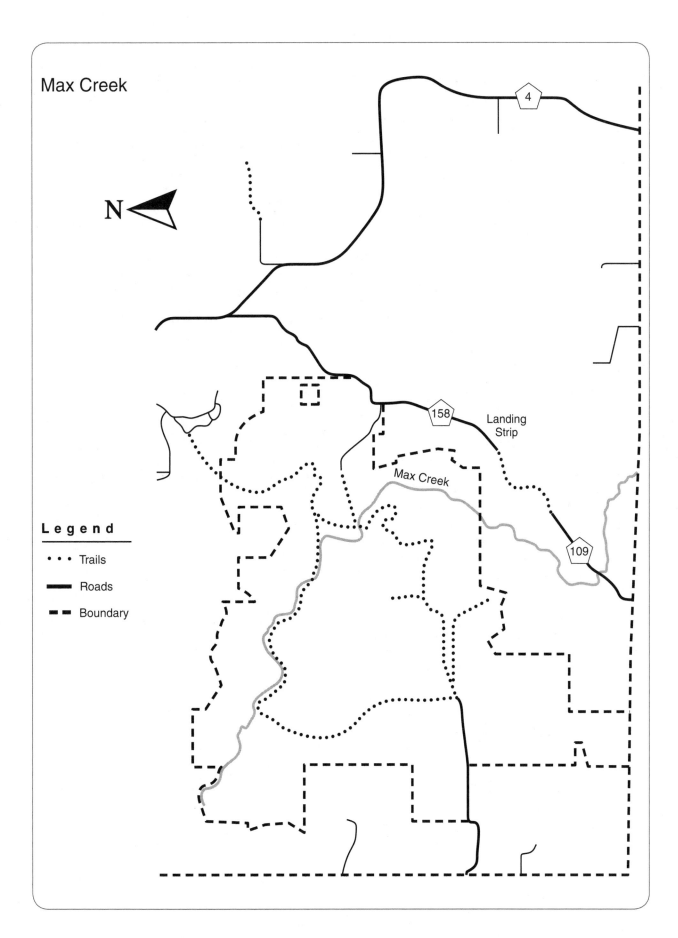

Max Creek

N

Legend

• • • Trails

━━━ Roads

▬ ▬ Boundary

4

158

Landing
Strip

Max Creek

109

# Max Creek

**Distance Round-Trip:** 4.25 miles
**Estimated Hiking Time:** 2 hours

*Take the vortex challenge as you hike this trail. Will you be pulled toward the creek? Maybe, if it is a hot day. Will you see illusions? Who knows what will happen if you don't keep hydrated on the trail. Will you feel the force? Yes, your body and mind should feel much better after experiencing the beauty and serenity of Max Creek.*

**Caution:** Parts of the trail are on sandstone and could be slick. There are several creek crossings that could result in wet feet. Rocks and roots jut out in the trail as well. Horses also use this trail.

**Trail Directions:** The trail begins at Brown Marker 1738, which is an old forest road [1]. The trail will be marked with periodic white diamonds and blue *I*s on the trees. The wide path soon narrows, and at .55 mi. the trail Vs; go right [2]. You will be hiking through a pine plantation with an occasional beech tree. Stay on the main trail, even though there are several offshoots; it is easy to follow.

Along the trail you will encounter large clusters and clumps of Christmas fern. These ferns stay green year-round; even when flattened by winter snows they are a welcome site. If you look closely at their leaves, called pinna, each has a distinct basal lobe, resembling the toe on a Christmas stocking. At 1 mi. the trail has narrowed again and begins to descend [3]. Oak trees are now prevalent as well. Switchbacks [4] (1.25 mi.) help you wind your way down into the valley and Max Creek. Don't forget to look for wildflowers on your way down and use caution because parts of the trail are on slippery sandstone. You are now in an oak-hickory woods; rock outcrops, which soon give way to rock crumbles, begin to appear on the left.

Finally at 1.5 mi. you have reached Max Creek [5]. Notice the pieces of rock in the water that stick up like shark fins. Cross the creek using flat rocks. As you cross, remember that wet moss is slick! After crossing, go left (do not follow the blue *I*s); you will be walking in an old creek bed. Cross the creek again at 1.75 mi. [6], using your rock-hopping skills. A beech tree on the other side has white diamonds, the correct trail mark.

You are now hiking amidst good-sized beech trees and are hemmed in by sandstone. Blue *I* trail markers appear again; don't forget to enjoy the sandstone escarpment on the right. At 1.9 mi. you will cross the stream again [7] and have close-up views of sandstone bluffs. Note how trees have gained a foothold on the narrow shelves.

A waterfall appears on the left [8] (2.05 mi.) where the creek undercuts the cliff. Cross the creek at least

two more times in the next .3 mi. At times you will be able to look down into the creek; also, the sandstone escarpments and beech trees begin to disappear. At 2.55 mi. the trail begins to ascend [9]; you are still following the creek, only higher up the slope. Cedars have now begun to appear.

Leave the creek behind at 2.9 mi. as the trail veers to the left and continues to wiggle its way out of the woods [10]. At 3.05 mi. you will cross a small tributary and begin the trek out of Max Creek Valley [11]. You are hiking through mixed hardwoods. The trail heads up and left as you pass some impressive oaks [12] (3.25 mi.).

Pine plantations appear again at 3.45 mi. [13]. At 3.8 mi. notice the large oaks on the right and left as the trail crosses sandstone [14]; you will hike on a sandstone shelf for a few steps. The trail then descends on a path lined with pine and cedar. Another path comes in on the left at 4.2 mi. [15]; continue straight, and soon you are back at the parking area.

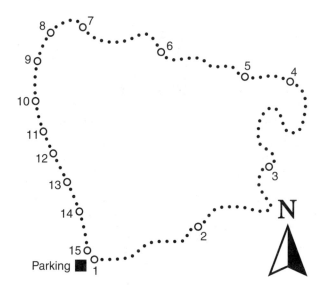

1. Start
2. Trail Vs, go right
3. Trail descends
4. Switchbacks
5. Max Creek
6. Creek crossing
7. Creek crossing
8. Waterfall
9. Trail ascends
10. Veer left
11. Start trek out
12. Ascend, left turn
13. Pine plantations
14. Sandstone shelf
15. Go straight

- Follow an ever-narrowing valley to a spectacular stream-carved gorge.

- View canyons, a natural stone bridge, and diverse rock formations.

- Look for grasshoppers that resemble lichens and eastern fence lizards camouflaged against rocks, soil, and lichen-covered trees.

- Search the nooks and crannies between giant boulders to discover some of the area's 700 species of wildflowers and ferns.

- Enjoy the profusion of redbud, dogwood, and early spring butterflies.

## Area Information

Bell Smith Springs is a world of vertical sandstone cliffs, clear rocky streams, outstanding rock formations, and a lush spring flora. Located in the Shawnee National Forest, Bell Smith Springs was named after its former owner.

The region is an area of contrasts. Sandstone ledges are windswept and scorched by the summer sun. Blankets of lichens and moss help to insulate the rock against the extremes of heating and cooling. Moisture brings slick, dark, algae-covered streaks (called dripways) to the sandstone shelves. In contrast to the harsh ledges, the canyons are dark, cool, and green. Beech trees, their gray tree trunks resembling huge elephant legs, occupy preferred spots next to the stream. Large clumps of yellow trout lily on inaccessible canyon shelves and boulder tops make hikers wish for the dexterity of a mountain goat to allow a closer inspection.

**Directions:** Drive south from Harrisburg on Route 145 and turn right (west) on Forest Route (FR) 402 at Delwood. After about 4 miles you will come to a T junction with FR 447. Turn left and proceed south past Teal Pond to FR 848. Turn right onto FR 848. At the park-entrance sign, go 1.6 miles farther to a right turn that leads down to Hunting Branch Picnic Area. To reach the main parking area for Bell Smith Springs, continue to the end of FR 848.

**Hours Open:** The site is open year-round. Teal Pond campground is open year-round and Redbud camp-

ground is open from March 15 through December 15. Hunting Branch Picnic Area is open March 15 through October 31 from 6:00 a.m. to 10:00 p.m.

**Facilities:** Camping, fishing, and picnicking areas are available. Restrooms are at campgrounds and parking areas.

**Permits and Rules:** The cutting of live trees, shrubs, and other vegetation is prohibited. Weapons, firearms, and fireworks are not to be discharged in campground or picnic areas. Pets should be leashed and are not allowed in the water.

**For Further Information:** Hidden Springs Ranger Station, 602 N. First Street, Route 45 North, Vienna, IL 62995; 618-658-2111.

## Park Trails

**General Area Trail or the White Trail** (👣👣👣, 1.5 miles). This trail can be accessed either at Hunting Branch Picnic Area or the parking area at the end of FR 848. The trail marked with white diamonds painted on trees or rocks goes through the center of the park and passes by Devil's Backbone, a cliff area. Farther on, deep spring-fed pools offer a welcome respite on hot summer days. The trail eventually leads to the site of the spring for which the area was named.

**Natural Bridge Trail or the Yellow Trail** (👣👣👣, 1.5 miles). This trail begins and ends at the parking area at the end of FR 848. The trail is marked with yellow diamonds on trees or rocks. It begins with a descent into Bay Creek Canyon, using a series of steps cut into the rock face. The trail explores the area above and below the natural bridge, a sandstone formation 30 feet high, 20 feet wide, and more than 125 feet long that was formed through centuries of water erosion.

## Other Areas of Interest

Accessed from FR 402, **Burden Falls,** a seasonal 100-foot waterfall, plunges into a deep canyon each spring but dries to a trickle by midsummer. A linear trail along the south bluff's bank allows the curious a closer look. For more information, call the Hidden Springs Ranger Station at 618-658-2111.

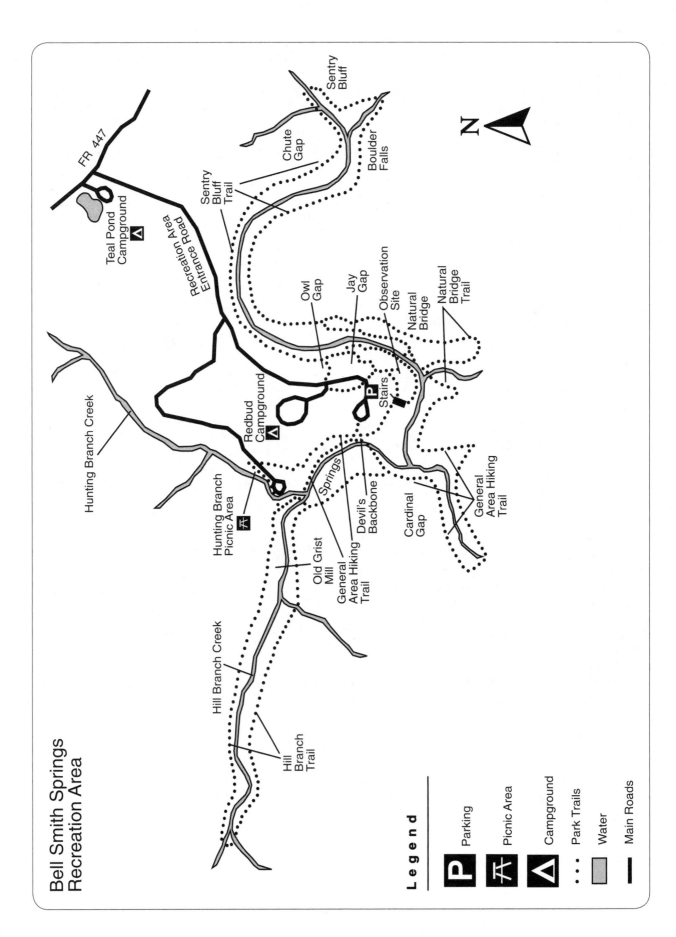

# Bell Smith Springs Recreation Area

FR 447

Teal Pond Campground

Recreation Area Entrance Road

Hunting Branch Creek

Sentry Bluff Trail

Sentry Bluff

Chute Gap

Boulder Falls

Owl Gap

Jay Gap

Observation Site

Natural Bridge

Natural Bridge Trail

Redbud Campground

Hunting Branch Picnic Area

Hill Branch Creek

P Stairs

Springs

Devil's Backbone

Old Grist Mill

General Area Hiking Trail

Cardinal Gap

General Area Hiking Trail

Hill Branch Trail

N

## Legend

**P** Parking

**⊼** Picnic Area

**⊿** Campground

⋯ Park Trails

▨ Water

— Main Roads

# Mill Branch Trail

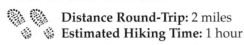 **Distance Round-Trip:** 2 miles
**Estimated Hiking Time:** 1 hour

*Mill Branch Trail offers the opportunity to play hide-and-seek with the lichen grasshopper and the eastern fence lizard (they will do the hiding) and to experience the unique habitat of a sandstone ledge.*

**Caution:** The sandstone ledges are slippery when wet. Stay off the cushions of lichens and mosses to help protect them.

**Trail Directions:** The trail begins near Hunting Branch Picnic Area at a parking lot across from the picnic grounds. The picnic area is on the other side of a concrete ford through the creek. Start your hike at a tree marked with both white and orange diamonds [1]. Immediately cross a creek, which can be a challenge in wet weather or in the spring. Mill Branch Trail is marked with orange diamonds.

After a few steps, the trail will fork [2]; proceed to the right. The trail climbs a series of rocky steps and crosses outcrops of lichen-covered sandstone with cushions of moss on either side. Look for trail markers on trees or painted on the rocks.

On your right is a dry oak-hickory woods with many red cedar trees. In the spring note the diminutive flowers of yellow star grass. In the fall single stems of blazing stars can be seen here. To your left is the flat-bottomed stream valley of Mill Creek that varies from a raging torrent in the spring to a series of quiet, leaf-strewn pools in the fall. As you proceed, note that the valley becomes deeper, narrower, and more rocky—very canyonlike. Along the trail be alert for eastern fence lizards, especially in spring when males have a bright-blue brooding patch on the throat.

At .5 mi. cross a series of small, intermittent streams that can be full in the spring [3]. The trail is just a narrow, rocky path at this point and the trail markings are very faint. Two large chunks of sandstone appear on your left at .8 mi. [4], providing a perfect place to observe Mill Branch Creek and to look for the lichen grasshopper (whose pattern mimics the colors of the lichens on which it sits).

After this brief side trip, the trail soon crosses the sandstone [5] (.9 mi.). Use caution when walking on the ledge, especially if there is a thin, dark layer of algae. The trail, still on the sandstone ledges, begins to descend toward Mill Branch Creek.

At 1 mi. the trail leaves the ledges to pass through the woods and, within a few steps, crosses Mill Branch Creek and heads up the other side [6]. You can expect to get your feet wet here during spring hikes. The trail on the south side of Mill Branch winds farther from the stream and into the woods. Temporarily off the hot sandstone, it passes through a cool woods composed mostly of oaks and hickories, but also maples with an understory of Christmas fern.

After about .5 mi. the trail descends onto a sandstone shelf [7], which is marked by diamonds. You should see a series of circular pools in the sandstone, one below the other—like stair steps—as you cross the feeder stream and come out of the woods to the right.

At 1.75 mi. cross a small, rock-strewn stream. From here the trail subtly forks. The oak tree on the left has both an orange and a white diamond; remember that you are on the orange trail, so head downward [8]. (The white trail continues straight ahead and becomes very narrow with a large drop-off to the left.) The orange trail winds its way down into the valley. Note the partridgeberry with its bright red fruit growing among the mosses. You now enter the streambed of Mill Branch Creek. Cross the stream [9], and at 1.95 mi. you return to [2]. Cross another stream and you'll arrive back to your vehicle.

1. Start
2. Right turn
3. Small stream crossings
4. Sandstone boulders
5. Sandstone crossing
6. Mill Branch Creek crossing
7. Sandstone shelf
8. Downhill slope
9. Stream crossing

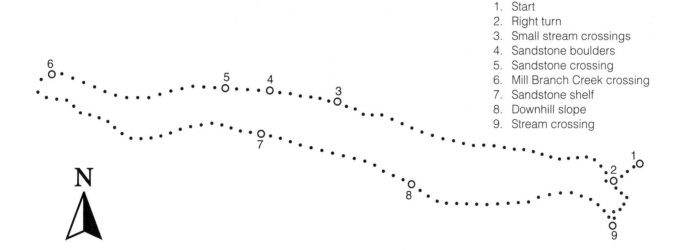

South

# Sentry Bluff Trail

**Distance Round Trip:** 3.5 miles
**Estimated Hiking Time:** 2.5 to 3 hours

*Make sure you take time to enjoy the sluggish, leaf-strewn stream called Bay Creek. The beech-lined banks, set against a backdrop of rocky bluffs and a brilliant blue fall sky, can be found only on the blue trail in the fall at Bell Smith Springs.*

**Caution:** Take extra care when crossing the creek because the rocks are slippery when wet. Watch your step on the trail. In a few places the trail comes perilously close to the bluff edge and at one particularly confusing spot descends a series of stone ledges that may be a small waterfall in spring.

**Trail Directions:** The trailhead is located off the parking area past Redbud Campground at the end of FR 848. A paved walkway leads down to a brown information board. Continue downhill from the sign on the asphalt trail. After a few steps the trail forks; go to the right. A yellow diamond will designate the beginning of a short hike on the yellow trail [1], which will soon lead to our destination, the blue trail.

At .05 mi. the trail descends into Bay Creek Canyon using a steep, rock staircase. At the foot of the steps find a shelter cave [2]. At the bottom of the staircase, go left and follow the yellow diamonds. The trail, now on bare sandstone, soon becomes a dirt path and leads through a beech-maple ravine forest. At .3 mi. cross a creek [3]. On the far side are stone steps leading up and to your left. The trail here carries both blue and yellow diamond markers. On your right you should see a massive stone cliff fronted with large beech trees.

As you walk along Bay Creek, skirting the bluff, note the huge boulders that have sheared off from the sandstone wall during some earlier time [4] (.4 mi.).

At .6 mi. the yellow and blue trails divide. The yellow goes right to the natural arch [5], whereas the blue goes left. A short side trip (.3 mi.) to the natural arch is well worth the effort. The trail to the arch is uphill and leads though the treetops of the ravine forest. Natural Arch [6] is a partially eroded shelter cave. The trail leads across the top of the arch; take care not to get too close to either edge. Then retrace your steps back to the junction of the blue and yellow trails [5].

At 1.25 mi. notice on the left that Bay Creek has undercut the rock face, creating shelter caves. In some places the stone walls abruptly end in the water [7].

At 1.5 mi. the trail narrows and runs near the edge of the bluff [8] before a slope downward into the ravine. At 1.75 mi. the trail skirts a sandstone wall that is being undercut, the early stages in the formation of a shelter cave. At the base of the wall are geological formations called Liesegang rings (colorful concentric raised rings in the rock) [9]. From here the trail again heads uphill. The valley floor soon comes up to meet the trail (2 mi.). The once-impressive ravine is now nothing but a boulder-strewn streambed [10]. Cross the stream on small boulders.

At 2.25 mi. you will come to a series of sandstone rock terraces that lead down into a valley. The trail is quite steep, requiring a little mountaineering, and can be treacherous. (Note that this area is confusing, so take your time and find the blue diamonds.) Walk across the ledge and climb carefully down on the terraces [11]. Blue diamonds are painted on the rocks to lead you downward. Cross a small creek, enter the woods on the other side, and go up a small incline. Turn left here. A blue, spray-painted NO to the right affirms that the trail proceeds to the left. Follow the blue diamonds emblazoned on trees along a dirt trail.

At 2.4 mi. Chute Gap [12] is marked by a brown forest service sign. A little farther along and to your left is an impressive view of the ravine [13].

At 3 mi. the trail heads uphill with a series of short switchbacks [14]. A trail to Owl Gap veers off to the right at 3.4 mi.; stay on the blue diamond trail [15].

At 3.5 mi. you will come upon the asphalt path by a metal sign for Jay Gap [16]. A few steps ahead are the brown park information board and parking area denoting the end of your hike.

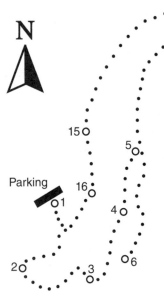

1. Start
2. Shelter cave
3. Creek crossing
4. Boulders
5. Right turn
6. Natural Arch
7. Sheer bluffs
8. Bluff edge
9. Liesegang rings
10. Streambed
11. Terraces
12. Chute Gap
13. Ravine
14. Switchbacks
15. Go straight
16. Asphalt path

N

Parking

South

- Discover Lover's Leap, Album Rock, Alligator Rock, Pluto's Cave, and Honeycomb Rock among the complex jumble of overhangs, outcrops, and cliffs.

- Take your rain gear because in rainy weather, rivulets are everywhere, cascading down the hills and creating hundreds of waterfalls—a spectacle not to be missed.

- Enjoy an idyllic setting—a babbling stream, large boulders cloaked with ferns, wildflowers strewn about, and large trees arching over the trail.

- Visit the Chocolate Factory across from the park entrance for a sweet treat at the end of your hike.

## Area Information

Dixon Springs State Park is located on a giant block of sandstone that extends northwesterly across Pope County. Rapid erosion has carved the rock into various forms (including giant streets and a canyon) and given rise to many imaginative names.

Native Americans who camped here called this area "the great medicine water," referring to the many springs. By the late 1880s a small community had grown up here and a large hotel had been constructed—the Dixon Springs Hotel Company. The area was a 19th-century health spa, and with the hotel open from June to September, visitors came from all around to take advantage of the springs that, according to one advertisement, "had been curing the ills of mankind for several years." If you couldn't afford the trip, you could have five gallons of this miracle water shipped to you for 50 cents.

The hotel no longer exists, and with the exception of the churches, the community has also disappeared. Swimming in the springs has been replaced with swimming in a modern pool. To modern-day visitors of Dixon Springs, however, another advertisement for the hotel still rings true: "The cool, quiet nights, invigorating mountain air, and sparkling spring water make this the ideal spot of recreation for the tired business man and his family."

**Directions:** Dixon Springs State Park is located 10 miles west of Golconda on Illinois Route 146, near its junction with Illinois Route 145.

**Hours Open:** The site is open year-round except on Christmas Day and New Year's Day.

**Facilities:** A campground has electricity and will accommodate both tents and trailers. A baseball field, a swimming pool with lifeguard and water slide, a concession stand, and picnicking are all part of the day-use area.

**Permits and Rules:** Pets must be leashed at all times.

**For Further Information:** Site Superintendent, Dixon Springs State Park, R.R. 2, Route 146, Golconda, IL 62938; 618-949-3394.

## Other Areas of Interest

Located 12 miles east of Vienna, **Lake Glendale Recreation Area** features swimming, boating, fishing, camping, and hiking. Two 3-mile hiking trails lead around Lake Glendale and around Signal Point Bluff. For more information, contact the Hidden Springs Ranger Station at 618-658-2111.

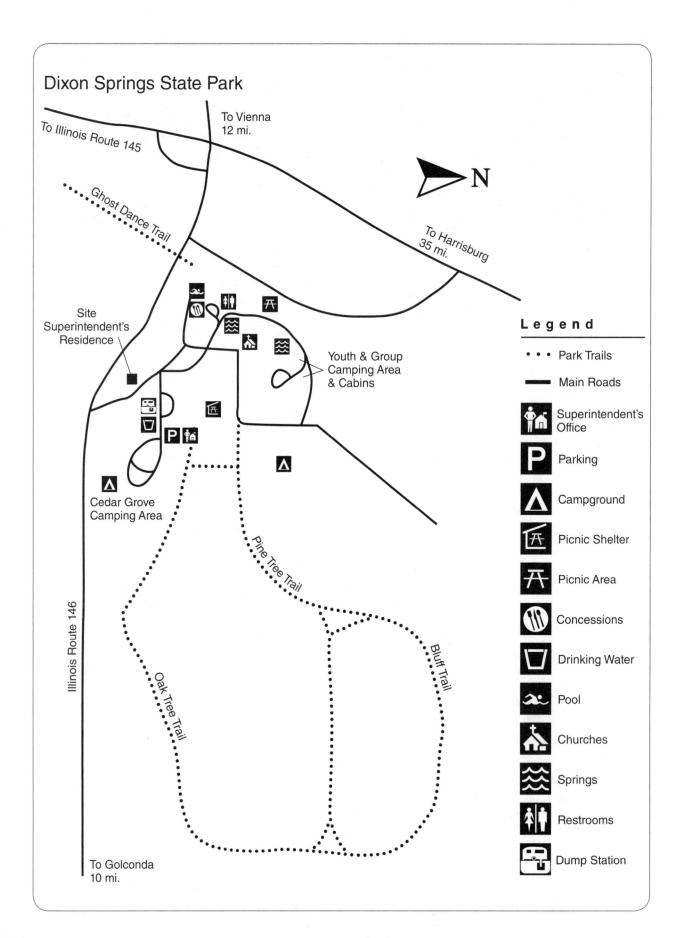

# Dixon Springs State Park

To Illinois Route 145

To Vienna
12 mi.

N

Ghost Dance Trail

To Harrisburg
35 mi.

Site
Superintendent's
Residence

Youth & Group
Camping Area
& Cabins

Cedar Grove
Camping Area

Illinois Route 146

Pine Tree Trail

Oak Tree Trail

Bluff Trail

To Golconda
10 mi.

## Legend

- - - Park Trails

——— Main Roads

Superintendent's
Office

Parking

Campground

Picnic Shelter

Picnic Area

Concessions

Drinking Water

Pool

Churches

Springs

Restrooms

Dump Station

# Pine Tree, Oak Tree, and Bluff Trails

**Distance Round-Trip:** 2.3 miles
**Estimated Hiking Time:** 1 hour

*The brown sandstone is quite striking, having weathered to fantastic shapes and with a gray-green patina caused by mosses and lichens. Small saplings try to set roots on precarious footholds—the soil is less than an inch thick.*

**Caution:** Tree roots are at the surface on some parts of the trail. During the rainy season, streambeds might be hard to cross.

**Trail Directions:** The trailhead is .2 mi. down the park road, past the white churches. Begin at a brown trail sign for Pine Tree Trail [1]. Trail markers and signs are infrequent, but the path is not hard to follow. The trail begins as a wide path through a pine plantation and a campground. The trail is carpeted with pine needles. At .3 mi. [2] you will cross a road; continue straight. A row of cedars will be on your right. The trail soon bears to the left; follow the marker for the Bluff Trail.

At .5 mi. the trail comes to a junction; go left [3]. You will cross a stream at .75 mi., and on the opposite side you'll begin to skirt a sandstone bluff [4]. The bluff is topped with cedars, and the forest on your right is mostly oak-hickory. After the stream crossing you'll find a mature second-growth forest of good-sized trees in place of the recovering forest.

Along this segment of the trail you are likely looking left at the bluff to admire honeycomb erosion and cigar-shaped mud dauber tubes. Don't neglect the right side, which gives a view into a stream valley. It is quite pretty in the fall, especially when the last rays of sunshine filter through the golden-brown and yellow leaves. At 1 mi. the trail skirts a small shelter bluff; as you walk by, touch the rock and feel it crumble in your hand [5]. Within a few steps you will recross the stream and enter a woods dominated by white oaks.

Ignore the arrow pointing downhill and straight ahead, go to your left, and continue to hike through an oak woods [6] (1.15 mi.). A large thicket of pawpaws is on your left and a grove of cedars is on your right. At 1.4 mi. you will pass a large white oak festooned with cablelike poison ivy. The oaks soon give way to vine-covered cedars (old farm site) and then return to oaks again. At 1.5 mi. the trail curves right through a grove of cedars [7]. You will come to an intersection at 1.8 mi.; go right [8] on a wide path lined with cedars and oaks.

At 2 mi. you have returned to [2]; go left and retrace your steps back to the parking area.

1. Start
2. Road crossing
3. Left turn
4. Sandstone bluff
5. Shelter bluff
6. Left turn
7. Curve right
8. Right turn

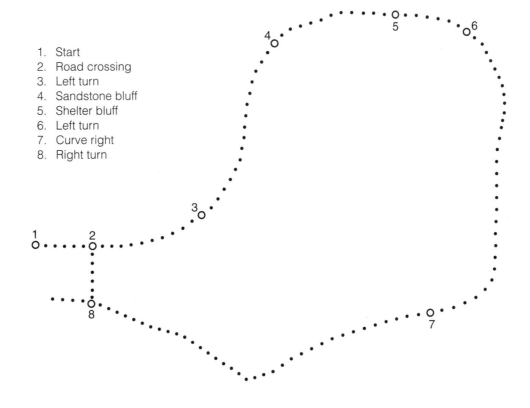

South

# Ghost Dance Canyon

 **Distance Round-Trip:** 1 mile or more, depending on how much you explore
**Estimated Hiking Time:** 1 hour

*I gained a unique perspective on a highway bridge as I prepared myself to be scared out of my wits as I hiked Ghost Dance Canyon. With its unique juxtaposition of boulders, lichens, and a rugged streambed, it did not frighten so much as inspire with its awesome beauty.*

**Caution:** There are plenty of opportunities to slip and slide on and across moss-covered boulders. Watch for roots and rocks in the trail as well as wet stream crossings.

**Trail Directions:** Park at the swimming pool; the trail begins at the bridge and immediately veers left [**1**]. The trail will be marked with red blazes. Notice the large tulip tree on the right. In less than .1 mi. the trail goes under an arched highway bridge [**2**]. Driving over the bridge, you have no idea that is it arched and quite stunning. Immediately on your left is Ghost Dance Canyon.

There are several side spurs that allow you to enjoy the views. At .2 mi. go left [**3**] at a double-trunked tulip tree, crossing the creek on slimy, slick rocks. You are now hiking in the canyon; note the walls on the right. The trail heads up [**4**] on rocks at .25 mi.—notice the overhang on the left—and then slithers through a rock jumble.

Squeeze through two large rocks at .35 mi. [**5**]. While wandering through this giant's playground of boulders, don't forget to enjoy the forest on the other side. At .4 mi. step onto a low rock ledge for an overlook [**6**], and from here follow the worn path down along the streambed. Follow the trail until it fades out, passing several large oaks. When the trail starts uphill, turn around [**7**] and retrace your steps. Take time to explore this frozen avalanche of tilted, skewed, and perched rocks as well as the sandstone walls. Once your curiosity is satisfied, retrace your steps back to the parking area.

1.  Start
2.  Under highway bridge
3.  Left turn, creek crossing
4.  Trail ascends
5.  Squeeze through rocks
6.  Overlook
7.  Turn around

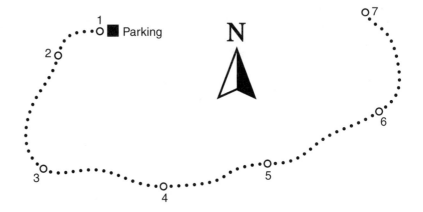

South

- Discover and explore the unique plant communities of barrens and glades.
- Meet the patriarch of the Shawnee Hills—Stone Face.
- While communing with Stone Face, enjoy one of the best scenic vistas in the Shawnee.

## Area Information

The original Shawnee Hills wasn't the solid forested land that we are familiar with today. Before European immigrants settled here, much of the landscape was quite open and grassy. They called these grassy openings in the forest *barrens,* rightly assuming that the soil must be poor to produce such a scanty growth of timber. Barrens are found on rocky, dry, south-facing slopes that have only a thin layer of soil covering the rocks. Vegetation includes small, gnarled, and twisted post and blackjack oaks. Prairie grasses and the occasional blazing star grow under the oaks.

Glades, another plant community found in forest openings, are open expanses of bedrock on a bluff top. Here the dominant tree is red cedar. Although prairie grasses such as little bluestem occur, the ground is just as likely to be covered with moss and lichens that crunch like eggshells as the hot, dry summer wears on.

Both communities, barrens and glades, were maintained by fire. In 1922 botanist H.A. Gleason observed, "Large areas of barrens were converted into forest by magic when the fires that had maintained them were stopped and the oak sprouts became trees." Look for both of these communities when you visit Stone Face, and don't be surprised if the ground is blackened: Diligent and patient volunteers are trying to restore and maintain this bit of botanical history.

**Directions:** Stone Face Recreation Area is north of the small town of Herod. Go north on Illinois Route 34 to the town of Rudiment. From here follow the directional signs to Stone Face for about 4 miles on a gravel road. The entrance to Stone Face is Forest Road 150 and is about .25 mile long.

**Hours Open:** The site is open year-round from dawn to dusk.

**Facilities:** None.

**Permits and Rules:** This is a natural area; do not remove any plants or animals from the site.

**For Further Information:** Hidden Springs Ranger Station, 602 N. First Street, Route 45 North, Vienna, IL 62995; 618-658-2111.

## Other Areas of Interest

Located southeast of Harrisburg, **Saline County Conservation Area** is a combination of Saline River bottomland and the northern Shawnee Hills. Springs, rocky creeks, and Glen O. Jones Lake are some of the area's highlights. The site accommodates camping, hunting, picnicking, boating, fishing, and hiking. Three trails are located here: Lake Trail, at 3 miles, encircles Glen O. Jones Lake; Wildlife Nature Trail, at .75 mile; and Cave Hill Trail, a 3-mile linear trail, ends at Cave Hill. An eight-foot-high bronze statue of Shawnee Chief Tecumseh is at the northeast corner of the Cave Hill Trail. For more information, call 618-276-4405.

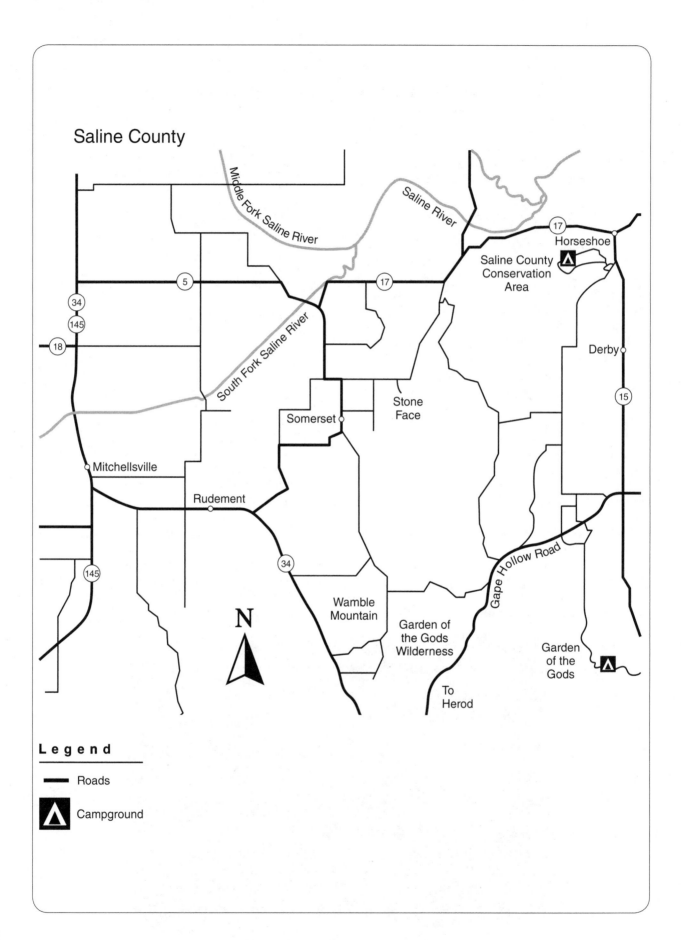

Saline County

Middle Fork Saline River

Saline River

17 Horseshoe

Saline County
Conservation
Area

Derby

5

34

145

18

South Fork Saline River

15

Somerset

Stone
Face

Mitchellsville

Rudement

145

34

N

Wamble
Mountain

Garden of
the Gods
Wilderness

Gape Hollow Road

Garden
of the
Gods

To
Herod

**Legend**

—— Roads

△ Campground

# Stone Face

 Distance Round-Trip: 1.6 miles
Estimated Hiking Time: 1 hour

*Here it's just you and Stone Face taking in the spectacular views of the Shawnee Hills and the Saline River Valley.*

**Caution:** Large chunks of rock and roots in the trail can trip you up. The downward route, after viewing Stone Face, is quite rocky and not well marked—use caution.

**Trail Directions:** The crushed-limestone trail begins at the parking area and forks within a few feet; go right and uphill [1]. As you trek upward through the oak-hickory woods, note the large sandstone boulders littering the hillside. At .15 mi. [2] you have come to the bluffs; go left. Look for walking fern and notice the small pebbles embedded into the bluff. From an airplane, this ridge looks like a thin gray line through a sea of green. From the ground, the bluffs are much more imposing and formidable.

The trail soon intersects with a path that will lead downward [3] (.25 mi.). Continue straight ahead. The trail is no longer crushed limestone and goes under a large chunk of sandstone. As you skirt the bluff, note the maze of moss that covers it. Pass a small shelter bluff. The trail curves right and leads uphill [4] (.4 mi.). You are soon walking on lichen- and moss-covered rock, the same bluff you skirted a few minutes ago, and you are eye-level with the treetops.

Soon you come to the first of several sandstone outcrops with great views. A wooden fence is provided to protect you from falling over the edge. Straight ahead is Stone Face [5] (.6 mi.), surveying his domain and guarded by scrubby sentinels of post oak and red cedar. After taking in the view and Stone Face (more impressive than New Hampshire's famous Old Man of the Mountains that collapsed some years back), continue walking on top of the bluff. The area to your left is a barrens community. Look for gnarled and stunted post oak (leaves have five to seven rounded lobes; the two middle lobes are the largest) and blackjack oak (leaves are broadest at the tip with three bristle-tipped lobes). In summer, look for blazing star and white prairie clover in this area.

Take advantage of the unobstructed view at the power line cut before the trail begins to descend until it comes out on bare sandstone [6] (.75 mi.). Continue straight. At .9 mi. [7], before going through a narrow notch, go down and head right, picking your way through the rocks. Approximately one-third of the way down, go to your right, skirting the bluff, and follow a faint rocky path. This might resemble bushwhacking because the trail is not maintained. Use caution on your way down. If you are hiking during a wet period, note the small waterfalls coming off the rocks. Look at the bluff, with its folds and faults, and note how they have been thrust upward. You will pass a shelter cave and pass under an overhang.

You will pass point [2] at 1.4 mi. (this is where you came up); retrace your steps to [3] and go left, descending back to the parking area. If you happen to hike at sunset, look up to see bats flying against an orange sky.

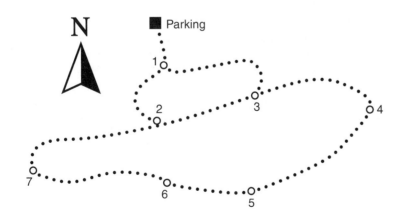

1. Start
2. Bluffs
3. Go straight
4. Trail ascends
5. Stone Face
6. Power line
7. Descend, right turn

# 57. Garden of the Gods Recreation Area

- Discover a fairyland of rock formations, including Camel Rock, Noah's Ark, Table Rock, and Mushroom Rock.

- Step onto the rock ledges, gaze over the vistas, and create your own nicknames for the fantastic rock formations.

- Wind through the woods and encounter not people but sandstone bluffs, huge boulders, and rugged sandstone knuckles.

- Spectacular fall color is provided by huge old-growth oak, maple, and tulip trees.

- Seek out fall hues of another kind—Liesegang rings, circles of eroded color.

## Area Information

The massive Pennsylvanian sandstone escarpments of Garden of the Gods stand ancient, weathered, and exposed. A visit during a southern Illinois summer can leave you thirsting for water, with only a hand-pump drinking fountain to be seen. Still, evidence is everywhere that water has influenced these formations. The sandstone was deposited by a warm sea some 270 to 310 million years ago. Glacial meltwater and rain moved along the joints and planes of the sandstone, expanding crevices into fissures and fissures into clefts, and eventually creating the pinnacles, curiously carved boulders, rock shelters, tunnels, and deep valleys.

In addition to the rock outcrops with exotic names, some cliff faces are decorated with dark, reddish swirls and raised designs with targetlike patterns. These circles of eroded color are Liesegang rings and are made of iron. Chemical changes caused the iron to solidify as rust between the rock particles; the sandstone is held together by these raised dark bands of iron and has resisted weathering.

**Directions:** Garden of the Gods is southeast of Harrisburg in Saline County. From Harrisburg follow Illinois 145/34 to Illinois 34. Turn east (left) onto Karbers Ridge Road (1065 N). At 2.8 miles turn east (left) at 250 E (Garden of the Gods Road). At 1.4 miles take another left into Garden of the Gods Recreation Area. There should be a national forest sign and several brown highway signs to indicate the way.

**Hours Open:** The site is open year-round. The picnic area and Observation Trail are open 6:00 a.m. to 10:00 p.m.

**Facilities:** A picnic area with grills, tables, and toilets and a 12-site campground with drinking water, fire grills, toilets, and tables are maintained year-round.

**Permits and Rules:** Pets are allowed only on leashes. No food or drink is allowed on the Observation Trail.

**For Further Information:** Hidden Springs Ranger Station, 602 North First Street, Route 45 North, Vienna, IL 62995; 618-658-2111 or www.fs.fed.us/r9/forests/shawnee.

## Park Trails

**Indian Point Trail** (👣👣, 1.7 miles). This hiking loop travels south along a ridge to Indian Point Overlook. It then curves back along a wooded east rim and through a pine plantation.

## Other Areas of Interest

Located between Garden of the Gods and Pounds Hollow, north of Karbers Ridge, **High Knob Recreation Area** provides picnicking and hiking. High Knob is a 929-foot hill of Pennsylvanian sandstone. A short trail follows the northwest side of the knob rim. The River to River Trail may be accessed at the base of the knob near the entrance. There are also several short, unmarked, interconnecting loops. For more information, call Hidden Springs Ranger Station at 618-658-2111.

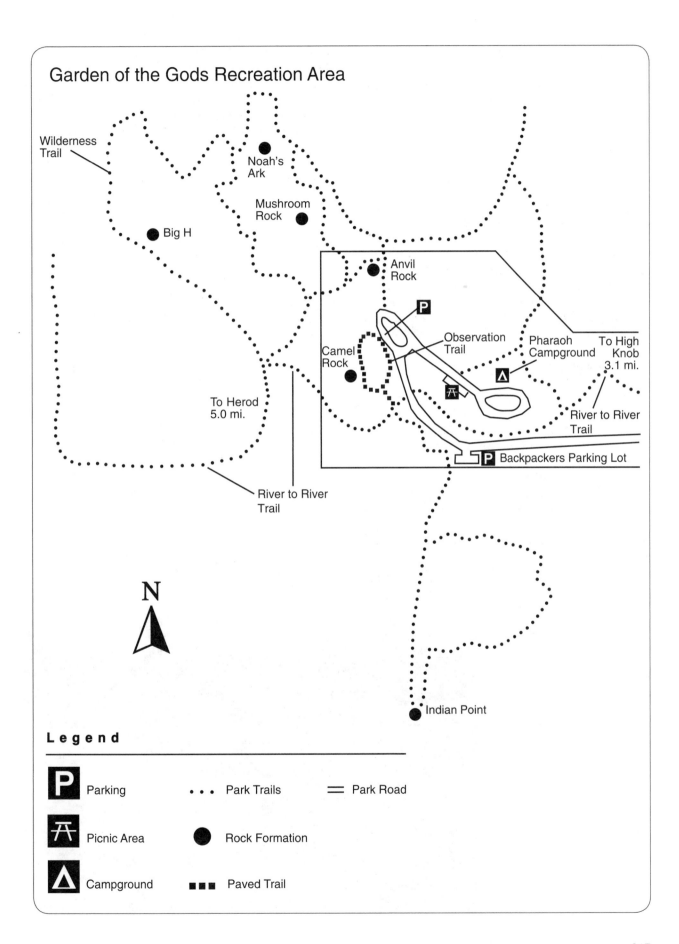

Garden of the Gods Recreation Area

Wilderness Trail

Noah's Ark

Mushroom Rock

Big H

Anvil Rock

P

Observation Trail

Pharaoh Campground

To High Knob 3.1 mi.

Camel Rock

To Herod 5.0 mi.

River to River Trail

P Backpackers Parking Lot

River to River Trail

N

Indian Point

**Legend**

P Parking    • • • Park Trails    ═ Park Road

Picnic Area    ● Rock Formation

Campground    ▪▪▪ Paved Trail

## Observation Trail

**Distance Round-Trip:** .25 to .6 mile (depending on whether you take in the various spurs)

**Estimated Hiking Time:** .75 hours

*Camel Rock is the poster child for the region. A trip to southern Illinois without viewing Camel Rock is like going to Yellowstone and not seeing Old Faithful.*

**Caution:** The trail and parking lot can be crowded during weekends in summer and fall.

**Trail Directions:** Begin the trail at the information signs off the parking lot [1]. The beginning of the trail is paved with flagstones. Take a right at the information sign. Although the walk won't be a "real" wilderness experience, the scenery is worth the effort.

Within less than .1 mi. [2] you will come to a narrow squeeze through the rocks. Give it a try! Down the path from the squeeze is a great example of Liesegang rings; an explanation of this phenomenon [3] is a bit farther down the trail.

At .15 the trail forks; go right [4]. This is a short side spur enabling you to take in the view—at one time it was only forest as far as the eye could see. The large bare slash on the horizon represents a strip mine. Retrace your steps back to the main trail.

At .3 mi. go right at a fork to another side spur [5]. Pause at Devil's Smokestack, a huge pillar formed when the softer sandstone around it washed away. The smokestack measures 30 feet. Retrace your steps and go to the left to begin a gentle climb to a rock-top vista.

The trail splits at .4 mi. [6]. Take the right branch for a view of Camel Rock. After viewing this most famous of southern Illinois' landmarks, head downhill. Table Rock appears on your left. Another observation spur leads to the right at .5 mi. [7] and provides a nice view of the forest to the south. Retrace your steps back to the original trail and head back.

Congratulations! Within .6 mi. you have seen and experienced the most prominent features of Garden of the Gods and warmed up your leg muscles for the more challenging Wilderness Trail.

1. Start
2. Narrow squeeze
3. Liesegang rings
4. Right turn
5. Devil's Smokestack
6. Camel Rock
7. Observation spur

N

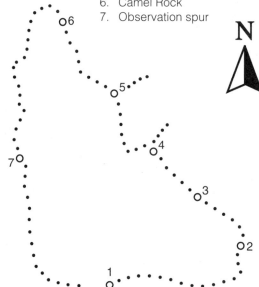

# Wilderness Trail

 **Distance Round-Trip:** 2.25 miles
**Estimated Hiking Time:** 1.1 hours

*Wind your way through the dense woods and encounter unique sandstone formations, rugged rock knuckles, and eroding outcrops framed against the backdrop of a blue fall sky and accented by the reds and golds of ancient oaks and maples.*

**Caution:** Parts of this trail are also used by horses (don't neglect to dodge the horse apples!), so the path can be uneven. The trail is also very steep in places, and don't be surprised if you must scamper over an occasional downed tree across the path.

**Trail Directions:** The trail begins to the north of the parking area for the Observation Trail. Enter an area enclosed by a split-rail fence, and begin the trail at the Garden of the Gods Wilderness Trail sign [1]. The trail starts out as a crushed-gravel road but soon gives way to a well-trampled dirt path. At a yellow marker (.1 mi.) take a left to Anvil Rock [2]. You can see this formation from the path or take a short spur to the left to examine the rock and its Liesegang rings more closely. Walk through the tunnel in the rock and rejoin the main trail—Bluff Trail 108E.

The trail is hard-packed and wanders through an oak-hickory forest with many sandstone outcrops. At .4 mi. take a short side spur to Mushroom Rock. Go left on this well-trod triangular path [3]. Backtrack again and continue on the trail. Take time in this area to step onto the ledges and use your imagination to name the many rock formations. At .6 mi. you have come upon Trail 001A [4].

The trail now goes up and down a series of small rock outcrops and comes to a junction at .75 mi. Go left onto the River to River Trail, which at this point is a deeply eroded path [5]. The trail will be marked with either a blue *i* or a large white diamond with a blue *i* in the center. This segment of the trail passes through large rock outcrops. At .85 mi. cross a creek and head up, skirting a honeycombed rock. At 1.05 mi. the trail begins an uphill climb [6]. Note the nice honeycomb pattern on the sandstone. A sandstone bluff is on your right; to the left are rolling hills with many sandstone knuckles and outcrops. At 1.2 mi. (the Big H sign) look around for a rock formation resembling an H. Go left after the sign on Trail 108C [7]. There will be periodic yellow natural area boundary markers and white diamonds to guide you.

You have now left the bluffs behind and are hiking through the woods. You will come to two junctions [8] at 1.7 mi. Continue straight ahead and then, within a few steps, go left. You are hiking in a valley that is

below the famous rock formations. The trail is labeled Parking Lot. You will soon ascend and cross two small rivulets and then wind through an oak-hickory woods. Climb up a series of rock boulders at 1.95 mi. [9]. Caution: These could be wet and slick. On your right is a mushroom rock in the making. Keep walking up this boulder-strewn valley. At 2.05 mi. you come out on Trail 108D [10]. Go right, retracing your steps to Anvil Rock. From Anvil Rock it is a short hike back to the wooden fence and the parking lot.

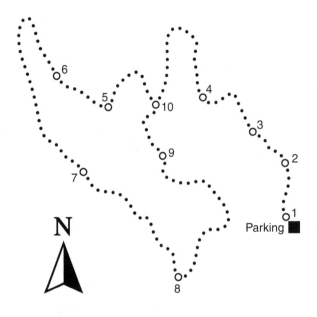

1.  Start
2.  Anvil Rock
3.  Left turn, Mushroom Rock spur
4.  Trail 001A
5.  River to River Trail
6.  Honeycombed rock
7.  Trail 108C
8.  Two junctions
9.  Climb up rock boulders
10. Trail 108D

# 58. Rim Rock/Pounds Hollow Recreation Complex

- Explore crevasses, streets, and shelter bluffs with names like Fat Man's Misery and Ox-Lot Cave, all "constructed" of Pounds sandstone.

- Look for the elusive beaver as you discover its dens, lodges, and favorite feeding areas.

- Enjoy vistas of the area—pretty anytime of the year, but when surrounded by fall colors, absolutely spectacular.

- Find out why this area is recommended by the Illinois Native Plant Society as a super site for spring wildflowers.

## Area Information

In earlier times before the recreation area was built, this area was known simply as the Pounds, a mesa-like rock structure with a rounded surface on top and sufficient soil for growing crops. Two valleys met at its north end to form Pounds Hollow. At the southern end and toward the top, mysterious rocks were strewn about and were said to be the remnants of a prehistoric fortification. Twenty families lived here during the late 19th century and kept their livestock in Ox-Lot Cave. The fertility of the soil soon gave out, however, and they abandoned the area.

The Rim Rock/Pounds Hollow Area you see today was developed by the Civilian Conservation Corps (CCC) during the Great Depression. The CCC planted a cedar grove on top of the Pounds to help stabilize the abandoned farmland, and they built steps and stone walls. The crown jewel of their work was the construction of Pounds Hollow Lake, covering the bed of a steam railroad that was used for taking logs out of the area during the 1800s.

The Rim Rock Recreation Trail was created in 1962-63 with money from the Illinois Federation of Women's Clubs. As you enjoy the area, experience a sense of the past while puzzling at the old stone fort, studying the layout of Ox-Lot Cave, and traversing the perimeter of Pounds Hollow Lake.

**Directions:** Rim Rock/Pounds Hollow is southeast of Harrisburg in Saline County. From Harrisburg follow Illinois 145/34 to Illinois 34; turn east (left) onto Karbers Ridge Road (1065 N), drive through the town of Karbers Ridge (4 miles from the area), and follow the national forest signs to the site.

**Hours Open:** The area is open year-round. The picnic area is open from 6:00 a.m. to 10:00 p.m. A swimming beach is open only in summer, and the campground is open April 1 to December 15.

**Facilities:** Picnicking, camping with drinking water, swimming, boating, and fishing are included. A con-

cession stand has row- and paddleboats for rent and is also in charge of the swimming area and showers.

**Permits and Rules:** Pets must be leashed. No pets, bottles, cans, or coolers are permitted on the beach. Rappelling and rock climbing are prohibited. No horseback riding is allowed on the Rim Rock National Recreational Trail or on the Beaver Trail between Rim Rock and Pounds Hollow.

**For Further Information:** Hidden Springs Ranger District, 602 N. First Street, Vienna, IL 62995; 618-658-2111 or www.fs.fed.us/r9/forests/shawnee.

## Park Trails

**Beaver Trail** (👣 👣, 7.5 miles one way). This trail can be accessed from Indian Wall Picnic Area. The trail descends into the hollow and goes right at an intersection, following Beaver Creek to Pounds Hollow Lake and the beach. It continues to circle the lake until reaching the dam, where it heads east, crossing Karbers Ridge. From the blacktop the trail uses old forest and gravel roads. Beaver Trail ends at Camp Cadiz, which has camping facilities, restrooms, and water.

**River to River Trail** (👣 👣 👣 👣 👣, 146 miles). The River to River Trail is an east-to-west trail that honors the routes of the pioneers, beginning at Battery Rock on the Ohio River and ending at Devil's Backbone Park on the Mississippi. This trail passes just south of the Rim Rock/Pounds Hollow Area and has a trailhead at Camp Cadiz. For more information, contact the River to River Trail Society at 618-252-6789.

## Other Areas of Interest

**Illinois Iron Furnace Recreation Site** is located 7 miles south of Karbers Ridge. The Illinois Iron Furnace was the first charcoal-fired iron furnace in the state. During the Civil War this furnace was the principal supplier of iron for the Union's ironclad ships. A .5-mile trail loop that follows scenic Big Creek is north of the site. For more information, call 618-658-2111 (Hidden Springs Ranger District) or 800-699-6637 (Shawnee National Forest Information Desk).

Located south of the intersection of Route 1 and State Route 146, **Cave-in-Rock State Park** offers a lodge, a restaurant, and a cave with a colorful history. Over the years it has been used by river bandits, outlaws and murderers, and Hollywood producers (appearing in *How the West Was Won*). The cave is a 55-foot-wide cavern overlooking the Ohio River. Two trails, Hickory Ridge and Pirate's Bluff, total 1.75 miles. For more information, call 618-289-4325.

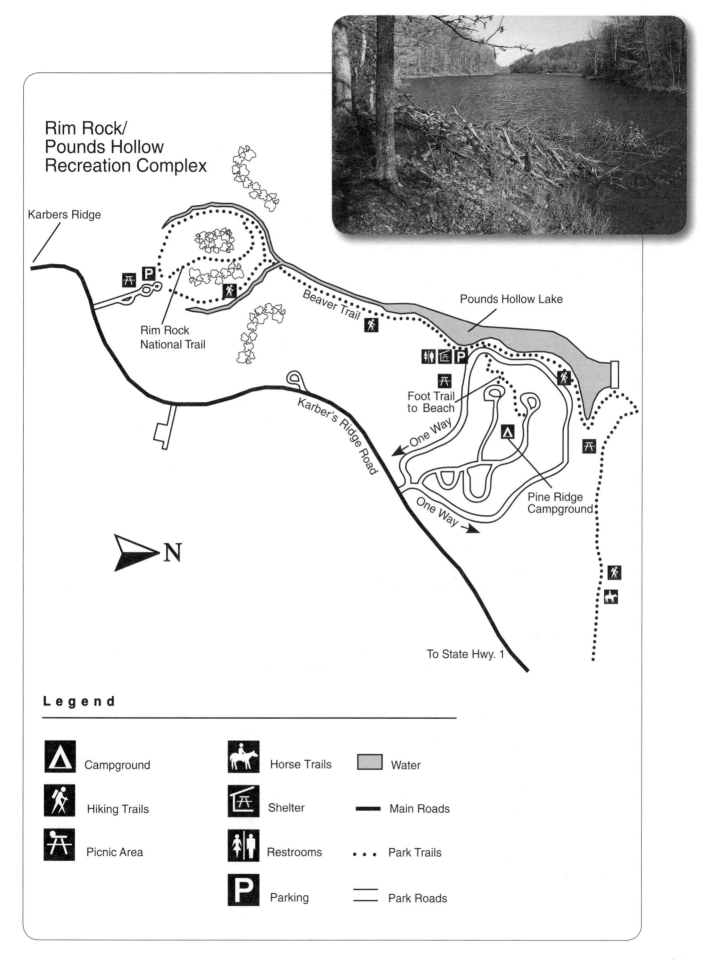

# Rim Rock/
# Pounds Hollow
# Recreation Complex

Karbers Ridge

Rim Rock
National Trail

Beaver Trail

Pounds Hollow Lake

Foot Trail
to Beach

One Way

One Way

Karber's Ridge Road

Pine Ridge
Campground

N

To State Hwy. 1

## Legend

△ Campground

🏇 Horse Trails

▨ Water

🥾 Hiking Trails

🏠 Shelter

▬ Main Roads

⛼ Picnic Area

🚻 Restrooms

••• Park Trails

P Parking

═══ Park Roads

# Rim Rock National Trail

**Distance Round-Trip:** 2.25 miles
**Estimated Hiking Time:** 1.5 hours

*Walk among walls built 1,500 years ago by Native Americans, 200 years ago by European settlers, and 60 years ago by the CCC. And, of course, walk along those walls "constructed" millions of years ago by geological forces shaping the Pounds sandstone.*

**Caution:** Once you have descended into the valley, be aware of many large tree roots and rocks in the trail. Be careful near bluff edges.

**Trail Directions:** Park at the Rim Rock National Trail parking area and take the middle trail from the informational kiosk. The trail is paved with flagstone and heads straight uphill [1]. Within a few yards encounter steps and an information sign explaining and speculating about the remains of an ancient stone wall built by Native Americans. The wall extends almost 150 feet across the bluff top.

Continue on the trail and pass through a cedar grove established by the CCC in 1939 to stabilize the soil. At .2 mi. [2] pause at a bench and look north. From here you can see Pounds Hollow Lake. Steps lead down to an observation deck [3] (.4 mi.) from which you can peer into the ravine forest below.

For an interesting side spur, take a few minutes to walk down and hike among the giant boulders. Squeeze through moss-covered rock walls and become lost in a maze of sandstone. Retrace your steps back up and rejoin the original trail (Ox-Lot Cave will be explored later). During the spring, along the neat flagstone trail, look for shooting stars and wood betony lining the way. Another name for wood betony is lousewort (farmers believed any animals that encountered it would be covered with lice).

As you hike along, look to your right, through the gnarly branches of ancient cedars, for the smooth gray upper branches of beeches. On your left is a dry oak-hickory woods; on your right at .7 mi. [4] is a plant community called a barrens. The term *barrens* often was applied to habitats perceived as unproductive. In truth, barrens are usually very dry with thin soil. The surface is often a mosaic of bare rock, plants that can tolerate the dry soil, and stunted, gnarled trees such as post and blackjack oaks.

You encounter the Indian Wall again, this time on your left [5] (.95 mi.), and the first half of the trail is completed. As you come off Rim Rock Trail, immediately go to your right and down Lower Pounds Trail. The first half of this trail is unmarked but fairly easy to follow. On your right are the bluffs, topped by barrens. Go right, up some fairly cryptic stone steps, and skirt the base of the bluff [6] (1.25 mi.). You are hiking between a huge boulder and the cliff. As you emerge from a jumble of rocks, the forest composition has changed; springtime brings the first installment of a multitude of wildflowers.

After you scramble over a boulder field and skirt the base of the bluff, another set of stone steps [7] (1.5 mi.) are hidden among the huge rocks. Like the last set, these were made by the CCC. Take the steps downward (up will take you back to the top of the trail) and come upon Ox-Lot Cave [8] (1.7 mi.). A sign provides details on the colorful past of this large rock overhang. Continue on the trail to an intersection at 1.8 mi.; go right and around the bluff. At this point the trail leads through a veritable garden of spring wildflowers [9]. From the earliest harbinger-of-spring to white trillium, all your favorites can be found.

As you skirt the bluff, note the smooth gray bark of the large beeches. They present a biography of the valley through the names carved in them, but please do not add yours! At 2.05 mi. [10] you will cross the first of a series of large and small bridges. The trail ends at 2.25 mi. and you are back at the kiosk.

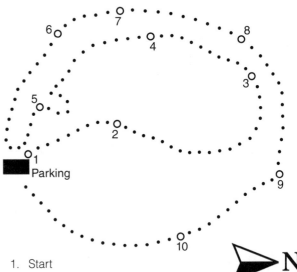

1. Start
2. Bench
3. Observation deck
4. Barrens
5. Indian Wall
6. Bluff base
7. Steps
8. Ox-Lot Cave
9. Wildflowers
10. Bridges

# Beaver Trail

 **Distance Round-Trip:** 3.9 miles
**Estimated Hiking Time:** 2 hours

*The trail is appropriately named—gnawed stumps, dams, lodges, and wood chips are everywhere. The only thing missing is a glimpse of the elusive rodent. Instead of the beaver, I had to settle for a path of wood chips leading from a fresh-cut stump to the beaver's dining table, the shallow water at the edge of the lake.*

**Caution:** Partway around the lake the trail will become very faint with many logs and rocks to negotiate. If the water is high, two places require log crossings. You might have to wade the stream to cross. When crossing sandstone ledges, remember the surfaces might be wet and slippery.

**Trail Directions:** From the kiosk at Rim Rock National Trail, take the trail farthest to the right at a sign indicating Beaver Trail [1]. The trail begins as a crushed-limestone path through a dry oak-pine woods. Look for Christmas ferns in the understory. Within the first .05 mi. [2] the trail crosses a series of wooden bridges and leads downward.

The forest in between the bluffs supports a profusion of spring wildflowers. As the trail nears the bluffs, both rocks and wildflowers tumble down the slopes. Along the path, note the shrubby trees called spicebush. These have aromatic, spicy bark and a small yellow flower that blooms in late March. A trail intersection is encountered at .5 mi. [3]; go right.

You will now cross a series of footbridges before reaching Pounds Hollow Lake. After the second bridge, note the huge beech tree on the left with its roots clinging for support. Go up the steps [4] (.7 mi.) and then left. You are skirting the backwaters of the lake. Take time to admire the bald cypress as you walk along a ridge that separates the wetland on the left from a dry oak-hickory forest on the right. Look for a beaver lodge on the left and also fresh gnawing.

Admire the stone wall built by the CCC during the late 1930s as you pass the wastewater-treatment plant [5] (1.1 mi.). You are now in the Pounds Hollow Recreation Area (1.15 mi.), and the trail passes a beach and bathhouse [6]. Follow the trail down the steps, along a sidewalk, and across a bridge; go left. You will skirt the lake on the left and picnic areas on the right. At 1.35 mi. [7] the final stone wall of a CCC picnic area will be on your right.

Continue along the lake. Although the path is not marked, a faint trail is present. Just keep the lake on your left! Don't forget to search for the elusive beaver, although you are more likely to see wood chips, stripped branches, downed trees, and at least one lodge. Find a convenient place to cross the narrow cove at 1.75 mi. [8] without getting your feet wet. On the other side go left and continue to hike around the lake.

At 1.9 mi. [9] you will come to the spillway and earthen dam; cross it and go left [10] (2 mi.). Continue to skirt the lake on the left. The trail here, although faint, is easily followed. While you may be drawn to the lake, take time to admire the oak-hickory woods and sandstone outcrops on the right. You will pass the picnic area and bathhouse on the opposite side at 2.6 mi. Close to the trail, find a beaver lodge [11], complete with its "deli"—submerged, newly cut branches and saplings stored for later consumption. A beaver's stomach produces an enzyme that enables it to digest these woody culinary delights.

On your left is a picturesque view of a large cypress, a beaver dam, and a pond (3 mi.). After the last cypress tree the trail heads down [12]. Where the stream narrows to a single channel [13] (3.1 mi.), head farther downward on a series of sandstone rock terraces. The trail now passes between the bluff and stream; begin to look for a narrow place to cross the stream [14] (3.25 mi.). (If the water is high, the only solution will be to remove your boots and wade.) From here you will rejoin the limestone path; at the intersection [3] go left, retracing your steps back up the bluff and to the parking area.

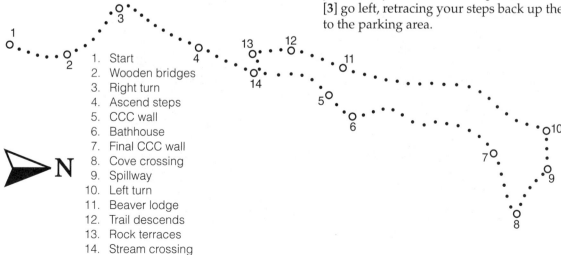

1. Start
2. Wooden bridges
3. Right turn
4. Ascend steps
5. CCC wall
6. Bathhouse
7. Final CCC wall
8. Cove crossing
9. Spillway
10. Left turn
11. Beaver lodge
12. Trail descends
13. Rock terraces
14. Stream crossing

South

# 59. War Bluff Valley Audubon Sanctuary

- Look for or listen to some of the sanctuary's 45 species of reptiles and amphibians.
- Participate in the annual fun-filled factual Insect Awareness and Appreciation Day in August.
- Don't forget a butterfly field guide—some of the state's rarest butterflies can be found here.
- Visit a special biological reserve maintained just for organisms.

## Area Information

War Bluff Valley Audubon Sanctuary was the former home of Richard and Jean Graber, ornithologists for the Illinois Natural History Survey. They gave the sanctuary to Illinois Audubon in 1990. War Bluff, the name of the sanctuary, comes from a prehistoric late–Woodland Native American "stone fort" site that is located in the Shawnee National Forest. This stone fort is on a ridgetop adjacent to and within view of the sanctuary.

Although War Bluff is adjacent to the Shawnee National Forest and appears to be the perfect wild-life habitat, it wasn't always so. When the Grabers purchased the first tract of land in 1965, it had been farmed with mules and horses for over 100 years. Jean commented, "The land was so worn out that it wouldn't even grow lichens." Concerned about the loss of habitat and its effect on birds and other wildlife, they managed the property for wildlife, allowing the reforestation of the old farm fields. Today, the old farm fields have reverted to native shrubs—sumac, winged elm, and blackberry—while tulip trees, sycamore, and river birch are along the creek. Large oaks still occur. Seven ponds have been constructed and have natural-ized with cattails. One of these, Dragonfly Pond, has no fish. Fish will routinely eat the eggs, larvae, and young of frogs, toads, and dragonflies.

The sanctuary, with its dense streamside and rasp-berry thickets, young regenerating deciduous wood-lands, brushy clearings, and impenetrable weedy tangles, is the perfect habitat for wildlife. Bobcats have walked through the caretaker's front yard. The spring is a chorus of frogs, including the uncommon crayfish frog. Numerous species of birds nest here along with countless insects. The area is such a great insect habitat that, since 1994, the local Audubon Club has held an Insect Awareness and Appreciation Day during late August.

In 1969 Dick Graber wrote, "It should be our hope for a long time to come, men will ponder their potenti-ality, learning to measure success not so much by what they had, but what they left behind." The Grabers have been very successful.

**Directions:** From Golconda, take State Route 146 north 3.5 miles to Bushwhack Road and turn left. Follow the road approximately 2 miles to the sanctuary entrance. (Look for brown wildlife-viewing signs.)

**Hours Open:** The site is open daily from dawn to dusk year-round.

**Facilities:** Toilets are on the site.

**Permits and rules:** Wildlife viewing only is permit-ted.

**For Further Information:** War Bluff Valley Sanctuary, R.R. 1 Box 216A, Golconda, IL 62938; 618-683-2222 or http://shawneeaudubon.org.

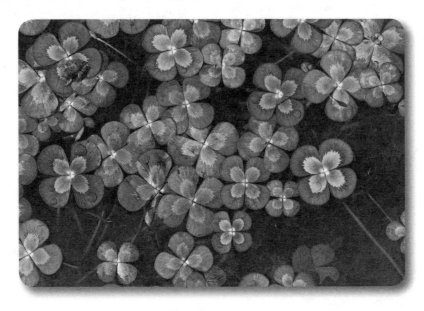

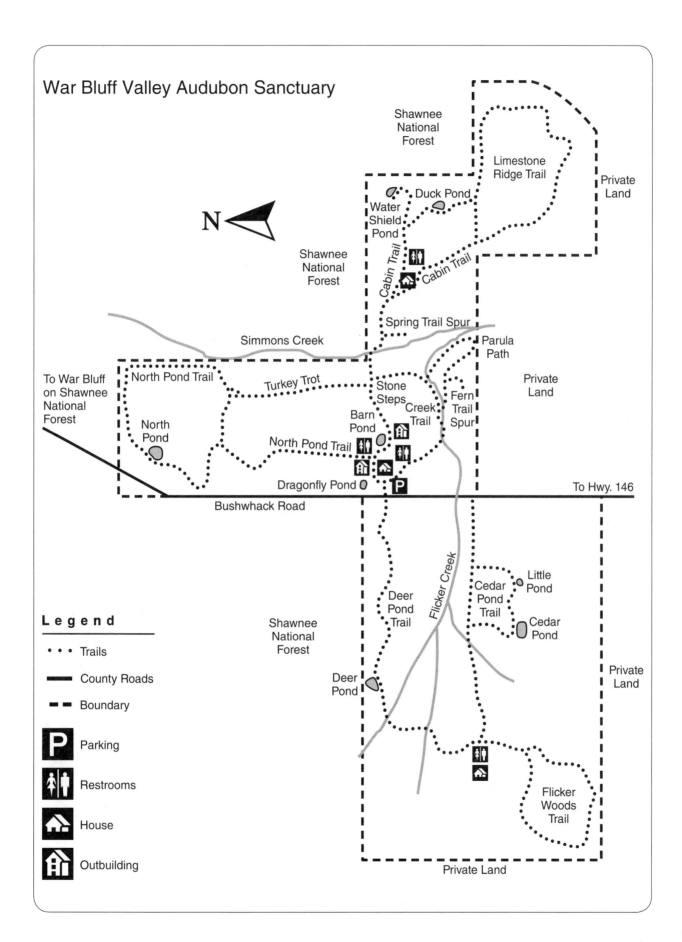

# War Bluff Valley Audubon Sanctuary

Shawnee National Forest

Limestone Ridge Trail

Private Land

Duck Pond

Water Shield Pond

Cabin Trail

Cabin Trail

Shawnee National Forest

Spring Trail Spur

Parula Path

Simmons Creek

North Pond Trail

Turkey Trot

Stone Steps

Fern Trail Spur

Private Land

To War Bluff on Shawnee National Forest

North Pond

Barn Pond

Creek Trail

North Pond Trail

Dragonfly Pond

To Hwy. 146

P

Bushwhack Road

Deer Pond Trail

Flicker Creek

Little Pond

Cedar Pond Trail

Cedar Pond

Shawnee National Forest

Private Land

Deer Pond

Flicker Woods Trail

**Legend**

- • • • Trails
- ——— County Roads
- – – Boundary
- P Parking
- Restrooms
- House
- Outbuilding

Private Land

# North Pond

 **Distance Round-Trip:** 2.25 miles
**Estimated Hiking Time:** 1.5 hours

*This trail is a lepidopterist's delight, whether you seek the commonplace (red admiral, tiger swallowtail, little yellow, and buckeye) or the rare (gemmed satyr and Carolina satyr). I constantly consulted my* Field Guide to Butterflies of Illinois *on this trail.*

**Caution:** There are several small stream crossings. Watch out for holes and molehills in the trail.

**Trail Directions:** Begin the trail [1] at the Welcome to War Bluff sign. Go left on the mown path. Continue to veer left, following the signs, and you will pass Kestrel Hall on the left and Barn Pond on the right. In less than .1 mi. you will come to Dragonfly Pond [2]. Take a short stroll over to check it out. The edges are ringed with cattail and willows while water lilies and water shamrock float on the surface. Frogs are all along the edge, usually trying to make a hasty getaway. In the fall, wood ducks roost here, so shy that they are usually gone before they are seen. Retrace your steps back to the trail.

You are walking in a perfect mosaic of habitat for wildlife—prairie plants mingle with shrubs and oaks, and viney tangles provide wildlife food and homes. The prairie supports a multitude of wildflowers, including bee balm, butterfly weed, black-eyed Susan, and St. John's wort. Check the milkweed for monarchs and milkweed bugs. At .3 mi. the trail curves left [3] at a bench. You might want to sit here and revel in the silence. You are a long way from any road, and the only sounds will be the scream of a red-tailed hawk or a fussing wren.

At .5 mi. go left at an intersection [4]. In the fall look for rare gemmed and Carolina satyr butterflies; both species are small, dead-leaf-colored butterflies. Don't be surprised if one leads you down the trail. The first

ones collected from Illinois were in 1994. Vines arch over the trail as a catbird calls from the rose canes and thickets. Go up a small incline at .65 mi., and North Pond appears on the right [5]. North Pond not only has several species of dragonflies but is also a home to beavers. Look for their holes in the side of the pond, their leftover gnawings on trees, and their trails to and from the pond.

The trail curves around the pond into an old field of goldenrod and grasses. There is a stream crossing [6] at .75 mi. with the possibility of wet feet. The trail soon curves right and a fence appears on your left. At 1 mi. you will pass a tulip and sweet gum plantation. Another stream crossing [7] is at 1.1 mi. and the trail curves right; stay on North Pond Trail. You will walk in a streambed for a few yards and then go left on a wide path with the stream on your right.

At 1.2 mi. you are back at [4]; go left, retracing your steps back up the hill. As you hike past the old field, don't forget to look for butterflies, especially in late summer. Turn left to explore Barn Pond [8] (1.6 mi.) and look for kingfishers and dragonflies. Skirt the edge of the pond and head left on Creek Trail. There will be a pair of benches at 1.75 mi., where you go down stone steps [9]. Within less than .05 mi. you will come to an intersection [10]; go right and do not cross the stream. You are hiking through a woods with a pawpaw understory, the food plant of the zebra swallowtail. In the spring look for Virginia bluebells, Dutchman's breeches, squirrel corn, and trout lilies. Several stone outcrops appear on your right.

At 2 mi. the trail heads near the creek and then to the right [11] on a faint rock-lined path. At the base of the hill, follow the white diamonds on the trees. Cross the creek (it is much narrower here) and then follow the red metal cardinal signs. You will emerge near the house; go left, and soon you are back at the Welcome to War Bluff sign.

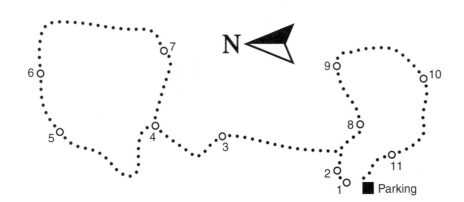

1. Start
2. Dragonfly Pond
3. Curve left
4. Intersection, left turn
5. North Pond
6. Stream crossing
7. Stream crossing
8. Barn Pond
9. Stone steps
10. Intersection
11. Creek, right turn

# Deer and Cedar Ponds

 **Distance Round-Trip:** 2 miles
**Estimated Hiking Time:** 1 hour

*Buckeyes were prevalent—not the trees but the butterflies. I saw more than 25 on this trail.*

**Caution:** The final quarter mile is on the road, so keep an eye out for traffic. There is also a small stream crossing.

**Trail Directions:** Begin at the trail's west sign [1]. Cross the road and enter the trail on the opposite side. You are walking through old fields with cedar trees, and periodically the trail will go in and out of the woods. At .5 mi. Deer Pond is on the right [2]. Take time to explore the pond, look at the tracks to see who has been there, and take advantage of the picnic bench. Rejoin the trail and head down.

You will cross a stream [3] at .9 mi. On your right will be an old house and a privy toilet. Within .05 mi. come to an intersection with Flicker Trail and go left. Look for butterflies along this section, especially buckeyes in the fall. The trail will fork at 1.3 mi.; go to the right [4]. You will pass bluebird nest box 12. These boxes are part of the Birdhouse Network, a citizen-science project of the Cornell Lab of Ornithology. Information is gathered and submitted to a national database. At War Bluff, bluebirds, tufted titmice, and chickadees are using the boxes.

Cedar Pond is on your right at 1.35 mi. [5]. The pond is ringed with yellow pond lily, and every tree around the pond has been downed by the resident beavers. Look for their holes in the sides of the pond. Within .1 mi. you will come to Little Pond. Here common yellowthroats hide among the grasses. The trail curves left at 1.55 mi. [6]. A line of shingle oaks will be on your right. Notice how their leaves have no lobes. The trail Ts at 1.6 mi.; go right [7].

At 1.75 mi. go right before the metal fence, then left and left again. You are walking up Bushwhack Road [8]. Look for box turtles in the road or eastern towhees scratching in the brush. Who knows what wildlife may cross the road in front of you? While white-tailed deer and squirrels are numerous, a bobcat is not out of the question. In April, this stretch of road is a gathering spot for tiger swallowtail butterflies. In a good year several hundred have been spotted. In the fall migrating monarchs stage here. Turn right into the sanctuary to finish the trail.

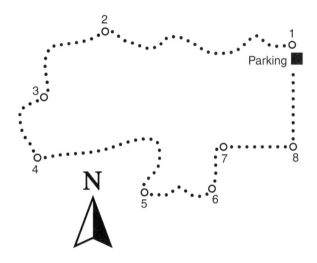

1. Start
2. Deer Pond
3. Stream crossing
4. Trail forks, go right
5. Cedar Pond
6. Curve left
7. Right turn
8. Bushwhack Road

# 60. Beall Woods State Park

- Discover one of the best examples of a near-virgin deciduous forest on the entire North American continent—the Forest of the Wabash.

- Bring a tree identification guide to help you identify the 60-plus species of trees that can be found along the trails.

- Listen for the call of the pileated woodpecker and look for these large woodpeckers throughout the park. Dusk and dawn are good times for a woodpecker encounter.

- Experience a sense of the past at the visitor center while viewing photos of the last great denizens (the giant trees) of these woods.

- Enjoy some of the premier fall colors in Illinois.

## Area Information

In presettlement days, the eastern border of Illinois contained the great trees that made up the last stronghold of the eastern deciduous forest. These primeval woods, considered by some to be one of the wonders of the world, had trees over 130 feet tall with trunks of 6 feet or greater in diameter. Poison ivy and wild grape hung like monstrous suspension cables from their branches.

Although not readily apparent to the casual observer, traces of this magnificent forest still remain in Beall Woods, a national landmark, in southern Wabash County. Over 60 tree species have been identified here, and some 300 trees have trunks with diameters greater than 30 inches at chest height. At least five state champion trees can also be found here.

Appreciating this region of Illinois requires a sense of the past. Here was the final citadel of the eastern deciduous forest before the onset of the endless prairie, a home to giant trees and lush vegetation. Beall Woods, a remnant of the Forest of the Wabash, helps to recapture the forest that our pioneering ancestors saw.

**Directions:** Beall Woods is in southeastern Illinois on Route 1 near Keensburg, about 10 miles north of I-64. From Keensburg, take a blacktop road 1.5 miles east to the park.

**Hours Open:** The site is open year-round except on Christmas Day and New Year's Day. The visitor center is open 8:00 a.m. to 4:00 p.m. Tuesday through Saturday and 12:00 noon to 4:00 p.m. Sunday and Monday. Trail conditions are posted outside the visitor center door.

**Facilities:** The visitor center has excellent photos of the ancient woods. Restrooms are also located here, as are picnic tables. A shelter and a 16-site campground with water and picnic tables are located near the small lake. Fishing is allowed in the lake.

**Permits and Rules:** The trails are located in the area of the park that is a dedicated Illinois Nature Preserve. Because of its status, no pets, bicycles, or horses are allowed on the trails.

**For Further Information:** Beall Woods State Park, 9285 Beall Woods Avenue, Mount Carmel, IL 62863; 618-298-2442.

## Other Areas of Interest

**Olney** is the now-famous home for the white form of the gray squirrel found around town and in Olney City Park. White squirrel symbolism is found everywhere in this small town. Bird Haven is a second attraction, a memorial to Robert Ridgway, an early Smithsonian ornithologist who documented the great trees that grew along the Wabash. Bird Haven is an arboretum with over 74 varieties of trees and is an excellent place to birdwatch. For more information about Olney City Park and Bird Haven, call 618-392-2241.

**Red Hills State Park,** located in southeastern Illinois between Olney and Lawrenceville, is an area of wooded hills, deep ravines, and Red Hill, the highest point of land between St. Louis and Cincinnati. The area has plenty of picnic sites with tables and grills, six playgrounds, and camping (complete with electricity, showers, and flush toilets). Hunting, fishing, and boating are allowed at the park. Six miles of hiking trails wind through the park. For more information, call 618-936-2469.

**Lincoln Trail State Recreation Area,** located west of Illinois Route 1 and 2 miles south of Marshall in Clark County, is named after the trail Abraham Lincoln's family followed en route from Indiana to Illinois. In addition to its historical significance, the area includes American Beech Woods, an Illinois Nature Preserve. Facilities include picnic sites, water, camping (both class A and D), boating, fishing, and a concession stand. Sand Ford Nature Trail is a 2-mile trail that explores an oak-hickory forest. For more information, call 217-826-2222.

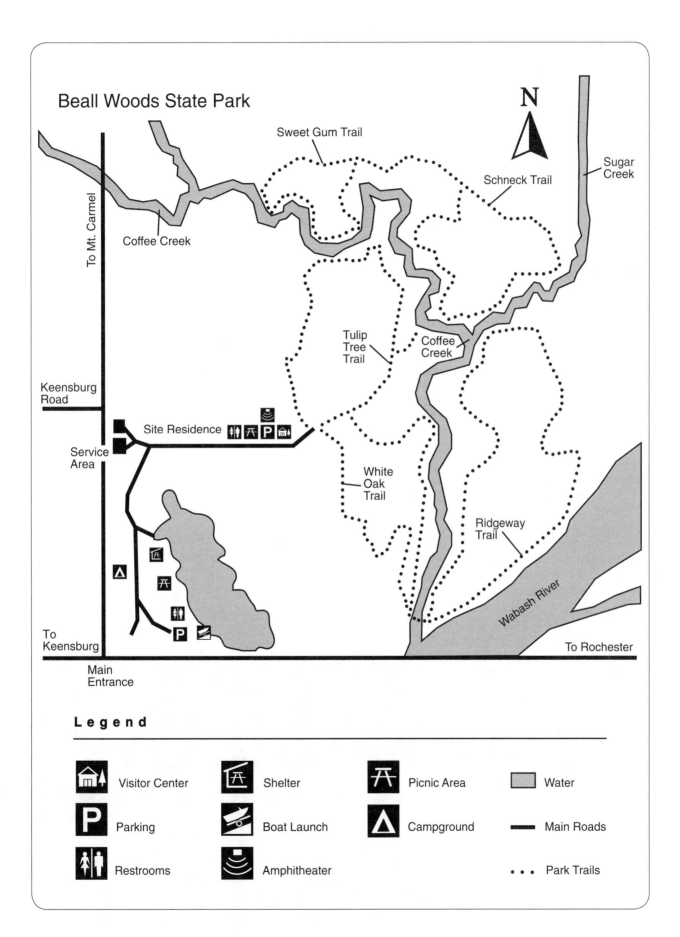

Beall Woods State Park

N

Sweet Gum Trail

Schneck Trail

Sugar Creek

Coffee Creek

To Mt. Carmel

Tulip Tree Trail

Coffee Creek

Keensburg Road

Site Residence

Service Area

White Oak Trail

Ridgeway Trail

Wabash River

To Keensburg

To Rochester

Main Entrance

**Legend**

| | | | | |
|---|---|---|---|---|
| Visitor Center | Shelter | Picnic Area | Water | |
| Parking | Boat Launch | Campground | Main Roads | |
| Restrooms | Amphitheater | | Park Trails | |

# Schneck and Sweet Gum Trails

 **Distance Round-Trip:** 2.2 miles
**Estimated Hiking Time:** 1 hour

*While this is a trail through the woods, Coffee and Sugar creeks are the stars. Look for river terraces, an oxbow in the making, a creek undercutting the bedrock, and even a small waterfall, all set against a backdrop of big trees.*

**Caution:** Poison ivy is present in large patches in some parts of the woods. Neck strain is a distinct possibility on the trail if you keep looking up to see the large trees.

**Trail Directions:** To reach the trailhead, leave the park and turn right onto 900 N. Boulevard, and immediately turn right again onto 800 East Road. Go north until you reach the parking area on the right (about a mile). Begin the trail at the fence and go left on the Schneck Trail [1]. The trail is the namesake of Dr. Jacob Schneck, a Mount Carmel physician and botanist who documented the huge trees during the mid-1800s. Within a few steps you will come to an intersection; stay left. You are walking through a mixed mesic (moist) woods with a pawpaw understory.

The trail heads up and to the right at .1 mi. [2] onto a river terrace. Soon you will come to two pairs of large oaks on your left. At the intersection at .25 mi. go left [3]. Note the torn-apart logs on the ground and the large, squarish holes in some of the trees, evidence of pileated woodpeckers. Listen for their call and staccato hammering on the trees. If you are quiet, you may be rewarded with a glimpse of these denizens of ancient woods. At .5 mi. the trail heads downward on a series of shelves and terraces [4]. The trail will curve right and Sugar Creek will be on your left. At .7 mi. note the oxbow in the making on your left [5].

Look for nurse logs in the understory. These decaying logs are a garden of mosses and mushrooms. The junction of Sugar Creek and Coffee Creek appears at .9 mi. [6]. The trail will now skirt Coffee Creek, meandering through the woods with sinuous curves and sweeps. Coffee Creek gets its name from leaf tannins that turn it brown. Gradually you will climb out of the floodplain, and soon you are back to [3] (1.4 mi.). Go left; as you retrace your steps past the pairs of large oaks, pause and reflect on the statement made by Dr. Schneck in 1876: "The time is not distant when there will scarcely be left a sample of those monuments of centuries of growth."

The trail splits at 1.6 mi. [7]; go left on Sweet Gum. Note the shagbark hickories. Their bark is a paradise for overwintering butterflies. At 1.8 mi. notice how Coffee Creek is undercutting the bedrock. For the next tenth of a mile marvel at the force this small stream applies to the adjacent bedrock. The trail curves right, and at 1.95 mi. a small instream waterfall, called Rocky Ford, will be on your left [8]. Note the exposed shelf of bedrock. The trail soon curves, leaving Coffee Creek behind, and all too soon you are back at the fence where you started.

1. Start
2. Right turn, river terrace
3. Left turn
4. Trail descends
5. Oxbow
6. Junction, Sugar and Coffee creeks
7. Left turn onto Sweet Gum Trail
8. Rocky Ford

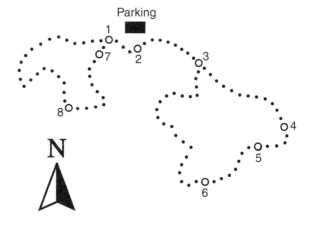

# White Oak Trail

**Distance Round-Trip:** 4.3 miles
**Estimated Hiking Time:** 2.5 hours

*Enjoy a ramble through the woods that Ridgway knew when looking for giants. Pick up a guide to the trees for the first part of the hike. During the second part you are on your own in identifying the tree names—they aren't labeled!*

**Caution:** Hiking the side spur during a wet spring could get your feet wet. Be careful not to walk into a ravine while looking up to see the canopies of the large trees.

**Trail Directions:** Begin the trail on the sidewalk north of the visitor center. The sidewalk will soon give way to a dirt path. At .1 mi. [1] there is a trail intersection. Go left on Tulip Tree and don't forget to pick up a guide to the trees. Orange-numbered posts along this trail indicate a tree described in the guide. Hiking might be slow in this section because you will constantly gaze upward at these impressive trees.

At .3 mi. [2] you will cross a bridge over a tributary of Coffee Creek. A floodplain woods is on your right. Within a tenth of a mile you will cross another bridge. At the beech tree (tree 10) [3] the trail winds left. At .9 mi. [4] you will come out into the parking area. Go left, skirting the parking area and the visitor center. Retrace your steps back to [1]. Once back at the intersection (1 mi.), go right on White Oak. Within a few steps you will go left on a wide path. A plantation of tulip trees will be on your right.

At 1.15 mi. [5] the path splits; go left. You are now walking on top of a ridge. After a few steps you will come to a series of wooden-platform overlooks with steps leading downward. During fall, winter, and spring, when the leaves are off the trees, you are able to see the huge grape and poison ivy vines—the "suspension cables" that Ridgway saw and marveled at.

The steps have brought you down to Coffee Creek. For the next .4 mi. the path skirts the creek [6]. Take time to look at the huge oaks arching over the path, the immense sycamores in the distant woods, or the tall straight sweet gums.

At 1.7 mi. [7] come to an intersection and go left (straight) across a wooden bridge over a small ravine. Within a few steps go left again, crossing Coffee Creek, and head uphill. At the top go left again; you have entered the Ridgway Trail [8] (1.75 mi.). You are hiking in a floodplain woods through an even-aged stand of silver maples. This section of the hike will be marked with yellow trail markers.

The trail curves left at 2.25 mi. [9]; a pair of large sycamores will be on your right, and soon the silver maples have disappeared to be replaced by large oaks. This part of the trail gives you a chance to experience a floodplain woods where the trees are something other than silver maples or sycamores. At 3 mi. the Wabash River is on your left [10]. Indiana is on the other side. At 3.4 mi. you are back at [8]; recross Coffee Creek.

Once across, go up and take an immediate left. The large straight tree on your left is one of the largest pecan trees in the state. Continue straight on this path, passing two large sycamores on your left. At 3.5 mi. [11] Coffee Creek empties into the Wabash River. Note the width of the Wabash while traversing its banks. Follow the path while walking under a large leaning cottonwood and passing a large sycamore on the right and an adjacent oil well. You will come to an intersection; go left and soon you are back at [7]. Go left and up a series of wooden stairs (64 steps); at the top will be a white oak (3.7 mi.).

The surrounding forest is now an upland forest, and the trail will snake through the woods for the next quarter mile [12]. Take note of the huge oaks with an understory of pawpaw and equally impressive tulip trees. At 4 mi. [13] you will cross a service road and then go left, following the sign for White Oak Trail. At 4.25 mi. the trail Ts; go left back to the visitor center and parking area, leaving the big trees but a memory.

1. Start, Tulip Tree Trail
2. Bridge over Coffee Creek
3. Wind left
4. Skirt parking area, left turn
5. Left turn
6. Coffee Creek
7. Left turn
8. Ridgeway Trail
9. Large sycamores
10. Wabash River
11. Coffee Creek empties into Wabash River
12. Upland forest
13. Service road crossing

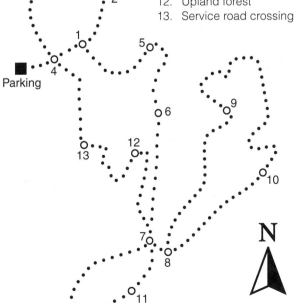

# About the Author

**Susan Post** has been a research biologist for the Illinois Natural History Survey since 1978, where she has worked on such jobs as biological control of purple loosestrife, sampling streams for threatened and endangered plants, and sampling horseradish fields for insect pests. Through her work, Susan has become well acquainted with the natural areas of Illinois.

Susan is the coauthor of *Illinois Wilds,* a book that showcases the state's natural areas. She is also the staff writer for the *Illinois Steward Magazine* and the author of "Species Spotlight" for *Illinois Natural History Survey Reports.*

She is the codirector of the Illinois Wilds Institute for Nature (IWIN), a joint project between the Survey and the University of Illinois Department of Natural Resources and Environmental Sciences that offers field courses to the public on various aspects of Illinois biology.